Writing From the Ground Up

Revised Second Edition

Leesther Thomas

Sherry D. Bailey

Margie Rauls

Ruth Sawh

Willie T. Williams

D0073812

Pearson
Custom
Publishing

Cover photo courtesy of Superstock, Inc.

Excerpts taken from:
The Writer's Brief Handbook, Second Edition,
by Alfred Rosa and Paul Eschholz
Copyright © 1996 by Allyn & Bacon
Copyright © 1994 by MacMillan Publishing
A Pearson Education Company
Needham Heights, MA 02494

The Allyn & Bacon Handbook, Third Edition,
by Leonard J. Rosen and Lawrence Behrens
Copyright © 1997, 1994, 1992 by Allyn & Bacon

The Practical Writer's Guide, by Susan X. Day,
Elizabeth McMahan, and Robert Funk
Copyright © 1997 by Allyn & Bacon.

This copyright covers material written expressly for this volume by the editor/s as well as the compilation itself. It does not cover the individual selections herein that first appeared elsewhere. Permission to reprint these has been obtained by Pearson Custom Publishing for this edition only. Further reproduction by any means, electronic or mechanical, including photocopying and recording, or by any information storage or retrieval system, must be arranged with the individual copyright holders noted.

This special edition published in cooperation with Pearson Custom Publishing.

Printed in the United States of America

10 9 8 7 6 5 4 3

Please visit our web site at www.pearsoncustom.com

ISBN 0-536-02432-4
BA 990792

PEARSON CUSTOM PUBLISHING
160 Gould Street/Needham Heights, MA 02494
A Pearson Education Company

Contents

Acknowledgments

We are grateful for the encouragement, understanding, and support given us by many people, as we prepared this book for use by our students. Many thanks are extended to Ms. Carol Challenger, Mrs. Ernestine Coley, Dr. Mary Diallo, Mr. John Hill, Ms. Delois Hollinger, Ms. Barbara Mallory, Dr. Evelyn Nash, Dr. Prettilal Sawh, Dr. Ralph W. Turner, and Ms. Cynthia Stokes Williams. We express special thanks to Mr. Alexander Williams, Mr. Kenya Thompkins, and to the following students who contributed writing samples for the book:

Gordon I. Barksdale, Jr.
Jerryl Bethea
Lisa Blankenship
Terrance Brisbane
Kia Byrd
Lavonne C. Cliff
Tasha Crichlow

Peggy L. Durant
Brian Echavarria
Shannon Glapion
Peter Holmes
Kelli V. Holsendolf
Sarah Hyde
Diemsk Jean

Jossalyn Johnson
LaToya N. Johnson
Davida Martin
Jermaine T. Robinson
Shawn Vann
Bryce L. Williams
Rosalyn Wynn

Introduction

Years of teaching experience have shown us that sometimes students do not write as well as we expect because they simply have not been taught the essentials of essay preparation and basic essay structure. Thus, in an effort to provide students with a thorough study of the essay, we begin our text, *Writing from the Ground Up* (2nd revised edition), with a plain, detailed explanation of sentence features, and progress from there to paragraph development, essay development (and rhetorical strategies), literature as a source in writing, the research paper, the essay examination, a glossary of usage, a concise handbook, English language skills exercises, and editing activities. We take special pride in using writing samples and activities prepared by our students as models to guide, motivate, and challenge other students to write. We also have sought to provide teaching illustrations and step-by-step activities related to ideas and concerns that run the gamut from contemporary matters to timeless concerns—all designed to cultivate confidence in students, motivate them to write, and provide sufficient experience to help them craft essays and other written correspondence of which they can be proud.

Chapter One is devoted to an extensive discussion of "The Sentence," the kernel of all good writing. This chapter addresses the following: "Sentence Patterns," "Sentence Sophistication and Expansion," and "Modifying Elements." The teacher who has a class of inexperienced writers may need to spend considerable time reviewing sentence patterns, while a class of more experienced writers may simply review modifying elements or skip the sentence review and proceed to paragraphs. The teacher can also make sentence skills assignments according to individual student needs in one class. The instructor's manual for this text provides suggestions and detailed activities for instruction for proficiency at each level.

In Chapter Two students are introduced to a treatment of "Writing Paragraphs." This chapter first entails a comprehensive discussion of the body paragraphs, with illustrations that relate to a plethora of subjects—from hairstyles, HBO comedy, shopping, and cosmetics, to soap operas and love. Practice activities are provided, with some requiring students to do peer editing and one requiring interviewing of fellow students. The second kind of paragraph discussed is the introduction, divided into a discussion of five lead-in strategies and then the thesis statement. Next is a discussion of the conclusion, with identification of the most common strategies used. And the final paragraph discussed is the transitional paragraph. A series of activities is provided for student practice. A checklist serves as a quick review of the basics regarding beginning, ending, and transitional paragraphs, and a similar checklist follows the discussion of the body paragraphs.

As its title implies, "The Essay in Summation," Chapter Three of the text, sums up all other basic features and steps involved in writing essays. The chapter begins with a comparison of the paragraph to the essay, informing students that they can write effective essays if they can write well-developed paragraphs. Next, students learn of the impact that audience, diction, and point of view have on writing and the steps involved in executing the actual writing process—from developing a positive attitude to prewriting and progressing to drafting, revising/rewriting, editing, and proofreading the essay. A thorough explanation of formal outlines is provided. Although formal outlines are not required as often today as they were perhaps ten or fifteen years ago, even in English classes, some teachers occasionally require them, and students at the senior level who have plans of attending graduate school often admit that they have no knowledge of outlining. Therefore, in addition to urging students to organize their thoughts better and write more coherent essays in composition classes, to some degree, we are helping them to excel in future graduate studies. We have chosen to use dual terms "revising" and "rewriting" for the third critical step in the writing process. We have discovered that students often consider *revising* to be checking over papers for a spelling error or two, or changing a word choice here and there, and maybe rephrasing a sentence—in other words, spending a few minutes with the draft before typing it or keying in these few changes in their text before printing it for submission. Apparently, they misunderstand or are resistant to doing any additional major work on the essay. We hope by using the term *rewriting,* more students will recognize that they are expected to make major changes, revising several sentences in one paragraph and possibly rewriting another entire paragraph or constructing a new one to add to existing text to strengthen the essay and receive a better grade than they might otherwise receive. You will note that there are limited practice activities in this chapter. Prior to the essay activities—completion of an essay and composing another from scratch—we have not included activities on other features discussed, except for point of view. We know that students will be able to incorporate major points about audience and prewriting, among others, in writing the essays. We have provided, however, three exercises on point of view because students' essays consistently reflect inconsistency and improper choice of point of view. Students' writing samples also often demonstrate weaknesses in word selection or word logic (diction), so activities in word problems appear in Chapter Five of the text, titled "Choosing the Right Words."

In Chapter Four, titled "The Portfolio: The Student's Brag Book," students will be challenged to prepare and maintain a *brag book,* a book of their own writing progression and mastery of skills during the course of their enrollment in composition. The students' comprehension of all instruction given prior to the beginning of the portfolio assignment, and that which will appear in subsequent chapters, will be reflected in this brag book. Documents from the book—or the portfolio itself—may be an impressive addition to, or serve as, the students' dossier when they seek employment after graduation. Teachers will also benefit from having a hands-on innovative strategy to teach their students about the writing process, and the brag book may even offer some teachers a more definitive means of evaluating their students.

Chapter Five, "Choosing the Right Words," discusses the main word problems that writers generally face. Students are cautioned about misused words, jargon, and euphemisms or pretentious language. They learn the significance of knowing when to use the specific versus the concrete and distinguishing between denotative and connotative meaning. They also learn that selective use of figurative language can bring vitality to essay writing. Of special note in this section is the inclusion of new groups of widely ill-chosen words which have been found in students' writing. Such expressions heretofore have not appeared in mainstream textbooks that treat diction. A variety of practice activities have been selected to help students become better informed about the significance of word choices and consequently to be more selective in their word options without denouncing or denigrating the significance of their familial or personal language (language used in social/peer settings).

Chapter Six provides instruction and practice in the "Rhetorical Modes." Discussion of rhetorical modes is divided into the four types of discourse, discussed here in this order: *description*, *narration*, *exposition*, and *argumentation*. This chapter provides instruction in making writing vivid, providing accurate details, and choosing the most appropriate details, all of which help to create sensory impressions and recreate experience(s) for audience. We have chosen to discuss "Description" first because there is a need to employ this strategy in almost all writing. While some English teachers seldom require students to write "Narration" essays, students do need to know how to chronicle events, whether for entertainment, information, or persuasion purposes. Narration, like description, may also be used in other types of discourse and thus appears at the outset of our discussion of writing strategies.

The next and most extensive section on modes is exposition, which provides simple explanations of how to use "Illustration," "Process Analysis," "Comparison-Contrast," "Classification," "Causal Analysis," and "Definition." *Illustration* is the first strategy in this section since examples are keystones of almost all writing activities, and *Definition* is the last to be explained because all of the other strategies are employed, in varying degrees, in definition. Each section on the modes seeks to provide students with thematic sample essays and topics that will appeal to students on a personal (cultural) or generational level. For instance, in the section on definition, students will be asked to define terms such as "Big Mama," "Word," and "hip hop culture," which have particular significance to them, but which would not appear in traditional texts. Some of the sample essays have been left unedited so that the students' untouched works can be examined, improved upon, or patterned after by those who need specific guides in formulating or reworking their own ideas. Instructors may use these samples to enhance any teaching unit, be it on organization and development, sentence structure, punctuation, or usage.

Finally, the last mode or discourse to be discussed is "Argumentation." Along with basic rules and tips about persuasive writing, we provide instruction in writing two types of persuasive communication: the position paper and the proposal. It is our hope that students will recognize the universal relevance of this writing strategy as well as others to which they are exposed or which they use in English composition classes.

After detailed discussion and practice in using critical thinking skills in argumentation, students should be well prepared to write essays using literature as source,

Chapter Seven. After an introduction to writing about literature, four common types of literary analyses—characterization, theme, symbolism, and imagery are described, with two sample essays of each literary type. A list of four writing topics is provided for each type of literary analysis. The next chapter of the text is devoted to the research paper, starting with an overview and detailing each step of the research process, from choosing a subject for study to typing the final paper. Two sample research papers, one on a literary topic and the other on a general topic, are presented.

The final writing assignment addressed is "The Essay Examination," Chapter Nine. Teachers in various disciplines often use one or more essay questions in their class examinations. Sometimes students need to answer in only one well-developed paragraph, but increasingly they have to write a 400–500 word response, and therefore need to know how to proceed in taking essay tests. However, an even greater reason for students to know how to approach essay examinations is the increasing importance of state-mandated tests that require college students to write a 500 word essay to demonstrate their mastery of composition skills. Thus, in Chapter Nine, we share the strategies and tips we have tried, and have found successful, in helping our students pass state-mandated tests.

Since writers everywhere will always have questions about usage, in Chapter Ten we have included a glossary of usage and a concise review on grammar, punctuation, and mechanics to benefit those students who have skill deficiencies. As college teachers, we prefer to teach our students developmental grammar, but in our concerted effort to reach the student, we have chosen to include whatever may be of the most assistance to teachers and their students; hence there are exercises on some of the most common usage errors. For the convenience of both the student and teacher we have also provided pre- and post-grammar tests as well as other editing activities, challenging the student to correct a multiplicity of errors and more closely simulating what students must do when they write their own papers—be they college essays, job correspondence, applications, or the like. It is this communicative empowerment that is the ultimate goal of the authors of this textbook.

1

The Sentence

SENTENCE PATTERNS

Knowing basic sentence patterns is a part of mastering the writing process. If you know the possible components of the sentence, you can structure your sentences more soundly and with greater sophistication.

Subject-Action Verb (S-AV)

S-AV is the most basic of all sentence patterns. (An action verb is any verb that does not indicate a state, as in the forms of the verb *to be*, *seem*, and so forth.) An adverbial often follows the action verb (AV) in this pattern.

SUBJECT	ACTION VERB (PHRASE)	ADVERBIAL
Sharon	ate	
Sharon	ate	*hurriedly*. (an adverbial follows the S-AV pattern)
Dave	was walking	*to the store*. (the adverbial in this sentence is in the form of a prepositional phrase— *to the store*)

Activity
Construct five sentences in which you use the S-AV (adverbial) pattern.

1. _____
2. _____
3. _____
4. _____
5. _____

Subject-Action Verb-Direct Object (S-AV-O)

The S-AV-O pattern contains a subject, an action verb, and a *direct object* (a noun or a pronoun that receives the action of the action verb). When using personal pronouns as direct objects, you must take care to use the objective case.

SUBJECT	VERB (PHRASE)	DIRECT OBJECT
Sharon	ate	the cake.
Bill	is having	a party.
Lucy	broke	a fingernail.

Activity 1

Complete the partial constructions below with an appropriate action verb. Make sure that your *action verb* is one that can take a direct object.
DIRECT OBJECT

1. Judy _____ the baby.
2. My mother _____ the train.
3. The teacher _____ the students.
4. Tina _____ crossword puzzles.
5. The policemen _____ some of the criminals.

Activity 2

Place a different *personal pronoun* in each space below. Try to avoid using *you* or *it*.

1. My children love _____.
2. I do not know _____.
3. We left _____ in the cafeteria.
4. The teacher met _____ in the classroom.
5. My mother feeds _____ every day.

Activity 3

Construct five sentences in which you use the S-AV-O pattern.

1. _____
2. _____
3. _____
4. _____
5. _____

Subject-Action Verb-Indirect Object-Direct Object (S-AV-IO-DO)

This pattern is much like the S-AV-O pattern. It too must use the *action* verb. However, the S-AV-IO-DO pattern can employ only certain action verbs, such as those listed below.

call	bring	steal
make	give	bake
write	mail	knit
leave	throw	wire
send	sell	buy
tell	save	find

The indirect object most often comes right after the verb and is *understood* to mean *to* or *for* something or someone.

SUBJECT	VERB	INDIRECT OBJECT	DIRECT OBJECT
1. Ralph	gave	the dog	a bath.
2. Mom	sent	*me	some cookies.
3. Helen	wrote	Henry	a long letter.

* All personal pronoun objects, either direct objects or indirect objects, are in the objective case.

Activity 1
Place an appropriate noun in the blanks below.

1. Carol baked _____ vanilla pudding.
2. The teacher gave the _____ passing grades.
3. My father wired _____ some money.
4. My uncle sells _____ used cars.
5. Every Christmas, Grandma knits _____ sweaters.

Activity 2
Place an appropriate personal *pronoun* in the spaces below. Try to avoid using *you* or *it*.

1. Sheryl bought _____ a sweater.
2. Dave mailed _____ a letter.
3. The witness told _____ a lie.
4. Jeff gave _____ some money.
5. Gabriel wrote _____ a letter.

Activity 3

Construct five sentences in which you use the S-AV-IO-DO pattern. Use personal pronouns in at least three of them.

1. _____
2. _____
3. _____
4. _____
5. _____

Subject-Verb-Subjective Complement (S-V-SC)

S-V-SC contains a subject, a verb—not an action verb, but a linking verb (see *linking verbs* under Parts of Speech), and an adjective or noun that comes behind the linking verb and either describes or renames the subject (subjective complement). When using a personal pronoun as a subjective complement, take care to use the nominative case.

SUBJECT	VERB	SUBJECTIVE COMPLEMENT
1. Katie	is	my friend (renames the subject)
2. The mango	tastes	good (describes the subject)
3. Your notion	seems	unlikely (describes the subject)
4. The guilty party	was	*she* (renames the subject)

Activity 1

Place an appropriate *linking* or *be* verb in each blank space below.

1. That piano _____ odd.
2. My sister _____ my best friend.
3. The teacher _____ ill.
4. Her hair _____ unreal.
5. The judge's sentence _____ unfair.

Activity 2

Place appropriate personal pronouns in each of the spaces below. Remember that personal pronouns used as subjective complements must be in the nominative case.

1. It was _____ who made the speech.
2. The winner is _____ .
3. These are _____ .
4. I am _____ .
5. The culprits were _____ .

Activity 3

Construct five sentences in which you use the S-V-SC pattern. Take care to use appropriate *linking* verbs.

1. _____
2. _____
3. _____
4. _____
5. _____

General Activity 1

Identify the pattern of each sentence listed below as one of the four that we have just studied in this unit. Be able to justify your answer.

S-V (AV)

S-AV-DO

S-AV-IO-DO

S-V-SC (adjective or noun)

_____ 1. Ken drives too fast.

_____ 2. The man gave his wife a ring.

_____ 3. The dean wrote the student an excuse.

_____ 4. Dr. Dawson's new car is really super.

_____ 5. Mr. Simpson seems unhappy.

_____ 6. The hermit lives far out in the woods.

_____ 7. Kelly mowed the grass for her mother.

_____ 8. Sherry's casserole tasted ghastly.

_____ 9. We worked in Jennifer's garage.

_____ 10. Nobody is having any fun.

Pattern Variations

Often, when a sentence is a question or begins with an adverbial (as one word or as a prepositional phrase), the pattern is not at first clear. In order to see the basic pattern more clearly, make the question a statement or take the beginning adverbial and place it at the end of the sentence; place the noun that follows the verb in front of the verb. If the word that seems to be an adverbial is *there*, you may rewrite the sentence, leaving *there* out completely.

EXAMPLES:

Question: Did Shannon feed the dog?

Statement: Shannon did feed (fed) the dog. (S-V-DO).

Question: Will they arrive on time?

Statement: They will arrive on time. (S-V-(adverbial))

Beginning Adverbial: In the front room sat a table and a single chair.

Restated: A table and a single chair sat in the front room. (S-V-(adverbial))

Beginning Adverbial: There is a roach in my bed.

Restated: A roach is in my bed. (S-V-(adverbial))

General Activity 2

Notice how the various patterns that we have studied work together to express clear, well-structured sentences in the paragraph on the next page. See how many of these patterns you can recognize. Discuss any minor modifications and tell how each change affects the effectiveness of the sentence and/or the paragraph.

1. On Sundays, the entire family lends Mom a hand in the kitchen. 2. My father is an amateur chef; 3. therefore, he makes the fanciest dishes. 4. Last Sunday, he made a squash casserole. 5. He gave each family member only a small portion of it. 6. My brother always prepares the salad. 7. He puts only lettuce, tomato, and cucumbers in the bowl. 8. He never deviates. 9. The poor fellow seems uncomfortable in the kitchen. 10. I prepare the dessert. 11. I am a great cook, 12. so I get lots of raves for my cherry and pumpkin pies, my red velvet cakes, and my apple turnovers. 13. My family loves the kitchen on Sundays.

```
 1. _____
 2. _____
 3. _____
 4. _____
 5. _____
 6. _____
 7. _____
 8. _____
 9. _____
10. _____
11. _____
12. _____
13. _____
```

General Activity 3

Construct a well-developed paragraph. After you have completed it, pick out the basic sentence patterns that you have used. Identify those that are *inverted* or *not written in their regular order*.

SENTENCE SOPHISTICATION AND EXPANSION

The sentences in the preceding section are all very simple. Most of them are basic patterns that lack sophistication. There are many ways that plain sentences can be embellished. The purpose of this section is to explore these ways and to help you learn to employ them in making your writing more mature.

Nominal Elements

The noun is a word that names a person, place, or thing. The noun can function as a subject, a direct object, an indirect object, a subjective complement, an appositive and in many other positions. Review these functions.

1. Her <u>plan</u> is unfair.

   the noun as the subject

2. We disliked <u>Mary</u>.

   the noun as the direct object

3. The children paid their <u>mother</u> no attention at all.

   the noun as indirect object

4. Charles is a <u>professional</u>.

   the noun as a subjective complement

5. Helen's idea, a very good <u>plan</u>, was accepted by the group.

   the noun as an appositive (a noun that comes immediately after another noun and renames it, as <u>plan</u> renames <u>idea</u>)

The Noun Clause

The *noun clause*, like all clauses, contains a subject and a verb. It can also contain other sentence elements such as direct objects, subjective complements, and appositives. (Note should be made here that, like the singular noun, a single noun clause, regardless of its content, takes a singular verb when it is used as a subject.) The noun clause, as its label indicates, can be used in most of the ways that a noun can be used. Take a look at various functions of the noun clause.

1. a. Her <u>plan</u> is unfair.

      the noun as subject

   b. <u>That she is so rich</u> is unfair.

      the noun clause as the subject

NOTE: Noun clause subjects, usually those beginning with "that," are often extraposed (moved) to the end of the sentence, and the expletive "it" is put in the subject's place.

---

c. It is unfair <u>that</u> <u>she</u> <u>is</u> <u>so</u> <u>rich</u>.

Even at the end of the sentence, the noun clause is still the subject, not *it*; the verb still agrees with the noun clause.

2. a. We disliked <u>Mary</u>.

the noun as direct object

b. We disliked <u>whatever</u> <u>Mary</u> <u>said</u>.

the noun clause as direct object

3. a. The children paid their <u>mother</u> no attention at all.

the noun as indirect object

b. The children paid <u>whatever</u> <u>their</u> <u>mother</u> <u>said</u> no attention at all.

the noun clause as indirect object

4. a. Charles is a <u>professional</u>.

the noun as subjective complement

b. Charles is <u>whatever</u> <u>he</u> <u>wants</u> <u>to</u> <u>be</u>.

the noun clause as subjective complement

5. a. Helen's idea, a very good <u>plan</u>, was accepted by the group.

the noun as appositive (Notice that this appositive is set off by commas. The commas are used because the appositive is only added information. It is not needed to identify the noun that it renames. If the appositive were needed for identification, no commas would be used.)

b. Helen's idea, <u>that</u> <u>we</u> <u>should</u> <u>go</u> <u>to</u> <u>the</u> <u>beach</u>, was accepted by the group.

the noun clause as an appositive (Notice that the noun clause appositive, like the regular noun, is also set off by commas because it is only added information.)

A noun clause is structured the same way that a simple sentence is. The major difference is that the noun clause is introduced by words that bring about subordination, and therefore cause the statement to be dependent. As a result, the noun clause must be used as a part of a sentence (as a subject, direct object), and cannot stand independently as a sentence can. Take a look at some of the words that can introduce a noun clause:

that	what	whatever
who	whoever	whom
whomever		

The words can be added at the beginning of complete ideas (sentences) to make them noun clauses. Notice how the added word (except when it is *that*) *takes the place of* a word already in the independent construction. *That* is simply added on. Notice the examples below.

6. a. Sentence: Paul said <u>something</u>.

   Noun Clause: <u>Whatever</u> Paul said.

   Noun Clause in a Sentence: <u>Whatever Paul said</u> upset his wife.

   Noun clause as the subject of a sentence

   b. Sentence: She should love <u>me</u>.

   Noun Clause: <u>Whom</u> she should love.

   Noun Clause in sentence: Gail does not know <u>whom she should love</u>.

   Noun clause as the object of the verb

   c. Sentence: John will come home soon.

   Noun Clause: <u>That</u> John will come home soon.

   (Notice that *that* is simply added; it does not replace a word in the original sentence.)

   Noun clause in a sentence: Mary's idea, <u>that John will come home soon</u>, is unfounded.

   Noun clause as an appositive for the noun, <u>idea</u>.

Activity 1

Rewrite each of the sentences below, replacing each underlined noun phrase with a noun clause.

1. Sheila paid <u>her young son</u> a lot of attention.

   REWRITE: _____

2. <u>Mike's story</u> did not sound true.

   REWRITE: _____

3. I do not know <u>her name</u>.

   REWRITE: _____

4. Tina's notions, <u>some insane ideas</u>, are never grounded in fact.

   REWRITE: _____

5. Jan named her baby <u>Sandy</u>.

   REWRITE: _____

Activity 2

Place appropriate noun clauses in the blanks below.

1. _____ was _____.

2. Shauna loves _____.

3. The students talked about _____.

4. Sylvia's secret, _____, will soon be public knowledge.

5. _____ made me sick.

The Gerund Phrase

The *gerund phrase*, like the noun clause, can be used in most of the ways in which a noun can be used. Its main feature is its *verb + ing* form. Also, the gerund, like the sentence and the noun clause, can contain objects or complements. Notice how another unit can be used in noun positions.

1. a. <u>Her</u> <u>plan</u> is unfair.

     the noun as subject of the sentence

   b. <u>His</u> <u>cheating</u> <u>on</u> <u>the</u> <u>test</u> is unfair.

     the gerund phrase as the subject of the sentence (a single gerund phrase subject, like a singular noun subject, takes a singular verb). The noun or pronoun that precedes the gerund is always in the possessive case.

2. a. We disliked <u>Mary</u>.

     the noun as the direct object

   b. We disliked <u>standing</u> <u>in</u> <u>the</u> <u>rain</u>.

     the gerund phrase as the direct object

3. a. The children paid <u>their</u> <u>mother</u> no attention at all.

     the noun as the indirect object

   b. The children paid their <u>mother's</u> <u>constant</u> <u>begging</u> no attention at all.

     the gerund phrase as the indirect object

4. a. Charles is a <u>professional</u>.

     the noun as the subjective complement

NOTE: The sentence above does not lend itself very easily to a gerund phrase as a subjective complement, but gerund phrases can be used in this position. Look at the following sentence.

---

   b. <u>Seeing</u> <u>Charles</u> is <u>seeing</u> <u>a</u> <u>professional</u> <u>man</u>.

     Here a gerund phrase is used as both the subject and as the subjective complement.

Activity 3
Replace each underlined noun phrase in the sentences on the next page with a gerund phrase.

1. <u>Tommie</u> is silly.

   REWRITE: _____

2. <u>The</u> <u>noise</u> got on my nerves.

   REWRITE: _____

3. The sign that the skirmish is over is a <u>white</u> <u>flag</u>.

   REWRITE: _____

4. My children love <u>the</u> <u>beach</u> in the summer.

   REWRITE: _____

5. Helen's idea, a very good <u>plan</u>, was accepted by the group.

   REWRITE: _____

Activity 4
Place appropriate gerund phrases in the blanks below.

1. _____ was _____.

2. Shauna loves _____.

3. The students talked about _____.

4. Sylvia's hobby, _____, can cost a lot of money.

5. After _____, I awoke refreshed and alert.

The Infinitive Phrase

The *infinitive phrase*, like the noun clause and the gerund phrase, can be used in most of the ways in which a simple noun can be used. Its main feature is *to + verb*; however, it can contain other components as well. A fully developed infinitive phrase can begin with *for + noun or pronoun* (in the objective case) *+to + verb + adverbial, direct object, subjective complement*, or any of the other sentence elements that you have already looked at in previous lessons. Take a look at the infinitive phrase being used as a noun.

1. a. Her <u>plan</u> is unfair.

      the noun as the subject of the sentence.

   b. <u>For</u> <u>her</u> <u>to</u> <u>make</u> <u>such</u> <u>plans</u> is unfair.

      the infinitive phrase as the subject of the sentence (The single infinitive subject, like the singular noun subject, takes a singular verb.)

   c. It is unfair <u>for</u> <u>her</u> <u>to</u> <u>make</u> <u>such</u> <u>plans</u>.

NOTE: Subject infinitive phrases, like subject noun clauses, are often extraposed (moved); and the expletive "it" is put in the subject's place.

2. a. We disliked <u>Mary</u>.

   the noun as the direct object

   b. We disliked <u>for Mary to say something untrue about our soror-ity</u>.

   the infinitive phrase as the direct object

3. The children paid their <u>mother</u> no attention at all.

   the noun as the indirect object

NOTE: *The infinitive phrase does not lend itself to being used in this position very easily.*

4. a. Charles is a <u>professional</u>.

   the noun as the subjective complement

NOTE: *The infinitive phrase also does not lend itself to being used in this position very well; however, in another construction, one in which balance is being shown, you may use the infinitive phrase as a subjective complement very easily.*

   b. <u>To know Charles</u> is <u>to know a professional</u>.

   the infinitive as both subject and subjective complement

5. a. Helen's idea, a very good <u>plan</u>, was accepted by the group.

   the noun as an appositive

   b. Helen's idea, <u>for us to go to the beach on Sunday</u>, was accepted by the group.

   the infinitive phrase as an appositive

Activity 5
Replace each underlined noun phrase in the sentences below with an appropriate infinitive phrase.

1. <u>My car</u> is <u>an old jalopy</u>.
2. <u>His accusation</u> hurt us badly.
3. Gina's thoughts, <u>mere reminiscences about boys</u>, trouble her mother.
4. Edie's son hates <u>apple pie</u>.
5. The thieves wanted <u>the loot</u>.

Activity 6
Fill in each blank below with an appropriate infinitive phrase.

1. _____ is_____.
2. Shauna loves _____.

3. The students talked about what _____.

4. Sylvia's hobby, _____, can cost a lot of money.

5. It is wrong _____.

General Activity 1

Read the paragraph below, paying very close attention to the underlined <u>noun</u> <u>clauses</u>, <u>gerund</u> <u>phrases</u>, and <u>infinitive</u> <u>phrases</u>. Then, reread the paragraph, reducing each underlined element to the <u>final</u> noun or pronoun (with its modifiers) of each construction. Read the paragraph a third time, commenting on the changes in meaning, specificity, and sophistication that you now observe.

> <u>To know Bob Durant</u> is <u>to know a gentleman</u>. First, he acts like a gentleman. For example, Bob loves <u>holding doors open for young ladies</u> and <u>giving his seat to the elderly</u>. He likes <u>to tip his hat</u>, and he deplores <u>using foul language</u>. Secondly, this young man's appearance is that of a gentleman. <u>Grooming his hair</u> and <u>shining his shoes</u> are daily considerations for Bob. He also puts a lot of time into <u>pressing his clothes</u> and <u>taking care of his personal hygiene</u>. Finally, Bob Durant is a man of considerable integrity. <u>What he says is the truth</u> is actually the truth. He hates <u>to tell a lie</u>. For <u>Bob to make a promise</u> is for <u>him to stick to a promise</u>. Everyone can always depend on Bob's word. Bob Durant is the epitome of a gentleman.

General Activity 2

Fill in each blank below with the construction requested on the right.

SUBJECT

1. <u>The cat</u>   frightened me. Noun phrase

   _____   frightened me. Noun clause

   _____   frightened me. Gerund (phrase)

   _____   frightened me. Infinitive (phrase)

DIRECT OBJECT

2. I like <u>a good movie</u>.   Noun phrase

   I like _____. Noun clause

   I like _____. Gerund (phrase)

   I like _____. Infinitive (phrase)

PREDICATE NOUN

3. Our error was our <u>fault</u>.   Noun phrase

   Our error was _____. Noun clause

   Our error was _____. Gerund (phrase)

   Our error was _____. Infinitive (phrase)

INDIRECT OBJECT
4. I paid my <u>husband</u> no attention.   Noun phrase

   I paid _____ no attention. Noun clause

   I paid _____ no attention. Gerund (phrase)

OBJECT OF PREPOSITION
5. We talked about <u>the class</u>.   Noun phrase

   We talked about _____. Noun clause

   We talked about _____. Gerund (phrase)

MODIFYING ELEMENTS

Modifiers are simply words, phrases, or clauses that modify, qualify or limit other words, phrases, or clauses. The *adjective* and the *adverb*, in their various forms, are the two modifiers that are used in the English language.

Adjectivals

The adjective qualifies or limits nouns and pronouns or words, phrases, or clauses that function as nouns. Take a look at the adjective more closely.

1. Dr. Lucas is an <u>old</u> lady.

   <u>Old</u> limits or qualifies <u>lady</u>, a noun.

2. <u>Only</u> you can make a significant difference.

   <u>Only</u> limits or qualifies <u>you</u>, a pronoun.

3. Ms. Bailey drives a <u>red</u> Toyota.

   <u>Red</u> limits or qualifies <u>Toyota</u>, a proper noun.

   The three sentences above would still be very legitimate sentences without <u>old</u> or <u>only</u> or <u>red</u>. However, you would know significantly less about <u>lady</u> or <u>you</u> or <u>Toyota</u>, if the modifiers were not present. Therefore, you can appreciate the limiting or qualifying roles that adjectives play in the English language.

Activity 1
Rewrite each of the sentences below, using an adjective to qualify or limit each underlined word. Feel free to consult your dictionary or thesaurus for the best possible descriptive words.

1. The <u>children</u> rode the <u>horses</u> at the <u>show</u>.
2. <u>People</u> often put off <u>tasks</u> that should be done immediately.
3. <u>Stars</u> in the <u>sky</u> can warm a <u>heart</u>.
4. My <u>sisters</u> think that their <u>boyfriends</u> are men.
5. Yesterday, a <u>snake</u> crawled into our <u>meeting</u> and scared all of the <u>ladies</u>.

> *SUGGESTION: You should read your sentences aloud to compare and contrast the effects that your chosen modifiers have had on the meanings that the altered sentences now convey.*

Thus far, you have looked at only single words that play the parts of adjectives. You should realize, however, that other grammatical units—clauses and phrases—can also function in limiting and qualifying capacities.

The Relative (Adjective) Clause

The relative clause, like all clauses, contains a subject and a verb, and can contain other sentence elements such as a direct object, a subjective complement, or an appositive. The relative clause functions the same way as a single-word adjective in that it serves to limit or qualify a noun or pronoun. However, unlike the single-word adjective, which usually comes *before* the word that it modifies, the relative clause comes *after* the word it limits or modifies.

The relative clause also differs from the single-word adjective in that the relative clause has special words that are used to introduce it. Take a look at these special words and the particular situations under which they are used.

Relative Pronoun Chart

PRONOUN	CASE	USAGE NOTE
which	nominative/objective	refers to nonhumans only
who	nominative	refers to humans only
whom	objective	refers to humans only
whose	possessive	refers to humans and nonhumans
that	nominative or objective	refers to both humans and nonhumans (the most commonly used relative pronoun)

Relative Pronoun Functions

The relative pronoun functions within the relative clause the same way that any other pronoun functions within a simple sentence. Although the relative pronoun is always fronted in the clause, the relative pronoun can act as a subject, subjective complement, direct object, and so forth. The best way to determine the function of the relative pronoun is to take it and place it in regular syntactical order.

1. The lady <u>whom</u> <u>Bob</u> <u>loves</u> works in my office.

    Bob loves <u>whom</u>.

    Bob loves the <u>lady</u>.

    Both <u>whom</u> and <u>lady</u> function as the direct object.

2. The family <u>that</u> <u>lives</u> <u>next</u> <u>door</u> is very noisy.

    <u>The</u> <u>family</u> lives next door.

    <u>that</u> lives next door

    Both <u>the</u> <u>family</u> and <u>that</u> act as the subject.

3. A person <u>to</u> <u>whom</u> <u>much</u> <u>is</u> <u>given</u> is very blessed indeed.

Much is given to a <u>person</u>.

Much is given to <u>whom</u>.

Both <u>person</u> and <u>whom</u> are the object of the preposition <u>to</u>.

4. The man <u>whom</u> <u>Terrie</u> <u>gave</u> <u>the</u> <u>letter</u> is the postman.

Terri gave <u>the</u> <u>man</u> the letter.

Terri gave <u>whom</u> the letter.

Both <u>the</u> <u>man</u> and <u>whom</u> function as the indirect object.

Activity 2

Read the sentence pairs below and discuss the difference in level of detail(s) between the <u>a</u> and the <u>b</u> sentences.

1. a. Dr. Lucas is an <u>old</u> lady.

   single-word adjective modifying <u>lady</u>

   b. Dr. Lucas is a lady <u>who</u> <u>is</u> <u>very</u> <u>old</u>.

   a relative clause modifying <u>lady</u>

2. a. <u>Only</u> you can make a significant difference.

   single-word adjective modifying <u>you</u>

   b. You <u>who</u> <u>are</u> <u>concerned</u> <u>with</u> <u>the</u> <u>plight</u> <u>of</u> <u>young</u> <u>people</u> can make a significant difference.

   a relative clause modifying <u>you</u>

3. a. Ms. Tate drives a <u>red</u> Toyota.

   a single-word adjective modifying <u>Toyota</u>

   b. Ms. Tate drives a Toyota <u>that</u> <u>is</u> <u>red</u>.

   a relative clause modifying <u>Toyota</u>

4. a. This has been a <u>hectic</u> day.

   a single-word adjective modifying <u>day</u>

   b. This is a day <u>which</u> <u>has</u> <u>been</u> <u>very</u> <u>hectic</u>.

   a relative clause modifying <u>day</u>

5. a. The <u>sick</u> man was rushed to the hospital.

   a single-word adjective modifying <u>man</u>

   b. The man <u>who</u> <u>was</u> <u>sick</u> was rushed to the hospital.

   a relative clause modifying <u>man</u>

6. a. <u>His</u> car is in the shop.

   a single-word adjective modifying <u>car</u>

   b. The man <u>whose</u> <u>car</u> <u>is</u> <u>in</u> <u>the</u> <u>shop</u> must walk home.

   a relative clause modifying <u>man</u>

7. a. The company gave the <u>diligent</u> worker a bonus.

   a single-word adjective modifying <u>worker</u>

   b. The worker <u>to</u> <u>whom</u> <u>the</u> <u>bonus</u> <u>was</u> <u>given</u> was Mr. Flint.

   a relative clause modifying <u>worker</u>

Notice the word that introduces the relative clause in each sentence above. Is each used appropriately? Recheck the usage and case note of each to make sure. Also, check to see if you could have used one of the other words in place of the one that was actually used. Why is there an option? Why is there no option?

The Relative Pronoun Deleted

Whom, which, and *that,* when used as a direct object, indirect object, object of the preposition, or in any other objective situation within the relative clause, can be deleted. However, if the preposition comes before its relative pronoun object, the objective relative pronoun cannot be deleted.

Determining Relative Pronoun Function and Deletability

Regardless of its function within the clause, the relative pronoun is always fronted—placed at the beginning. Therefore, it is sometimes difficult to determine the way in which it is functioning within the relative clause. Three suggestions to follow are

1. If *no* noun or pronoun comes between the fronted relative pronoun and the verb of the clause, the relative pronoun is in the nominative case (usually the subject of the clause). The relative pronoun is *not* deletable.

2. If a preposition comes at the very beginning or at the end of the clause, the relative pronoun is most often the object of the preposition. If the preposition begins the clause, the relative pronoun is not deletable.

3. If a noun or pronoun *does* come between the relative pronoun and the verb, more than likely the relative pronoun is in the objective case—a direct object or an indirect object. The relative pronoun is deletable. See examples below.

EXAMPLES:

1. a. The man <u>whom</u> <u>we</u> <u>saw</u> was wearing green trousers.
   We saw whom.
   whom = direct object = deletable

   b. The man <u>we</u> <u>saw</u> was wearing green trousers.
   Relative clause with the relative pronoun deleted

2. a. The students <u>that</u> <u>we</u> <u>gave</u> <u>the</u> <u>free</u> <u>samples</u> were delighted.
   We gave <u>that</u> the free samples.
   that = indirect object = deletable

   b. The students <u>we</u> <u>gave</u> <u>the</u> <u>free</u> <u>samples</u> were delighted.
   Relative clause with the relative pronoun deleted

3. a. The merchants <u>that</u> <u>we</u> <u>traded</u> <u>with</u> all gave discounts to college students.

   We traded with that.

   that = object of preposition (prep. not fronted) =deletable

   b. The merchants <u>we</u> <u>traded</u> <u>with</u> all gave discounts to college students.

   The relative clause with a deleted relative pronoun

Activity 3

Keeping the above explanations and helpful hints in mind, determine the function of each underlined relative pronoun below. Your answers should be discussed in class.

1. The star <u>whom</u> we all love is Denzel Washington.
2. The words <u>that</u> stayed on my mind had been spoken by my mom.
3. The physician <u>that</u> we spoke to was Dr. Trehenski.
4. In the middle of the crowd was a girl <u>who</u> had forgotten her own name.
5. After the prom, we went home with the girl <u>whose</u> house was closest to the school.
6. The two people to <u>whom</u> you must speak are Katie and Delores.

Activity 4

Underline the relative clause(s) in each sentence below, and then, if possible, delete the relative pronoun. Be able to justify your identification of each relative clause and your deletion, or failure to delete, each relative pronoun.

1. The girl who sits next to me sleeps in class.
2. The bandits whom I saw ran north on Tharpe.
3. The girl whom I gave very clear directions to still did not know which way to turn.
4. Some students whom I know never study.
5. The man that I will marry must have a personality that will complement mine.

Activity 5

Construct a sentence in which you use the indicated word as a relative pronoun. Then, *if possible*, rewrite each sentence and delete the relative pronoun.

1. Who
2. Whom
3. That

4. Which

5. Whose

NOTE: Review the form and function of a relative clause, and review the case of each relative pronoun before you begin to construct your sentences.

Restrictive and Nonrestrictive Relative Clauses

Restrictive relative clauses (those that are needed for the identification of the noun or pronoun) are *not* set off by a comma or commas, and nonrestrictive relative clauses (those that give only additional information) are. In addition, restrictive relative clauses *usually* modify common nouns, and non-restrictive relative clauses *usually* modify proper nouns.

1. a. The girl who just walked by is my cousin.

   common noun

   Who just walked by is a relative clause that is essential for the identification of girl.

   b. The girl is my cousin.

   Without the relative clause, *girl* lacks specific identification.

   c. Betty, who just walked by, is my cousin.

   proper noun

   Because the name Betty already identifies the girl, the relative clause is nonrestrictive (not essential for identification); there-fore, commas are used to set off the relative clause.

   Notice the same basic difference in the sets of sentences below.

2. a. The man who won the Oscar has starred in many movies.

   b. Mel Gibson, who won the Oscar, has starred in many movies.

3. a. The river which runs through our town is now flooding.

   b. The Flint River, which runs through our town, is now flooding.

There are some exceptions to these basic rules.

A. *That* Usage

   A relative clause that begins with *that* can never be nonrestrictive (set off with commas); it must always be restrictive (not set of with commas).

   The story that I wrote was published.

B. Relative Pronoun Deletion

   A relative clause with a deleted relative pronoun can never be nonrestrictive (set off with commas); it must always be restrictive.

   The song (which) she sang was "Black Gold."

C. Restrictive Clauses with Proper Nouns

When there is more than one person or item with the same name and there is a need to make a distinction between/among them, *the* is placed before the person or item and a restrictive relative clause is used.

1. <u>The</u> Susan White who went to school with me works at Sears.

   The restrictive relative clause is needed to distinguish one Susan White from other women by the same name.

2. The Rockie Mount <u>from</u> <u>which</u> <u>Bob</u> <u>hails</u> is in Virginia, not North Carolina.

   Same distinction

D. Nonrestrictive Clauses with Common Nouns

When a common noun has already been identified by a possessive noun or when specific knowledge about a common noun is already shared by the speaker and listener, a nonrestrictive relative clause is used.

1. Tim's watch, <u>which</u> <u>is</u> <u>very</u> <u>expensive</u>, was given to him by his father.

   <u>Tim's</u> already identifies <u>watch</u> (a common noun); therefore, a nonrestrictive relative clause is used.

2. My brother, <u>who</u> <u>lives</u> <u>in</u> <u>Atlanta</u>, is coming to visit me.

   If the listener knows that the speaker has just one brother, then a nonrestrictive clause can be used with brother, a common noun.

Activity 6

Each sentence below contains at least one relative clause. First, underline the relative clause. Second, circle the word that it modifies. Third, determine whether the relative clause is restrictive or nonrestrictive and punctuate it accordingly. Be able to give a reason for each of your choices.

1. One of the songs that Whitney Houston sings in the movie is "I'll Always Love You."

2. Sam's father who is a medical doctor is on staff at Meigs Memorial.

3. The Dr. Hugo who won first prize is from Chicago.

4. I spoke to Francis Hill who was reading a book that her sister had written.

5. The movie we saw starred John Denver.

6. Atlanta which is located in northern Georgia is often said to be a city that is growing by leaps and bounds.

Activity 7

Combine the two sentences in each set below so that the *b* sentence functions as a relative clause within the *a* sentence. Be careful to place your relative clause as closely as possible to the word it modifies and punctuate it correctly. Also, be sure to use appropriate relative pronouns.

EXAMPLE:

    a. Mr. Thompson is my English professor.

    b. Mr. Thompson has written several novels about slavery.

    Combined: Mr. Thompson, who has written several novels about slavery, is my English professor.

1. a. Sidney's car is that red convertible.

   b. Sidney's car was involved in an accident.

2. a. My alma mater is known for graduating all of its athletes within five years.

   b. My alma mater is located in north Florida.

3. a. The heart belongs to me.

   b. You stepped on the heart.

4. a. Mrs. Henderson loves to work crossword puzzles.

   b. Mrs. Henderson is confined to a wheel chair.

5. a. The hungry students appreciated our efforts.

   b. We cooked a big meal for the hungry students.

Adjective Phrases

A phrase is a group of words that work together as a unit. The participial phrase (present and past), the prepositional phrase, and the infinitive phrase are all word groups that can function in the same manner as a single-word adjective or a relative clause. That is, each of these units can modify a noun or noun substantive by limiting, qualifying, or specifying the noun.

    A. *Participial phrases* come in two basic forms, present and past. The present participle is made by adding *ing* to the basic form of the verb. The past participle is often marked by adding *ed* to the basic form of the verb or by changing the verb to its past participial form. The phrases can contain direct objects, subjective complements, and other sentence elements.

EXAMPLES:

    a. <u>playing</u> in the rain   present participial

    b. <u>sitting</u> on the step   phrases

a. <u>baked</u> by Jane   past participial

b. <u>stung</u> by a wasp   phrases

Notice the differences in the verb forms in the examples above. Take a close look at the sentences below. Notice that participial phrases give more specific information than regular adjectives alone do.

1. a. The <u>naughty</u> children will catch cold.

   a regular adjective modifying <u>children.</u>

   b. The children <u>playing in the rain</u> will catch cold.

   a present participial phrase modifying <u>children</u>

2. a. The <u>sick</u> man was rushed to the hospital.

   a regular adjective modifying <u>man</u>

   b. The man <u>stung by a wasp</u> was rushed to the hospital.

   a past participial phrase modifying <u>man</u>

As the examples above show, a restrictive (essential for identification) participial phrase most often comes immediately after the word that it modifies. However, if the phrase is nonrestrictive (used only to add information), it may be found not only immediately behind the words that it affects, but also at the beginning or at the end of the sentence as well. A comma or commas are also used to set off the nonrestrictive participial phrase. When placing a nonrestrictive participial phrase at the beginning or end of a sentence, you must be careful to make sure that the relationship between the phrase and the word that it modifies is unmistakably clear.

EXAMPLES:

a. <u>Grinning from ear to ear</u>, Shirley broke the news of her engagement to Sidney.

b. Shirley, <u>grinning from ear to ear</u>, broke the news of her engagement to Sidney.

c. Shirley broke the news of her engagement to Sidney, <u>grinning from ear to ear</u>.

In sentences *a* and *b*, the relationship between Shirley and the participial phrase, <u>grinning from ear to ear</u>, is quite clear. You would readily assume that it is Shirley who is grinning. However, in sentence *c*, the relationship is not as clear. In fact, it seems that Sidney is the one grinning. You should be careful not to cause such confusion.

B. *Prepositional phrases* consist of a preposition, the noun it governs, and any modification of that noun.

EXAMPLES:

a. <u>behind</u> me

b. <u>after</u> lunch

c. <u>at</u> the mall

The sentences below show that prepositional phrases give more specific information than regular adjectives give, but less information than participial phrases do.

1. a. The <u>pretty</u> girl is my sister.

   a regular adjective modifying girl

   b. The girl <u>behind</u> <u>me</u> is my sister.

   a prepositional phrase modifying <u>girl</u>

   c. The girl <u>standing</u> <u>behind</u> <u>me</u> is my sister.

   a present participial phrase modifying <u>girl</u>

2. a. A <u>quick</u> nap is refreshing.

   a regular adjective modifying nap

   b. A nap <u>after</u> <u>lunch</u> is refreshing.

   a prepositional phrase modifying nap

   c. A nap <u>taken</u> <u>after</u> <u>lunch</u> is refreshing.

   a past participial phrase modifying <u>nap</u>

C. An *infinitive phrase* usually consists of *to* plus a verb, with a noun that it governs and any modifiers of that noun. However, it can be expanded to include *for*, plus a noun (in the objective case). The infinitive phrase also gives more specific information than the regular adjective does.

EXAMPLES:

Basic infinitive phrases

a. to leave (early)

b. to sleep (late)

c. to believe (him)

expanded infinitive phrases

a. for them to leave early

b. for the children to sleep late

c. for his wife to believe him.

The following sentences show that the infinitive phrase, like other adjective phrases, gives more specific information than the regular adjective alone does.

1. a. The <u>best</u> game is the one between Dallas and Oakland.

   a regular adjective modifying <u>game</u>

   b. The game <u>to</u> <u>watch</u> is the one between Dallas and Oakland.

   a basic infinitive phrase modifying <u>game</u>

2. a. The storm was a <u>good</u> reason.

   a regular adjective modifying <u>reason</u>

   b. The storm was a reason <u>for</u> <u>him</u> <u>to</u> <u>leave</u> <u>early</u>.

   an extended infinitive modifying <u>reason</u>

Activity 8

Identify each underlined construction below as a participial phrase (pp), a prepositional phrase (pr), or an infinitive phrase (ip). Be able to justify your answer and to point out the word in the sentence that each construction modifies. Use the symbol in parenthesis after each phrase type to indicate your choice.

_____ 1. The essay <u>written by Gena</u> earned an "A."

_____ 2. The man <u>sleeping on the sidewalk</u> is homeless.

_____ 3. The student <u>in the middle</u> works for Dr. Hill.

_____ 4. The movie <u>to see</u> is *A Place in the Sun*.

_____ 5. Being hungry was no real reason <u>for him to do that</u>.

_____ 6. The roll <u>called by Sgt. Finderson</u> included my name.

_____ 7. The space <u>between his eyes</u> has turned blue.

_____ 8. The road <u>to freedom</u> must pass through the land of suffering.

_____ 9. They were sitting beside the lady <u>playing the piano</u>.

Activity 9

Construct five sentences in which you use the indicated phrasal construction as a modifier of a noun. Underline each targeted construction.

1. present participial phrase
2. expanded infinitive phrase
3. prepositional phrase
4. past participial phrase
5. basic infinitive phrase

Activity 10

Reduce the *b* sentence in each set below to its participial phrase or infinitive phrase. Then embed that construction into the *a* sentence. Be careful to place the targeted element so that it clearly modifies the word whose meaning it best enhances.

EXAMPLE:

  a. The children loved the role.

  b. The role was played by their mother.

    embedded: The children loved the role *played by their mother.*

    past participial phrase modifying <u>role</u>

1. a. The store is Ross.

  b. The store is frequented by teenagers and adults alike.

  embedded:

2. a. At the corner of Thinnes and Vine, I saw a drunk man.

   b. The man was leaning against the street sign.

   embedded:

3. a. Hannah had a special mission.

   b. Hannah's mission was to learn all that she could about life after death.

   embedded:

4. a. I do not know the reason.

   b. The reason is for Henry to stay out so late.

   embedded:

5. a. Everyone loved the fruit cake.

   b. The fruit cake was baked by Patty's mother.

   embedded:

Adverbials

The adverb, like the adjective, is a modifier. The adjective modifies nouns, pronouns, and noun substantives. The adverb, on the other hand, modifies verbs, adjectives, and other adverbs by answering such questions as how? when? where? why? to what extent? and so forth. Adverbs, especially adverbs that modify verbs, are the most movable parts of speech in the English language; therefore, they may be found in different places in the sentence.

   EXAMPLES:

1. a. Charles made the phone call <u>hastily</u>.

   b. Charles <u>hastily</u> made the phone call.

   c. <u>Hastily</u> Charles made the phone call.

   <u>Hastily</u>, an adverb which answers the question

   <u>how</u>, clearly modifies the verb *made*, regardless of its different positions in the sentences.

2. a. <u>Every day</u> Katie goes to church.

   b. Katie goes to church <u>every day</u>.

   <u>Every day</u> clearly modifies the verb <u>goes</u> and answers the question when, regardless of its different positions in the sentences.

At times, however, the writer must take greater care in placing the adverb in the sentence. This is especially true when the adverb can possibly modify more than one word or word group.

3. a. The man announced hurriedly that he would be leaving.

   It is difficult to determine whether <u>hurriedly</u> is modifying <u>announced</u> or <u>would be leaving</u>.

   b. <u>Hurriedly</u> the man announced that he would be leaving.

c. The man <u>hurriedly</u> announced that he would be leaving.

In sentences 3b and 3c, <u>hurriedly</u> is more clearly indicating that the announcement was made in a speedy fashion.

d. The man announced that he would be <u>hurriedly</u> leaving.

e. The man announced that he would be leaving <u>hurriedly</u>.

In sentences 3d and 3e, <u>hurriedly</u> is more clearly indicating that the departure would be done in a speedy fashion. Remember that a clear and obvious relationship is a must in constructing effective sentences.

The Adverb Clause

A clause is a group of words which has a subject and a verb, just as the sentence does. It may also, like the sentence, contain elements such as a direct object, subjective complement, or even adverbs. The characteristic that makes it unlike the sentence is that it is subordinate; it cannot stand alone; it functions within the sentence the way that individual parts of speech do. The adverb clause modifies words within the sentence the same way that regular adverbs do. Such words as *if, since, when, although, after, before, as if, because,* and *while* introduce the adverb clause and render it subordinate. Because they are clauses, they give more information and make a sentence more complex—and thus more sophisticated—than regular adverbs.

1. a. Marion registered for classes <u>yesterday</u>.

   A regular adverb (of time) modifying <u>registered</u>.

   b. Marion registered for classes <u>when</u> <u>she</u> <u>returned</u> <u>from</u> <u>vacation</u>.

   An adverb clause (of time) modifying <u>registered</u>.

Each adverbial element modifies *registered*, but it is obvious that sentence 1b is more specific and that its clausal structure makes the sentence more complex and sophisticated. In fact, in sentence 1b, the reader is given two major ideas in one sentence construction. This is not the case in 1a.

Movability

Like the regular adverb, the adverb clause can often be placed first, last, or in the middle of the sentence.

2. a. <u>Because</u> <u>they</u> <u>were</u> <u>on</u> <u>extended</u> <u>maneuver</u>, the soldiers from Ft. Bragg were forced to walk ten miles.

   b. The soldiers from Ft. Bragg, <u>because</u> <u>they</u> <u>were</u> <u>on</u> <u>extended</u> <u>maneuver</u>, were forced to walk ten miles.

   c. The soldiers from Ft. Bragg were forced to walk ten miles <u>because</u> <u>they</u> <u>were</u> <u>on</u> <u>extended</u> <u>maneuver</u>.

   The relative clause in the sentence above fits well into all three positions.

3. a. <u>Although</u> I <u>make</u> <u>only</u> <u>six</u> <u>thousand</u> <u>dollars</u> <u>a</u> <u>year</u>, I do not want any public assistance.

   b. I, <u>although</u> I <u>make</u> <u>only</u> <u>six</u> <u>thousand</u> <u>dollars</u> <u>a</u> <u>year</u>, do not want any public assistance.

   c. I do not want any public assistance, <u>although</u> I <u>make</u> <u>only</u> <u>six</u> <u>thousand</u> <u>dollars</u> <u>a</u> <u>year</u>.

Sentence 3b seems a bit awkward with the clause in the middle, mainly because the placement of the clause disrupts the rhythm of the sentence. Writers must use their own discretion in making their sentences more effective. Writers must always make sure that their adverb clause has a focused function and modifies the entire main clause or some word or word group within the main clause. Notice that the adverb clause in sentences 2a to 2c modifies *were forced to walk* and that in the sentences 3a to 3c, the adverb clause modifies *do (not) want*. Such clarity is imperative in writing effective sentences.

Comma Usage

All *introductory* adverb clauses are set off with a comma, regardless of length. The placement of commas with middle and final adverb clauses depends on whether or not the clause is essential to the reader's understanding of a word or word group in the main clause; if the adverb clause is essential (restrictive), no comma or commas are needed; if the adverb clause is not essential (nonrestrictive), then a comma or commas are needed. The point should be made that this is not a standard rule, and many variations are found among writers. Notice the varied treatment of the middle and final clauses in sentences 2b–c and 3b–c above.

Activity 1

Add a word that introduces an adverb clause to either of the two sentences in each set below; subordinate the sentence that sets forth a condition for an action or situation within the other sentence and then add it to the remaining sentence. Be careful to place and punctuate your clauses correctly.

EXAMPLE:

   a. Michael Jordan bagged a three-pointer.

   b. The fans cheered.

     Combined: *When* Michael Jordan bagged a three-pointer, the fans cheered.

1. a. I was washing my hands.

   b. My ring slipped off.

     Combined:

2. a. The scouts were all asleep.

   b. A bear entered their camp.

     Combined:

3. a. They still love each other.

   b. They have been divorced for years.

   Combined:

Activity 2

Construct five sentences in which you use adverb clauses. Vary the placement (beginning, middle, or end) of your clause in each sentence.

1. _____

2. _____

3. _____

4. _____

5. _____

Adverb Phrases

The *absolute phrase* is the present or past participial form of a verb, which is fronted by its own subject. It is understood to have the same full meaning that an adverb clause has, but the predicate verb in the absolute is not complete; there is no helping verb to accompany the present or past participial form of the verb.

ADV CLAUSE:

   1. a. If the <u>weather</u> <u>permits</u>, we will be in Dallas by noon.

AB PHRASE:

   1. b. The <u>weather</u> <u>permitting</u>, we will be in Dallas by noon.

     Both the clause and the phrase modify <u>will</u> <u>be</u>.

ADV CLAUSE:

   2. a. The parents stayed up late <u>because</u> <u>their</u> <u>children</u> <u>had</u> <u>gone</u> <u>to</u> <u>visit</u> <u>their</u> (the <u>children's)</u> <u>grandparents</u>.

AB PHRASE:

   2. b. The parents stayed up late, <u>their</u> <u>children</u> <u>having</u> <u>gone</u> <u>to</u> <u>visit</u> <u>their</u> (the <u>children's)</u> <u>grandparents</u>.

     Both the clause and the phrase modify <u>stayed</u> <u>up</u> <u>late</u>.

ADV CLAUSE:

   Sheila, <u>because</u> <u>her</u> <u>arm</u> <u>was</u> <u>bandaged</u> <u>from</u> <u>her</u> <u>fingers</u> <u>to</u> <u>her</u> <u>shoulder</u>, drove with considerable difficulty.

AB. PHRASE:

   Sheila, <u>her</u> <u>arm</u> <u>being</u> <u>bandaged</u> <u>from</u> <u>her</u> <u>fingers</u> <u>to</u> <u>her</u> <u>shoulder</u>, drove with considerable difficulty.

   Both the clause and the phrase modify *drove*.

Notice that the absolute phrase, like the adverb clause, is movable. Also notice that it is set off with a comma or commas, regardless of its place in the sentence.

The *infinitive phrase* can also function in an adverbial capacity. Most adverbial infinitives have the same meaning as adverb clauses beginning with *so that*.

ADV CLAUSE

   1. a. We left church early <u>so</u> <u>that</u> <u>we</u> <u>could</u> <u>beat</u> <u>the</u> <u>traffic</u>.

INF PHRASE

   1. b. We left church early <u>to</u> <u>beat</u> <u>the</u> <u>traffic</u>.

       Both the clause and the phrase modify <u>left</u>.

ADV CLAUSE

   2. a. <u>So</u> <u>that</u> <u>they</u> <u>could</u> <u>get</u> <u>to</u> <u>the</u> <u>far</u> <u>side</u> <u>of</u> <u>the</u> <u>river</u>, the children fashioned a canoe out of sticks, tree bark, and old wire.

INF PHRASE:

   2. b. <u>To</u> <u>get</u> <u>to</u> <u>the</u> <u>far</u> <u>side</u> <u>of</u> <u>the</u> <u>river</u>, the children fashioned a canoe of sticks, tree bark, and old wire.

       Both the clause and the phrase modify <u>fashioned</u>.

ADV CLAUSE:

   3. a. Lewis moved back to Chicago <u>so</u> <u>that</u> <u>he</u> <u>could</u> <u>be</u> <u>closer</u> <u>to</u> <u>his</u> <u>elderly</u> <u>parents</u>.

INF PHRASE:

   3. b. Lewis, <u>to</u> <u>be</u> <u>closer</u> <u>to</u> <u>his</u> <u>elderly</u> <u>parents</u>, moved back to Chicago.

       Both the clause and the phrase modify <u>moved</u>.

All introductory and middle adverbial infinitives are set off with a comma or commas (see sentences 2b and 3b). Final infinitives are usually not (see sentence 1b). Notice in sentence 3b that middle adverbial infinitives can be somewhat awkward; therefore, the writer should take a close look at all aspects of placement in order to construct the most effective sentence.

When using adverbial infinitives, many writers tend to omit the performer of the action that is expressed in the main clause. Such an omission makes for a vague and faulty sentence.

EXAMPLES:

   1. a. <u>To</u> <u>make</u> <u>the</u> <u>best</u> <u>use</u> <u>of</u> <u>your</u> <u>time</u>, an activity schedule should be made each week.

     b. A shorter route must be taken <u>to</u> <u>get</u> <u>to</u> <u>school</u> <u>on</u> <u>time</u>.

A good way to avoid the weakness of the sentences above is to start the main clause with the most probable performer of the action.

NOTICE:

2. a. <u>To make the best use of your time,</u> you should make an activity schedule each week.

   b. <u>You</u> must take a shorter route <u>to get to school on time</u>.

Because the performers of the actions are clearly stated, sentences 2a and 2b are much stronger than sentences 1a and 1b.

The *prepositional phrase* is one of the most common phrasal forms in the English language. It is made up of a *preposition* (a word such as *after, over, around, among, in*), the *object of the preposition* (a noun or pronoun in the objective case), and any modifiers of that noun or pronoun.

EXAMPLES:
–around the world

–in a red sports car

–by the side of the road

–in an effort to get to the church on time

–after the storm

–before lunch

All of the constructions above are prepositional phrases, and each can be used as an adverb that modifies a verb.

They sailed <u>around the world</u>.

They arrived <u>in a red sports car</u>.

The stranded motorist sat <u>by the side of the road</u>.

Adverbial prepositional phrases are most often found behind the verbs that they modify; however, they can also introduce the sentence. When they come at the beginning and are long (usually five words or more) or proliferated (two or more prepositional phrases joined together), they are set off with a comma. Short introductory prepositional phrases are usually not set off with a comma, unless the omission of the comma could cause the sentence to be misread.

–<u>In an effort to get to the church on time</u>, the groom thumbed a ride with a total stranger.

–<u>After the storm</u> the sun came out.

–<u>Before lunch</u>, rooms are cleaned and beds are made.

The phrase in the first sentence is long (nine words) and proliferated (several phrases included); therefore, a comma is needed to set it off. The phrase in the second sentence is short (three words), so no comma is needed. Although the phrase in the third sentence is very short (two words), a comma is used in order to prevent a possible misreading. Notice that *lunch*, without the comma, could be read as the object of *before* or as a part of the compound word, *lunch rooms*.

Before lunch rooms are cleaned and beds are made.

Thus, we use a comma to set off the prepositional phrase.

If an adverbial prepositional phrase interrupts a sentence to add non-essential information, it is set off with commas.

The groom, <u>in</u> an <u>effort</u> <u>to</u> <u>get</u> <u>to</u> <u>the</u> <u>church</u> <u>on</u> <u>time</u>, thumbed a ride with a total stranger.

That same phrase, however, is not set off with a comma at the end of the sentence.

The groom thumbed a ride with a total stranger <u>in</u> an <u>effort</u> <u>to</u> <u>get</u> <u>to</u> <u>the</u> <u>church</u> <u>on</u> <u>time</u>.

Activity 1

Construct five sentences, placing an adverbial construction in the indicated position.

1. Introductory infinitive phrase

2. Final absolute phrase

3. Interrupting prepositional phrase

4. Introductory absolute phrase

5. Interrupting or middle adverb clause

Activity 2

Indentify the phrase or clause type underlined in each sentence below. Circle the word or word group in the sentence or main clause that it modifies. Be able to justify your choices.

IDENTIFICATION

_____ 1. Tina went to the library <u>to</u> <u>study</u> <u>for</u> <u>her</u> <u>French</u> <u>test</u>.

_____ 2. <u>If</u> <u>you</u> <u>want</u> <u>to</u> <u>see</u> <u>a</u> <u>beautiful</u> <u>sight</u>, you must see my rose garden.

_____ 3. <u>The</u> <u>weather</u> <u>being</u> <u>cold</u> <u>and</u> <u>dreary</u>, we stayed inside all day.

_____ 4. Sherry moved closer to the front of the class room <u>so</u> <u>that</u> <u>she</u> <u>could</u> <u>see</u> <u>the</u> <u>board</u> <u>better</u>.

_____ 5. <u>On</u> <u>a</u> <u>small</u> <u>cot</u> <u>in</u> <u>the</u> <u>back</u> <u>of</u> <u>the</u> <u>room</u>, three small children lay huddled together.

_____ 6. <u>His</u> <u>eyes</u> <u>filled</u> <u>with</u> <u>tears</u> <u>of</u> <u>joy</u>, Charles embraced everyone in the room.

_____ 7. <u>To find out what all of the secrecy was about</u>, Milton crept into the office and went through everyone's personnel files.

_____ 8. The president discontinued his speech, <u>his voice being drowned out by the jeers of protesting students</u>.

Activity 3

Add a clause, absolute phrase, infinitive phrase, or prepositional phrase that acts as an adverbial to each of the sentences below. Be able to justify your choice of construction, its placement, and its punctuation in regard to sentence effectiveness. For comparison, you may want to write two or more versions of each sentence, each time using a different construction.

1. Few people vote in state, county, and city elections.

2. Most of the students participated in a university-wide protest.

Compounding

Compounding is the connecting of two or more separate parts to act together as a unit. In speech there are several means by which connections are made. Among these means are hand gestures and facial expressions. The connectors below are the main ones that are employed in the writing process.

Coordinating Conjunctions: and, but, or, nor, for, so, and yet

Correlative Conjunctions: neither . . . nor, either . . . or, and not only . . . but also

Conjunctive Adverbs: however, moreover, nevertheless, therefore, thus, and so forth.

Both the semicolon (;) and the comma (,) are marks of punctuation that are usually employed in the connecting process; most often, in conjunction with one of the connectors listed above, they can help ideas in a sentence to flow more easily and show better relationships.

When you connect ideas, you must make sure that they are parallel in both grammatical structure and content. That is, all items being paired together—sentences, clauses, phrases, words—should be of equal importance and of the same kind.

1. a. Shannon is a full-time student, and she is a full-time wife and mother.

   Notice that the comma (,) and "and" are used here to connect these two sentences. Also, notice that the two ideas are equal in importance.

   b. Shannon is a full-time student, but she is also a full-time wife and mother.

The difference in the choice of connectors shows a difference in the relationship of the two ideas. Sentence 1a focuses on the likeness of the two ideas; sentence 1b focuses on the differences in the two ideas.

Coordinating conjunctions, as you have seen illustrated above, can show different relationships between ideas. Conjunctive adverbs and correlative conjunctions can also make similar distinctions.

> c. Shannon is a full-time student; <u>however</u>, she is also a full-time wife and mother.

> d. Shannon is a full-time student; <u>therefore</u>, her time as wife and mother is very limited.

In 1c, *however* prepares the reader for a contrast in ideas; in 1d, *therefore* prepares the reader for a result. Thus, in making effective sentences, the writer should choose his connectives carefully to make his point clear.

We should also focus on the difference between the punctuation of the conjunctive adverbs when they come between two sentences. Notice that the sentences in 1a and 1b are connected by a comma and a coordinating conjunction. The sentences in 1c and 1d are connected by a semicolon, a conjunctive adverb, and a comma. The conjunctive adverb can also interrupt the second sentence and show the same relationship between the two ideas. In such instances, a comma should precede *and* follow the conjunctive adverb. Both the coordinating conjunction and the conjunctive adverb may be preceded by a period; however, many writers frown upon using the coordinating conjunction after a period.

> e. Shannon is a full-time student; she is, <u>however</u>, also a full-time wife and mother.

Notice the change in punctuation when the conjunctive adverb interrupts a sentence.

Correlative conjunctions indicate a reciprocal or complementary relationship. They come in pairs, and the writer should be especially careful to make sure that the items that they connect are paired equally.

> f. <u>Either</u> Shannon is a full-time student, or she is a full-time wife and mother.

Each component of the *either . . . or* combination comes before a complete sentence. This set of correlatives shows an *alternative* relationship. Other pairs can make other distinctions. More will be discussed about equal pairing with all conjunctive elements later in this unit.

The comma, semicolon, and the coordinating conjunction *alone* can sometimes come between two sentences. If two sentences are closely related and are parallel, a semicolon can be used between them.

> g. Shannon studies in the morning; she cooks and cleans in the afternoon.

Each sentence generally follows a subject–action verb–prepositional phrase (as an adverbial modifier) format. Thus, the constructions are parallel.

If two sentences are parallel and short (about three words), either a comma *alone* or a coordinating conjunction *alone* can be used between them.

>   h. Shannon cooks <u>and</u> she cleans.

>   i. Shannon cooks, her husband cleans.

There are several ways of showing coordination between sentences. The same, to some extent, can be said about smaller elements—words, phrases, and clauses. These items can come in pairs, but they are quite often found in a series. In either case, you must still take care to make sure that connected constructions are parallel—that they have the same or similar grammatical formats and that they manifest ideas that are equal in meaning.

The sentences below show the balance or parallel structure that connected items must have if a sentence is to be effective and your ideas are to be correctly conveyed. Ideas are first paired and then used in a series to point out the variations in punctuation that can occur.

>   *WORDS*

>   2. a. We ate ice cream <u>and</u> cake.

>   b. We ate ice cream, cake, and bananas.

Notice that the two nouns in sentence 2a are joined by *and*; no comma precedes the connector. However, it is the usual practice of good writers to insert a comma before *and* when more than two items are listed in the series, as in 2b.

>   c. We ate <u>neither</u> the ice cream <u>nor</u> the cake.

>   d. We ate <u>neither</u> the cake <u>nor</u> the ice cream <u>nor</u> the bananas.

Each component of the correlative, even when more than two items are being connected, comes before parallel units—nouns—in the sentences above. This same practice holds true with larger units.

>   *PHRASES*

>   3. a. Charles must learn <u>to read</u> and <u>to write</u>.

>   b. Charles must learn <u>to read</u>, <u>to write</u>, and <u>to think</u> logically.

>   c. Charles learned neither <u>to read</u> nor <u>to write</u>.

Notice that only infinitive phrases are being used to express the coordinated ideas above.

>   *CLAUSES*

>   4. a. I believe in <u>what he says</u> and in <u>what he does</u>.

>   b. I believe in <u>what he says</u>, <u>what he does</u>, and <u>what he promises to do</u>.

>   c. I believe not only in <u>what he says</u> but also in <u>what he does</u>.

These noun clauses are treated in the same manner as the words and phrases above.

The examples above seem to be clear enough; however, there are times when handling sentence elements can be a bit puzzling. The treatment of compound predicates can present such a problem. The situation can be made clear, however, if you remember that a predicate is only the verb plus its modifiers and/or complements; it is not a sentence; therefore, it should not be treated as if it were. It should be handled in the same manner that words, phrases, and clauses are handled.

COMPOUND SENTENCE:

Betty goes to school in the morning, and she works for her father in the afternoon.

In most compound sentences, a comma is placed before *and*, especially if both sentences are relatively long. However, a comma is seldom placed before the *and* that connects a compound predicate, regardless of the length of each predicate.

COMPOUND PREDICATE:

Betty goes to school in the morning and works for her father in the afternoon.

Notice that the compound sentence has a subject for each verb: *Betty* for *goes* and *she* for *works*. The compound predicate, however, has just one subject—Betty—for both verbs, *goes* and *works*.

Some instances of using punctuation with coordinating conjunctions can be even fuzzier than the ones that have just been discussed. For example, *but*, when it is used to point out opposition or a significant contrast, can be paired with a comma between two *non-sentence* items.

COMMAS NOT NEEDED

a. I slept most of the night but didn't feel refreshed the next morning.

b. Mike asked Debbie to marry him several times but never got an answer.

But in each of the sentences above points out a difference, but not opposition or a significant contrast; it is not disjunctive. Therefore, we use no comma to separate the two parts of the predicate.

COMMAS NEEDED:

c. We are very poor, but very proud.

d. Lorna Dean is warm and friendly with her audience, but cold and distant with her family.

Sentences *c* and *d* need a comma before *but* because of the contrastive nature of the two elements that are being paired. *Poor* and *very proud* are unexpected mates that are in significant opposition to each other. The same can be said for *warm and friendly* and *cold and distant*. *But* separates in these two instances; it is disjunctive.

Another deviation from the basic rule can be found with *and*. *And*, when it is used to place emphasis on the second element of the pair, can be accompanied by a comma between two non-sentence constructions.

COMMAS NOT NEEDED:
  a. Lewis is tall <u>and</u> dark.

  b. Melvin is a doctor <u>and</u> a lawyer.

And is used in the sentences above simply as a device to show *connection* or *addition*. No particular emphasis is placed on either item.

COMMAS NEEDED:
  c. Tom's new wife is tall, <u>and</u> very pretty.

  d. He is a medical doctor by day, <u>and</u> a race car driver by night.

Commas are needed with *and* in sentences *c* and *d* because of the emphasis that is placed on the second element in each sentence. An intensifier (very, extremely, exceptionally, and so forth) is often placed before the second element to help highlight it.

A final departure from a customary practice can be seen with the use of the semicolon. You have learned in this unit that sentences can be combined by different means. However, until now, the semicolon has not been paired with a coordinating conjunction. The combination of these two is usually used when one or both of the sentences contain internal commas.

  1. a. Mrs. Tillman prepares lunch for her husband, her son, and her son-in-law, <u>and</u> her daughter prepares lunch for the children.

     b. Mrs. Tillman prepares lunch for her husband, her son, and her son-in-law; <u>and</u> her daughter prepares lunch for the children.

  2. a. At the reunion we saw Tess and John, my husband's friends, but we didn't see any of my husband's relatives.

     b. At the reunion we saw Tess and John, my husband's friends; but we didn't see any of my husband's relatives.

In 1a, the comma before the underlined *and* might cause you, upon your first reading, to think that *her daughter* is a part of the series of people for whom Mrs. Tillman prepares lunch. The final comma does not signal that the first sentence ends there. The semicolon in 1b gives that signal and prevents a misreading. In 2a, the second comma used to set off the appositive, *my husband's friends*, must also function as the comma used before the coordinating conjunction *but*, which separates the two independent clauses. Thus, you could very easily think that the phrase *my husband's friends* is in addition to Tess and John, *not* the same as Tess and John. Sentence *2b* prevents such a misunderstanding.

Activity 1
Write two different versions of the sentence sets below, using a different connector or means of connection in each version. Then compare the two versions to determine the effectiveness of each and their differences in meaning.

EXAMPLE:
  a. They will behave.

   b. They will go to their room.

     Either they will behave, or they will go to their room.

           Connected by correlative conjunctions

     They will behave; in fact, they will go to their room.

           Connected by a conjunctive adverb

1. a. Tom studies very hard.
   b. He seldom passes a test.

2. a. Lois and Roger will get married in Las Vegas.
   b. They will move to Honolulu.

3. a. The train from Atlanta will arrive at noon.
   b. The train from Miami will arrive at midnight.

4. a. The twins will practice with the chorus every day.
   b. They will not go on any road trips.

5. a. Sarah works very hard.
   b. She will go far in life.

Activity 2

Complete each of the partial sentences below with the indicated grammatical structure in a series (at least three). You may need to revisit the previous unit in an effort to refresh your memory of certain constructions. Remember to punctuate properly.

EXAMPLE:

   Lulu wants _____. (Infinitive Phrases)

   Lulu wants to learn to play the piano, to learn to fly a jet plane, and to learn to scuba dive.

1. Our team will take the train_____._____.
_____(Prepositional Phrases)

2. _____
   _____Margie joined the Army. (Infinitive Phrases)

3. When we went to Red Lobster, Katie ordered _____
   _____. (Noun Phrases)

4. _____
   _____Lena burst into tears. (Absolute Phrases)

5. _____
   _____are all that most teenagers think about. (Noun Clauses)

6. The man _____
   _____ is now in jail. (Relative Clauses)

7. The _____
   _____dress is the one that Monica wanted. (Adjectives)

8. _____
   _____Keisha calls her mom. (Adverb Clauses)

9. Rachelle likes _____
   _____(Gerund Phrases)

10. The man _____
    is LaTressa's uncle. (Relative Clauses)

General Activities

Activity 1

Enhance each basic sentence below by adding at least two sentence elements—absolute phrases, relative clauses, prepositional phrases—to each. Make sure that you punctuate properly and that each addition is meaningful to the sentence.

EXAMPLE:

The woman hit the man.

The woman (a) in the silver Mercedes hit the man (b) who was trying to cross the street.

Additions: (a) a prepositional phrase to modify woman.
(b) a relative clause to modify man.

1. The team left the court.

2. Mr. Fields loves Mrs. Fields.

3. Tina borrowed my dress.

4. We all went to the restaurant.

5. The sun came out.

Activity 2

Combine each of the sentences below so that you will have one sophisticated sentence. You may combine some sentences through various modes of connection, or you may reduce some sentences—deleting repetitive information—and make them function as a word, phrase or clause within another sentence. Remember to place and punctuate all additions correctly.

EXAMPLE:

    a. Sheila is a girl.

    b. Sheila wants to have her way about everything.

    c. Sheila is my best friend.

    d. I love Sheila.

I (d) love Sheila, (c) my best friend, although (a) she is a girl (b) who wants to have her way about everything.

(d) the main clause

(c) an appositive for <u>Sheila</u> in (d)

(a) an adverbial clause modifying <u>love</u> in (d)

(b) a relative clause modifying <u>girl</u> in (a)

1. a. Dictionaries cannot be brought into the testing arena.

    b. Notebooks cannot be brought into the testing arena.

2. a. My husband sent me a gift.

    b. The gift was perfume and lacy handkerchiefs.

    c. My husband sent a gift last week.

    d. My husband is a very thoughtful man.

3. a. The car sped down Elm Street.

    b. Its lights were flashing.

    c. Its horn was blowing.

    d. Its wheels were smoking.

4. a. The man gave us a lift.

    b. The man was generous.

    c. The man was Christian.

    d. The man was on his way to Miami.

    e. The lift was much-needed.

5. a. Kelso bought a suit.

    b. Kelso is a snappy dresser.

    c. The suit was blue.

    d. The suit was expensive.

    e. The suit was designed by Rudini.

Activity 3

Rewrite the paragraph below, combining and embedding sentences so that the paragraph will seem less choppy and the ideas will show better relationships. Feel free to add connectors of your choice.

Several of the English teachers at National State University have written popular novels. Dr. Horace Filburn wrote *Star Dust*. *Star Dust* is a novel about the antebellum South. Dr. Filburn is an assistant professor. His novel has sold two million copies. Mrs. Azeene DeJesus has also written a popular novel. Mrs. DeJesus is an instructor. Her novel is titled *El Lobo*. It is a novel about the plight of the Mexican American in American society. Both teenagers and adults alike buy and enjoy this novel. Dr. Geraldine Jones has written *Up from the Ghetto*. She is an associate professor. Her novel is very popular among African Americans. Her novel is about a woman. The woman overcomes her meager beginnings in a New York City ghetto. The woman in the novel becomes a medical doctor. National State University has its share of popular novelists in its English department.

Activity 4

Compare the two paragraphs below to determine if one is more effectively written than the other. Discuss their specific differences.

PARAGRAPH ONE

I put a lot of effort into keeping my closet neat. I put all of my shoes into the shoe rack. The shoe rack hangs on the door of my closet. I put my shoes in the rack as soon as I pull them off. My shoes are all lined up according to color. The black ones are at the top. The white ones are at the bottom. I make sure that every item of clothing is hung neatly on a hanger. I arrange my clothes in a particular order. I hang my blouses in front. My skirts come next. My pants come after my skirts. My dresses come after my pants. My coats come last. My hats are stacked neatly on the top shelf of the closet. My purses are stacked there also. My umbrellas are placed in a stand. The stand is in the back of the closet. My closet could win an award for neatness.

PARAGRAPH TWO

I put a lot of effort into keeping my closet neat. As soon as I pull my shoes off, I put them into the shoe rack, which hangs on the door of my closet. My shoes are lined up according to color, with the black ones at the top and the white ones at the bottom. Every piece of my clothing, which is hung neatly on a hanger, is also arranged in a particular order, with the blouses coming first, and the shirts, pants, dresses, and coats (in that order) coming next. My hats and purses are stacked neatly on the top shelf of my closet. My umbrellas are placed in a stand at the back of the closet. My closet could win an award for neatness.

Discuss specific paragraph differences:

Activity 5

Write a paragraph of seven to ten sentences. When you have finished with the first writing, read the paragraph to see where you can use connectors (or change some) and embed ideas so that your paragraph will read more smoothly. Rewrite the paragraph, incorporating the changes that you deem necessary.

2

Writing Paragraphs

BODY PARAGRAPHS

In this textbook we begin our discussion of writing with the sentence because the sentence is the kernel of all good writing. An idea means little if you are not able to couch it in some orderly, comprehensive pattern. After the sentence, the paragraph is the next basic component of written communication.

Of the several types of paragraphs, the body paragraph, or basic paragraph, is the one which we will review first. Understanding the purpose and basic features of the paragraph will help you in writing the other types, but more importantly, you will be equipped with what you need to communicate effectively in any kind of written correspondence.

In simplest terms, a paragraph is a group of sentences that clearly define, describe, defend, or explain a central point. Normally, the paragraph is composed of three parts: the topic sentence, the supporting sentences (evidence), and often a concluding sentence.

THE TOPIC SENTENCE

The topic sentence explicitly expresses the central point of the paragraph. Ambiguous topic sentences confuse the reader. For instance, what will the writer discuss if he writes this construction?

> Shopping at Henderson's Department Store can be a frustrating and time consuming experience, but also save you money.

Will the paragraph discuss the frustrations of shopping at Henderson's, or will it discuss the amount of time one spends there? Perhaps both of these will be discussed. Or does shopping become frustrating because it is time consuming? Will the writer give equal treatment to both the frustrations and the time involved? Just how long will the paragraph be? And what about a discussion of the money saved?

The preceding topic sentence is vague; the writer goes on a tangent in writing, inevitably commenting on *three* central ideas instead of developing *one* central point as a *paragraph* dictates. Always keep in mind that the topic sentence *controls* the content of the paragraph and therefore should clearly identify the subject and focus of it. With this in tact, the writer knows how to proceed in his discussion, choosing only details and examples that support the topic sentence, and the reader knows what to expect, as in these revised topic sentences.

1. Shopping in Henderson's Department Store can be frustrating because of the way merchandise is displayed.

2. Not only is the arrangement of merchandise a problem for shoppers, but also frustrating is the inordinate amount of time spent in trying to select the merchandise.

3. Rivaling both the arrangement and time wasted in selecting merchandise is the price that one pays for it.

Each of the sentences above would make a fitting topic sentence for a paragraph. The writer has directions in knowing how to proceed with his discussion, and the reader knows what to expect in the paragraph. One of the topic sentences is developed below.

> *Not only is the arrangement of merchandise a problem for shoppers, but also frustrating is the inordinate amount of time spent in trying to select the merchandise.* With two different price-slashing signs appearing above the clothing display, you certainly would like to buy one of the cheaper items, but the salespeople are usually nowhere to be found to answer questions about price. Then, when you finally find a salesperson, the employee cannot tell you whether the garment you want is being discounted at 30% or 40%. Thus, you must wait for her to find the manager, who she reports is taking a "repast" in her office and apparently will not answer any questions until she finishes the last morsel of her dinner. By the time you ascertain this information and decide to make the purchase, you must stand in one of three long lines, with approximately ten to twelve people in each one, despite the fact that the store has ten check-out aisles. There are two cash-only express lanes that invariably are closed. As if these inconveniences aren't enough to annoy you, the closer you get to the checkout counter, the slower the cashier moves, often needing check approval for the fourth customer in front of you; or she runs out of receipt tape the moment you put your goods on the counter. *Assuredly, if time is of essence to you, start checking out those mail order catalogs that you have been tossing aside or go shopping on the Internet, even if there is a Henderson's near your neighborhood.*

All of the sentences address the time issue. Each sentence—from finding a salesperson to paying for the merchandise—supports the idea that shopping at Henderson's is time consuming. The concluding sentence reiterates the topic sentence. Not all paragraphs need a concluding sentence; however, including one is a way of emphasizing the central point, especially if the topic sentence is the lead sentence in the paragraph and the paragraph is lengthy, as this one is.

Topic Sentence Position

There are three different positions for the topic sentence: at the beginning, at the end, or in the middle. You might omit an explicit topic sentence and present that main idea by implication.

At the Beginning

The traditional body paragraph begins with the topic sentence. The writer wants to plant his point about a given topic firmly in the reader's mind, and he then proceeds to present the evidence to substantiate his position.

> *Apparently, some women have forgotten that cosmetics, makeup in particular, are supposed to enhance a woman's natural beauty, not distort it.* Walk around any campus, state government building, church, and, surprisingly, the track or jogging trails, and you will see females of every age group and race plastered with foundation, pressed powder, lipstick, mascara, and eye shadow. While these so-called "beauty aids" are supposed to be applied moderately to give the illusion of effortless, natural beauty, one frequently notices excessive application of all of the above or superfluous application of one. For example, full lips are naturally beautiful, and gingerly applying a complementary shade of lip color enhances that beauty. However, some women seemingly attempt to *anoint* their lips; they apply so much color—often the wrong shade—and this act, accompanied by some ill-understanding of why and how to use the lip liner, causes them to transform voluptuous lips into an unattractive feature, laughable, not appealing. At other times, women misuse makeup by choosing improper shades for their complexions, resulting in noticeable disparities between face and neck or face and other exposed body parts, leaving the onlooker wondering, "Does she have a skin disorder?" And at other times, too much blush is applied, leaving the onlooker pondering whether the woman has been assaulted or whether she is preparing for a circus act. Certainly, women have the right to wear makeup if they choose, but when will they realize that too much detracts from, rather than adds to, their beauty, making them look *silly,* at best, instead of *sophisticated,* as they desire?

At the end

When the topic sentence appears first, the writer more or less seeks to report his conclusion or interpretation of some situation right away. He, in essence, says, "This is the way it is; now I am going to show you and you will reach the same conclusion." The reader can usually predict what is to come, spending limited time, if any, in contemplation. However, when the writer presents supportive material first and the topic sentence last, he presents data that creates or recreates a reality or experience that arouses the reader's curiosity and causes him to contemplate the significance of it. He discovers how right or wrong he was in the final sentence, which sums up that significance.

> What a pleasure it is to awaken in the morning at 7:45 in my rustic home and not hear the engines of neighbors' cars as they speed off to work, or to nap at noon during July and not hear the chatter and screams of children enjoying their summer vacation. Moreover, I certainly can appreciate the silence on Friday nights without having to be jolted awake by shrilling sirens, which can be heard at all hours of the day in the city and especially on Friday nights. Oh, doubly blessed am I, not to have to endure that noise. Furthermore, I do not have to be disturbed by uninvited guests who habitually visit at the most inopportune times, such as when I am showering, sitting down to eat, or just relaxing on Sunday afternoon. Thanks to higher gasoline prices, no one wants to risk coming thirty miles outside of the city limit and not finding me at home. Even door to door salesmen and church groups leave me to my solitude. *Oh, Countryside, dear Rustic Life, how I welcome the peace you bring.*

In the Middle

Sometimes a writer provides background information on a given topic prior to writing the topic sentence and subsequent supporting details. This places the topic sentence in the middle of the paragraph. The topic sentence remains the controlling sentence. The preceding information introduces or describes it, while those sentences that follow substantiate it.

> Attitudes and laws governing the place of children have changed tremendously over the last five decades. In decades past, most adults accepted the adage that children should be seen, not heard, and that sparing the rod would most certainly spoil the child. Unfortunately, in an effort to duly chastise unruly children, some parents, caretakers, and guardians have resorted to using abusive tactics that today are punishable by law, finally establishing and protecting the rights of those who previously had no objective voice. *Yet, the very laws that were established to protect children against undue punishment are now being used by some children themselves as punitive measures to control parents.* For instance, a child who does not get the trendy object he desires may have a temper tantrum. If scolded and threatened with punishment (non-corporal, in fact), the child may threaten to call authorities and file charges against the parent(s). This parent, fearing retaliation by the child, may decide not to punish the child, even though he or she may become profane and combative. In some other instances, when the parent has not ignored the child's threat and given reasonable corporal punishment, the parent has been arrested because of a simple phone call that the vengeful child made. This action creates havoc in the parent-child relationship and, ultimately, in the family, as the indignant, mortified parent, more often than not, wishing to avoid a

repeat performance, asks the child (usually a teenager) to leave home or stoically resolves to feed, clothe, and provide shelter alone for the child, abandoning any previous notions about nurturing him/her. Incidents like these are increasing every day, evident by daily talk show topics. This behavior is such a sad commentary on the state of the family—such colossal irony on the laws of humankind.

By Implication

At other times, writers do not deem it necessary to include a topic sentence in a paragraph. In instances such as these, they rely on precise explanations, details, and descriptions to reveal the central point of the paragraph overtly. Their point, they believe, is so painfully obvious that readers will immediately grasp its purpose.

> The day after Halloween it all begins. Each store in the mall becomes a collage of red, green, and gold, with Victorian pink quietly appearing in the background. Retailers yield to the temptation and quickly abandon the traditional easy listening sounds for more spirited tunes about joy, hope, and partridges; sacred muted tunes that fill patrons with wonder and awe; or toasty nestling lyrics about the approaching wintry season. Due to media blitzes, throngs of shoppers begin their procession through the mall, some lighthearted and festively dressed, others reluctant victims of peer pressure, all with giddy children running ahead in search of the jolly saint himself. The store clerks adorn their emmy award winning smiles and chant the well wishes of the season, as plastic slides in and out of credit card machines and gullible, smiling patrons lug away their purchases, reveling in the notion that though they have spent much, they have saved threefold what they spent at last year's preseason sales. And they will probably save even more this year, since there are approximately six weeks remaining before the big day arrives.

The writer of this paragraph expresses concern about how contemporary society rushes to celebrate Christmas, seemingly ignoring Thanksgiving altogether. You may use any one or more of these strategies in placing your topic sentences. The last one, the implied topic sentence, is used sparingly in essays, often appearing in narrations and in descriptions for emphasis, but almost always written by experienced writers. If you have limited experience in writing, you should always write explicit topic sentences, placing them at the beginning so that you will stay focused in your writing.

Activity 1
Write an explicit topic sentence for each idea listed below.

1. the character trait that I like least in people
2. a fashion trend that is a disgrace
3. the one act that will most likely destroy a friendship
4. the room that I like best in my house

5. the song that motivates me to do house (school, car) work

6. the reward that house plants afford

7. one reason a popular sitcom should be canceled

8. the first thing I notice in a romantic interest

9. the best advantage in dining out

10. the worst disadvantage in moving

Activity 2

The topic sentence for each paragraph below has been omitted. Fill in the blank that follows with an appropriate topic sentence.

> Kim Wilson, a court attorney with the Bronx Supreme Court, chooses sophisticated business apparel for the hardnosed legal scene. Mellody Hobson, a senior vice president with Chicago-based Ariel Capital Management Inc., prefers classic suits with a whimsical flair for the high-powered world of finance. Ertharin Cousin, director of the White House Liaison Office at the State Department, sticks with very classic, comfortable clothes for the Washington, D.C., power scene. On the West Coast, Yvette Lee Bowser, executive producer and creator of *Living Single*, chooses avant-garde power wear for her Tinseltown meeting. Freida Wheaton Bondurant, vice president and associate general counsel of Citicorp Mortgage Inc. in St. Louis, customizes her professional style in a business-casual setting. Atlanta secretary Cheryl Morgan expresses her personal style through sensible separates and suits. And Teresa Fleming of Detroit succeeds in maintaining a crisp, feminine image although she works in the gritty atmosphere of an auto assembly plant. (Lisa Jones Townsel, "Working Women: Dressing for Success," *Ebony*, September 1996: 61)

1. TOPIC SENTENCE:

_____

_____

_____

> After the 1992 election, he and Clinton drafted a written agreement that guaranteed Gore a major role in policymaking and appointments; particularly early on, the new president depended on the veteran senator to explain Washington to him. Gore is often the one to press Clinton to make a final decision. He pushed Clinton to take the environment seriously. Over the objections of tobacco sensitive political advisers, he won the president's commitment to pursue the ban on cigarette sales to teenagers . . . (Bill Turque, "What Mr. Smooth is Teaching Mr. Stiff," *Newsweek*, September 2, 1996: 26)

2. TOPIC SENTENCE:

_____

_____

_____

Frequently this means introducing human interest into your writing. Most of us, at any educational level, have an interest in other human beings and in human personalities. Most writers for lay audiences recognize this interest and use it to gain acceptability for their subject matter. For example, an article in *Time* about unemployment will give us statistical information about the numbers of people out of work. But the writer of the article knows that many of us do not relate very well to bare, abstract statistics, even when they affect us deeply, as do the facts about unemployment. Therefore, the *Time* writer will also usually introduce people into the article. Perhaps Bill and Mary Gould, a "typical" couple living in Detroit, Michigan, will be cited. We'll learn what effect Bill's being unemployed has had on their lives. We are interested in learning about what happens to real people, and through such knowledge we can better understand the problems unemployment creates. (Kenneth W. Houp and Thomas E. Pearsall, *Reporting Technical Information*, 1984, 5th Ed.: 23)

3. TOPIC SENTENCE:

_____

_____

_____

Activity 3

Write well-developed paragraphs for topics assigned below.

1. Place the topic sentence you wrote for #1 or #3 (in Activity 1) at the beginning and write a well-developed paragraph.

2. Place the topic sentence you wrote for #5 or #7 in the middle and write a well-developed paragraph.

3. Write a well-developed paragraph for #6 or #8, placing the topic sentence at the end.

4. Without including the topic sentence itself, write a well-developed paragraph that supports your central point for #2 or #4.

UNITY

All sentences in a paragraph must clearly relate to a central point. A reader must be able to see the significance of each sentence in relation to the central point.

Read the following paragraph; then analyze it for unity.

> (1) Many students attend my alma mater because of family tradition. My roommate's grandmother graduated with a degree in mathematics in 1952. (2) Then, in 1970 her mother matriculated at this institution, and it was here that her mother met her father. (3) They dated throughout their four years of school and got married shortly after graduation. (4) During the last four decades, cousins, aunts, and uncles have followed suit, earning degrees in a variety of areas, including biology, art, economics, and sociology, and a number have earned both the bachelor's and master's degrees here. (5) Hearing her loved ones talk about the university marching band, the hallowed campus hangout, and the challenges of this or that professor, my roommate, at an early age, developed a yearning to attend City University, collect her own stories, and, consequently, continue the family's educational legacy. (6) I know she enjoys walking around this big campus. (7) I can just imagine how she is going to talk about this when she starts telling her CU tales.

What is the central point of this paragraph? Does each sentence address family tradition? No, you should have questioned sentence 3. It is not necessary to write about the dating life of the parents. Did you find other unrelated sentences? Of course. Sentences 6 and 7 should not appear in the paragraph. While sentence 7 does make reference to the tradition, it is an extension of sentence 6, and thus it will not be needed after sentence 6 is removed. At other times, unity of a paragraph is destroyed because the writer either forgets to indent for his new paragraph idea or is so excited about the general topic of discussion that his thoughts leap ahead to another point before he completes his first thought. Such an example follows:

> Students should not be forced to attend classes because they have paid their money to go to school. If a student does not go to class, who loses? The student suffers, not the teachers and definitely not the school. If a student fails a class because he was not present to take notes and pass the examinations, then the student can accept his failure. Most class periods are repetitious any way. Students sit there listening to the teacher drone on and on about the same point. We do not do anything worthwhile. Just last week, for instance, I sat in English 1101 while the teacher explained pronoun agreement. They [sic] did not do anything but talk about pronouns. Can you believe that? I learned about it [sic] in grammar school.

Where does the first idea end? What is the second central point?

Sometimes a writer introduces a new idea at the end of a paragraph. The following paragraph demonstrates this third kind of common violation of paragraph unity.

> When the term "addiction" is mentioned, the average person immediately thinks about a dependence on drugs, alcohol, or cigarettes, but one can be obsessively attracted to any substance or activity, for that matter. One such addiction can be the soap operas. Some people organize their daily lives around the soaps. Some students are often more concerned about the time a class meets than they are concerned about who teaches

it. Why should one attend Composition I at 12:30 when she has not missed a single episode of *The Young and the Restless* (*Y and R*) since she was twelve years old? Of course, the VCR has proven to be her loyal friend in the past, but what if the tape breaks or she forgets to set the tape? You have guessed it. Her 12:30 hour is devoted to a light lunch and the *Y and R* cast. In addition, some housewives plan their day around the soaps. Contrary to what many believe, these women do not sleep until their favorite soap comes on. No, they arise early with two missions in mind: to get their daily work completed and to make certain that it is completed before their soap comes on. Housewives, students, and others like them (men too) become addicted to watching soap operas because there is something missing in their personal lives.

Clearly, the final sentence introduces a new idea. The focus of the paragraph is the effects of soap opera addiction, but the final sentence identifies a cause, which, if discussed at all, should appear in a separate paragraph. Careful re-reading of writing assignments will help you to prune irrelevant details from paragraphs.

Activity

Consider the word groupings below for each topic sentence. Select the word or phrase that most likely would be irrelevant in a paragraph about the topic sentence. Then, write a paragraph. Exchange the paragraph with a neighboring student. Has she or he violated unity? If so, how?

1. Football games can be therapeutic for those suffering from boredom on Saturday evenings.
   (a) the sound(s) of music
   (b) stadium seat players
   (c) fashions
   (d) concession prices

2. People who have several children habitually end up spoiling the youngest one because of several reasons.
   (a) self-centered individuals
   (b) financial security
   (c) sibling caretakers
   (d) wisdom through experience

3. Buying food at fast food restaurants is becoming increasingly frustrating.
   (a) slow employees
   (b) microwave food
   (c) wrong orders
   (d) multiple orders

4. My cousins, Jennifer and Jeraldine, criticize others who do not attend worship service on Sunday morning, but their behavior during church reveals their disinterest in worship itself.

   (a) staring and pointing at cute guys

   (b) nodding off occasionally during the sermon

   (c) never missing a Sunday, even on holidays

   (d) laughing when someone leads a solo

DEVELOPMENT

Another salient feature of effective paragraphs is development. In addition to making all ideas relate to the topic sentence, the writer must provide sufficient information to support the central point. It is a good idea to think of every paragraph as an argument. After writing your paragraphs, ask yourself whether you have provided enough details to prove whatever you have written in the topic sentence. If you find yourself asking, "What is the point here?" or "yes?" in a confused, expectant manner, then your paragraph is underdeveloped. The reader may not agree with your position on a given topic or idea, but he must be able to concur that you have provided ample discussion of your point.

An example of an underdeveloped paragraph follows.

> A teenager who commits heinous crimes should be treated as any other criminal. When one violates an individual, that individual suffers. Before he commits the crime, the adolescent knows that the potential victim will suffer because the teenager knows he is planning to do something that is wrong. Suffering is painful.

And? The preceding paragraph is a series of repetitive sentences. The writer alludes to the pain that the teenager's victim experiences. Granted, if one is a victim, he indeed suffers. The question that arises is whether the writer can be more specific, more convincing. Without becoming sensational in his discussion, can the writer make the reader *sense* the severity of the pain or loss and thus the *seriousness* of the offense, despite the *age* of the victimizer?

Contrast the preceding paragraph with the one below.

> A teenager who commits heinous crimes should be treated as any other criminal who commits the same or a similar offense. A young single parent who is beaten with a baseball bat and has her biweekly paycheck snatched from her by a fifteen year old has to find other provisions for her children or neglect their needs for another two weeks. Is it fair that her twelve and fifteen year old children be deprived of basic essentials while the truant youth squanders the money and, when caught, is given only a verbal reprimand and returned to his parents' custody? When one fires a gun at another individual at close range, that wounded person usually dies, whether the assailant is thirteen or forty-five years old. In those few instances when the victim survives, he is usually maimed for life—dependent upon family or some support person for assistance in

taking care of personal needs—and forced to become another government ward, destroying all hopes of ever realizing the American dream of prosperity. Even though the individual survives, is he not—in a sense—defeated for the remainder of his life? Is he less traumatized by his loss when he discovers his assailant was a thirteen year old girl? The answer is obvious, and so is the retribution set by the court system at large for anyone—whether thirteen or older—who so carelessly and intentionally destroys the life of another.

In the second paragraph you see not only a hurt victim, but also one that is permanently scarred, or, even dead. You see how a life can be altered at every level by one who wittingly commits the wrongful action, cognizant that his or her punishment will be minimal, if he or she is arrested at all. Having read the second paragraph, you may maintain the position that the teenager be treated as a confused and mischievous individual, but you must concur that the writer has provided sufficient details to support his position to the contrary.

Failure to provide *specific* details to support generalizations is the most common error in underdeveloped paragraphs. The writer moves from one generalization to another as indicated below.

> Comedians of the 90s cater to the baser instincts of their audiences. Unlike comedians of the 60s, such as Bill Cosby, whose routines were insightful vignettes on family life, or comedians of the 70s, like Richard Pryor, whose routines were seriocomic social commentaries, today's comedians often use sex and mean-spirited ridicule as the basis of their humor. And the audiences love it. Mainstream comedians also tell mean-spirited jokes.

How mean-spirited are they? Whom do they ridicule? How do we know that audiences love this type of comedy? Specific details incorporated below answer all of these questions, yielding a *discussion* of topic, not a mere *comment* on it.

> Comedians of the 90s cater to the baser instincts of their audience. Unlike comedians of the 60s, such as Bill Cosby, whose routines were insightful vignettes on family life, or comedians of the 70s, like Richard Pryor, whose routines were seriocomic social commentaries, today's comedians often use sex and mean-spirited ridicule as the basis of their humor. Programming torch-bearer of the future, HBO, airs *Def Comedy Jam* and *Loco Slam*, two ethnic oriented half-hour showcases in which up-and-coming comedians do five minute sets rife with profanity and sexual gesturing. The comedians, males and females, use their five minutes to graphically relate "stories" about sexual experiences, to explicitly proclaim their sexual prowess, to insensitively insult audience members, and to exploit the cruel misfortunes of the famous. And the audiences love it. They cheer; they whoop; they bark their approval. These cable comedians have only marginal competition from those comedians relegated to network television. These mainstream comedians, forced to use cleaner language, compensate by increasing the sexual innuendo and the mean-spir-

ited reference to those larger-than-life celebrities among us. Reviewing the "news of the day," they hardly ever miss an opportunity to exploit a misfortune or connect the dots of sexual happenstance implicitly in any of those news tidbits. Of course, comedians have always used sex and the famous as part of their routines, just not as explicitly or as cruelly. And, it seems, once upon a time, there was a point to it. Perhaps today's bright and industrious comedians simply have nothing else to say.

A common complaint of some students is that they cannot find enough to write about—that they do not have enough information about the topic of discussion. Of course, one solution is to avoid choosing unfamiliar topics to write on. But occasionally, when they choose topics of interest and *assumed* familiarity, they still encounter writer's block during invention. If you experience these problems, do not panic. Draw upon your personal experiences, case studies, observations, statistics, television programs, experiences of loved ones, and your imagination, to some degree. Anticipate questions that readers might raise and answer those as illustrated in the last example. And finally, use words, phrases, and explanations that will make your writing come alive, that will appeal to your reader's senses. Consider the following pairs of sentences.

Use of Concrete Details

Sight

Weak: John looked at Marlena for a long time, wondering if she were real or an apparition.

Improved: John halted in his steps, eyes stretched wide and wild, as if searing through the female that had to be Marlena or her twin whom he had never met.

Hearing

Weak: Suddenly the clock's alarm went off, awakening me from my catnap.

Improved: Suddenly the clock's alarm made a "bong, bong" noise, jolting me awake from my catnap.

Smell

Weak: Awakening to the strong scent of household cleansers, Denise frowned, for she knew in a few minutes her mother would begin calling her to get up and join her in the Saturday morning cleaning ritual.

Improved: Awakening to the pungent scent of lemon-scented Pinesol and the stench of ammonia, Denise frowned, for she knew in a few minutes her mother would begin calling her to get up and join her in the Saturday morning cleaning ritual.

Taste

Weak: As she stood in the lane at Dairy Mine, my diabetic aunt fidgeted, hoping none of us would spot her, and drooled in anticipation of the divine Peanut Butter Temptation that had been forbidden to her.

Improved: Hoping none of us would spot her as she stood in the line at Dairy Mine, my diabetic aunt fidgeted and drooled in anticipation of her favorite confection: bitter sweet chocolate, cascades of whipped cream with flakes of crushed pineapple, creamy peanut butter, topped with tantalizingly crunchy, salty nuts combo—the Peanut Butter Temptation.

Touch

Weak: The victim shuddered in memory of the abductor's uncomfortable hands around her neck.

Improved: The victim shuddered in memory of the abductor's scaly and clammy hands around her neck.

At other times, it is necessary to use adjectives to describe your subject under discussion. In this case, a phrase such as "*paint-chipped, mildewed walls* greeted the tenants" is more specific than a lukewarm expression such as "worn walls." Dramatic verbs also make writing come alive, as in this construction:

The teenage girl *strutted into the class late.*

instead of

The teenage girl *came to class late.*

Now note how the sentence—the experience itself—comes alive when additional specific information is included:

Wearing only a red halter, mustard Daisy Dukes, and three-inch metallic thongs, the adolescent girl strutted into class twenty minutes late.

An experience! Specific, complete, clear. These are the manifold purposes of the paragraph. Those who write paragraphs begin with the premise that something needs to be communicated—whether it is to present a philosophy, elaborate on an idea, or recreate an experience.

Activity 1
Read the underdeveloped paragraph that follows and then write a well-developed paragraph. Exchange your paragraph with a classmate's and critique it for development. Also look for errors in sentence structure and spelling.

Jacob is a generous person. All one has to do is let him know he has a problem, and he will come to the rescue. Jacob is planning something real nice for the senior citizens in his neighborhood here in Tallahassee. I hope he plans the activity on a day when I can help. It is such a blessing to know a sweet guy like that.

Activity 2
Interview one of your classmates. Ask questions about his or her major, hobbies, musical tastes, political affiliation, and organization memberships. Look at details gathered; make a general assessment about the personality of your interviewee, and then write a well-developed para-

graph about your study. Pay special attention to sentence structure, spelling, and grammar.

Activity 3

Turn each phrase below into an *experience* for the reader by writing a sentence with concrete details.

1. man at bus stop
2. crying baby in church
3. the hall (in your house) at 2:00 a.m.
4. Your roommate's side of the room
5. local student hangout
6. an arrogant young man
7. the love of your life
8. a hair trend
9. your favorite food
10. a grocery store you frequent

Activity 4

Now, using the sentences you wrote for #2, #5, or #7 (or a modification of one of these), write a well-developed paragraph.

COHERENCE

> To see the extent that our society prides itself on being liberated and urbane, one needs only to look at our youth who no longer look like youths. Quickly and deliberately, the physical traces of softness and inno-cence that only time normally alters are ransomed for hardened, unnat-ural, or seductive images. More baby girls' ears are pierced now. Little girls' hairstyles are like teenagers' styles, and adolescent girls mimic women. Parents must pay for their cosmetics and their children's. Parents and teenagers wear the same clothes. What do these teenagers have to look forward to when they become adults?

Having read the preceding paragraph about the grooming styles and appearance of young people today, would you say the ideas flow from one to another? If you see some connection, could there have been smoother transitions from one idea to the next? More than likely, your response is that there needs to be a better *flow* between ideas. The preceding paragraph has unity because all of the sentences are related to the topic sentence and there are ample details to support the central point, but the paragraph has a "jerky" effect or, at best, a kind of "hurry-up-and-let-me-list-these-points" effect. A diagram of the reading pattern of such a paragraph would appear thusly:

BEGIN -. STOP

- -. STOP

- -. STOP
- -. STOP
- ... STOP

In essence, the paragraph has a telegraphic effect rather than the controlled voice that a *discussion* brings. Keep that thought in mind; paragraphs should discuss an idea, not simply *mention* or *enumerate* some concern.

Coherence, the third major feature of effective paragraphs, connects ideas in a paragraph, thereby creating a discussion rather than a listing. The reader is able to see the relationship of one sentence to the preceding one or see connection between one paragraph and another. Otherwise, writing will appear to be disjointed, confusing the reader about the relevance of some sentences or the central idea itself. Now read the revised paragraph.

> To see the extent that our society prides itself on being liberated and urbane, one need only to look at our youths who no longer look like youths. Unfortunately, quickly and deliberately, the physical traces of softness and innocence that only time normally alters are ransomed for hardened, unnatural, and, too often, seductive images. For some time now—at least the last two decades—some mothers have pierced their baby girls' ears instead of allowing the girls to decide later, around age sixteen, whether they want to pierce their ears or not. However, during the last decade this beauty rite for infant girls has become about as commonplace as the medical procedure of circumcising male infants. And by the time these young girls reach age thirteen, many have several additional holes in their lobes. But more incredible than this practice is the more recent tendency of some mothers—and fathers, too, no doubt—to pierce their male infants' or toddlers' ears! In addition to ear piercing, some hairstyles of children are as sophisticated as those of their parents, sometimes even more mature. For instance, the French roll, formerly a chic or occasional hairstyle of women, but now an everyday hairstyle for some women, is sported by teenagers as young as thirteen; however, the simple French roll is not sufficient for them. It must be a towering construction, often streaked with red, purple, blonde, or green dye. Thirteen years old—imagine! Of course, the hairstyle itself—no matter how tall or dramatic—is of little stylistic value without the makeup to complete the "diva" look, a look which too often also includes clothing that is much too revealing for adolescent females, clothing such as tight fitting or low-cut blouses and skirts with incredibly high splits. One wonders what remains to be altered or enhanced for these young people once they reach twenty-eight or thirty years old.

The revised paragraph is coherent. The relationship between sentences is clear. Words like "however," "unfortunately," "for instance," "of course"—transitions—provide the connections. Synonyms like "infant" for "baby" and "adolescent" for "teenager" —pronoun usage, and repetition of key terms—provide still further continuity and a discussion of relevant ideas. A diagram of the reading pattern of the latter paragraph would resemble the following sketch.

BEGIN $\longrightarrow$
$\longleftarrow$
$\longleftarrow$
$\longleftarrow$
$\longleftarrow$ S - - - - T - - - - O - - - - P

The writing flows as a discussion should. To give your writing cohesiveness, use the same devices as those utilized above: repetition of key terms, correct pronouns, synonyms, and transitions. A more detailed explanation of each follows.

Repetition of Key Terms

To keep readers focused on the main point or general subject of a paragraph, it is a good practice to repeat key words. You should not repeat a word so many times that the paragraph becomes boring, but you must keep the reader on target about the purpose of your writing exercise, as in this example.

> One of the most *beneficial* technological aids of the twentieth century is the *answering machine*. It is a time-saver for the caller and the recipient of the call. No longer does the caller have to spend precious time redialing a number when the other party is not at home. He can simply leave his message on the *machine* and have the recipient return the call once she receives the message. Imagine how *beneficial* the recorder is if the caller is using a pay telephone. The rewards that the *answering machine* affords the owner are even more *beneficial*. Finally, the owner can take that afternoon nap without being disturbed by the shrilling ring as soon as he begins to doze. He can simply turn off the ringer and let the *machine* record the latest gossip. In addition, the owner can screen calls so that he can avoid another solicitor requesting only a small donation for his special interest group, or he can delay making a decision about some troublesome situation, or dodge that effervescent, aimless chattering relative or friend who ritualistically calls at the wrong time. To be sure, the diverse *benefits* of the *answering machine* make it more of a necessity now than the luxury item or "toy syndrome" many first believed it to be.

Repeating the words *answering machine (machine)* and *benefit (beneficial)* reminds the readers of the main point of the paragraph.

Synonyms

Another option is to use synonyms for key words to connect ideas in a passage or paper. Subtly, the reader stays focused on the main subject without being bored or bombarded by the sight or sound of the same word. In the preceding paragraph, for instance, "recorder" is used for "answering machine," and "machine" itself is used for the same. For practice, identify the synonyms in the paragraph below.

> Current clothing styles prove that some people will wear anything. Apparently, it means more to be trendy than to be decent. This has to be the goal

of those young people who choose to wear their pants half way down their buttocks, baring underwear and at times baring even more. It is not uncommon to see young men in church with their shirts hanging outside their pants, halfway down their thighs, all in the name of being fashionable. Meanwhile, some young ladies walk proudly into church or class dressed in thigh-length, tight skirts and dresses more appropriate for parties, according to etiquette standards. But, surprisingly, young people are not alone in this "with-it" quest. Many women in their twenties and thirties don these same ill-fitting clothes to make others think they are chic dressers. How revolutionary these styles must appear to senior citizens.

Pronouns

Pronouns are words that act as substitutions for nouns or noun phrases. Therefore, it is imperative that correct pronouns be used to replace or refer to key words in paragraphs. Note the use of pronouns in the selection that follows. Identify each pronoun below and its antecedent (the object, person, or place referred to). You will note that each pronoun clearly refers to some specific person or thing. The correct use of pronouns in number and gender eliminates *needless* repetition of key words and *connects* the ideas so that the reader is able to follow the writer's train of thought without having to stop to question who or what is being referenced.

The room in which the boys were fed was a large stone hall, with a copper at one end: out of which the master, dressed in an apron for the purpose, and assisted by one or two women, ladled the gruel at meal times. Of this festive composition each boy had one porringer, and no more—except on occasions of great public rejoicing, when he had two ounces and a quarter of bread besides. The bowls never wanted washing. The boys polished them with their spoons till they shone again; and when they had performed this operation (which never took very long, the spoons being nearly as large as the bowls), they would sit staring at the copper, with such eager eyes, as if they could have devoured the very bricks of which it was composed; employing themselves, meanwhile, in sucking their fingers and most assiduously, with the view of catching up any stray splashes of gruel that might have been cast thereon. Boys have generally excellent appetites. Oliver Twist and his companions suffered the tortures of slow starvation for three months: at last they got so voracious and wild with hunger, that one boy, who was tall for his age, and hadn't been used to that sort of thing (for his father had kept a small cookshop), hinted darkly to his companions, that unless he had another basin of gruel *per diem*, he was afraid he might some night happen to eat the boy who slept next [sic] him, who happened to be a weakly youth of tender age. He had a wild, hungry eye; and they implicitly believed him. A council was held; lots were cast who should walk up to the master after supper that evening, and ask for more; and it fell to Oliver Twist. (Charles Dickens, *Oliver Twist*, New York: Bantam, 1982:12.)

Transitions

The use of transitions to connect ideas in writing is a very effective means of achieving coherence in writing. Transitions serve as signals to let readers know what to expect next. In other words, they show the relationship between one sentence or idea and another. Below is a listing of the most common transitional words and phrases and the kind of relationship they represent.

Addition: also, and, besides, moreover, furthermore, in addition, too, first, second, next, finally, similarly

Contrast: but, yet, however, nevertheless, on the other hand, in contrast, while, still, otherwise, instead

Comparison: similarly, in like manner, also, likewise, moreover, in comparison, not only . . . but also

Illustration: for example, for instance, to illustrate, as a case in point, specifically, such as, in particular

Time: now, then, first, last, during, immediately, while, next, meanwhile, previously, afterward

Space: above, below, next to, beneath, across, to the (your) right, to the left, beside

Result: therefore, hence, consequently, thus, as a result, accordingly

Conclusion: in summary, in short, in brief, finally

Concession: granted that, conceivably, of course, admittedly

Emphasis: indeed, to be sure, in fact, undoubtedly, assuredly, certainly

While transitions are effective coherence devices, they are effective only when used correctly. Always make certain you choose the most appropriate transition to lead into another sentence or idea, and do not make the common mistake that inexperienced writers often make—using superfluous transitions in paragraphs. From the listing provided, you will note that some transitions may be used to signal a number of different relationships. An illustration of effective use of transitions follows. Pay special attention to punctuation used with transitions when they appear at the beginning of a sentence, in the middle, or at the end.

> The idea that the American society is infatuated with violence is no longer as controversial as it once was. Signs of this infatuation loom before us at every hand, starting with that most innocent and commonly accessed resource in our homes, the television. Of course, a die-hard opponent of the violence issue might concede that the cable stations frequently televise movies that contain violent action and profane language, but he would argue that such movies are given an "R" rating to warn parents not to allow their youngsters to see these movies and to make self-righteous adults aware of the bawdy and bestial nature of some films so that they, like the youngsters, will not be traumatized or tainted. Certainly, this much is true. However, what the die-hard refuses to admit is that undue violence surfaces in television shows that are normally considered child-safe or, in fact, in children's cartoons. *Road Runner* and *Bugs Bunny*, for example, two of the most popular, long-running cartoons loved by children and adults

alike, are fraught with violent gestures and violent blows. What crime, pray tell, has little Tweetie committed to stir the wrath of Sylvester, the titular name of another children's program? In addition to watching these cartoons that contain violence, children and adults encounter a disproportionate amount of violence in programs such as *In the Heat of the Night*, which airs before prime time, or *New York Undercover*, or the daytime soap operas, whose storylines about rape, homicide, and aggravated assault now rival stories about romance and its ensuing sentimentality and sensuality. The expected smidgen of combative intrigue in these soaps has mushroomed. Even the news media now aggressively pursue and present violence, releasing graphic ravages of war and homicide, stalking *victims* of violence to gather and report every gruesome detail of their ordeal(s), all in the name of keeping the public informed. After all, someone out there may just want to make a movie—another cinematic production of violence—out of some helpless person's mishap. That some people might disagree about America's infatuation with violence, even in light of such damnable documented evidence, is a strong probability. That that number of believers is dwindling daily is a certainty—a certainty, indeed!

Identify the transitions used above to help keep the flow of ideas moving smoothly, even though this is a lengthy paragraph. Although there are numerous transitions used, they are not monotonous, nor do they make this a stilted, pretentious piece. However, if you are an inexperienced writer, you need to exercise caution in using too many transitions in one paragraph or in one paper.

Transitional sentences are sometimes used to connect paragraphs so that the reader will sense the continuity of thought as the writer moves from one point to another. Consider the following paragraph.

Selfish people can wreak havoc on their friendships because they bring nothing but themselves to the relationships. For one thing, they are constantly talking about their concerns, their day, their needs, or their successes, leaving very little time for their friends to express their feelings. These self-centered folks impose upon others for all kinds of favors but always find excuses when it is time for them to reciprocate. My friend Kelsia is a perfect example. It is not uncommon for her to ask me to pick up her dry cleaning for her on Saturday morning, pick up her contact lenses before the optometrist's office closes at 3:00, and pay for the lenses until she gets paid a week later, pick her up from her part-time job at 4:00, and take her to her fiancé's apartment later on that night. However, if I should ask her to drive me to work (I'll have someone else bring me back home) when my car is in the shop, she sighs and complains, quickly checking her calendar to see if she can fit me in. Now, if this behavior alone were the extent of selfish friends like Kelsia, the friendship would be bearable. But, oh, no! *While the spoiled "me, me" bratty behavior is annoying, the selfish competitiveness can be outright dangerous.*

The last sentence is transitional; the reader looks forward to finding out just how dangerous the selfish, competitive friend can be.

Parallelism

When two or more ideas have the same significance in writing or are integrally related in some way, those ideas should also have the same grammatical structure. This grammatical structure gives the ideas balance and rhythm. Repetition of such grammatical structures several times in a paragraph helps to connect ideas and sentences, thus establishing coherence.

> The most painful part of ending a romantic relationship is the actual parting itself. *It is painful to say* "we have grown apart." Though both partners may have recognized that fact for some time, neither wants to verbalize it, for *it is painful to think* of something emphatic and positive to say, yet acknowledge the problem that must exist to necessitate separation in the first place. *It is painful to stand* there, fighting back tears that threaten to engulf you because there is still some measure of affection left and memories of heretofore considered insignificant moments inundate the brain in what seems like a fleeting second. "Can't We Try?" "It Hurt So Bad." "I'll Never Love This Way Again." "Where Did Our Love Go?" "Touch Me In the Morning." "I'll Always Love You"—songs permeate the mind until the inevitable happens. Someone mouths some empty expression, and the door opens and closes, leaving you on one side and the love of your life on the other. Maybe tomorrow, maybe this weekend, maybe next month, the pain will go away. But, at this moment, as lukewarm tears slither down your chin, you know that it is painful—undescribably painful—ending a relationship.

Were the subject itself not a compellingly sad one, the repetition of the phrase "it is painful to" would move the reader along, clarifying the subject, setting the tone, and tying the sentences together. Like transitions, this coherence device is more effective if used sparingly—in one paragraph or two at the most in a lengthy essay.

LOGICAL ORDER/ORGANIZATIONAL PATTERN

Chronological Order

Some writing tasks dictate that sentences and paragraphs follow a time sequence. *Narration*, for example, often requires that one present a written account of an occurrence in sequential order as events or actions unfold(ed). Failure to write sentences that are outgrowths of one another causes undue confusion for readers, preventing them from readily comprehending the point of the written exercise. When the occurrences are recorded in natural sequence, the writing flows. Chronological order also is normally required when one writes process analysis, especially directional process (giving instruction to someone to perform or complete some action) as indicated below.

> While academics, as well as social concerns, are of utmost importance to you during your college experience, you, like any other college student, may often find yourself challenged to complete the everyday mundane responsibilities that come with living on your own. One such task is doing the laundry. However, you need not fret. You can master this task

if you follow a few instructions. First, gather supplies. You will need detergent (Cheer is a good brand), bleach, fabric softener, and a measuring cup. Next, gather dirty clothes, and then separate them according to colors and fabrics. Place similar colors together to prevent fading. [Some fabrics should be washed on a gentle cycle, while other fabrics may require a permanent press setting.] After sorting clothes, you are finally ready to begin washing. Thus, you should set the gauges on the machine to accommodate the first load of clothes. These gauges normally are related to water level (low, medium, high), temperature (cold, warm, or hot), and fabric (gentle/knit, cotton/sturdy, permanent press). Place the amount of detergent required for load (See detergent box) in machine, being careful not to overload the washer so that the clothes will get clean. Turn on the machine to desired setting and water temperature. When the rinse light appears, add fabric softener. After the wash cycle stops, place the clothes in dryer, setting the temperature and other appropriate gauges on dryer to accommodate laundry load. Then, turn on the dryer. Take the clothes out immediately after the dryer stops to prevent further wrinkling of clothing. Fold the laundry before putting it away; this also helps reduce the amount of ironing that has to be done, if any. Complete these steps for each load, and you will discover that that which may have appeared to be a formidable task becomes a simple weekly activity that you can perform as you work on your lap top, listen to music, or watch that favorite sitcom.

What would happen if the writer had presented the sentence about supplies after the sentence about sorting the clothes or placed the rinse routine before instructions about the detergent and bleach? The reader would have been confused, and any effort to follow these instructions to do laundry would have been futile. It is clear that chronological order is often necessary to make sense in writing. You will note that the chronological strategy for achieving coherence also incorporates the use of transitions, a means of maintaining coherence device discussed earlier.

Spatial Order

While some writing tasks dictate that sentences and paragraphs follow a time sequence, others require a spatial ordering of details. This arrangement is more often used in descriptive writing, a rhetorical pattern in which the writer attempts to recreate a picture or scene and to give coherence at the same time.

Students hate going to their English 101 class in Shucks Hall. Yes, they dislike writing papers each week and reviewing grammar. But one of their biggest complaints is about the room in which the class is held—the dreary chamber (D.C.)—as students call it. Walking into the room, a visitor turns to the right, searching for the light switch, but before touching it, his hand grazes a memento—a thick black wad of gum left by some previous visitor. When he finally flips the switch, only one set of lights shines, those on the left side of the room, and one of those bulbs needs to be replaced. Immediately the visitor's eyes sweep the room, noticing its cell-like proportions for a class of forty people. Then, suddenly his eyes shift straight across to the wall where splotches of paint that have been splattered to cover up obscene language have begun to chip. As his eyes shift from the left wall on around toward the corner back wall, the visitor spots a piece of ply board, cut unevenly and held up in front of the open window by several pieces of duct tape. To the right of the window is the remnant of a cork board with peace signs and faint scribbling of the words "We shall Overcome" underneath a yellowed newspaper clipping of a riot scene from the sixties. "Yes, we shall overcome this *room*," students often sneer as they look at the gaping hole in the right wall where apparently a couple of students evidently gave up on *peace* and sought to settle their dispute violently. Canvassing the room further, his eyes zoom toward the front wall upon which rests a slick blackboard and nubs of chalk, with no eraser in sight. In front of this wall sits the teacher's desk—one leg missing—thus explaining its diagonal position and a weatherbeaten chair, rough splintered edges and all. As his eyes drift downward from the chair, the visitor gets a whiff of a sour smell stirred by the breeze that sneaks in ever so often from the broken window. Having analyzed the smell, he returns his eyes to the floor where he notices worn brown carpet stained with big circles that could only have been created by the leaking ceiling with exposed, torn, wet insulation sagging overhead. "D.C., D.C.," he grunts. "Even basketweaving would be difficult to learn in this classroom."

Emphatic Order

Sometimes it is necessary to discuss the most important supporting point last in order to persuade or impress the reader. The rationale is that people remember what is said or written last. This strategy for organizing details and sentences is most often used in argumentative discourse but also is effective in all types of written discourse, which in and of itself is persuasive communication. An example of emphatic ordering follows:

> Relationships often fail because two people fail to be honest with each other. If a young man dislikes the cologne that his beloved wears or dislikes some quirk of hers, he should let her know—in a tactful way, of course—early on in the relationship rather than wait until two years later to express his displeasure. By that time, what at first was a simple annoyance may seem so detestable that an argument ensues when this dissatisfaction is divulged. In another situation, a young lady sees an ex-lover and decides to eat lunch with him. She should feel comfortable telling her current mate about the luncheon, if, in fact, she knows about it the day before. On the other hand, if she meets the former friend and suddenly at that moment decides to eat lunch, she should not hesitate to tell her current mate about it. When she arrives home, she should not hesitate to acknowledge the truth. Failure to be honest about *who* one is can have even more traumatic effects on a relationship. For example, if she dislikes drinking alcohol or smoking cigarettes or dressing flamboyantly,

she should not assume the persona of someone whom she believes her mate would find more desirable. One can pretend for just so long before the true self emerges, and when that happens, her loved one might begin to question whether the woman he has been dating has several personalities or wonder why she suddenly changed. Consequently, he may end the relationship, only to begin dating someone who is honest about her likes and dislikes. He might begin dating someone who has the basic character, taste, and temperament of the *real* woman whom he earlier dated.

Conceivably, failure to be one's true self is more damaging to a relationship than not being honest about one's preference of perfume and even lying about talking to or dining with a former love. Thus, one sees the benefit of using the emphatic strategy and recognizes numerous other devices used to achieve coherence, indicating an important point: most of the paragraphs and essays that you will write should have a combination of strategies and devices to provide clarity and connect ideas. Just remember to use these devices correctly and sparingly.

Activity 1
For each topic below, write a paragraph, utilizing the coherence tool recommended.

1. Describe your bedroom (spatial order).
2. Explain your morning routine in preparing to go to class (chronological order).
3. Tell why you prefer one season to the others (emphatic order).

Activity 2
The writer of the paragraph below has made numerous errors in trying to achieve coherence. Rewrite the paragraph, correcting these errors so that the main idea and sentences in the paragraph will flow smoothly.

Once considered the answer to the serious shopper's prayers, today's mall has become a temporary roosting den for a myriad of personalities. The first person one sees is a leather clad, half-shaven head, one shoulder length-earring-dangling, nose-pierced tattooed teenager, stomping his way across the food court to a table with three or four similarly leather clad young people, who seemingly sneer at passersby. Screaming near the fountain you see a couple of eleven or twelve year old girls. These girls could not have come here alone. These girls must have been dropped off by parents. These girls run all around the mall screaming and shrieking, enjoying the startled looks and frowns of older mall patrons who look at these girls. Older patrons understand. Older patrons were young years ago. He remembers when his sister ran up and down the aisles of the Bee Kay Dime Store screaming, having the time of their life. Soon these girls will be the leather clad young adolescents of the mall, or whatever is trendy then. Homeless people come to the mall, especially on rainy days, they can tell the homeless people because they are unshaven, unkempt. The homeless people dress shabbily. The homeless people sometimes ask me for money. The mall is a kind of home to the homeless people, if only temporarily. There are dressed up people there, professionals at lunch time. You can recognize them. First, the male professionals wear suits and ties.

Second, the professional women wear suits and expensive looking blouses or chemises with stockings and pumps. Some may wear flat shoes. They just are dressed up and act proper. You conclude they must be professionals who have come to the mall simply to eat lunch. Some people are doing some serious shopping some days. You see people with two to three shopping bags, darting in every store in the mall; their children have packages. Some people don't come to shop. Some people don't come to exercise, like the old people do. Some don't come to eat lunch. Some teenagers meet their leather clad friends in grocery store parking lots or on the school grounds after school hours. A man or woman may approach you trying to sell gold watches or earrings, even shoes or purses. The mall is not what it used to be. The mall is filled with all kinds of people. The mall is a convenient place and even a dangerous place and an interesting place.

Activity 3

Write a paragraph about one of the subjects below. The paragraph should have an explicit topic sentence and a concluding sentence. Use a combination of the following transitional devices: synonyms, transitional words and phrases, correct pronouns, and parallelism.

1. sanguine people
2. angry people
3. dull people
4. melancholy people

CHECKLIST FOR BODY PARAGRAPHS
1. The paragraph has one central point.
2. The paragraph has an explicit topic sentence.
3. All sentences are clearly related to the topic sentence.
4. There are vivid, specific examples, details, and background information provided to support the topic sentence.
5. The paragraph is a discussion, not a simple listing of points.
6. Ideas and sentences are coherent.
7. The reader, who may have a different opinion about the topic than the writer of the paragraph, can earnestly say the writer has defended his position well.

WRITING OTHER PARAGRAPHS

In addition to the body paragraphs, most papers (essays and themes) contain two or three other types of paragraphs. These include the *introduction* (beginning), *conclusion* (ending), and *transitional* paragraph (between body paragraphs).

THE INTRODUCTION

The introductory paragraph is the first paragraph in an essay or theme. It identifies the subject of the essay and the central idea or *thesis* on that subject, which is often followed by a listing of key points—a plan of development for that thesis. Sometimes it is necessary to provide synoptic but salient background details to help the reader understand the discussion to follow. Sometimes that background information will be a definition of a key term, in one or two words, or it may be an explanation in a couple of sentences. At other times, an individual paragraph is needed to provide historical or sociological data necessary for the reader to understand the subject at hand. This individual paragraph is included in very long papers, not the typical 500–700 word freshman composition. In such a short paper, the lengthy discussion of historical data would shift the focus away from the main point to be discussed.

Caution should be exercised in giving brief definitions as well. It is imperative that you do not use tiresome phrases such as "According to *Webster's*" or "*Random House* states." If you decide a key word needs to be defined, use a paraphrase of the dictionary explanation. In addition to providing the thesis, the introductory paragraph should arouse the reader's interest in the written piece. A "ho-hum" introduction in an essay has the same effect that a "dry" introduction in a speech has: the reader, like the listener, develops a negative attitude and places little merit on what follows; that is, if he reads or listens in the first place. An example of an effective introduction follows:

> Can a professional woman have a meaningful romantic relationship with a man who is a nonprofessional? For some successful, cynical, arrogant women today, this question would elicit a laugh, followed by a curt "of course not" response. And perhaps they are right. After all, their salaries might far exceed that of the nonprofessional male, not to mention the different level of ambition each might have, their different tastes in friends, and different general interests. But would these differences keep the couple from being happy? Not necessarily. The most meaningful romantic relationships—whether between persons with like or dissimilar professions or the lack thereof—survive because they are built on love, respect, and trust.

The paragraph above meets the criteria identified for effective introductions: (1) A question is a fairly common strategy raised to make the reader pause and contemplate the issue. Then, a response is provided, a response that leads the reader to think that the writer takes one position but then shifts to the opposing one—"not necessarily." The reader's curiosity should be stirred by now as he waits to discover how an apparent mismatched pair might indeed develop a meaningful relationship. (2) The writer provides an explicit thesis statement, asserting that a relationship between people with dissimilar jobs can work, and indicates a plan of development—the need for love, respect, and trust—to prove the point. You will note that there are no definitions or historical details given. The subject of "love and relationships" is commonplace enough not to warrant such definitive clarification. Also, note the length of the introduction. Normally, the length of an introduction is about three to five sentences, considered sufficient for a 500–700 word essay. With a three to five sentence introduction, the actual body paragraphs in an essay must be longer. In essence, what you actually discuss in a paper—the body of the paper—must be longer than your thesis statement and/or plan of development. The preceding sample introduction is longer than five sentences; thus, the reader should expect to find body paragraphs longer than or at least as long as the introduction.

Introduction Strategies

There are numerous ways to write effective introductions. Five of the most common strategies used in writing introductory paragraphs follow.

General to Specific

Start with a broad generalization that in itself could not be used to develop a classroom essay but that serves as a lead-in to a *specific* point about a *specific* aspect of the generalization. The writer narrows the broad subject until he progresses to the question or issue at hand, providing pertinent background as he moves, filtering his thoughts, more or less, until he reaches a *specific* conclusion or makes a *specific* assessment of the topic.

Example

Women in general are fond of saying that there aren't any good men left. Normally, comments such as these are made during discussions on the cruelties suffered by women, which are meted out by men. The statement is hardly ever meant to be taken literally. The women only mean that good men are hard to find. But what is a good man by their standards or anybody else's, for that matter? Some people say that a good man is one that doesn't cheat on his wife. Others say that a good man is one that takes care of his family and responsibilities. Still others say that he is one who provides a good example for younger generations of males. All of these statements have the same basic meaning. A good man must be an asset to his community.

Questions

Another common strategy used in writing introductions is to use one provocative question or a series of rhetorical questions on the general subject and then follow the question with a thesis that indicates your answer to the question or a thesis that makes some pointed conclusion, analysis, or takes a position on the topic. In the case of the latter, the essay (body paragraphs) will no doubt answer the question, or, if nothing else, the provocative opening question(s) arouses the readers' curiosity and makes them look forward to reading the essay, as he contemplates his own response to the question(s). This method—use of question(s)—and the "general to specific" method are considered the easiest of the various strategies to employ, especially during essay tests or in other "timed" writing situations when stress is great and writer's block delays invention.

Remember, however, that a *provocative* question is essential. Students sometimes use this technique and use the most boring questions that the whole paragraph seems contrived and motionless. For instance, if they had to define love, they might begin with the obvious: What is love? Now read a model introduction using a question.

Example

Is America really the strongest nation in the world? Wait before you answer this question with a resounding "Of course." Many experts believe that a strong nation *might* have a formidable military force, but it *must* have a sound economic system. If our judgment is based upon what the experts espouse, then it is Japan, not America, which is the stalwart country of the world. Because of its global export business, its socialistic welfare system, and its stronghold on electronic technology, Japan, without a doubt, is economic ruler of both the eastern and western hemispheres.

A Quotation

When your muse does not answer right away and inspire you to write an original opening, it is good to draw upon the wisdom and eloquence of others: Use a quotation, an *appropriate* quotation, for the topic. Consider what great poets, novelists, playwrights, politicians, historians, activists, family sages, and the mouths of babes have said. A familiar line of a popular artist (comedian, singer) may be used; however, it is best not to use cliches or trite expressions. Always remember that you want to capture the reader's attention and keep it, not bore him or her at the outset with tiresome expressions. Another important reminder in using quotations is to quote accurately, giving proper credit to the author, when such is known.

Example

"To every thing there is a season, and a time to every purpose under the heaven:" (Ecclesiastes 3:1). Usually, when we think about good things such as love, marriage, or the birth of a child, we reflect on the Biblical lines above. However, there are times or seasons to consider the bad or negative things of life, such as, believe it or not, hatred. Hate does have a place in the world. Specifically, when it comes to the ugly plagues of racism, discrimination, and political misconduct, all of humankind should find these social ills despicable.

An Anecdote

Everyone enjoys an interesting story. The natural inclination is to read further to find out more. Thus, the story stimulates reader interest. This story, which has to relate clearly to the thesis statement, might recap a personal experience or narrate the story of someone else. Keep in mind that the story must be brief, since you do not want the reader to forget the main topic of concern, and you do not want the introduction to rival the support paragraphs in length and in development.

Example

"Gary, why did you set fire to that old sofa on the front porch?" screamed an angry mother. Eyes stretched as wide as saucers, Gary whined, "It was not none of me, Mama. It sho' wasn't me. I didn't do it!" Standing squarely and powerfully over her son's head, Mama leaned forward and explained coldly and slowly, "G-a-r-y, I K-N-O-W you did it. DON'T LIE!!"

"How you know? *Who* told you? Gary inquired.

His mother did not say a word. A good mother always knows when her child misrepresents the truth. A responsible mother teaches her child that lying is unacceptable, telling the truth is virtuous, and accepting blame for one's actions is necessary.

A Controversial Statement

Use of a controversial—debatable—statement immediately engages the readers, especially if they choose to respond to the question. If nothing else, most will feel compelled to read further. Once you write your controversial statement, provide one or two related sentences before you write your thesis statement.

Example

The Confederate flag is indeed a symbol of the courage and honor of American southerners. The sight of it brings pride to some people who are too often misunderstood and consequently criticized or condemned. In fact, it is as American as baseball, Thanksgiving, and apple pie. So why, then, does it incite such rage in the hearts of other Americans? No doubt, some Americans are incensed because the symbol—the Confederate flag—represents an ethos that is un-American.

THE THESIS STATEMENT

Up to this point, emphasis has been on the strategies for beginning introductions—attracting the reader's attention, with only references to the thesis statement of the paper. Granted, the lead-in is significant, but it loses relevance when the thesis is questionable, confusing, or missing. A *good* thesis makes an explicit point about a given topic, as the example below illustrates:

Contrary to popular opinion, people who have dissimilar professions and interests can have meaningful relationships.

The general subject here is relationships, which alone would be too broad to develop in a brief essay. The writer has limited the topic to relationships between people who have apparent differences, then narrowed that key concern to the thesis above. The writer's position is explicit. He could leave the thesis as is and begin development on the first supporting point for this thesis, or he could add additional information to it—divide the thesis into three parts, indicating his plan of development for the central idea. When this plan of development is added to the position one takes on a topic, the construction is called a *three-pronged* thesis statement. See below:

> Contrary to popular opinion, people who have dissimilar professions and interests can have meaningful relationships if they have love, if they have respect, and if they have trust.

> With love, respect, and trust, two people can have a meaningful romantic relationship, despite personal and professional differences.

With this added information in the thesis, the reader knows that the first support paragraph will discuss the importance of love; the second, the importance of respect; and finally, the importance of trust. When the three-pronged thesis is used, the writer must develop points in the order mentioned. If he changes his mind about the order during the drafting or revision of the paper, he must remember to change the order in the thesis. Note the ordering of points to develop the central point; that is, the most important point—trust—will be discussed last. The writer suggests that one can have love; one can have respect, but without *trust*, most relationships soon end. Always order your points for desired effects.

Next, note how distinct each point is. There is no overlapping of ideas. If "trust" and "respect" were the same or too similar, the writer would end up writing the same ideas in both paragraphs. To avoid this, if you are an inexperienced writer, you should spend time brainstorming the topic, jotting down ideas, at least four or five, and considering each before choosing the three distinct ones—sometimes there may be four points in a paper, occasionally two—that you will write about to support your thesis.

Also note the grammatical structure of points in the three-pronged thesis: "if they have love," "if they have respect," and "if they have trust" —all dependent clauses—or the three nouns: "love, respect, and trust." These points have the same significance in development of topic and thus have the *same* grammatical structure; they are *parallel* as all points in the plan of development should be.

The placement of thesis in an introduction is of great importance. In the preceding introductory paragraphs, the thesis statement is the last sentence in the paragraph. It is often best to write a three-pronged thesis statement last so that you do not forget what you initially planned to discuss and end up writing underdeveloped essays. In long essays, it may be necessary to place the thesis in the second paragraph of the paper or whichever paragraph precedes the body of the paper. You will observe that some essays have an implied thesis. This practice should be limited to experienced professional writers.

Errors to Avoid

The following are examples of the most common mistakes writers make in writing thesis statements.

Announcements

Do not simply make a declaration of your plans to write the essay. Do not make an announcement.

This essay will discuss the reasons why adolescents lose interest in school.

I am going to write about the differences between my two sisters.

Apology/Defense

Whatever you write will more than likely consist of your opinion as well as general knowledge of subject, interpretation of existing data, and perceptions of others. You synthesize information and make an assertion about a topic. *Assert* that point; don't apologize or become defensive, expecting others to challenge your thesis.

In my opinion people have every right to live together without marriage if they choose to do so.

I think talk show hosts are as gifted as clergymen.

Do you fear objections by most people because of your view? If you have a basis, some evidence to support either idea, assert your position.

Broad Statement

Always keep in mind the amount of time and word requirement of your writing assignment. Never attempt to develop in 500 words an idea that might more reasonably be developed in a 500-page book.

Technology has had a great effect on our society.

Are you referring to automobiles, microwave ovens, computers, VCR's, electric clocks? Are those effects good or bad? The possibilities for discussion seem almost endless.

Doctors today are so different from doctors years ago.

Do you plan to begin with doctors of the Middle Ages, or will you begin with those of the Victorian era? Will you discuss bedside manner, clothing, competency, or research efforts? The possibilities for discussion are too varied for this thesis to be workable.

Narrow Statements

Just as some ideas are too broad to discuss in 500 words, some are too narrow. The writer who chooses a narrow statement, usually a fact, ends up repeating himself.

Elderly people normally go to bed before 10:00.

I am saddened to see homeless people on the streets.

Yes, many elderly people go to bed before 10:00, but what else can be said or written about that point? And, yes, most people are saddened to see homeless people on the streets. These are facts with no room for a 500-word discussion.

Vague Statements

Do not confuse the reader by identifying two or more possible ideas for discussion.

Vacationing in a tropical paradise can be relaxing, and it can be very expensive.

Which point will be discussed, the expense or the relaxation?

The teachers at my high school played a major role in helping me develop self-esteem; also a couple of my neighbors.

Did the teachers help you more than the neighbors? Will part of the essay be devoted to the teachers and part to the neighbors? Did someone help you with the neighbors as well as help you develop self-esteem?

Questions

The thesis is a declarative sentence, one declarative sentence, not a question.

Why do people gossip about others?

What causes people to become selfish individuals?

These questions would be effective lead-ins for introductions, not theses. If you learn how to choose eye catching lead-ins and write explicit thesis statements, you will be able to write effective introductions for most topics.

Activity 1
Choose one thesis statement from each of the six types of errors identified above and write effective thesis statements.

Activity 2
Listed below are ten broad topics/subjects. Limit each subject; then write an explicit thesis statement for each, five of which should be three-pronged thesis statements.

1. hair
2. grocery
3. music
4. violence
5. sports
6. humor
7. manners
8. restaurants
9. dating
10. habits

Activity 3
Identify each thesis below as effective (E) or ineffective (I). For each ineffective sentence, write an effective sentence.

1. Stress can be reduced by getting adequate rest, taking time out to play, and can be helped by improving dietary habits.
2. This paper will analyze the way Lorraine Hansberry develops characterization in *A Raisin in the Sun*.

3. Modeling can be a very rewarding career.

4. While they are indeed very different, middle aged people and teenagers experience some of the same unique problems.

5. Jogging helps individuals develop their bodies and improve their health, but they should not limit their exercise to jogging.

6. In their day to day interactions, people prove that Jonathan Swift was correct in asserting that man is capable of reason but seldom uses it.

7. In my opinion more people are getting divorced because of a lack of communication, lack of compatibility, and lack of fidelity.

8. Shouldn't corporal punishment be allowed in school if it helps students to behave, discourages them from disrespecting their teachers, and reinforces values parents teach them at home?

9. Music is a universal language.

10. Coaches are usually good role models for their players.

Activity 4
Write a thesis statement for each of the essay topics below.

1. What students can gain from working with the elderly.

2. A time when people take chances.

3. An inexpensive activity that the whole family can participate in.

4. A person whom you met early in life that you will never forget.

5. Where to go when you need consolation.

6. An individual whom you would like to insult.

7. The best way to spend the weekend.

8. The one luxury everyone should have/buy.

9. The satisfaction that artwork brings.

10. What I would like to change about myself.

Activity 5
Keeping in mind what you have learned about effective introductions, write introductory paragraphs for five (5) of the thesis statements you wrote for Activity 4. Indicate the strategy you use. You must use at least three of the different strategies identified: general to specific, questions, a quotation, an anecdote, or a controversial statement. Pay special attention to sentence structure, usage, and punctuation.

Activity 6
The introductory paragraphs written below are unsatisfactory. Revise them so that they will be effective introductions.

1. People often complain about how much money professional athletes earn. Professional athletes earn a lot of money. They buy all kinds of cars

and expensive homes. But doctors make a lot of money too, and they can afford the most expensive possessions. Teachers are professionals, but they do not make a lot of money, nor are they respected as much.

2.   Riding through small towns you usually see people who wave heartily, as if they recognize you. If you stop at the local gas station or choose to dine in one of the few restaurants on the main street of the town, people often speak and smile, and some will even ask you about your hometown and destination. As you leave their establishment, they will bid you a fond farewell as though they have known you for quite some time, and you leave with a smile on your face, thinking about the warmth and kindness of human beings, earthly creatures with more than a smidgen of celestial grace. But then when you return home to your semi-large metropolitan hometown, you quickly awaken from this dream about the milk of human kindness. You are assaulted by the cold, rude, almost brutish behavior of people you see every day. For instance, as you go to your mailbox, you look next door, ready to wave at or greet your neighbor, but he and the children look straight ahead, ignoring your presence six feet away. Even when you aggressively yell your greeting, you see a quick nod, never a smile, nor do you hear any verbal response. Was that, in fact, a nod or an involuntary movement? You get on the elevator at your workplace with a cheery "Good Morning," only to have one of the four sleepy looking employees mumble a curt, barely audible "morning." And when the elevator stops on your floor, the man that works right down the hall from you scurries off, head bowed, hoping you will not try to make any conversation with him. This he has done for the last seven years since his employment. Even adolescents attending the same school or college walk around looking upward, to their right or left—any direction away from the approaching student—hoping to avoid speaking. What is wrong with people? Why are they indifferent to each other's presence? Where have manners gone? If not speaking is the trend today, what do we have to look forward to tomorrow?

3.   People with good incomes and all of the imaginable family values often refuse to adopt children themselves, but object to homosexuals adopting children, disabled people adopting children, or people of one race adopting children of another. Anyone who loves children and can provide for them should be eligible to adopt.

THE CONCLUSION

The concluding paragraph reiterates the central idea of a writing assignment and makes some kind of emphatic final statement on the topic at hand. It might be said that while the introductory paragraph acts like the appetizer in dining, the conclusion is comparable to the after dinner mint. In other words, while the purpose of the introduction is to impress the reader and arouse his curiosity, the conclusion reminds one of the purpose, the significance of what was discussed, leaving the reader with a provocative thought or satisfaction in having grasped the writer's message, creating a kind of "ah" sensation.

Like the introduction, the conclusion is brief, approximately two sentences. Since you have written detailed supporting paragraphs, there is no need to delay the ending, and since your primary purpose is to summarize key points made in the essay, all effort should be made not to introduce *new* material that would also add length. For that reason alone, it is imperative that you proofread the concluding paragraph very carefully to make certain that you have not omitted any key words. Omission of what appears to be a simple word like *not* can contradict the argument you put forth in three to four well-developed paragraphs.

While it is true that in the conclusion you end your discussion on a given topic, it is not necessary to trumpet that fact by using trite phrases such as "In conclusion" or "In summary." This kind of lead-in to the conclusion is as pedestrian as the "announcement" approach in writing thesis statements. It is also overused by students and creates a carbon copy or xeroxed effect. Find a way to close your discussion so that the reader quickly recognizes closure. An example of an effective conclusion follows.

> An informal polling of your park bench lovers, middle aged spouses at a school affair, or an elderly couple holding hands and napping on their veranda would attest to the fact that romantic relationships are difficult at best, but normal difficulties are often aggravated when a couple has different careers. Yet, with further discussion, many would add that despite these career differences and many other differences, couples can have lifelong gratifying relationships. And a few pollsters, hesitant at first to reveal their joyful secret, lest they appear like braggarts, would finally acknowledge that though they and their spouses have very different careers—white collars married to blue collars—the source of their joy and longevity of their relationship stems from the commitment to nurturing the love, respect, and trust they share.

Conclusion Strategies

The following are three of the most common strategies for writing concluding paragraphs.

Summary

Perhaps the easiest conclusion to write is one that restates the central idea and the main points to support that central idea. However, do not cite thesis and plan of development verbatim. Use synonyms and different phrases. Along with the summary, writers of this strategy usually include one final emphatic statement on topic.

Example
In order to be considered a good man, you must be an asset to your community. If you are at least trying to do what was discussed, then your community will support you.

Because of its simplicity, this strategy is often more appropriate in stressful timed-writing situations.

Recommendation

Following a restatement of or reference to the thesis, the writer makes one or two suggestions about what should be done to alleviate the problem discussed or to positively modify some situation or matter.

Example

Finding that perfect vacation spot does not have to be a long task. Cancun has many wonderful things to offer. The next time your family can't decide where to go on that family vacation, go to Cancun, Mexico. You will not regret it!

Remember not to get so involved with providing solutions that you divert attention away from the main point of your discussion.

Prediction

Following reiteration of the thesis, you should make an educated guess of what will occur if those who are in a position to rectify the given situation refuse to do so. Or you might concur that continued positive responses to an already profitable venture or stance can only yield more positive results.

Example

If the welfare system is abolished, there will be no problem with its being misused. Instead, everyone will have to work and find a way to make ends meet. Without welfare, hard-working taxpayers will not have to spend their money meaninglessly to help freeloaders who do not want to help themselves. Consequently, the nation will see a reduction in the looming deficit that now exists, and the soon-to-be former recipients will gain self-respect.

Activity 1

Write a concluding paragraph for each of the five introductory paragraphs you wrote for Activity 5. Use all three strategies and identify the type used for each paragraph. Pay special attention to sentence structure, usage, and mechanics.

Activity 2

Revise the ineffective concluding paragraph below.

In conclusion, people must not allow themselves to become victims of burglary. They must buy weapons, join the neighborhood watch program, and add proper lighting around their homes. No one wants to go through the window of a home that has a bright light right beneath that window. And surely, one can stop a burglar in his tracks if he has a gun to shoot once the perpetrator enters his home. We must begin to search for ways to help people who victimize others this way. Perhaps they had an unhappy childhood, or they may be homeless. Can't we do something to help them now before it is too late? I know I want to help my former classmate who got into trouble last week. In short, burglaries can be prevented.

TRANSITIONAL PARAGRAPHS

Essays/Themes with four to five paragraphs do not need transitional paragraphs. Long essays, 1200–1800 words or more, often need a paragraph to relate what was discussed during the first half or two-thirds of the paper to what follows in the rest of the paper. Sometimes it may be reiteration of a thesis; at other times there may be a need to provide a very brief summary of material discussed earlier before continuing your discussion; or it may be necessary to provide some kind of brief discussion of what is to follow. Consider this paragraph from the discussion on sentence sophistication that summarized the first half of a discussion and prepares the reader for what is to follow.

> The sentences in the preceding section are all very simple. Most of them are basic patterns that lack sophistication. There are many ways that plain sentences can be embellished. The purpose of this section is to explore these ways and to help you learn to employ them in making your writing more mature.

Checklist for Other Paragraphs

1. Introductions are brief, approximately 3–5 sentences long.

2. Introductory paragraphs arouse the reader's interest and present the thesis statement.

3. The thesis statement may include a plan of development, referred to as the three-pronged thesis statement.

4. All points in this plan of development must be parallel and must not overlap.

5. Concluding paragraphs reiterate the main point of the paper, without introducing new material.

6. Conclusions should be brief, approximately 2–3 sentences long.

7. Transitional paragraphs are needed to connect parts/ideas in very long papers; they summarize what has been discussed earlier and identify what will follow in the discussion.

3

The Essay in Summation

THE PARAGRAPH VS. THE ESSAY

Having mastered writing the paragraph, you should have minimal, if any, difficulty in writing well-developed essays. After all, the paragraph is often called a "miniature composition." To be more exact, the essay is a series of relevant organized *paragraphs* supporting and clarifying one central idea, whereas the paragraph is a series of *sentences* that support or clarify a central idea. A more detailed comparison of both follows.

PARAGRAPH		ESSAY
Topic Sentence (Serves as introduction)	[CENTRAL IDEA]	*Thesis Statement* (Appears in Introductory Paragraph)
Supporting Sentences (Examples, details, facts, statistics, case studies and observations)	[EVIDENCE]	*Supporting Paragraphs* (Filled with sentences containing examples, details, facts, statistics, case studies, and observations)
Size (Five to seven sentences of moderate length)	[LENGTH]	*Size* (Three body paragraphs or more, each with five or more sentences of moderate length)

PARAGRAPH		ESSAY
Closure (A final sentence reiterating topic sentence idea)	[SUMMARY]	*Concluding Paragraph* (A final paragraph of two to three sentences reiterating the thesis idea or offering a solution or recommendation)
Subject Matter (All sentences clearly related to topic sentence)	[UNITY]	*Subject Matter* (All paragraphs clearly related to thesis statement)
Discussion (Subject [topic sentence] developed in detail)	[DEVELOPMENT]	*Discussion* (Subject [thesis statement] developed in detail)
Organization (Key ordering of and transition between sentences)	[COHERENCE]	*Organization* (Key ordering of and transition between paragraphs)
Structure (Conventional syntax along with individual polish)	[STYLE]	*Structure* (Conventional syntax along with individual polish)
Editing Check (Grammar, mechanics, punctuation, and spelling)	[USAGE]	*Editing Check* (Grammar, mechanics, punctuation, and spelling)

Considering the general definition given earlier and the analogy presented above, you are correct in concluding that the primary difference between a paragraph and an essay is the length. Thus, most definitely, if you can write well-developed paragraphs, with practice, you will also be able to write well-developed essays.

Model Paragraph and Essay

For further clarity, study the sample paragraph and sample essay below.

> As Patrick Ewing, superstar basketball player of the New York Knicks, said: "Children develop their work ethic at home." Therefore, parents must teach their children the importance of doing every work detail as accurately as possible. If parents instill in their children the idea that they should take pride in their work, the children learn to perform each task meticulously. For instance, children who are assigned the chore of

washing dishes must be told to wash both the inside and the backside of the dishes as well as the rims. They must be instructed to wash between the prongs of the forks and must be encouraged to apply moderate pressure to remove gritty food particles that may cling to dinner dishes and cookware. Children must also be told how much dish detergent to use and why it is important to rinse the dishes with hot, instead of scalding, water. If, for some reason they do a poor job of washing one plate or one fork, the parent should require them to wash that item again, consequently simulating the workplace, which should demand the same action or more punitive action when an employee's productivity is less than expected. Of course, some people discard the values instilled during their childhood once they leave home, but observation has shown that the majority will subscribe to those lessons long after they have left the proverbial "nest."

Do the paragraph check at this point. Is there an explicit topic sentence? What about the reiteration of that idea? Is there unity in this paragraph? Is coherence achieved? Are there any grammatical problems? Is the main point developed?

Now read the essay that follows.

After securing the phone number of a popular restaurant one fine Sunday afternoon, I called the establishment, only to hear the phone ring fifteen times."Evidently," I thought, "I must have written down the wrong number." After rechecking the number and redialing, this time allowing the phone to ring twenty times, I again received no response. Thus, I drove over to the place—less than ten minutes away—only to find the restaurant open for business as usual and staff just sitting around the counter—near the phone—fraternizing as if they were on the veranda of some local social spot enjoying their day off. Smoldering, I ordered, thinking to myself, "Now I'll have to sit here for fifteen minutes." Finally, actually ten minutes later, I left with my mouth-watering cuisine (or so I thought), only to arrive home and discover that I had been given someone else's order which included a sauce that had been inadvertently placed in the bag without a lid, thus spilling onto my car seat. That was enough! I vowed never to return to that restaurant. The work ethic of the proprietor and his staff is dismally lacking, too much like that of many other proprietors, professionals, and craftsmen. How refreshing life would be in this age of retro fashions, retro songs and dances, and retro movements if we also readopted the serious work ethic of yesteryear when people approached a job—any job—with seriousness of purpose, utilized their maximum potential, and consistently produced quality work.

Attitude is important to the success of any venture, and work is foremost among these endeavors. Having a serious attitude toward work means willingly accepting the responsibility to which one has been entrusted. The serious-minded worker is conscious of the time involved in doing the job and puts forth every effort to begin the job at the time designated, working steadfastly on the task, and working (instead of breaking frequently) until quitting time. This worker is willing, on occasion, to work past the "written" quitting time to meet crucial deadlines. The serious worker is cognizant of time only in regard to job performance, unlike the clockwatcher who makes waiting for break time, waiting for lunch, waiting for the work day to draw near to an end—so that he may leave just ten minutes early—his primary goal.

Preparedness for the job is a *must* if one is to take his job or responsibility seriously. School is a responsibility that should be approached with the same commitment given to salaried employment. Consequently, the student who arrives to class on time but continually fails to bring appropriate supplies does not take his education seriously. What happens if an assignment requiring pen and paper, calculator and compass, or textbook is made? Because of his non-serious attitude, the student is unable to complete his task.The same assumption can be made about the teacher who comes to class regularly without notes, text, some plan for the day's discussion, nor any plan for the next class meeting. In both cases, someone fails to do a satisfactory job, a job which each should have understood upon acceptance of it, and it is, in fact, this *understanding* of what one's job entails that is perhaps even more crucial. The serious worker finds out specific responsibilities or objectives of the job during the interview (the student finding out objectives from the course syllabus) and seeks additional information about mastery of job after employment. This concerned employee wants to know how he might actually excel in his position. Maybe the student forgets his tools occasionally, and maybe a teacher occasionally becomes too exhausted to plan properly the night before class and ends up rambling for an hour, but when either of the aforementioned actions repeatedly occurs, the likelihood increases that these people, and others like them, have, for whatever reason, an indifferent attitude about their obligations.

Once an employee finds out the duties of his job, he must utilize all of the knowledge and skill that he has to execute his responsibility. For example, a waitress greets her customers, takes their orders, and brings food to the table. She walks back and forth by these diners during the course of their meal but never pauses to ask if there is some other need she can fulfill. One of the diners tries to get her attention, but is unsuccessful, for she does not even look in their direction. Finally, the waitress returns and absentmindedly tosses the check on the table and mumbles what the guests later surmise to be "Have a Good Day." How would you rate her job performance? Sure, she brought the food ordered and the check, but she did not provide full service to customers who ultimately pay her salary, customers who may have wanted dessert or looked forward to enjoying a cup of cappuccino or needed additional napkins. Likewise, the hairdresser who fails to follow the proper routine of shampooing, conditioning, and styling hair does not complete his job with efficiency. Nor does the pharmacist who hurriedly fills a customer's prescriptions, neglecting to caution against alcohol consumption while taking the medication, use all of his knowledge. In the former example, the customer may be disappointed with the "sorry" hairstyle or may infrequently suffer hair and scalp damage because of a professional's negligence, but there is imminent danger for the customer who takes the medicine prescribed and drinks, and he places others at risk if he decides to drink and drive as well. The same hazard exists when automobile craftsmen fail to test key parts of each vehicle properly and take short-cuts to save money. Too often, consumers lose money, pride, time, and sometimes life because of lazy or negligent employees.

Sometimes consumers are just left feeling baffled as well as angry because of the inconsistent productivity of workers. A career woman who frequently visits the bakery shop near her job may conclude that the proprietor is a sorry excuse for a baker because some days he has delec-table pastries, and some days he has unappetizing ones. The baker might just have a bad day. Though she eats there regularly, mainly because of convenience, she would not dare buy pastries from there for her soror-ity meeting. The same anxiety is experienced by the woman whose hair-dresser's work is inconsistent. On some visits the woman's hair is beau-tifully styled, but on other visits, the same customer leaves the salon "steaming," cringing with shame because her hair is styled ridiculously or fearing hair loss because the chemicals remained in her hair too long. For this reason, she would not dare visit this stylist prior to an impor-tant engagement. In earlier times, after years of patronage, people could expect the same excellent care and attention that they had received dur-ing their first business transaction with a person or company. A profes-sional's reputation was then tantamount to a brand name.

Change can be a many splendored thing, and sometimes it can produce multi- FEARS. But too many of the changes in work ethic have wrought unnecessary physical, mental, and financial losses to too many people. Professionals referred to in this discussion have been used as examples, with no attempt to make an indictment against all persons in these professions, but those in these and other professions, businesses, and crucial positions—from politicians to parents, from midwives to morticians—who have taken lackadaisical attitudes about their jobs should adopt the work ethic of their foreparents. That work ethic is best summarized in these lines penned by an unknown but very insightful author: "Every job is a self-portrait of the person who did it. Autograph your work with quality."

Using some of the same questions that you raised about the paragraph, critique the essay. What about sentence variety? Do all of the sentences begin the same way? Do you recognize colloquial language or words that are too pompous for the subject matter discussed? Do any of the words confuse you? These are additional concerns that you the writer must consider as you compose paragraphs, essays, letters, and other types of written communication. And *always* keep in mind that regardless of the unity of ideas, support of main point, connection of ideas, usage problems such as incorrect spelling, verb tense, and modifier placement, cause confusion for your audience. Such confusion can consequently defeat your purpose for writing, which ultimately will be to communicate some idea—whether you are attempting to inform, persuade, explain, or entertain. (See Glossary, Part Ten, for clarity on rules about grammar, punctuation, and mechanics.)

The following is a discussion of important features and concerns that you must understand and address in writing polished essays.

AUDIENCE

As indicated, the audience—the readers—of any written text must be considered as you prepare to write. Just who will read your essay? How informed will the audience be about the subject to be discussed? What language should be used? These are just a few questions that you or any writer should ponder in preparing to write. Of course, since all writing is persuasive to some extent, you do not want to write anything that would offend your audience, even though they may take a different position from yours. You want to use language and ideas that will be understood and that will be of interest to your readers. You also want to include content that will capture their attention and make them want to read further and at least consider what you have to say.

Therefore, if your audience for an essay about happiness is a group of teenagers, your examples, references, and some word choices used might only appeal to teenagers. For instance, the thesis might state: Happiness is "chilling" with the gang at the mall on Friday evening, being surprised with a car on your sixteenth birthday, or going on a shopping spree with your father's bankcard.

However, an essay written on the same subject for a more mature audience (thirty years and above) might offer the following thesis:

> Happiness is bonding with a loved one(s) on a rainy Saturday afternoon, taking a three-day cruise, or renewing a friendship after several years of estrangement.

The writer here anticipates the speech as well as the values of his audience. True, some adults may use the colloquial expression "chilling" and cherish the acquisition of material goods more than memorable experiences, as implied, but the writer has aptly identified the preferences of most people in these two age groups. At other times, gender may also be a variable, with predictably larger numbers of males than females—all age groups represented—declaring happiness to be "spending a weekend feasting while watching the NFL playoffs."

These and similar interests notwithstanding, you should consider your reading audience to be anyone with basic reading and comprehension skills and average intelligence, someone who could read the local newspaper, or magazines like *Time, Newsweek, Essence, Sports Illustrated, Glamour, The Reader's Digest*, or *Soap Opera Digest*. You would provide the same kind of information and employ the same informal language you would use in talking to a family member, teacher, clergyman, doctor, or retail salesperson. If a classroom assignment demands that you use a specific audience for your essay, you usually will be made aware of this expectation by the very nature of the assignment itself. For instance, an assignment that instructs you to adopt the persona of an apprenticed mechanic who must present a proposal to automechanics on how to rebuild engines faster would dictate that you use jargon of the trade. On the other hand, an assignment that requires you to address the same subject but this time to lay people would force you to use the most simplified terms and provide background material that would not be necessary in the proposal to automechanics.

DICTION

Again, use informal diction—simple everyday vocabulary with clear sentence structure—in the essays that you write. Do not use the flowery, pretentious language that some inexperienced writers use in their attempt to appear polished and intellectual. And do not take that opportunity to use the language that you use with peers during social settings, even if the topic assigned lends itself to personal choice or opinion. When in doubt, ask yourself this question: "Will the average young person or elderly individual with average reading skills be able to comprehend my expressed thoughts? If the answer to this question is a resounding "NO" or an apprehensive "MAYBE," you need to review word choices and phrases. For further instruction and review on diction, see Chapter Five, "Choosing the Right Words."

POINT OF VIEW

In addition to considering audience, you must decide on point of view for your written discussion. Whose ideas, experiences, or knowledge are you writing about? How close are you to your audience? Do you know your readers very well, or are you addressing people in general? Whichever point of view/reference you choose to use, be *consistent*. Consider the following approaches.

First Person Point of View

"If you have heard it once, you have heard it a thousand times (trite but true): 'Never use 'I' in essays.'" That English teachers have made this statement throughout the years is true, but the principle is false. You as any other writer may use first person— I, me, my, mine—in an essay if the writing topic dictates that you do so. Such occasions arise when topics like these are assigned:

"Would you prefer to live in the country or the city?"

"Are you a morning, midday, or evening person?"

"What would cause you to break a law?"

And you may use first person in almost any essay—regardless of topic phrasing—to cite a personal testimony as an illustration to support your point. However, you should exercise caution in using first person frequently in essays. The "I prefer," "I function," "I could never" type of responses throughout an essay can be boring, may be construed as unreliable and/or egotistical, and sometimes prove to be unenlightening. Granted, your opinions have merit, but audiences usually want to know that your conclusions and evaluations are the result of a synthesis of personal experience, observation, reading, and *thinking*, which, in itself, is such a vital component of *good* writing. Consequently, to give writing more credibility and sharpen your critical thinking and analytical skills, avoid using first person frequently.

Second Person Point of View

The writer who uses *you* in addressing audiences has made two basic assumptions about his purpose in writing. First, he assumes the same level of familiarity with the reader of the essay as he does with a friend in a friendly letter. Second, this point of view implies some kind of mutual understanding between the writer and his audience. For some readers, repetition of "you" in essays may be as odious as the "you know" banter is in oral communication. Reserve second person point of view for friendly letters and for process analysis paragraphs and essays (see "Process Analysis" in Chapter Six).

Third Person Point of View

The third person point of view (he, she, they, it) is more commonly used by scholars, journalists, business people, and politicians. The writer who uses this point of view places a certain distance between his personal feelings and the subject that he writes about, even though he may be in agreement with the position or attitude conveyed in the written text. He becomes a reporter, an observer, a researcher—finding and reporting truths, secrets, results, and occurrences. He seems reliable or trustworthy in his analysis or discussion of an issue. Whenever possible, use the third person approach in your writing activities.

Activity 1
Read the following paragraph which uses first person. Now rewrite the paragraph using third person point of view. How do the paragraphs differ?

> Some people say that window shopping may appear to be a harmless activity, but it can cause serious problems for some people like me. I see the most gorgeous outfits that I cannot afford on my tight budget. Then I end up worrying during the remainder of my shopping trip and later at home, worrying about how I might manage to buy the dress-to-die-for and pay rent and my car note. I drop hints to my boyfriend when he is with me, but he ignores me completely. However, sometimes I just take the plunge and buy what I like. Then I worry later about how I am going to pay the charge card bill. At other times I end up buying some items just because I see them. Needless to say, these end up in a corner of my closet because I am too ashamed to take them back to the store. The clerks already tease me when I make purchases. "See ya soon," they chortle. I am ashamed that I have allowed a carefree activity to cause me so much stress.

Activity 2

Read the paragraph below, which uses *second person* point of view. Then rewrite it, using *third person* point of view. What is the difference in the messages conveyed?

Whether most people will admit it or not, living together before marriage is necessary today so that couples can determine if they are compatible. You and your partner discover if the two of you can live in the same space for weeks and months, maybe even years, at a time and get along well. You know how it is when your significant other spends the night every now and then. You are both on your best behavior, carefully choosing topics of conversation, acting as if you are interested in what to you actually sounds like a boring day, and not spending excessive time in the bathroom. You pretend that you do not mind watching *Seinfeld* instead of your favorite program, *Star Trek*. However, when you move in together, you get a chance to see the real person—who may not stay in the bathroom forever in the morning, but who might bore you with shop talk or neighborhood gossip every evening or make you question what is wrong because of monosyllabic responses like "no," "yeah," and "huh" when you attempt to communicate. And finally, you get an opportunity to see if your heart-throb is as amorous as you have been led to believe when you spent those weekends together at your co-worker's beach house or at the Love Nest Cabin. You know the effects such settings can have on each of us, and you wonder about the reality. The only way you can discover if your sole mate is truly your soulmate is to live together before you say those "I do's."

Activity 3

The brief paragraph below has a number of shifts in point of view. Revise the paragraph for consistency in point of view.

When we the people decide to be kind to one another, we will all get along, as Rodney King pleaded for us to do. I try to speak to people whom I meet and offer assistance when I see someone in need of help. I allow people to get in front of me when their blinking signal light suggests they need to get in my lane. People can do simple things like holding a door for another person who may have an armload of packages. We can start by encouraging people when we know that they are attempting some feat or task that is new to them. You can allow that elderly person or mother with a baby and small children to get the park bench that you spotted first. There are just so many good deeds that one can do to help others have a better day and less frustration in their lives in general.

GETTING READY TO WRITE

Armed with all of this information, you are *almost* prepared to write. Why *almost*? There are a number of other important factors to be considered. These include developing a positive attitude, choosing the appropriate topic, then performing the physical act itself, prewriting, which includes brainstorming, freewriting, making a jot list and/or outline.

Attitude

Even the most experienced writers—acclaimed novelists, poets, and journalists—have problems getting started writing. They experience anxiety before sitting down with paper and pen or sitting at the computer to compose, but the advantage that these writers have that inexperienced writers do not have is that they *know* they can write. If you are an inexperienced writer, you must first believe that you too can write. Sure, writing is not an easy task, but neither is playing the trumpet, playing chess, or learning how to swim. Yet, just as knowledge of *do's* and *don'ts* about these challenges, as well as courage to try them, is the first step to mastering them, so it is with writing. Believe that you, too, can write.

Topic Selection

The next step is to decide on the subject for your discussion. Suppose you were one of seven people sitting at a table in a cafeteria where the following topics were discussed: oceanography, Denzel Washington, kinetic energy, Oriental rugs, Gloria Estefan, Bruce Springsteen, and hockey. Would you take an active part in the discussion of *all* of these topics, *some* of these, only *one* of these, or *none* of these? Chances are that you'll know more about one of these than you will know about others, and you will comment, maybe even at length, about the subject familiar to you. Your response to a writing topic will be the same as your response to the table talk. You cannot write about what you cannot talk about. Therefore, whenever possible, choose the writing topic with which you are most familiar.

Prewriting

Sometimes you may find it difficult to write, even after you choose a topic of interest to you. At other times you may be slow to begin writing because none of the writing topics appeal to you or only one seems vaguely familiar to you. However, write, you must. Do not panic. You can write that paper by utilizing one or more of the most common prewriting strategies discussed below.

Brainstorming

In brainstorming, you raise a series of questions about the topic, and one of your responses to the questions generates an idea to write about. This strategy is very effective when you are assigned a *broad* topic that you must limit to write a 500 to 700 word essay, the fifty (50) to sixty (60) minute in-class essay. Simply ask these six questions: who? what? why? when? where? and how? Note the following questions raised for this broad topic, Denzel Washington.

> *Who* have been the most influential people in this famous actor's life?
>
> *What* are Mr. Washington's best movies (or *which* one is his best movie?)?

Why does Mr. Washington appeal to so many women?

When did Mr. Washington recognize his potential or value as an actor?

Where did this incredible actor learn his trade?

How does Mr. Washington prepare for tough roles?

Surely, responses to one of these questions or maybe a couple will generate ideas for discussion in a class essay.

Freewriting

Another common prewriting strategy is freewriting, that is, writing whatever comes to mind about a subject without worrying about grammar, punctuation, spelling, sentence structure, and other conventions. In employing this strategy to generate ideas for a writing assignment, you write as fast as you can for ten to fifteen minutes, even indicating in writing that you cannot think, if such a moment should occur. The point of this exercise is to tap into what you know about the subject or discover your true attitude about it. Writing freely will help you sharpen your focus. Compare the freewriting sample below to the model essay on work ethic that grew out of a freewriting exercise.

> I am tired of being taken advantage of by people who don't want to do their jobs. My friends are too so I know I can't take it personally. But people should not take jobs when they don't care how they affect others like in stores, and restaurants and even hairdressers too. What can I say about these people with these bad job attitudes always messing up when they do try to do their job, and that doesn't happen often. Why can't people work like they used to work when my mama and older people used to work they always did what their bosses said they were supposed to do on those jobs and cared about how their jobs were done. Something needs to happen and soon cause I am tired about not knowing what to expect when I go into a business these days.

The writer above indicates a desire for change in work attitude and performance of today's employees. His next task is to decide on a plan of development.

In writing essays, you will find that brainstorming works very effectively when you need to limit a subject. Freewriting works equally as well when you are trying to limit a familiar subject or determine what you know about what appears to be a vague subject, and it is helpful in organizing thinking in any writing situation.

Making a Jot List

The jot list is also an effective step to use when you are asked to write about a broad topic or when you are given a particular question to address. Simply write down whatever comes to mind. See how many details you can think of that are related to the topic. Then sort your ideas. Check to see if there are similarities in the ideas that you have jotted down. If you do not see a group of related ideas or thoughts expressed, continue to think and jot down ideas that come to mind. Soon you should identify a series of ideas or related thoughts on the subject. Read the list of ideas and thoughts drawn up while someone contemplated "roommates" as a topic for writing.

some good times

some problems

money

late money (no money)

differences

cleanliness vs. filth

responsible vs. irresponsible

adjustments

some good lessons

slumber parties

long talks

tolerance

snoring

sharing space

studying late

patience

diplomacy

This list of ideas about roommates led the writer to a focused idea that could be worked into a thesis statement—lessons or virtues gained from living with room-mates. These virtues included tolerance, patience, adjustment (later changed to adaptability), and diplomacy. After further thought, the writer chose to develop this thesis: Living with a roommate teaches you tolerance, adaptability, and patience.

Making a Scratch Outline

Brainstorming often arouses the writer's curiosity. Freewriting often jogs the memory and exposes subconscious feelings and desires, and it comes closer to simu-lating the writing process with its usual paragraphic format and series of sentences, rather than words or brief phrases generated by the other pre-writing strategies dis-cussed. Nevertheless, freewriting sometimes causes writers to go around in circles, repeating the same generalizations, and brainstorming can lead to questions for which there are no answers, or at least none readily available for the student who has to complete a timed-writing assignment. But the jot list is felt by many teachers to be the most definitive prewriting strategy in helping writers choose ideas for discussion more quickly.

Not only do student writers identify major ideas for discussion with this strategy, but they also are reminded of examples—supporting details—to develop the ideas. With these ideas recorded, a third of the writing challenge has been met. Selection of crucial ideas identified and organization of these remain before the actual writing process occurs. And the next step, the next strategy, is to develop a scratch outline. The scratch outline forces the writer to select main ideas, discard irrelevant ones, choose more appropriate ones, if necessary, and choose the most appropriate arrangement for discussion of ideas to support the thesis statement. *Suggestion*: Often, planning for timed essays ends with a jot list or scratch outline. The sample jot list on roommates led to this scratch outline.

Scratch Outline
Thesis: Living with a roommate teaches you tolerance, adaptability, and patience.

    I. Tolerance
        1. Snoring
        2. Slamming doors
    II. Adaptability
        1. Little space
        2. Change in study time
        3. Housekeeping
   III. Patience
        1. Dealing with money problems
        2. Dealing with sensitive feelings

You will note that there are three divisions above. These divisions represent main points for the body of the essay. They tell you what you must write next. You may change a subtopic as you write, but with this scratch outline you have a plan for an essay. The next step is to begin drafting the essay.

Formal Outline

While scratch outlines provide the writer with an immediate plan for writing, the formal outline primarily informs the audience of what to expect in the body of an essay. While the scratch outlines may not reflect all of the subtopics discussed in the essay, whatever is mentioned in the formal outline must appear in the same order identified in the outline. In essence, the formal outline in the essay serves the same purpose as the table of contents in a book. At some point in your academic studies you will be required to submit a formal outline along with your essay. Thus, you need to be aware of the requirements of this outline.

Unlike the scratch outline, the formal outline, as the name implies, has rigid guidelines concerning the physical structure itself and the divisions/and order of ideas to be discussed. *Consistency* is essential in this arrangement. There are two main types of formal outlines: the topic and the sentence outlines. *Never mix topics and sentences in a formal outline.* Traditionally, English teachers have requested that students submit a sentence outline when outlines are required. Study the basic outline pattern below, paying special attention to *numbering, indentation, punctuation, and spacing.*

Thesis: _____

_____

  I. _____

    A. _____

      1. _____

      2. _____

        a. _____

        b. _____

    B. _____

You should have made the following observations: placement of thesis statement; use of Roman numerals for main headings (often equivalent to a topic sentence for each body paragraph); use of capital letters for subheadings; use of Arabic numbers for second subheadings; use of lower case letters for third subheadings. You should have also noted spacing and indentations for subheadings.

Always indent approximately five spaces or make certain that the subheading appears directly under the first letter of the first word of the preceding heading. If you are unable to complete a heading (for example, A) on one line, indent the second line of that heading so that it appears under the first word of the preceding line. Unless stated otherwise, always double space headings. In addition, punctuate sentences with periods at the end. Capitalize the first word in each sentence, and as always, capitalize proper nouns. In a topic outline, capitalize only the first letter of the word that begins the heading, and, of course, capitalize proper nouns. No punctuation is needed at the end of an entry in the topic outline.

Make certain that each heading on a particular level addresses an idea of equal significance. Headings should not overlap, for example, I, II, and III should address different points relevant to thesis development, and, likewise, the subheadings should be different ("A." should be different from "B."). Also, make sure that headings are parallel. Main headings should have the same grammatical structure, and all sub-headings for each main heading/division should have the same grammatical form. Thus, main headings in a topic outline might look like this.

    I. Eating the right foods . . .

   II. Exercising three times a week . . .

  III. Getting six to eight hours of sleep . . .

If the first main heading began with a prepositional phrase, so would all other main headings. (See section on parallel structure.) Of course, in a sentence outline, each heading will be a declarative sentence. Finally, keep in mind that there must be at least two divisions for each heading. There cannot be a main division "I." without division "II." There cannot be a subheading "A." without an accompanying "B." and so forth. This simple rule applies: If anything is divided, there will be at least two parts.

For further clarity on formal outlining, see the two examples below.

<u>Topic</u> <u>Outline</u>	<u>Sentence</u> <u>Outline</u>
Thesis: Living with a roommate teaches you tolerance, adaptability, and patience.	*Thesis*: Living with a roommate teaches you tolerance, adaptability, and patience.
I. To tolerate others	I. You must learn to be tolerant.
A. Snoring loudly	A. You have to tolerate snoring.
B. Slamming doors	B. You have to tolerate slamming doors.
II. To adapt to changes	II. You must adapt to unexpected situations.
A. Change in space	A. You may have less space.
B. Change in study	B. You may need to change your study schedule.
C. Change in housekeeping	C. You may have to modify your housekeeping practices.
III. To develop patience	III. You must develop patience.
A. Wait for money	A. You must wait for your roommate's share of the expenses.
B. Avoid hurting feelings	B. You must learn to avoid hurting your roommate's feelings.

You will note that only two levels, main and one level of subheadings, are provided in these outlines. Normally, this is the minimum requirement for short to average length essays. Although there are only three major divisions identified in these outlines, I., II., and III., you may have additional headings, but normally no more than five for a given essay. You will also note that the terms "introduction," "body," and "conclusion" do not appear in the outline and should not unless you are given specific instructions to include them by your teacher. The main divisions (headings) represent only the body. It is understood that all essays naturally have a beginning and an ending.

DRAFTING

With planning behind you, you are ready to write the essay. Place a dictionary, a thesaurus, several pens, adequate paper and other resources before you. You do not want to have to interrupt the composing process to look for something once you begin. Also, make certain that your jot list, scratch outline, or whatever prewriting materials used are in your immediate view. This is of utmost importance when you are composing during the class period.

Keep in mind the rules for writing effective introductions and conclusions and be certain to provide ample supporting details for each main point discussed. As you write, if you are writing an in-class paper, you must pay close attention to usage, sentence structure, and punctuation, even though you will allot five to seven minutes to proofread your paper before submitting it. However, if you are writing an out-of-class essay, consider conventional rules as you compose, but spend more time with writing the essay—developing content. Do not approach your out of class essay with a "sink-or-swim-immediately" attitude. You will revise the essay. It is okay to scratch out or type a whole paragraph that may be discarded later. You may see the need to change one of the main points identified in the scratch outline; do so. Just remember to rewrite the thesis statement—provided you wrote a three-pronged thesis statement—to reflect those changes.

If you are typing your essay on a computer or word processor, be certain to save material occasionally. You do not want to touch the wrong key and lose what you have already produced. You also should not wait until you have finished the essay to print a hard copy. Sometimes taking the draft away from the computer or academic scene can help you with further drafting and/or revising of ideas.

If you are writing the essay first and typing it later, you should feel free to write notes to yourself, if necessary, about certain words or phrases; draw arrows when you need to insert ideas that occurred to you later; write in margins or on the back side of your paper, if necessary. As you write more, you will develop your own style or system of drafting. Do not be afraid to experiment with drafting procedures. Some people write long hand first; others type; some cut and paste from handwriting or typing. Never forget that you may have to draft and revise several times before the final paper is produced. Take comfort in knowing that thousands of writers do the same thing daily.

REVISING/REWRITING

Some teachers might tell you to draft and then revise. The truth is, however, that all of us make some revisions as we write. We write a word, then scratch it out or delete it and make other minor changes. Yet there is another step involved in the writing process that could only best be described as REWRITING. During drafting you seek to place ideas and supporting details down on paper. During the rewriting stage you attempt to critique what you have written. You, the creator/writer, become the critic–doing a job which is very difficult for the average student writer who so often, after having received a "C" or lower grade on a paper, whines, "But I spent five hours on this paper. I know it's a good paper."

To make the transition from creator to critic, you must distance yourself from the writing. Of course, if you are doing a timed-writing assignment, you do not have this option, but still you must try to allot a few minutes—five to seven—before the end of class to critique your essay for glaring errors. But when you are given time to prepare an essay out of class, you must devote enough time to drafting and allow sufficient time to revise/rewrite it. Five to eight hours is normally considered enough time between the drafting and revision stages. Sleep, go to the park, or do something relaxing before returning to the draft. Then, armed with your check sheet and additional paper or computer space for revising, ask yourself the following questions:

1. Do I have an explicit thesis statement?
2. Do my points (areas of development) overlap?
3. Do I support my thesis or position on the assigned topic?
4. As a matter of fact, have I responded to the assigned topic?
5. Do I provide enough evidence in each body paragraph, or is the topic sentence underdeveloped or unbalanced in its response or support of my thesis?
6. Am I logical in my assumptions and conclusions?
7. Should the first point discussed appear last?
8. Have I used the most appropriate organizational plan for this topic?
9. What about my audience?
10. Is the statement in paragraph # _____ too general, confusing?
11. Am I showing the similarities or differences that I claim in my introduction?
12. Does this paper reflect sound reasoning?
13. Have I insulted my audience?
14. What about the term in paragraph # _____, sentence # _____?
15. Have I used someone else's data without giving proper credit?
16. Are the sentences too long? too short?
17. Do most of the sentences start the same way?
18. Is my conclusion emphatic enough?
19. What about coherence? Is there a connection between ideas? Paragraphs?
20. What can I do to produce a more polished essay?

You may need to change a few words and phrases, or you may need to rewrite half of the essay. As you write more, you will become more familiar with your individual writing errors and tendencies, and you will not have to consider each question above. You may need to spend more time polishing or varying sentence length. In case you do have to make major revisions or rewrite an essay two to three times, give yourself enough turn-around time to revise and complete other steps in the writing process before you submit your essay for evaluation or send written correspondence any place.

EDITING

Even experienced writers sometimes make errors in such areas as verb tense or spelling. They even have been known to write a dangling modifier occasionally. But they have learned to edit their writing carefully to eliminate these errors before others see them. You too must edit your essays to correct errors in grammar, punctuation, syntax, and diction.

If you tend to make errors in certain areas of usage, for instance, subject verb agreement, then you should read your revised draft carefully to find grammatical errors in general, but subject verb agreement errors in particular. If you question your placement of a comma or omission of an apostrophe, do not hesitate to check handbook rules governing these marks. If a sentence does not make sense to you, assuredly, it will not make sense to others. When in doubt always check resources, both material and human.

PROOFREADING

After having planned, drafted, revised, rewritten, edited, and prepared the final draft of your essay, you are ready to present it, right? Wrong! There is one final step: proofreading! Read the final draft two to three times, but seldom will you need to read it more than this because your anxiety might cause you to change too much and create undue problems. Space your readings of this final draft so that you can be more alert and consequently be more likely to spot typographical errors and careless omissions, sometimes omission of a word and at other times omission of a line or two. Omission of what appears to be a simple word like "not" may contradict your argument entirely.

Be certain to read the paper aloud slowly. Point to each syllable or sound as you read aloud. Doing so will help you to *see* what you are *saying* or bring your attention to the fact that what you are *saying* is not what is actually on your paper. In reading silently, you may assume endings are included that are not. Reading aloud helps you to recognize omissions, incorrect usage, or inclusion of the wrong material. With correction of errors and final check of manuscript submission requirements (which vary from teacher to teacher), you are ready to present your essay.

Activity 1
You have seen the outline about roommates. Now you have an opportunity to see the draft of the essay written from it. Read the essay carefully. Then, using the revision/rewriting checklist, critique the essay for effectiveness.

A ROOMMATE

At least once in life, most people will share an apartment or a dorm room with others. In most cases, the persons involved will have been friends, living in separate environments, who decided to try living together. Two or more different personalities under one roof, from my experience, can only lead to problems. However, if you are lucky, as I was, you will solve those problems and learn some important lessons. Living with roommates taught me tolerance, adaptability, and patience.

Firstly, I learned how to be tolerant. When I lived in the complex last year, I had three roommates, two of whom were in the band. The four of us were inseparable and many "outsiders" were jealous of our friendship. All of my roommates snored and enjoyed slamming doors.

Because we were so close, I learned to tolerate their disturbing antics, and eventually got used to them. My only choice in that situation was to either learn to tolerate them or pull all of my hair out.

After I developed tolerance, I then had to learn adaptability. All of my life I had slept in a queen-size bed located in a room that was all mine. With a roommate, I had to learn to make do with the space available and not be a floor-closet-wall hog. I had to adapt to studying earlier in the evening because lights late in the evening would disturb my roommate. I also had to adapt to the notion that on many occasions one side of the room—my side—would be clean and the other filthy. Although adapting takes time, I quickly made the adjustments needed to make our stay together all the more pleasant.

The final lesson I learned was how to be patient. I never realized that the old cliche "Patience is a virtue" was true until I met the roommate I am currently living with. She never has any of the bill money on time, even though she works at a local department store earning well over $160 a week. She is an immature baby who can't take constructive criticism. I find myself calling home almost everyday so that my younger brother can calm me down after a heated argument with my roommate. If I had not learned to be patient, I probably would have had a fight with my roommate.

I have experienced living with numerous types of roommates. Each year brings a new experience that I never thought I would encounter. I am just happy that I learned to tolerate, to adapt, and to be patient with others. If I had not developed these important qualities, I might be living alone right now.

Activity 2
Below, an introduction and conclusion are provided for you. Complete the essay by writing the first, second, and third body paragraphs. After you finish composing, be certain to revise, edit, and proofread your essay.

THE LOVE OF MONEY
The appropriation of money is one of the major driving forces in modern day society. Without money, survival is almost impossible. With this in mind, people base their lives around money and methods by which to obtain it. Often people get high paying jobs, not because they enjoy the occupation, but rather so that they can make the big money. Thieves do what they do because they are trying to stay afloat in our materialistic and money-hungry society. Basically, Americans are so preoccupied with money that they so some unorthodox things to get it.

(First Supporting Point)

(Second Supporting Point)

(Third Supporting Point)

This lustful preoccupation with money is extremely damaging to many people in our society. Because of it, many things are taken for granted. The unfortunate part is that the things that Americans take for granted are things that they could not live without. For most people, it takes a near death experience or the death of someone close to them for them to realize the important things in life. For the others, money is the only important thing.

Activity 3

Write an essay (out of class) on one of the four topics listed below. Submit a copy of prewriting material, rough draft, and a final draft along with a formal sentence outline. (91-93) Due Wednesday 209 A

A. A character trait(s) that you find detestable in people.

B. A group of professionals who do not get the respect that they deserve.

C. A movie that was overrated (or underrated).

D. What causes young lovers to break up.

E. What it means to be eighteen years old today.

4

The Portfolio

All of the sections in this text should help you in reaching your writing goals and putting together a portfolio that is well worth bragging about.

Modifications of the portfolio method of enhancing writing development can most definitely be made. For instance, some programs may opt to use two notebooks instead of three, or to include three or four entries in the portfolio rather than one or two. Often you, the student, alone decide which papers to place in your portfolio and/or whether or not to include two or three drafts of a particular paper to testify to your progress. Surely, no two portfolio programs will be identical, and they need not be. The focus of such a project is to help you to become more attuned to your ideas and to manipulate them in such a way that your reader will appreciate your efforts.

THE STUDENT'S BRAG BOOK

Each story that I tell is pieced together from the fabric of my soul—a checkered rag from times gone by, a flowered patch from times to come, and a striped scrap from the stark reality of the here and now—all padded with both hope and despair and stitched together with the threads of my musings and imagination.

Margie Rauls

Do you know what a *brag book* is? It's nothing more than snap shots a person has taken of special people, scenes, and/or events. These are the shots that the owner of the brag book feels show his best side, her stunning new figure, the grandchildren's biggest and best birthday party or the bride's beautiful wedding. They are the best shots—no out-of-focus ones, no unflattering shots of the bride tripping over her veil, or a little one running around in a soggy diaper.

Not all brag books contain snapshots, and many individuals have one, or a portfolio, as such a special collection is more commonly called. An artist with a book of select sketches, a chef with a notebook of special recipes, or a lawn care person with a scrapbook of the yards he cares for and a list of satisfied customers to match the pictures in it, all have brag books—collections of their very best efforts.

When you come to college, you are asked to write something in just about every class that you take, and you most likely will write extensively in your college composition classes. Often it is in your first college writing course that you will realize your *like* or too often your *dislike* for putting pen to paper. You find that ideas to write about don't come easily, and at times you have to produce an essay, even when you have no feel for the given topic or rhetorical mode assigned by your teacher. You might think back to your high school days and to all the mediocre to poor grades that you made on your essays. You might even start to believe that you hate the entire writing process. It probably never would occur to you that, like an artist, a model, or an engineer, you—a freshman college student—can produce work good enough to put in a portfolio, a brag book. In the freshman English programs at many universities, maintaining a portfolio is a basic requirement for each student. If this is the case at your school, you are lucky. Your relationship with the writing process can be off to a very good start. The entire process of becoming a better, more enthusiastic writer is easier than you could ever imagine.

What's Needed to Get Started?

In order to begin keeping a portfolio and writing better, you should buy yourself three inexpensive note binders—one small (pocket book size) and two of standard size (larger ones). The small binder and one of the larger ones should be filled with loose-leaf notebook paper of appropriate size. The second large binder will remain empty for a while. Each binder should have at least five tabbed dividers in it. Each tab should reflect a different category. The various categories may be determined by certain themes, topics, or rhetorical modes.

Your teacher will probably determine the means of categorization. One section must be labeled GENERAL. An example of tab entries categorized according to rhetorical patterns follows:

Classification	Process	Narration
Comparison/Contrast	Cause/Effect	General

You should stencil or write your name, the teacher's name, the number of the course and section, and the semester or quarter in which the course is taken in a prominent place on the front of each of the three binders. Some students paste pictures of themselves or a dear relative, a favorite pet, or a peaceful scene on their binders. This act is usually optional. After all of this is done, the large empty binder should be given to the teacher.

NEEDS: THREE NOTE BINDERS

(1) Small—filled with note paper

(2) Large—filled with note paper

(3) Large—empty

How Are These Binders Used?

Each binder will serve a special purpose as you change your writing habits and your attitude toward the process.

The Small Binder

The small binder is your constant companion. It, as well as your first large note-book, can be looked upon as your "bragging 'writes'" books. Each is done in preparation of your portfolio, your brag book. You should take the pocket size binder in your pocket, purse, or book bag where ever you go. In it you will scribble down anything that you see or feel that is of special interest to you. Below are some scribblings from the small binder of a former freshman English student.

- Ms. Crocker's eyes are always red on Mondays
- I need money; I must buy my chemistry book
- I think I've lost Joey altogether
- I hate this place
- "Nothing is worth dying for"—J. Copelands, The Rising Cost of Life
- Rainy days are my favorite
- ----------------------------▶ (A snake)
- My mom had a car like that when I was around ten; hers was blue; I loved that car.
- Why? ? ?
- What will my children look like?
- Losing it, losing it, losing it! ! !
- I met a new guy today—WOW—he's a real looker.

As you can see, scribbles can come in various forms (words, sentences, drawings, etc.) and in various stages of development (words, phrases, sentences or short paragraphs). They are your observations: they belong to you.

The small binder takes the place of the napkin, the gum wrapper, or the torn paper scrap on which you once wrote your fleeting observations, which you frequently lost or misplaced. Now you have a safe place for your rambling ideas. Keep the following suggestions in mind; they will help you later in the writing process.

- Try to place only one observation on each small sheet. You may later want to take a particular observation from its present position and place it under a different category. Two or more observations on the same page may make such a move difficult.
- Date each observation and give the place where it happened or the circumstances under which it occurred. Such data will help you remember

the event or idea later and assist you in recreating the mood or atmosphere you were in when you made the observation.

– If you scribble down an idea or quote from a published source, also write down the publication information. This way you will have your reference material at hand if you should ever use the information in your own writing and will not run the risk of plagiarizing.

– If you are writing down an observation from the writing of a particular author, you may want to comment (on the same sheet) on his/her writing style, word choice, persona, etc. If you are very impressed, you may want to jot down a few sample sentences or words.

– Try to read over your day's notes each evening or night. You could embellish them a little, making them clear and more detailed. You may also want to reclassify a thought.

– At times you may want to read over all the notes in your binder, following the same steps that you take on a daily basis. Remember that some of the notes you will use right away, some much later, and some you may never use.

The First Larger Binder

This binder is your "work book." In it you keep your more formal writings—essays, research papers, and fully developed paragraphs. It also contains your drafts and various editing and rewriting efforts. You may also keep preparatory activities here, such as exercises in subject-verb agreement, sentence structure, or vocabulary building—any activity that you perform to help improve your writing. The papers in this binder often reflect the ideas jotted down in your small notebook. Such thoughts are carefully selected, organized, and placed in the developmental order dictated by a certain rhetorical mode or theme and/or topic. It is also good to keep a course syllabus pasted to the front inside cover of this binder. The specific guidelines that are listed within the syllabus can guide you in understanding your writing needs, as well as help you to remember the seriousness of the grammatical, structural, or mechanical errors that you tend to make.

The Second Larger Binder

This binder is your portfolio, your brag book. In it you will place only selected papers—your best efforts. Not all of your drafts, not even all of the ones submitted to the teacher, will be placed in your portfolio. And not all of your submitted essays will even be revised. Usually you and the teacher together decide which ones lend themselves to revision and/or placement into the portfolio. The teacher sometimes dictates the number of essays (and often the theme, topic, and/or rhetorical mode of the essays) that you place in your portfolio; your folio will be evaluated and given an overall grade by a special committee of English teachers at the end of the quarter or semester. (More will be said about the evaluation process later in this unit.)

Illustration

Step I	<u>First</u> <u>Draft</u> (and perhaps drafts *2* and *3* or even more).
Draft(s)	— This draft is *or* these drafts are evaluated by peers. (Evaluation involves the entire class or a small group within the class.)
Step II	<u>An</u> <u>Ensuing</u> <u>Draft</u> (considered to be worthy of submission to the teacher by you and your peers).
Draft	— This draft is analytically evaluated by the teacher and assigned a grade.
	— This draft may or may not be revised.
	— This draft may or may not be placed in the portfolio, even if revised.
	— Graded entries not placed in your portfolio will be kept in your large binder with ungraded drafts, exercises, and other activities.
Step III	<u>Portfolio</u> <u>Entry</u> (should reflect your best possible writing efforts).
Draft	— Entry into the portfolio depends upon the teacher's assessment and/or a certain pre-determined theme, topic, or rhetorical mode.
	— A portfolio entry can be revised many times, even after being placed in the portfolio.
Step IV	<u>The</u> <u>Portfolio</u>
	— Contains a reflection statement and two or three essays or other pieces of writing.
Portfolio	— The portfolio is holistically scored, and the overall portfolio (not individual entries) is assigned a grade by a select committee.

Who Keeps the Binders?

a) You always keep the small notebook of observations. You should try to keep it with you at all times, or at least most of the time.

b) You keep the first binder, usually in your apartment or dorm room, working in it when you are writing or doing exercises. You may often bring it to conference sessions with the teachers and review various drafts and exercises that preceded the writing of a particular draft.

c) The teacher keeps the second large binder, the portfolio. However, the student has ready access to any paper that has been placed there.

How Are You Evaluated?

You read the first draft of your essay to the class or to a select group within the class. Your peers give you feedback on the strengths and weaknesses of the paper. The process of reading a draft and receiving criticism from your peers can be repeated as many times as necessary. When you, together with your peers, feel that a paper is polished enough, you then submit it to the teacher for an analytical reading and the assignment of a grade or score.

A particular paper evaluated by the teacher may or may not be placed into your portfolio, or even revised any further. The determination of what's included may depend upon the teacher's discretion or on selections that have been predetermined according to theme, topic, or rhetorical mode. Usually, the teachers of a particular course make these specifications before each term begins. Remember that only a few papers—two or three—will serve as entries into the portfolio and that these chosen selections can be rewritten many times, even after they have been graded by the teacher and placed into the portfolio. Thus, you can try to make your portfolio the best that it can be.

At the end of the semester, the teacher sends your portfolio to a committee—a team of usually two teachers who teach the same or a similar course. The members of this group will each grade the portfolio (not individual entries) holistically, using criteria such as those found in the rubric on page _____ .

The grade and comments are placed on separate sheets, never on or within the portfolio. An average of these two evaluators' grades will constitute your portfolio grade. The classroom teacher is never involved in this aspect of the evaluation process.

The graded essays that were not placed into the portfolio will also constitute a significant percentage of your final grade. Exercises, ungraded drafts, and other activities included in the workbook, binder #2, and even conferences with the teacher can make up a percentage of your overall grade as well.

A SAMPLE GRADE ALLOTMENT SCALE

1. Graded essays not placed in the portfolio   30%
2. Various exercises and other activities   20%
3. The portfolio   50%

The small notebook, which contains your daily observations, is never evaluated. However, the teacher may have to do a word count of the entries to satisfy certain university or state-mandated regulations, such as those set forth by the Gordon Rule in the State University System of Florida.

Where Does the Portfolio Go After You Have Completed the Course?

The teacher might keep the portfolio for one or two terms after the course is completed. Then it becomes your personal property. In other instances, the portfolio is sent to the teacher of the next English course that you take. For example, after you exit your first Freshman Composition course, your teacher for the second part of Freshman Composition may request your portfolio from your first part. The portfolio often wends its way to your area of concentration, where your major professor keeps it and periodically deposits applaudable assignments, such as lesson plans, class projects, or creative productions into it. Eventually, you, usually upon graduation, will be able to collect your portfolio and present it to potential employers. You will have a finished product well worth bragging about.

How Does Preparing a Portfolio Improve Your Writing?

You, the student, will also be able to make an assessment of your experiences in preparing the essays for your portfolio, as well as collecting and organizing your ideas, sharing them with peers, and writing and rewriting your many drafts.

Your reflections should be put in the form of a memo, business or friendly letter, an essay, or a fully developed paragraph. In preparing this piece of writing, you will indicate what you now understand about how you handled the writing process, how you have strengthened your writing skills, how preparing the portfolio has helped you to change your attitude toward writing, and how you plan to improve your writing even more in the future. Your statement of reflections should not be taken lightly. It will be submitted with the portfolio and constitute a significant part of its grade.

5

Choosing the Right Words

Every writing assignment begins with the idea because the idea is basic for communication; however, we forget sometimes that the right words are essential if the intended idea is to be expressed and if communication is to be achieved. As a writer, you use words as the main tool to communicate your ideas to your audience, for, ultimately, your effective use of words is the element that will determine if your audience understands what you are trying to convey.

Appropriate word choice, or diction, requires that you make decisions about which words will most effectively serve your subject, your purpose, and your audience. In making those decisions, you must consider how formal you need to be, when you need to use abstract or concrete terms, or general or specific terms, to say exactly what you want to say. You must try to avoid vague and ambiguous words and to reject cliched and trite expressions. Your word choice must be precise in order to ensure conciseness in your writing. Such attention to word choice will help to eliminate the possibility of misunderstanding and miscommunication.

Because your writing represents you—your thinking, at least—you must be conscientious in selecting words that will best convey your ideas.

BEGIN WITH DENOTATION AND CONNOTATION

Denotation refers to the dictionary or literal meaning of a word. That meaning is objective, factual. *Connotation*, on the other hand, refers to the emotional responses associated with a word. Take the word *tradition*, for example. It is a word which most of you can define objectively as "something that is handed down from generation to generation." As you consider the emotional association that you have in connection with *tradition*, the meaning of the word may be expanded and enhanced by those associations. That expanded and enhanced meaning is the connotation. Connotations may be favorable, unfavorable, or neutral. Words similar in denotative meanings (synonyms) may have connotations that alter the tone and meaning of a sentence. Note the examples below.

> He is an *eccentric* little man who has long, dark hair.
>
> He is an *odd* little man who has long, dark hair.
>
> He is a *bizarre* little man who has long, dark hair.
>
> He is an *unconventional* little man who has long, dark hair.

To some degree, the *words* in the sentences above have the same denotative meaning and might even be suggested as synonyms. However, because of the connotative meanings of these words, some may be more suited to your purposes than others. Unless you intend to offend, insult, or ridicule, you will avoid choosing *bizarre, eccentric*, and perhaps even *odd*, as each has a negative or unfavorable connotation. *Unconventional*, on the other hand, has a more favorable or neutral connotation and is less likely to cause problems for your audience. This does not mean, however, that you should always avoid words with negative or unfavorable connotations. On the contrary, if your purpose demands such choices, or if your point will be more effectively conveyed by making such choices, you should make them. For instance, if your purpose is to offend, then you will most likely choose *bizarre* or *eccentric* instead of *odd* or *unconventional* in the examples above. As you compose, your attention will be focused on getting your ideas on paper—as it should be. However, as you edit and revise you should make sure that you have considered connotation as well as denotation in your word choices. A good dictionary or thesaurus will help you with choices about which you are uncertain. Be careful, however, when selecting and using synonyms that the word you choose has both the denotative and connotative meaning that will make your ideas clear. Synonyms are *nearly* the same in meaning; it is usually the connotation that makes the difference. Another word of caution: Be sure you know the meanings of the words you use. Look them up if you are uncertain. Words used incorrectly or inappropriately hinder communication. The sentence below illustrates:

A real friend *portrays* a positive attitude that shows he can be trusted.

The general definition of *portray* is "to represent or depict." For most of us, however, the connotation of the word recalls *acting*. Clearly, *portray*, as it is used in this sentence is not the best choice. It isn't even the right choice. The sentence contradicts itself denotatively and connotatively. If we derive our meaning denotatively, then the *friend* in the example is "representing" or "depicting" an attitude that may not be authentic and therefore should not be trusted. Likewise, should we accept the connotative meaning of *portray*, the example describes a friend who *pretends* to be positive and who probably should not be trusted either. The results of such ill-chosen words are often mildly amusing, but sometimes they can be hilarious. Keep a dictionary handy to prevent such mishaps.

The activities below provide practice in distinguishing denotative and connotative meaning.

Activity 1

Arrange the words in each list below from the the least favorable connotation to the most favorable.

a. friendly, congenial, cordial, approachable

b. house, domicile, residence, home, crib

c. fat, plump, obese, pudgy

d. unyielding, stubborn, resolute, bull-headed

e. smart, bright, brainy, knowledgeable

f. filthy, unclean, soiled, dirty

g. pretty, beautiful, gorgeous, stunning

h. frightened, timid, nervous, terrified

i. slender, scrawny, slim, thin

j. disciplined, strict, rigid, stringent

Activity 2

Indicate the difference in meaning of each word in the pairs below. Explain whether the difference in meaning is denotative or connotative. Write a sentence using each word according to its connotation.

1. humid, sultry

2. embarrassed, humiliated

3. love, adore

4. unusual, extraordinary

5. foolish, ignorant

6. alone, isolated

7. aloof, reserved

8. dreamer, idealist

9. economical, frugal

10. ecstatic, happy

11. belief, opinion

12. adversary, opponent

13. famous, notorious

14. ability, capacity

15. fate, destiny

CONSIDER LEVELS OF FORMALITY

Your choice of words should serve both your audience and subject effectively. Therefore, in determining the level of formality, you should consider the demands of the subject and of the audience. There are three generally accepted levels of formality used in writing: formal, informal, and colloquial. *Formal* language uses correct grammar and sometimes uses inverted sentence order; neither contractions nor slang is acceptable in formal language; the tone is elevated to accommodate the formal documents and speeches in which such language is generally used. Similarly, *informal* language also uses correct grammar and generally avoids the use of slang or contractions. Sentence order is usually conventional. The informal level is appropriate for academic and professional writing. *Colloquial* language is used in everyday conversation; it includes contractions, fragments, some slang, and shortened or abbreviated words. Colloquial language is appropriate for writing personal letters and for note-taking, but should be avoided in academic writing. *Slang* is generally unacceptable in academic and professional writing because slang terms have a short life span. In addition, some slang terms are regional and your use of them may leave your audience baffled.

Formal: One should not fail to consider other viable options.

Informal: We should consider other workable options.

Colloquial: We're not gonna overlook the choices.

Once you have decided on the level of language you will use, be consistent in using it. Avoid mixing levels, which your audience may find annoying or distracting.

Activity 3
Label each sentence below as formal, informal, or colloquial.

a. Stan returned to his residence inebriated and prepared for a confrontation.

b. We'll be jetting outta here around 5.

c. You'll have to cook your own dinner.

d. Although I read the poem five times, I still didn't get it.

e. Enclosed are copies of the contract for your perusal and approval.

Activity 4
Revise the letter below for consistency in level of language.

Dear Editor of the Spartan:

I would like to discuss with you our beloved school. It seems we have a lot of problems going on that no one's checking out. Complaints filed are the usual ones—late financial aid checks, no housing, high tuition. I'm kinda tired of hearing the same gripes about our school, so I can't imagine that you aren't as well.

Perhaps, then, you can answer a few questions for me that will help me get to the bottom of my complaint. How come the transportation to the school is so lousy? I could sojourn to my hometown in less time than it takes to secure reliable transport to the school. "Why do I live off campus," you may ask. I reply—"There's no place on campus to live." This leads to my second question—Why would you guys bring more students here than you can accommodate? We're kids! We don't all have the wherewithal to live comfortably and healthfully off campus.

This question forces a segue into my final question. Why is this place so boring? Of course I know that an answer to such a question is far beyond your domain. However, I would not broach the subject had not so many of us been lured here with hype. We heard about how we'd party everyday, about how there's never a dull moment at this school. Hello? All I've had are dull moments.

Someone should take these complaints seriously and try to fix the things they refer to.

Sincerely,

Dwight Bailey

CHOOSE CONCRETE AND SPECIFIC WORDS

As you write, be conscious of your use of abstract and general terms. Abstract words refer to ideas, emotions, and qualities (*democracy*, *joy*, *gentleness*), general words to classes of things (*trees*, *books*, *humans*). Concrete words appeal to the senses and are often more tangible than abstract words (*soft*, *whisper*); specific terms name a particular element of the class or type (*oak tree*, *math book*, *small child*). Most of the time, the more concrete and specific your word choice, the more precise your writing. Of course, not all of your word choices will be concrete and specific, nor should they be. There are situations in which the abstract or general word is the best word, or even the only word. You should seek the effective balance.

Activity 5
Replace the words below with more concrete or specific ones. In some instances, you may need to use phrases in order to make the changes.

furniture	music	compassion
automobile	generosity	beverage
honor	school	integrity
evil	athletics	wealth

Activity 6
Revise the paragraph below to eliminate unnecessary abstract and general terms.

The afternoon was so nice that I could not resist skipping class. Besides, Professor Knight is so dull that I can hardly avoid napping during his lectures. So I decided I wouldn't miss any more than I usually did. On this day I thought I might have some fun. As I relaxed outside, I noticed the people walking by and reacted to some of the interesting things I saw. Finally, one young woman came by and lingered in front of me. I looked at her intently because her attire was so bizarre. She noticed my staring and smiled. As she walked over to me her clothes made noises. When she was in front of me she said, "You think I'm strange, don't you?" I simply smiled. She said, "That's okay. Perhaps I think you're strange too." She smiled again and walked away. It dawned on me later that I had learned something that day despite my efforts not to.

Your efforts to make your writing more precise will require you to avoid several word choice "bad habits." As you proofread, try to substitute more precise words or phrases in place of those that are vague, ambiguous, and dull.

Clichés

Clichés are metaphorical phrases that have become worn from overuse. Most cliches are vague and the imagery they contain has lost its crispness. The imagery in "My father *worked like a dog to support us*" has no real meaning, even though we all understand the intended meaning of the sentence.

Consider, however, your most common image of a dog. Is the image one of a lively dog that prances and yelps as its owner nears? Or is it of a dog that lies around in the warmth of the home waiting to be fed or taken for a walk? Which dog, then, is the father in the sentence above being compared to? Cliches are too vague and ambiguous to add real information to your essays. Avoid them.

Activity 7
Below are some of the more common clichés. Select five of them and write one sentence using each cliché and one substituting more precise language for the cliché.

last but not least	grass is always greener
dry as a bone	cold as ice
never a dull moment	pretty as a picture
clear as a bell	few and far between
white as snow	green with envy
better late than never	beat around the bush

Sexist Language

Sexist language is terminology which uses masculine nouns or pronouns to refer to whole groups; such terminology usually excludes any reference to females who may also be part of the group. Once an acceptable traditional usage, such language today is considered offensive by many. If possible, avoid terms that are gender specific unless they are absolutely necessary. For instance, use *police officer* instead of *policeman*; *humankind* instead of *mankind* or *man*.

Activity 8
Choose a gender neutral term for each term in the list below.

Anchorman	Salesman
Maid	Congressman
Fireman	Weatherman

Stewardess   Mailman

Forman   Housewife

Euphemisms and Jargon

Euphemisms are words or phrases that serve as pleasing or inoffensive substitutes for words we prefer not to name directly. Sometimes we use them to avoid discomfort; sometimes they are tools of deception (for example, *pre-owned*). For instance, our loved ones do not die; they "pass away." We ourselves do not lie; we "stretch the truth a bit." Euphemisms only hamper the conciseness and precision of your writing. Although they may seem a kinder way to express an unpleasant concept or idea, they detract from the vitality of your writing. Below is a partial list of euphemisms you may wish to avoid.

senior citizen

chemically dependent

economically disadvantaged

physically challenged

writing resource center

correctional facility

pre-owned

Jargon is language used among members of a profession, trade, or group. You should avoid such language unless your audience is one that will understand the terminology you use. Jargon is usually technical language, but it can refer to language used by groups with common interests. For instance, non-basketball fans might be stunned to read that "Alonzo Mourning gave Michael Jordan a facial." So, write, instead that "Mourning slam dunked the ball while Jordan was standing under the basket."

Activity 9
The following sentences are from students' essays: revise them to eliminate inappropriate language.

1. Children at school may pick on other children because of where they live.

2. Some people will go out with clothes on that are too small for them.

3. Parents always back up the student even if the student is in the wrong.

4. Never go with your friend's ex-boyfriend.

5. A true friend goes overboard to help a friend who loses a loved one.

6. American moviegoers are always willing to come out of their pockets to see a good movie.

7. Violence is not right and it should not obtain respect.

8. Lies have a way of coming back on you.

9. Americans spend thousands of dollars on diets so they can have the ideal weight in which models portray.

10. People don't realize that their actions can rub off on their children at the age of one.

6

Rhetorical Modes

DESCRIPTION

Have you ever heard the ancient Chinese proverb which states that a single picture is worth a thousand words? The wisdom of this saying has probably proven itself to you repeatedly. For example, the delight in a child's eyes as he or she reaches into a forbidden cookie jar may be more concisely and effectively conveyed in a photograph than in a writer's attempt to explain the incident. There are times, however, when pictures may not be the appropriate medium for expressing yourself. In an essay examination, for instance, to draw a picture in answer to describing a place, a person, an emotion, an object, or any other thing, will be equal to failing the exam. That is definitely one time that a picture will not represent a "thousand words," for it will be not only ineffective but inappropriate as well.

Types of Descriptions

In many instances, a description will be a part of a narrative or of an essay that has used some other rhetorical mode or pattern of development. In general, however, there are two types of descriptions—those for which you will not use a dominant impression, the *objective* description, and those for which you will need a dominant impression, the *subjective* description. The dominant impression is the mood or atmosphere that you want to create in your writing. Consider first your purpose for the description and the audience for whom you are writing. Such consideration will help you to decide whether to use a dominant impression. Usually, a dominant impression will be necessary for descriptive and narrative writing, and in some instances exposition and argumentation may require that you use this technique. However, in technical and scientific writing, it is unlikely that you will need to create a dominant impression, since such information will normally be factual.

When no dominant impression is required, you will need to describe the person, place, activity, emotion, or object in a factual manner. For instance, if you were reporting an experiment or incident, giving directions to someone who was interested in duplicating the experiment, gaining knowledge about the incident, or following the directions, for objectivity, you should not create a dominant impression. To avoid creating a subjective description, choose precise terms. An objective description follows:

> The Spanish styled house at 24 Apple Pie Road has been freshly painted in white with green awnings. Twelve stairs lead to a gallery that is 14' × 6'. The door that leads to a 14' × 12' foot living room is made of oak and steel. A spacious dining hall and kitchen of 10' × 10' is located to the left of the living room. Five bedrooms, each measuring 10' × 8', with three intermittent bathrooms, are to the right side of the living room.

If you were describing this house as your house in a narrative and wished to create a dominant impression, you would include your feelings about the house. Was it a happy place? Was it full of sorrow? Did you feel alienated? You will need to decide and select clusters of words that express those feelings.

Activity 1

What dominant impression do you get from the following description of a house?

> Our Spanish style home stood alone at the edge of a small tropical forest. It had no street address like most normal dwellings, and the postman never ventured that far. He always left our mail, what little we received, with our closest neighbor a half of a mile away from us. In fact, we lost friends because of where we lived. They always said it was too far behind everyone's back, including God's.
>
> I don't know, however, whether I could blame potential visitors, because I too experienced tremors in my stomach over the possible creatures that could come creeping, crawling, roaring, jumping out at me, especially in the thick black night. Because I was so disturbed by horrible imaginations, uneventful nightly slumber was never easy. Every creak on the wooden floors of that monstrously old Spanish house was cause to send my heart racing. I dreamed of snakes that could swallow the twelve stairs that led to the gallery of my house, of tarantulas so black that I could not see them at night until they had wrapped their multitude of stinging hairs around my throat, and of devils that would come to usher my soul into the deepest pits of hell.
>
> The structure of the house lent to my fears. The attic, for instance, was a world unto itself. It was inaccessibly high above our heads and at night we would hear the bats on their way out, and the tarantulas would sometimes, ever so tauntingly, crawl into our presence through small ceiling ventilators. We never visited the basement either, because creatures that could not manage the heights of the attic or could not survive with bats and tarantulas, found their niches in the "underworld." An occasional snake had been known to show itself, and three-inch roaches and spiders gained territorial rights in the dry, dusty areas.

In later years, when I viewed the outside of the house, I understood why so many nonhumans had found homes in it. Its rough, unfinished boards made for good burrowing and camouflaging against the hues of the forest. We should have willed it to the creatures of the forest.

Activity 2

Underline synonyms which you think demonstrate the dominant impression in the above description.

Creating the Dominant Impression

Depending on the atmosphere or mood you wish to create for your reader, you will select words that will describe such an atmosphere or mood. Words that evoke certain moods have been divided into generally positive and negative categories only to assist you as you choose appropriate words for your description. You will need to remember that some positive words could be used with negative connotations and vice versa.

POSITIVE WORDS	NEGATIVE WORDS
happy, pleasant, carefree, warm, lively, joyous, caring, fostering, felicitous, fitting, suitable, cheerful, fortuitous, favorable, propitious, benign, opportune, auspicious, appropriate, apt, proper, effective, efficacious, efficient, effectual, cogent, seasonable successful, affluent, right, nice, compatible, gay, contented, satisfied, gratified, delighted, pleased, gladdened	sad, unpleasant, dense, hot, stifling, deathly, stinking, gloomy, distasteful, unharmonious, stiff, malignant, unhappy, depressed, weighty, oppressed, despairing, despondent, desperate, forlorn, hopeless, melancholic, blue, mean, low-spirited, deprived, difficult, arduous, incompatible, dense, callous, sinful, doleful, baneful, indurate, obstinate, unfeeling, losing

Selecting the exact word for any type of writing is a skill that comes with tireless devotion to reading high quality literature or listening to effective oratory. To be able to select words wisely, you must recognize the difference between denotative and connotative meanings of words.

Denotative Meanings

To use the denotative meaning of a word is to use the word as it is defined in a standard dictionary. For instance, *The American Heritage Dictionary* defines the term "skinny" as "pertaining to, or resembling skin" and "very thin." The definition does not indicate that "skinny" is not a good word to use under certain circumstances, but if you know the connotative meaning of the word, you will be able to determine when it could be used appropriately. *explicited, objective, devoid of personal feeling*

Connotative Meanings

In addition to the denotative meanings found in standard dictionaries, good writers will also know the connotative meanings of words. Connotative meanings are the suggestive or associative implications, created by different societies, of a word. If you knew that the word "skinny" is more negative than positive, then you would recognize that it should not be used under certain circumstances. For instance, if a young man were interested in a young lady who was thin, and he wanted to secure a date with her, he would know not to call that lady skinny, which has negative connotations. He would prefer to call her slim or slender, both of which have pleasing connotations. To call the lady skinny would be tantamount to saying "good-bye."

For effective descriptions, an understanding of connotative meanings is necessary. Many words and their synonyms could be ranked on a continuum from positive to negative. In other terms, words have shades of meaning and you must determine the best meaning that will suit your purpose.

> ### Activity 3
> In the following excerpt, George Orwell writes about Charlie, a young man he met in Paris. Choose the bracketed expression you would use to fill in the blanks. Why did you choose the expression? What connotations do your choices convey? Discuss your choices in class.
>
>> Charlie was a youth of family and education who had run away from home and lived on occasional remittances. Picture him very _____ {flushed and childlike, young}, with the fresh cheeks and soft brown hair of a _____ {nice little boy, cute lad}, and lips _____ {excessively red and wet, like cherries; like berries}. His feet are _____ {small, tiny}, his arms _____ {unusually, abnormally} short, his hands _____ {wrinkled, dimpled like a baby's}. He has a way of _____ {dancing and capering, shifting from foot to foot} while he talks as though he were too _____ {happy, ecstatic}, and too full of life to keep _____ {quiet, still for an instant}.

Paying Attention to Parts of Speech and How They Affect Description

Many inexperienced writers overly associate adjectives with descriptive writing. While it is true that the adjective is probably the most commonly used part of speech in descriptions, it would be unwise to ignore the power of other parts of speech.

Nouns and Pronouns

In a description, the subject (noun or pronoun) should be as specific as possible. Notice the following sentence: *I told my friend to come to my house.* "Friend" and "house" could become more specific and therefore more valuable to your reader if you wrote: *I invited Susan to my home at 26 Bancroft Street.* In the rewritten sentence, the reader will have more specific information with the details you have provided. Of course, many more details can be added to describe Susan and your house.

In strong descriptions, carefully chosen significant details will create effective pictures. It is often possible to expand on nouns and pronouns with meaningful details.

Abstract nouns that express ideas (intangibles) should be made clear with concrete (tangible) nouns. Observe the following sentence: *My younger brother's <u>intelligence</u>* (abstract noun) *was limited to his appetite.* To expand on the quality of intelligence you are describing, you will need to use concrete images. For example, you may write, "*Jamie, my fifteen-year-old brother would shove his homework aside and spend up to a half of an hour perfecting a sandwich. First, the bread had to be stripped of its crust. This was a tedious task of sawing along the foot-long bread that mom would buy for him. After the loaf was completely white, he would pile on butter, mayonnaise, ketchup, mustard, lettuce, tomato, pickles, olives, ham, turkey, chicken, corned beef, jam, chocolate pudding, and whatever else he could find in the refrigerator.*"

These details provide the proof (why you think Jamie's intelligence is in his appetite) of your first summarized sentence.

Activity 4
Expand the following sentences, with meaningful details, into a paragraph.

1. The day began well.
2. Our trip was fine.
3. We had a nice picnic.
4. On our way home, we ran into trouble.

Share your version with your classmates and listen to their versions.

Verbs

Action verbs, which suggest mental or physical activity, always cover more ground than stative verbs, which are the state-of-being verbs. Observe the different effects.

Action Verbs

My roommate <u>introduced</u> me to my first boyfriend.
The bull <u>gorged</u> the fighter to death.

When you read these verbs, you will picture the action that corresponds with the word. Observe the stative verbs.

Stative Verbs

We <u>were</u> at the ball game yesterday.

The description of your room <u>is</u> delightful.

These verbs do not suggest an action but a state of being. It is possible to convert these sentences with active verbs. For example, we might say, "We <u>cheered</u> at the ball game yesterday." Do you see some action?

Some verbs such as "to be" and "to have" and their conjugations are overworked verbs. If you tend to use them too often, you should try to find action verbs to replace them.

> ### Activity 5
> In the following paragraph, change the stative and overused verbs to action verbs.
>
> > Mr. Jones <u>had</u> tickets for his wife, their two sons, Jack and Joe, and himself, to go to the Bahamas for a summer holiday cruise. This trip was <u>to be</u> one of the highlights of their family life as they had planned to celebrate Jack's graduation from college. They <u>got</u> information from the travel agent about where to board the Miss Fantasy, the liner that would take them to the Bahamas; what time to board the ship; what documents they needed to take with them; what type of cabin they would <u>have</u>; and the different types of entertainment and food they would <u>have</u>.

Adjectives

Because adjectives make the meaning of a noun or a pronoun clearer, they are important to descriptions. They answer three questions about the noun or the pronoun: What kind? How many? Which one? Note how the adjectives modify the nouns or pronouns in the following sentences.

1. "The hills across the valley of the Ebro were <u>long</u> and <u>white</u>." (Ernest Hemingway) "Long" and "white" answer what kind of hills.
2. "The woman brought <u>two</u> glasses of beer and <u>two</u> <u>felt</u> pads." (Ernest Hemingway) "Two" answers the question, how many? "Felt" answers the question, what kind?
3. The girl bought the <u>last</u> dress. "Last" answers which one.

Avoid overused adjectives such as *good, bad, nice,* and *beautiful,* and select high quality adjectives that convey the exact shade of meaning you have in mind. It will be helpful to have a thesaurus, but be certain to make appropriate choices.

Adverbs

Even though adverbs are useful, you should be suspicious about them in descriptions. Challenge their use in your writing because they often color a description when you don't want them to do so. For example, note the adverb in the following sentence.

> Mr. Joe, the violinist, played *flamboyantly* as he read the music.

Does this sentence mean that Mr. Joe's mannerisms were flamboyant or that he played the music itself flamboyantly? Even though "flamboyant" more likely refers to Mr. Joe's style, the reader may be confused.

> ### Activity 6
> In the George Orwell excerpt (Activity 3), find all the adjectives and adverbs, and discuss their functions with your peers. Are they appropriate?
>   Do you have suggestions for more apt adjectives or adverbs? Can you rewrite the paragraph to describe a child in a different setting?

Interjections

Interjections (such as *Oh! Wow! Great! Ouch!*) are used more in speech than in writing and should be reserved to express strong emotion.

Imagery—Using Your Five Senses

Successful descriptions will appeal to at least one or more of your five senses: sight, hearing, touch, smell, and taste. You will create imagery that will activate your reader's vital senses. Read the essay titled "Yearning to Go Back" at the end of these instructions and underline the sentences that appeal to the various senses. Observe the effect that they have on you. What if they were not used? Would the essay have been as effective?

> ### Activity 7
> Appeal to your readers' senses as you describe, in one or two paragraphs, your favorite hangout, pizza, dessert, car, or dream home.

Using Figurative Language

Figures of speech always add depth to meaning, help to compress expression, and paint pictures that aid understanding. Because skill and experience are necessary in using figurative devices, the beginning writer will want to try using some of the simpler devices first. One of the simplest devices is comparison as used in a *simile* or a *metaphor*. In the example below, a person is compared to a cookie.

> Simile: After sitting in the hot sun for an hour, I felt like a cookie coming out of an oven.

A simile uses the word "like" or "as" in its comparison of one thing with another.

> Metaphor: After sitting in the hot sun for an hour, I was a baked cookie.

The metaphor makes the same comparison as the simile but it omits "like" or "as" in its comparison.

Personification is another simple device that can be useful. If you write about something inanimate as though it were a person, you would have used personification. Here is an example: "After I kicked the desk, I heard its heart crunch." The desk—an inanimate object—is given life-like characteristics.

Activity 8

Make a list of a few things you have seen today, then write a sentence in which you use a simile, or a metaphor, or personification.

Avoiding Cliched Descriptions

Stereotypical or trite descriptions will detract from high quality writing. Your aim is to provide descriptions that are fresh to the mind and to the senses of your reader. If you try to describe, for example, stock characters (overused descriptions) such as the absent-minded professor, the male chauvinist pig, or the cruel stepmother, readers will tend to say, "I have read this before." To avoid this pitfall, read plenty so that you will be informed about how stock characters have been described, and then practice writing descriptions, using your own words and observations. A keen observation will help you to detect details that others might not notice.

Organizing a Description

The description should be organized in a logical manner. To do so, the following methods may be used either separately or in combination: *chronological, emphatic, simple to complex*, and *spatial*. The pattern of organization you choose should be appropriate or logical for your description. A description of a school function, for example, could use chronological organization and begin from the time the idea was born to the time the idea was implemented. You might describe a lecture, using the emphatic arrangement, saving the most important point of the lecture for last. An engineer might describe a piece of machinery by beginning with the simple and progressing to the complex. To describe a sunset, you may want to use spatial organization, beginning from as far as your eyes could see, and then closing in space by space until you get up close to where you are. Top to bottom, bottom to top, right to left, left to right descriptions also follow spatial organization.

Chronological

A description that is in a chronological order follows a timeline, usually beginning with the first or earliest event, and then progressing to subsequent events, until the last event is described. An autobiography that describes a person's life from its beginning to its end, a report of an incident from its start to its finish, a description of an experiment that uses a timeline to reveal its progress, all follow chronological order. The following description is short and compressed into one paragraph. It is possible to extend the paragraph below to a novel using chronological organization by providing many more details for each period of Adam's life.

> Adam was born on June 4, 1948, in Charlotte, North Carolina. His parents wanted to provide him with the best kind of childhood possible, but since they worked hard for a living, Adam did not get all the attention he needed as a young toddler. Instead of being able to run outdoors, he had to be kept in a playpen every day. It was not until he turned five years old that he was allowed to walk to a nursery close to where he lived. That made him so happy that he skipped to school in the fresh air every day. When he entered

kindergarten, he was the fastest runner in his class. He kept that record in every class from kindergarten through twelvth grade. More than that, when he entered college, he was invited to run the 200-mile dash at the 1972 Olympics for the U.S. He won that race and felt ready to win many more races, but that was not to be. He injured his legs in a skiing accident in 1973 and was never able to run again. He went on, however, to become an ambassador to Mexico where he died in a car accident in 1976.

Emphatic

To use emphatic organization, you must describe at least three objects, events, people, or emotions, beginning with the least important point and progressing to the most important point. Readers tend to remember the last idea better than those discussed earlier in an essay.

Emphatic order may be used for description, narration and all expository modes, but it is especially effective in argumentation. For example, let's say you were trying to convince your friend to attend the same university you are attending. You may describe your most enticing point last. When your friend reads that most persuasive last point, he or she may be likely to accept your point of view. That descriptive appeal will linger with him or her.

To further exemplify emphatic order in description, say you like the university you are attending for the following reasons: (1) You have met people from several countries, and can gain firsthand multicultural enrichment; (2) You have made lasting friendships; (3) You like the sorority parties; and (4) The education you are receiving is of high quality. If you know your friend will value the sorority parties more than the other points, then you will want to appeal to his or her senses in that final point where it will be given the most thought.

Activity 9
Write an emphatic description of a sports event, a series of examinations, some experiences, or another cumulative activity, which led to enlightenment about some aspect of life.

Simple to Complex

Descriptions of complicated experiments or activities are usually given in a progressive manner so that a person may be able to start with a simple step and then go on to a more difficult one. In fact, all of our education operates on that principle. Take mathematical problems, for example; first, we learn simple basics such as addition, subtraction, division, and multiplication, and then we progress to more challenging problems. The following exemplifies the simple to complex organization. Identify transitions that help you to detect the simple to complex organization.

> If you should observe babies learning to talk, you will notice that they start with the gurgling, babbling, cooing and the more aggressive bahing sounds that come from vocal chords that have not been developed sufficiently to

manage so-called words. Babies repeat those simple sounds and then progress to a definitive "da" sound, which fathers precociously interpret as an abbreviation of daddy. No one knows for certain. As the vocal chords develop and as their intelligence increases, babies are able to say some of the words they have heard and make the association between the words and their objects. Words such as *milk, juice, cat,* and *dog* are popular, mid-level baby vocabulary. With time, the baby's vocal chords become strong and more complex, and soon babies are able to make complete sentences. Sentences are usually simple at first, consisting of one or two words such as "Go." "Come here." "Bad dog." "More milk." As the vocal chords strengthen, probably when the children are from two to four years old, sentences with multi-syllabic words may be added. This process of language acquisition often continues into adulthood, where the language becomes so complex that only a few lucky fellow beings may be able to understand it.

Activity 10

Write a descriptive paragraph on a topic of your choice using simple to complex as your pattern of organization.

Spatial

This type of pattern uses space as its strategy. If you want to describe your room, for instance, you may describe it from the point where you enter the room to the spaces farther away. You may choose, however, to describe the farthest corner and then come up close, or from top to bottom, or vice versa. The following is an example of a description that uses spatial organization. Underline spatial transitions.

Even though my neighbors had told me that our abandoned house in the forest was now dilapidated, I wanted to revisit it. I drove down the old dirt road and braked at the front stairs that were to my left. I climbed each one, counting as I ascended. All twelve steps were still there. The porch was dusty and littered with leaves. I was afraid to turn the leaves for what might have been living beneath them. The front door led to the living room, which had become an expansive nothingness with holes in the floor boards and shattered glass where panes had been. I tiptoed to the rooms down the hall. To the right was Ma and Pa's bedroom, another expanse of nothingness of dusty corners and piles of leaves. As I looked to the left, I saw a similar scenario in the other bedrooms. Finally, I looked straight ahead to my own bedroom at the end of the hall. I lingered in my bedroom to reminisce about some of my silly bygone fears.

Activity 11

Describe your campus, your mom's dinner table, your favorite or most hated restaurant, a friend's home, or a special spot, using spatial organization.

Sample Descriptive Essay

YEARNING TO RETURN

In 1984, my husband, two sons, and I decided to visit Caracas, Venezuela. We thought that the people there would have been able to converse with us in English—the language of progress. How insensitive of us! Why should anyone who has grown up speaking any language want to give up his or her prized tongue for anyone else's? Can people change their skins for those of other races? Anyway, the people were comfortable in their language, and we realized that we would have to get by as best as we could. Gestures instantly grew in importance.

After fanning our noses at the head clerk at the hotel desk to show him that we could not sleep in a room that smelled of cigarette, we were settled into another room on the sixth floor that overlooked a street full of activity at noon on Saturday. We looked out on doll-like figures dressed in reds, yellows, turquoise, and many dazzling colors that were popping into small sidewalk stores and cafes and then popping out again. Since we were so removed from the bustle, we could only imagine the noises of cars going by and of people chatting in that beautiful rolling tongue that Spaniards speak.

We were eager to join the activities—to pop into some of those shops and eateries—so we donned shorts, tees and sandals that felt just right for the moment and boarded the elevator that took us to the level of the very street we had been looking down upon. We were lucky to find a cafe that displayed its food. We could go up to the attendant and wave insistent fingers at the food and say "*Yo quiero, yo quiero.*" Each of us took turns at waving our fingers at the food and smiling at the tolerant waiter. Of course, he wanted our dinero. I ended up with a corn muffin and smoked herrings cooked with fresh tomatoes. The crustiness of the corn muffin with the tartness of the smothered fish was so right for my stomach that it is still easy to recall that taste, even though so many years have passed. The sour sop drink was also exquisite with its distinct fruitiness, but the dessert was the best. It was a delicate snowy hybrid of ice cream, frozen yogurt, and whipped cream, served in a sugar cone. Even though many years have passed and I have traveled to several places with the hopes of finding a dessert of that taste and texture, I have not been successful. I must return to Venezuela soon.

Activity 12

The following paragraph contains several errors in description. Find the errors and improve the paragraph. Label the organizational patterns you have used.

Panama City Beach is okay as far as beaches go, but I have heard that university students from all over the United States go there to socialize during their Spring Break. I went to all of the MTV productions and wanted to get myself on the stage when the host asked for a student with an amusing burp, but someone beat me to it. When I first saw the beach, it was nothing spectacular, but when I saw how many fellow university students were there to make friends with, I was ecstatic. It was wild when the music started to play and we all tried to dance on the sand.

Activity 13

Take a walk over a small area of your campus, and then describe the area with as many details as you can. Make a list of the details you discovered, and then select only the significant details to include in a finished paragraph. Explain to your classmates why you decided to omit the details you did not use.

Activity 14

Here is the introduction to a descriptive essay. Improve it and write a clear thesis statement.

Graduations are usually portrayed as wonderful times, but they can also be scary. If you were not offered a job previous to that day when you march across the stage to collect your bachelor's degree, you may not be wearing the same type of smile that others may be wearing. You may be wondering about what should go into your resume, whom you should ask for a job, and what you should wear when you go for an interview.

Assignment I

1. Describe a relative you admire/do not admire.
2. Which animal traits resemble those of some people?
3. Recount your feelings of your first day on a college/university campus.
4. Describe your hometown.
5. What type of people would you like to become close friends with?

Assignment II

1. Describe a day in the life of a slave.
2. Describe each step you would take in performing a biological or chemical experiment such as dissecting an animal or observing chemical reactions.
3. Select a great artist and describe some of his or her works.
4. What are some of the most common skills that prove to be useful to all college/university students?
5. The life of a great pioneer.

Assignment III

1. Choose one of the Assignment II topics to write a description of about 1000 words. Research the topic and provide accurate details.
2. Write a 1000 word autobiography of some period in your life.

NARRATION

Narration is a sophisticated term for a story, a genre that you have been familiar with since your mom read *The Three Little Pigs*, *Red Riding Hood*, *Heidi*, *Brer Rabbit*, a Bible story, or some other tale to you.

Our lives are full of stories; almost everything we do is a story, although we don't usually think of everyday occurrences as stories, but rather as a variety of personal experiences or episodes. Many times we relate these daily events, be they amusing, sad, instructive, cruel, or otherwise to our friends, relatives, ministers, lawyers, counselors, roommates, and others, to convey some point about daily living. This is the same way that narration is used in essays—to make a point—to clarify an idea. The point you intend to make should be the focus of your story and of your thesis statement.

Thesis Statement

The narrative essay must have a thesis statement just as any other essay, as discussed in Chapter Three. In the narrative you must think of the significance of the event. Here are some activities that could lead you to an idea for a story.

1. *Reading*   Reading can take you anywhere and provide you with an abundance of ideas.

2. *Discussions, conversations*   Some discussions/conversations are not worth your time, but a discussion/conversation that makes you think can stimulate ideas for stories.

3. *Travel*   Readers are always interested in the differences found in other countries.

4. *Personal Experience*   Even though your experiences may be common to many, they are hardly ever identical. On the other hand, an experience that has been retold too many times could become trite, mundane, or insignificant.

5. *Another Person's Experience*   Parents, great grand parents, grand parents, elderly people, younger people, people of your age, friends, classmates, and teachers all tell stories. One may be worth retelling.

6. *Imagination*   Think of a point you would like to illustrate, create some characters, plot the events, provide a setting and atmosphere, and you may obtain one of your most fulfilling stories.

Here are examples of thesis statements developed by narration.

The closeness we once felt among our uncles, aunts, and cousins disappeared quickly after our grandmother's funeral.

It was difficult for me to stop smoking, but my father's battle with lung cancer convinced me to quit the habit.

I must warn you of several cultural differences you will experience when you travel to China next summer.

Using Rhetorical Modes to Achieve Your Purpose

Consider the rhetorical modes that are usually used for essay writing, and you will find that for each of those modes a story may be used to achieve your purpose. Examples follow:

Rhetorical Mode	How a Story May Be Used
Description	Describe a memory, such as your most embarrassing moment, your graduation from high school, or a family union with a story. Your point may be to show the quality of a moment and what it meant to you.
Illustration	A story could be used to illustrate a visit to a foreign country. You may want to illustrate different customs. The custom of siestas in Spain, for instance,could well be made clear with a narrative.
Comparison/Contrast	A story could be used to show the differences and/or similarities among the educational systems of different countries by telling the stories of school children from several countries.
Division/Classification	A story could be used to classify animals.
Process Analysis	A story could be used to explain how to travel to Europe, purchase a house, or prepare a French meal.
Definition	A story could be used to clarify, define, or describe a term.
Cause/Effect	A story could be used to explain some occurrence or show results of that occurrence.
Argument	A story could be used for emotional appeal in an argument.

These are only a few examples to prompt your thinking of many other applications.

Point of View

As the writer, you must decide how close you want your readers to get to the people in your narration. The first person point of view indicates that you are one of the participants in the narrative. The third person point of view shows that you were an observer. The second person, "you," is not frequently used in narration.

Example of the First Person

> I (first person) visited Tobago during the Easter holidays. It was perfect timing, for I had the opportunity to see congeniality at its finest. When

Lucy, my hostess, took me to the goat race, we were empty-handed, but when we returned to Lucy's home that evening, we had brown paper bags full of sugar cakes, peanut cakes, fish, pone, sapodillas, and banana fritters. All Lucy's friends had shared their picnic baskets with us. I was stunned by this display of kindness.

Example of Third Person

My mother told me that she visited Tobago during the Easter holidays. To her it was the perfect time because she had the opportunity to see congeniality at its finest. When Mrs. Murray, her host, took her to the goat race, they went empty-handed, but when they returned to Mrs. Murray's home, they were carrying brown bags full of sugar cakes, peanut cakes, fish, pone, sapodillas, and banana fritters. All their friends had shared their picnic baskets with them. She was stunned by that display of kindness.

Activity 1
Which point of view seems more effective? Relate a short event in the first person point of view and then in the third person point of view. Which seems more appropriate?

Providing Significant Details

Vivid descriptions must contain specific, telling details. It may often be possible to write many details about your subject, but to include every small detail may insult your readers' imagination and knowledge. Only the significant details that move your story forward at a moderate or fast pace should be selected. When you are ready to write a narrative, list all of the details you can think of, then read through them carefully and eliminate the ones that seem too elementary for your readers.

Activity 2
Look around your classroom and list all the details you can. Which ones do you view as significant for a complete but sensible description?

Most of your descriptions in the narrative will involve your five senses. Notice how you can improve a vague sentence with significant details.

Sight: The setting sun lit the sky.

Improved: The golds, pinks, reds, and purples of the sun blazed the evening skies.

Scent: My mother's potato salad smelled good.

Improved: My mother's potato salad smelled as though the freshness of the outside had walked into our home.

Hearing: I heard the loud bell.

Improved: Even though I was a mile away, I heard the clang of the bell.

Touch: My prom dress was soft.

Improved: My black prom dress was as soft as my kitty's fur.

Taste: My meat tasted terrible.

Improved: As soon as I tasted my steak, I was sorry that I had spent so much money on what tasted like water that came from a rusted tin cup.

Activity 3

Improve the following sentences with details. Edit the words that have little value.

1. Jim was a good boy.
2. The flowers were beautiful.
3. The picture was exquisite.
4. The apple smelled terrible.
5. Broken glass is more than rough on the feet.
6. My milk shake wasn't the flavor I ordered.
7. I can't stand the look of the oatmeal.
8. I was suspicious of the sounds outside my window.

Organizing the Narrative

Chronological Organization

In most cases, narratives are written with a chronological organization; that is, they follow a strict progressive timeline with the beginning of the story relating the earliest event and then progressing to subsequent events in an ordinal manner. If we should take the events of a day to illustrate timeline, we may diagram it as follows:

Episode 1—>	Episode 2—>	Episode 3—>	Episode 4
(morning)	(midday)	(afternoon)	(evening)

A skillful writer, however, may not choose to relate his or her story in a chronological manner. Such a writer may want to begin with episode 4 and then return to episodes 1, 2, and 3 (whatever arrangement is best for the effect he or she wants to create). A graduating student, for instance, may want to begin with the culmination of his bachelor's degree and then go back to the first day he walked on campus and his successive days of study. His purpose may be to start with the satisfaction he found at the end of his persistence and then relate the details from the beginning.

Emphatic Organization

An emphatic organization may be used if the writer chooses to relate several episodes that lead up to the most important event. The story that follows illustrates emphatic organization.

ADAGES

I have heard many adages in my life such as "Act in haste, repent in leisure," and "A stitch in time saves nine." However, I never paid very much attention to such catchy sayings until one day, when I was seven years old, one actually slapped me in the face. The moment I disobeyed my mom and took a big bite of my granddaddy's giant plug of Blood Hound Chewing Tobacco, I realized that "Experience is the best teacher."

My mom had warned me many times to stay away from Grandpa Ellis' big plug of chewing tobacco, but her warnings fell on deaf ears. After all, Grandpa seemed to enjoy it so much. Every day, right after supper, he and I would sit on the back steps of our old house. He would pull from his pocket a closely woven wad wrapped in cellophane, which had a red dog across the front of it. Grandpa would carefully unwrap the wad, bite off a huge chunk, and wallow it around in his mouth until he found the perfect place for it inside his jaw.

After a few minutes of holding this gigantic parcel in his mouth, Grandpa would begin to spit. I have never seen anyone—before or after—who made such an art of spitting. Grandpa Ellis could spit his tobacco juice a distance of six feet, his juice always landing in the same place. He never dribbled, and he never wiped his mouth. All the time he had the most placid and serene look on his face. I felt that I just had to have this feeling—this experience of ultimate pleasure. My opportunity came one day when I found my Grandpa asleep on the sofa with his trusty brown wad of Blood Hound sticking from his pocket. I eased the plug out, opened my mouth wide, and bit off the largest piece I possibly could, just the way Grandpa did it. I then slipped out under a pecan tree to relax and enjoy my stolen pleasure.

I rolled the big bundle around in my mouth, but instead of finding a snug place inside my jaw, it kept getting larger and kept rolling around in the back of my throat. Soon the juice would either land on the front of my shirt or slip back down my throat, and I would wind up swallowing this nauseating liquid. I became sick! My head started to whirl and pound, and it was difficult for me to keep my balance. My stomach balled up in knots and my throat started to fill with a mixture of tobacco juice and salty water. I spat out the wad and rinsed out my mouth at the faucet in the yard, but nothing helped. I soon lost my breakfast, lunch, and supper. Only then did I begin to feel a little better.

My mom found me about an hour later draped over a lawn chair in the backyard; my half chewed tobacco was sticking to the toe of one of my sneakers. She looked at my sneakers and she looked at me; she smiled and walked away. I had learned my lesson. I have never touched tobacco again since that day.

Activity 4

Here is the first paragraph of a story. Finish the story. Feel free to make changes as you wish.

CULTURE AT A REASONABLE PRICE

Traveling is one of my expensive hobbies. Most of the time, I have to work harder and live cheaper than many students, just so that I can afford a trip to some foreign place every summer. When I do arrive on foreign shores, I also search out ways to stretch my pennies. One time I went to _____ (You may use a real country or create one.) and managed to save pennies by _____
(Fill in the rest of the story).

Activity 5

Read the following story, written by a student, then discuss ways to improve it. Rewrite the narrative.

MOMENT OF FEAR

To drink was viewed by those in my circle of friends as the "cool" thing to do. We were a group of high school seniors who liked to party; a party was incomplete without a keg of beer, a fifth of Courvoisier or Hennessey. There could be no holiday or social event that went without a round of drunken debauchery. The "buzz" that I got from alcohol was irresistible. I was unable to see that I was heading down a darkened path. It would seem that I would still be upon this path of self-destruction if things had not begun to collapse around me. Friends who have been long and diligent users of alcohol started to fall by the wayside. Those whom I had viewed as invincible began to feel the sting of the law. Arrested for underage drinking, many of my friends were jailed, and I knew that my time was coming soon, and soon it did. It was a night that changed me.

On this particular night, I had done some excessive "partying". I got into my car thinking that I could drive; I later learned that I barely had the faculties to walk. As I sped down the dark highway, I was oblivious to my weaving badly across the yellow lines. I thought I was in total control. Of course I wasn't or I would have seen the state trooper that was driving closely behind me. He didn't stop me immediately. It seemed almost as if he were trying to determine just what I was doing. He allowed me to weave a while longer, and then the expected happened. That is, I did the expected and so did he.

The flashing blue lights alerted me, and as they flashed I felt my life ending. I somehow managed to pull over. A tall policeman walked up to my car. He asked me if I were aware that I had been crossing the double lines in the highway. Too drunk to have the sense to be polite, I replied that I was not aware of my weaving, but that I assumed he knew the reason for my weaving or could at least smell it. He gave me a strange look, told me to get out of the car and to go over to a nearby telephone and call someone to come and take me home. I have never been so relieved— nor have I ever been so afraid. I should have been arrested that night, but a kind cop gave a stupid kid a break. My "brush" with the law had a happy ending. Too many of us are not so lucky. I never have and never will put myself in that sort of position again.

Assignment I

Write a narrative essay of 500 words on one of the following topics.

1. A moment you wish you could relive
2. An acquaintance's battle with a bad habit
3. A relative's visit
4. What your favorite pet taught you

Assignment II

For a writing project that may take the entire semester, chronicle the events that have taken place since you began your university education. You may think of making diary entries, writing memoirs, or writing letters to various university people, writing daily anecdotes, humorous quips, poems, or some other form that you will enjoy. Save them all in a portfolio (see Chapter Four on The Portfolio) to share with your class and your teacher at the end of the semester.

EXPOSITION

The difference between loving someone and worshiping someone is ...

Why should we become more
concerned about the environment?

He is handsome: tall, lean ...

E
X
P
O
S
I
T
I
O
N

There are three types of friends

Learning to foxtrot is easy. First,

"Chilling" means ...

Of the four written types of discourse—narration, description, argumentation, and exposition—exposition is the one that is the most frequently used in daily communication, written and oral. *Exposition* is that mode of discourse that ultimately seeks to *explain*, *clarify*, or *inform*, often leading reading and listening audiences to get a clearer understanding (illustration); develop some skill (process); make some judgment or preference (comparison-contrast); understand or recognize types of divisions that exist (classification); discover the why's and results (causal analysis); and, finally, learn meanings (definition). The information cited may result in acquisition of information, provide entertainment, or stir audiences to take action. Though we treat each of the six strategies of exposition as a separate rhetorical mode, seldom will you develop an essay by employing only one of these strategies. Therefore, while we focus on numerous strategies in this chapter, the essays that you will write, like the sample ones other students have written, will incorporate, to some degree, various strategies.

ILLUSTRATION

Consider these lines from one of the world's most popular love sonnets:

How do I love thee? Let me count the ways.
I love thee to the depth and breadth and height
My soul can reach, when feeling out of sight
For the ends of Being and ideal Grace.
I love thee to the level of everyday's
Most quiet need, by sun and candlelight.
I love thee freely, as men strive for Right;
I love thee purely, as they turn from Praise...
I love thee with the passion put to use
In my old griefs, and with my childhood's faith...
I love thee with a love I seemed to lose
With my lost saints—I love thee with the breath,
Smiles, tears, of all my life!—and, if God choose,
I shall but love thee better after death.

Now consider this dialogue overheard between two young ladies one recent morning in the elevator at work.

> "Girl, where are you going dressed like that?
>
> "What you mean? To work."
>
> "Yes, I bet. *Who* is he? Why are you dressing so fine these days?"
>
> "Well, there's this guy. Child, I have met Mr. *Right*. Yeah, Mr.
>
> *Right*, and that's the only name I'm telling you right now.
>
> He's a *good* man, girl!"
>
> "Stop holding back. Explain what you mean by "good."
>
> "He goes to church on Sunday and midweek too. He even cut my
> mama's grass the other day for free, and he makes me feel so special
> and alive. Yeah, child. I've found myself a *good* man."

What do these two pieces of writing have in common? They both express a woman's admiration for a very special man in her life. And they reveal this admiration by citing *specific* examples. In the first example, Elizabeth Barrett Browning illustrates that she loves her husband, Robert, with her very being, her soul: the very "depth and breath and height my soul can reach." Her love is reflected in her "smiles," "tears," "life" here and in the hereafter. In the second writing sample, the young lady says that she has found a *good* man. Since such a common term means different things to different people today, the term needs to be clarified, and the speaker does just this. When she cites her examples, her listening audience readily understands what she means by using the term "good." Whether through eloquent, poetic speech or the informal language used in heart to heart conversations with friends and associates, we all use the illustration strategy every day.

The use of examples helps others to understand our feelings and clarifies our ideas and thoughts. In writing, illustrations are tantamount to pictures, but are not always sensory depictions. If you support another student for SGA president, it is not sufficient to say simply that he or she is the right candidate because he or she "cares about the school." You need to explain, to clarify, what you mean. Perhaps the student volunteers to help other students prep for the state-mandated examination, volunteers to pick up litter around the school on Saturday mornings, and always speaks positively about the school when others—students and outsiders alike—make complaints. While some of your reading or listening audience may still prefer another candidate, these examples have persuaded some in your audience to vote for your candidate. Why? You clarified the term "care." Examples can be used to *persuade* as well as *clarify*. Those already not convinced of your candidate's eligibility probably would have just shrugged had you provided only *one* example.

Always be certain to cite examples that your audience can relate to and only those examples necessary to clarify, inform, or persuade. Students readily relate to the examples cited above. And it would be unnecessary to state facts, such as the candidate's selection of your school out of five, the fact that his or her tuition was paid there, and other similar, obvious facts which indicate nothing about "concern" for the school. After all, many students choose a school and pay tuition but complain from thereafter until commencement exercises four years later. Always use examples that are representative of the total group being discussed.

Writing Tips for Writing the Illustration Paper

Organization

Use *specific* examples and details to support each topic sentence. You may do this by using a series of related examples or by using an extended example to support your main point. See samples below.

> My first cousin has done a poor job of rearing her children. She brought them with her when she attended the Mary Kay party at my house two weeks ago, and I am still seething because of the damage those urchins did to my home. For instance, the oldest two kids—ages eight and seven—decided to continue their game of catch ball and in the process hit the inexpensive but cherished vase my best friend gave me several years ago. That vase is irreplaceable. Then, they—these big kids—decided to romp around on my sofa, somehow managing to rip the fabric on the arm of the sofa, leaving me with this big glaring beige circle on my green and burgundy plaid sofa. To make matters worse, the baby of the family—the five year old—had entered drinking a grape soda, wasting part of it on the carpet and then smearing his soiled hands along the basement casing of the wall. To my horror, when I told my cousin what her children had done, she merely shook her head and said they all were still fairly clumsy.

> My cousin has done a poor job of rearing her children. Her youngest son, Chad, ruined my wall on his last visit. He entered the house with a grape soda, which I thought he could handle since he is five years old. But he could not and ended up dropping the soda on the carpet. Then he tried to wipe up the spill with his hands, only making matters worse. To illustrate, he then wiped his hands on his clothes and proceeded to walk around touching my figurines, the lampshade, and the remote control before returning to the spill on the floor, to dance in the spot, grinding the soda into the carpet, and touching the baseboard with his sneaker shortly thereafter, leaving his mark there too. When I showed my cousin what he had done, she shrugged and said, "Chad, you are so clumsy!"

The first paragraph is developed with a series of examples, while the second has an extended example. Try to mix these approaches in your essays. Pay special attention to the length of the paragraphs. You must remember to provide enough *specific* details.

Coherence

Keep in mind that you are presenting a *discussion*, not a listing. Always use transitions or some connecting phrase to make ideas flow. The most commonly used transitions for signaling examples include: *for example, for instance*, and *to illustrate*. However, if you cite several examples, there is no need to use a transition every time you cite an example. Also keep in mind that in a discussion, you will need to provide details and commentary on some of your examples. Do not cite example after example without providing any discussion or further clarification of those examples. Read the paragraph below that does not include any transitions and that does not include any details or commentary. Note the telegraphic or jerky effect.

> My cousin's son Chad is a bad boy. He spilled his soda on my carpet. He wiped his smeared hand on my figurine. He danced in the puddle he had made. He touched the baseboard with his stained sneakers. I hope he never returns to my home.

Sample Essay #1

WHAT IS AMERICAN HUMOR?

Humor is a concept that is not easily explained, as it exists within a system of personal beliefs. However, it is generally agreed upon that it is definitely evident in things with which we are familiar and within those elements that are relevant to our lifestyles. Therefore, humor which is indigenous to an area has evolved and is categorized by its uniqueness to other types. This is especially true of American humor in that even though much of it developed in different regions and certain elements appeal only to certain types of people, there are several links which tie all American humor together. American humor, in the early days, was imported from various parts of the world and simply made over. It was not considered an important part of the "American Experience." Actually, no 17th or 18th century writers devoted their effort to humor exclusively, although chronicles did describe the incongruities of colonial life and draw humor from regional types they encountered. [The humor of Oscar Wilde, a British humorist, and Benjamin Franklin constitutes similarities in that both employed the practice of wit.] Wilde's saying "I can resist everything but temptation: tends to elicit the same-grin as Franklin's popular quote "Fresh fish and new-come guests smell by the time they are three days old."

American humor, as such, took root in the exaggerations of tale-telling. Mark Twain, a comic lecturer of the late 1800s, gained fame as he used exaggerations to burlesque things ranging from women's fashions to various vernacular accents. Furthermore, the history of Black humor may have had its inception on the Southern plantation. Slaves had their own orally transmitted humor, which their white owners believed was carefree and high-spirited. The owners missed the sly deceptions and covert protests in the humor. This form of humor has carried over into the present-day.

American humor, as a whole, is categorized by its willingness to "poke fun" at the incongruities and foolishness of a typical American situation. Regardless of background, most would tend to find humor in a married woman who has yet to lose her virginity trying to figure out why she cannot become pregnant as illustrated in Joseph Heller's *Catch 22*.

Also, as the Harvard *Lampoon*'s parody of *Time* magazine satirizes President Bush, we as Americans can find humor in the mockery of one of our prominent national leaders.

Nevertheless, there are types of humor which exist for certain groups. Occupational humor, for instance, in the form of doctor, dentist, or lawyer jokes, sometimes contains significance only for those either in the profession or for those closely associated with one who is. Also, some humor is regarded as having special meaning for Blacks only. The humor of Langston Hughes in *The Best of Simple*, as it speaks, comically yet with overt hints of seriousness about military integration and forms of oppression of the Black man, may have more meaning for those who may have experienced the prejudice of the early and mid-1900s. Similar, is the humor of Dick Gregory as he says in reference to a new walking fad, "I can't get too excited about Bobby Kennedy walking fifty miles. Down south, we walked farther than that just trying to find a restaurant that will serve us" would be bittersweet for those who lived during the Civil Rights Era.

On the other hand, there are several "recurring themes" in American humor which provide a common ground upon which humorists often work.

> Being adored is a nuisance. Women treat us just as Humanity treats its Gods. They worship us and are always bothering us to do something for them.
>
> Oscar Wilde

> "Virginia is where I was born", said Simple. "I would be born in a state named after a woman. From that day on women never gave me no peace."
>
> Langston Hughes

As shown in the previous illustrations, even men of different eras and different backgrounds and nationalities can appeal to an American audience with a common theme—nagging women. This type of humor is further evidenced in Eddie Murphy's monologues which from time to time focus on dumpy, nagging women who are only after a man's money.

Furthermore, there are consistencies in the theme of ethnic humor. This type of humor may be found in the TV sitcom, *All in the Family*, as Archie Bunker degrades Blacks, Jews, Women and Polish people. George Jefferson also shows his prejudice in the series, *The Jeffersons*, as he reveals his negative attitude toward white people. Similarly, in Joseph Heller's *Catch 22* the character Chief Halfoat resents being treated like a "nigger," "kike," "wop," or "spic," for he feels he is far superior to them. These aforementioned characters contain humorous elements for Americans as they are representative of the ignorance shown in prejudice nationwide in all sectors.

In conclusion, American humor is not categorized as one type; yet, it is comprised of many different elements giving it its distinctive character. American humor, with its many different facets, has come to be a part of our national heritage and is an integral part of many of our day to day lives.

Sample Essay #2

GIVE ME THE SCORE

Today, the sports information and entertainment industry is a necessity to the American sports fan. Newspapers provide coverage of local teams and athletes. However, since 1979, ESPN has been the number one source of sports action, having become the most-watched sports information show—ESPN *SportsCenter*—in the world. Whatever their interest, fans now can keep track of their favorite franchises from the comfort of their own home.

Local newspapers that include the sports section give fans the opportunity to read accurate details of every game the day after they occur. For instance, the *Washington Post* provides readers with the most comprehensive information on Washington metropolitan teams and athletes. No where else other than the local newspaper can citizens find in-depth reports on both professional and high school athletic performances. The *Washington Post* presents articles on the Washington Redskins (football), the Washington Wizards (basketball), the Washington Capitals (hockey), the Baltimore Orioles (baseball), as well as high school events from the District of Columbia and its three surrounding counties.

The largest reason fans enjoy reading the sports page is the acknowledgment of criticisms by the columnists. These columnists react to various situations involving the local sports organizations. These columnists themselves are fans, a factor which is of great importance to their readers. Fans love the opportunity to disagree and debate their differences. Columnists often mimic sports fanatics in expressing opinions about sports. This situation is also apparent in the pages of the Post. The staff of the *Washington Post* have two of the most respected and admired columnists in the country, Michael Wilborn and Tony Kornheiser. These two men truly represent the fans of the Metro DC area. Just like fans, they are diverse, but share one thing in common, their love of sports. Wilbon is black and baldheaded, while Kornheiser is white and balding. Wilborn is seen on television shows such as *The Sports Reporters* and the *Redskins' Report*, but Kornheiser, who is rarely seen on television, maintains his own radio talk show. The newspapers and their columnists bring fans to the games even when the game is being played in another time zone.

In 1979 ESPN changed the way sports were viewed forever. In that year, the first 24-hour all sports network called ESPN was launched.

Nineteen years later, ESPN has become the most-watched channel for sports action and information in the world. From its top ranked show, *SportsCenter*, to its investigative series, *Outside the Lines*, ESPN has emerged as a source for the everyday athlete. The network has enhanced its outreach by launching two new channels since 1993. ESPN2 premiered in 1993 as the sister network to the older network (ESPN). ESPN2 focuses on issues such as health and fitness, as well as sports that are often not seen on other sports channels. Last year, ESPN News began operation as the first 24-hour all sports news network. Its main purpose is to report sports scores and reports as soon as they occur. ESPN News is compared to CNN Headline News, but all of its topics are based on athletics. ESPN, which is owned by Disney/ABC Co., has extended its coverage to other continents with the establishment of ESPN Europe, ESPN Asia, and TSI (Canada).

The total sports network, as it is often referred to, has a fan base that touches every creed of American society, if not the world. This is due to the diversity of the anchors on *SportsCenter*. *SportsCenter* is the highest rated sports show in the world. It is believed that the popularity of the show is due to the superb skills of its anchors. These anchors report all the latest information as well as highlights in their own personal style. For instance, Dan Patrick, the two-time winner of the Cable Ace Award for Best Sports Anchor, is one half of what was believed to be the best studio duo in sports. His former "tag team partner," Keith Olbermann, recently left ESPN for his own show on MSNBC. Before the separation of this duo, fans of the show sent more than 100,000 e-mail letters wishing Olbermann the best of luck. This illustrates how personal the relationship between sports reporters and their viewers tends to become. Even after the separation of its most popular team, the show still remains number one in every ranking in the sports information field. The addition of a new anchor, Stewart Scott, has propelled the show to new heights. Scott, a graduate of the University of North Carolina, represents the urban influence in sports with his use of slang and references to popular rap lyrics. At the same time, Chris Berman, one of the most recognized sports figures in the world has been with ESPN since its inaugural show. He is host of the *NFL Game Day* and can be found on ABC at halftime on *Monday Night Football*. These figures represent the core of the televised sports information industry. They are the essential link between the action and the fans. Without people like Dan Patrick and Steward Scott, the American sports scene would seem bland and distant.

Sports information closes the gaps between those who are attending the game and those who are sitting at home. Sources such as the *Washington Post* and ESPN are services to the public. The sports fans can have all their desires fulfilled through the ever-expanding sports information industry. This expansion includes the recent duets of ESPN2 and ESPN News. It is truly rewarding to be able to follow one's favorite teams without having to pay over twenty-five dollars for a basketball ticket.

Activity 1

Essay Completion

Use illustrations to develop the thesis statement/topic below.

PEOPLE HELPING PEOPLE

Everyday people are interacting with one another to get over a particular obstacle or to overcome a trying situation. If people did not help others, what kind of world would this be? Often time, it is difficult for human beings to ask for help in their time of hardship. But whether people know it or not, they need one another to survive in this world. The situation could be a natural disaster, governmental conflict, or something community-related.

First Body Paragraph

Second Body Paragraph

Third Body Paragraph

Therefore, knowing that people are going to need one another at some given time, we should try to get along and overcome all prejudices. We need others to survive—to cope with our problems and to enjoy our good times.

Activity 2

MINI FIELD EXERCISES

1. Think of as many specific details and examples as possible to support the following generalization: Today is a good (bad, boring) day. Write your analysis in a paragraph of 150 to 200 words. Exchange paragraphs with a classmate; critique the paragraphs for development.

2. Select a job listing for which you are qualified from the classified ad section of a recent newspaper. Then write a paragraph illustrating how your experiences are relevant to the position. Attach the ad to your paragraph.

3. Write a short poem, as Elizabeth Barrett Browning did, citing special examples to reveal your love, admiration, or annoyance with someone. Remember to be specific and try to be poetic.

4. Imagine that you have been asked to serve as the public relations person for a political candidate. Write up the flyer, no more than a page, citing examples of this candidate's work or service history that make him or her eminently more qualified than the other candidates seeking the position. Include specific information, not generalizations.

Assignment I

Choose one of the topics listed below and write an essay of 500 words.

1. Silence can convey many messages. Explain some of the messages that are expressed through silence.

2. In his essay titled *An Essay on Criticism*, Alexander Pope wrote these lines: "A little learning is a dangerous thing; Drink deep, or taste not the Pirerian spring ...." Write an essay illustrating that a little learning can often prove to be a dangerous thing for some people.

3. Current fashions prove that some people will wear anything.

4. Some television programs present the _____ (some group or population) in a negative light.

5. Unlike most magazines, _____ offers informative and entertaining reading for all types of people.

6. The first few weeks of school have been hectic (boring, frightening, disappointing, or challenging).

7. _____ is a regular television program that is primarily informative.

8. Illustrate that "love conquers all."

9. Our society is infatuated with _____ (winning, beauty, food, or collecting).

10. Though it is convenient, the cellular phone is fast becoming a _____.

Assignment II

Choose one of the topics listed below and write a 700 to 1000 word illustration essay.

1. In the seventeenth century, John Donne, a famous poet, wrote the following lines in his prose piece titled *Meditation 17*:

   No man is an island, entire of itself; every man is a piece of the continent, a part of the main. If a clod be washed away by the sea, Europe is the less, as well as if a promontory were, as well as if a manor of thy friend's or of thine own were.

   Any man's death diminishes me, because I am involved in mankind; and therefore never send to know for whom the bell tolls; it tolls for thee.

Consider these lines. Was Donne right? Using examples, write a paper proving that what happens to one human being affects another or that human beings need one another to survive. Draw upon personal experiences, knowledge of others with whom you are associated, or situations in movies, songs, or news stories.

2. Conduct research on some person who has made significant contributions to popular culture. Write a paper substantiating those contributions.

3. Over the ages, the quest for equality in America has been a resounding cry. However, in modern times, equality is often taken for granted. Write a paper illustrating that our society has achieved minimum, moderate or optimum equity.

4. Study your family tree—starting with the earliest known relative or the youngest member. Gather data about habits, features, accomplishments, and the like. What do you all have in common? What is the common link in this family? Is it attitude? Is it a certain talent or gift? Consider the positive attributes of your family. Now write an essay illustrating that your family is *great*.

Assignment III

1. It has often been said that what we say can hurt us; thus, it is often better to keep silent than to speak. However, sometimes what we refuse to say leads to more pain and anxiety than we might imagine. "In the Living Years," a song by Mike and the Mechanics, expresses regret that the speaker did not tell his father how much he cared for him before his father died. Evidently, some time long before his father's death, the young man and his father had had a disagreement and had never made up. "One Sweet Day," by Mariah Carey and Boyz II Men, expresses a similar sentiment.

   Consider these songs and similar songs, or a movie, short story, novel, drama, personal experience, or experience of others. Write a paper illustrating the point that what goes unsaid can often have traumatic effects.

2. Write a one act play illustrating one of these themes:
   a. People take kindness for weakness.
   b. Kindness can be infectious.

PROCESS ANALYSIS

Directions: Remove contact lens from your eye and place three drops of daily cleaning solution on it. Gently rub the lens between the thumb and index finger (you do not want to tear lenses). Rub the lens for three seconds. Now rinse the lens thoroughly by … .

Directions: Take two tablets every four hours as needed. If symptoms persist after four days, see your physician immediately.

Every day when we read directions or instructions or give directions or instructions, we use process analysis, the second of six types of exposition. The process *essay* tells a reader *how to do something* (directional process) or explains to him *how something is/was done* (informational process). With directional, you are expected to *follow* instructions and produce something, whereas with informational process, you *learn* how something occurs. The process analysis essay is developed through a close description of certain actions or activities that are set forth in chronological or "step-by-step" order. Most process analyses are serious in tone because the purpose is to direct someone about how to do something; however, some range from light to humorous in tone. You should remember that if specific instructions or steps are not involved, or if your major ideas can be developed in any order, then you are not developing a process paper.

The following are steps you should complete in writing a process essay.

1. Choose a topic with which you are very familiar.

2. Write a thesis in your introductory paragraph that indicates why understanding the process is important or provide an adjective to indicate your assessment of the process (for example, easy, difficult, expensive, challenging).

3. Arrange steps in chronological order (in the body of your paper). You may have to integrate related minor steps into a major step. Do not attempt to explain fewer than three steps or more than five (if you are writing a timed essay).

4. Explain the systematic stages or steps as completely and accurately as possible, citing the correct quantity of material, the right amount of time, and the appropriate approach to take.

5. Define and describe all unfamiliar terms and procedures. Base the choice of terms and extent of instruction on the interest and levels of sophistication of your audience.

6. Warn the reader of possible difficulties that completing the process might present or possible mishaps that might occur if steps or instructions are not followed as directed.

7. Give the reader alternative steps to follow in case some specific tasks are difficult or impossible for him/her to follow or complete.

8. Use the second person, "you," in writing the essay.

9. Use transitions to signal new steps in the process (transitions like *first, second, next, then, after, finally*).

10. Write a concluding paragraph, reiterating the significance of knowing how to do the process or understanding how it is done.

Sample Essay #1

A PARTY DISH TO DIE FOR

After you decide to host a party, the next concern is what to serve your guests. Perhaps you want to create at least one memorable dish that your guests will leave talking about. Hawaiian curried chicken is just the dish. To prepare this dish, follow the steps below.

The first step to making Hawaiian curried chicken is to shop for fresh ingredients. Go to a reputable grocery store where you have checked to see which day(s) and what time chickens are usually delivered to the store. Be sure to arrive at the store when the truck rolls in and the poultry department begins to display its fresh chickens. Check the dates on the packaged chickens and select a package with the most recent date. Look for a plump chicken that has a rich pink color. Be suspicious of and do not touch any chicken that has any dark traces of any type on its back or between its wings or legs. If you do not have much time for cutting up a chicken, buy one that is already cut up, but you do have to pay more for this kind of chicken. You may request that the skin be removed or remove it yourself before cooking the meat. After your chicken is bagged, make sure to pick up the seasonings you will need. Some curry powder, salt, pepper, thyme, garlic, and onions should be sufficient for seasoning the chicken. In addition, you may purchase some pineapple circles or pieces and some red or green maraschino cherries.

When you get home, wash your chicken in cold water with a few drops of lemon or lime juice or vinegar. Cut the chicken into fairly large pieces and then sprinkle the fellow with each of the seasonings that you bought at the supermarket, except the curry. Start first with a little salt; then go to a pinch of pepper and thyme. Bruise two or three heads of garlic and chop one large onion and mix those condiments into the bowl with the chicken. Marinate the chicken overnight, if possible, to ensure that you will have a tasty birdie.

The next step is to cook the delicacy. It is not difficult even if you are a beginner. Select a heavy pot to lessen your chances of burning your precious dish. Set the temperature on the stove between medium and medium high; place your pot on the stove with about four tablespoons of oil. When the oil is hot, you will see slight ripples; that means it is time to place your meat in the hot oil. Be certain to remove the large pieces of garlic and onion before placing the chicken into the pot. A big sizzle will occur, so protect yourself by standing away from the stove and wearing elbow length mits while you stir the pot with a long handle cooking spoon. Let the chicken fry for a few minutes; then take the remaining garlic and onion mixture and add a little water to it and about one and a half tablespoons of curry powder. Stir the curry powder in the water, and then pour that mixture over the cooking chicken. Reduce the temperature, cover the pot, and allow the meat and seasonings to simmer for about half of an hour. Next, take a fork and pierce the chicken to see if it is done. If it is done, a clear liquid will ooze out, and the meat will be tender to the touch. If the meat appears only partially done, continue to simmer until it becomes tender.

The best step in preparing this dish is garnishing it. Get out your fancy platter and place the pieces of chicken in a pleasing arrangement; then garnish it with pineapple pieces and cherries. Not only will this dish be delicious and the talk of your party, but it will also be an excellent center piece for your special table. Remember to prepare several chickens if you are having a crowd because this dish will disappear in one "lickety-split" moment.

It is easy and inexpensive to prepare Hawaiian curried chicken. To add to that, it will be the party platter that all of your guests will want. They will ask you for the recipe, but that will be no trouble because you will then be the expert.

Sample Essay #2

SIDDHARTHA'S QUEST FOR SALVATION

Is salvation really important to you? Have you ever considered how you might achieve it? Well, chances are that it is important to you and that you have considered a method of attainment. However, there are so many different religions that the decision becomes rather difficult. However, despite all of the outside influence and the many religions, the most important thing is to be satisfied within your own soul. In the story, *Siddhartha*, a young man searches for salvation until he has satisfied himself. He tries Hinduism; then, he tries Samanaism, and finally, he resorts to the river.

Firstly, the young man tries Hinduism. This is the belief that he is born into. However, because of his "intelligence and thirst for knowledge," he isn't satisfied. Though he has always been happy, he feels that "the love of his mother and father will not always give him peace." In Hinduism, the worshiping of idol gods is practiced. The gods are sometimes made of flesh and many are made of stone. Siddhartha is not content with worshiping either of these because he knows that man could lead him wrong and that stone could not give him a reply. Siddhartha feels that belief in the gods is not a central part of salvation, but being happy within is most important. After he finds no satisfaction in Hinduism, he moves on to another method of attaining salvation.

Secondly, Siddhartha turns to Samanaism, which does not provide him with salvation. In Samanaism, he learns a lot, but he's still not satisfied. He learns what he considers to be very important, "losing the self." He travels the way of self-denial through meditation, through emptying the mind of all images. Although he loves being able to deny himself for the sake of peace, he's still not happy. He feels that there should be more to salvation than just being able to stay calm, so he continues to search. Nothing less than absolute blessedness will suffice. Siddhartha feels that salvation requires a very thorough change in character. His character does change in that he learns patience, which is a very important factor in any religion because one is always awaiting a reward. Although Siddhartha believes in his heart that he has tasted the best fruit of the reward with the Samanas, he goes on because he is still distrustful of the words that come from teachers.

Finally, Siddhartha goes to the river. He finds peace and serenity in communicating with the river, seeing it as a beautiful specimen with "pearls rising from its depths" and with a thousand eyes of blue, green white, and crystal. Of course, the river doesn't actually communicate or have eyes, but Siddhartha "animates it because of his passionate desire and regard for truth." Siddahartha, through meditation, learns to interpret the many voices of the river. He views the river as having the "voice of a king, or a warrior, of a night bird." Upon discovering the secrets of the river, Siddhartha becomes very happy. He is content with having the river as a god and believes that he will not be misled by such a peaceful god. He believes that he has reached Nirvana or received salvation and, to Siddhartha, the river is very strong and symbolic. He gets his impressions and sensations of life from it.

In conclusion, salvation cannot be attained by others for you. You must be satisfied within your own soul. The search might be long and tedious as it was for Siddhartha, but it will be worth it.

Activity 1

Essay Development

Directions: Complete the process essay below by identifying appropriate steps and detailed instructions to complete the process indicated in the thesis statement. If you wish to modify the introduction and conclusion, please do so.

TO MEET THE PERSON OF YOUR DREAMS

Imagine you and your friends are at the biggest party of the year, and all of a sudden, you see the perfect male (female). He (She) is instantly at the top of your list of priorities. It is mandatory that you meet this individual and nothing will stop you. This situation occurs quite often in the lives of young people. If you plan to meet the person of your dreams, you must make a thorough search, then flirt with the person you desire, and next, prove to him (her) that you are the perfect companion.

First Body Paragraph

Second Body Paragraph

Third Body Paragraph

We all understand that it is not an easy task finding the person of your dreams. However, along with cooperation from the opposite sex and these three steps, it should be quite easy.

Activity 2

MINI FIELD EXERCISES

1. Provide directions from downtown (or from the biggest shopping mall in your town) to your English classroom.

2. You will need a partner for this exercise. Write down the steps and movements one must make to do a new dance. Then choose a classmate to read these steps and perform accordingly. This is an in-class assignment. Provide appropriate music. Have class critique the instructions and the performance.

3. Visit your campus library during study time for one hour for several days and observe fellow students. See if you can detect the students who just sit and waste time instead of studying. If you witness this, write a well-developed paragraph explaining how some students waste time when they could be studying.

4. Find at least five different types of process analysis from everyday life situations or concerns. Critique these to determine their effectiveness in providing important instructions and clarification.

Assignment I

Choose one of the topics listed below and write an essay of 500 words. Pay special attention to sentence structure, grammar, punctuation, and mechanics.

1. How to be a good neighbor
2. How to become and remain a member of your university band (student government association (SGA), sorority or fraternity, dance troupe, gospel choir)
3. How to plan a romantic date
4. How to prepare a special meal
5. How to plan a successful moving venture
6. How to overcome shyness (or some fear)
7. How to gain and maintain respect
8. How to keep up with the "Joneses"
9. How slang becomes popular
10. How a star (famous singer, actress, group, hero) is born

Assignment II

Choose one of the topics listed below and write a 700–1000 word process essay.

1. In one of his songs George Benson sings, "I believe the children are our future/Teach them well and let them lead the way/Show them all the beauty they possess inside/Give them a sense of pride..." Considering this song by Benson, R. Kelly's "I Believe I Can Fly," and a version of "The Impossible Dream," from the Broadway production of *The Man of LaMancha*, write a paper explaining how to achieve in life (or how to believe in one's innate potential).
2. Using two movies that focus on friendship, explain how to be a good friend to another person.
3. Consider the careers of several professional athletes from different sports (such as Michael Jordan, Larry Bird, John Smoltz, Ken Griffey, Jr., John Elway, Tiger Woods, and Michael Chang). Then explain how to succeed once you enter the pros.
4. Research the process of student government elections at your school. Explain what one must do to run a successful election campaign.

Assignment III

1. Produce a guide—in pamphlet or brochure format—giving extensive details on how to do one of the following:

    a. How to cater a social event

    b. How to adjust to college (from arrival to graduation)

    c. How to plan some major activity

    d. How to become _____ (some kind of professional)

2. Write the script for a 30-minute "how to" video on some skill or process with which you are familiar.

COMPARISON-CONTRAST

When you compare, you examine the ways in which two or more objects are alike, or the ways in which they differ. You exercise this thinking process in an effort to make some final decision about the subjects you are comparing or contrasting. For instance, you might compare or contrast two family restaurants to determine which one will better meet your needs if you want a satisfying, nutritious meal that won't cost much money. Or you might want to recommend to your friend that she purchase one brand of sneakers rather than another. Perhaps you are trying to convince your best friend that one professional golfer is more gifted than another. Any one of these instances is likely to occur in everyday conversation. So, comparison and contrast, as a thinking process, is something with which you are already familiar.

When you use comparison/contrast as a method of development in your writing, you will employ the same analytical techniques that you use in your everyday discussions or decision-making processes; you will point out similarities or differences in order to make a point about your subjects.

The first thing to keep in mind when you use comparison/contrast as a strategy for development in your writing is that you are not writing simply to show your audience how your subjects are similar or different; neither are you writing to show how your subjects are similar *and* different. Therefore, unless your subjects are completely unfamiliar to your readers, a simple listing of the similarities or differences between or among your subjects is often useless, or worse, a waste of your readers' time. Even if you are certain that your subjects are unfamiliar to your audience, you should offer some critical judgment about those subjects based on the comparable/contrastible elements you provide. That judgment becomes your thesis statement, which indicates the purpose of your discussion, as well as your point-of-view on and attitude about, your subject.

As you begin your essay, first make sure that the subjects you discuss are comparable, that is, that they belong to the same class. For example, a hot dog stand is not likely to be among your choices if you are recommending an eating establishment where your favorite couple can have a romantic dinner. You should find at least three criteria, or *points of comparison,* on which to base your discussion. Select only those criteria that serve your purpose, regardless of any additional similarities or differences that you may find interesting between or among your subjects. Superfluous discussion will only detract from the main point of your essay.

Once you have determined the criteria on which your comparison will be based, you need to decide the most effective way to organize your details. There are two common patterns of organization to consider: *point-by-point* and *block*. The complexity of the subjects compared or contrasted and the amount of detail that you provide will help you to determine the most effective pattern of organization.

The block pattern of organization presents all of your details about *Subject A* in one paragraph, then all of your details about *Subject B* in the next paragraph, and so on with the other subjects that you may have. Discuss your criteria in the same order in each paragraph to avoid confusing your readers. The sketch outline below uses the block pattern of organization:

> Thesis:
>
> I. Subject A
>
>   A. Point 1
>
>   B. Point 2
>
>   C. Point 3
>
> II. Subject B
>
>   A. Point 1
>
>   B. Point 2
>
>   C. Point 3

In using the block pattern, you must remember to make brief references to Subject A when you are discussing the same criteria about Subject B and so on. Such references will lend to the coherence of the essay and will eliminate the readers' sense of having read two or more "mini" essays.

The point-by-point pattern of organization allows you to make the points of your comparison or contrast the more prominent feature. Using this pattern, you will discuss the details of the first criterion with reference to both Subject A and Subject B (and other subjects, if you have more) in a single paragraph. You will develop each criterion similarly in succeeding paragraphs. Transition words and phrases are most important in this pattern of organization, as they will signal to your readers a change in focus of subject. The outline below illustrates the point-by-point pattern of organization.

> Thesis:
>
> I. Point 1
>
>   A. Subject A
>
>   B. Subject B
>
> II. Point 2
>
>   A. Subject A
>
>   B. Subject B

III. Point 3

    A. Subject A

    B. Subject B

If your details are extensive and complicated, you should organize them according to the point-by-point pattern, which facilitates the readers' understanding of your complex discussion by eliminating the need to remember all of the details of the discussion about previous subjects. Nor will they have to keep returning to that previous discussion to see exactly how the subjects compare or contrast.

Whichever pattern you decide is more appropriate for your purpose, you must remember to give equal attention to each subject. A lop-sided discussion which gives more attention to one subject than to the other(s) may appear biased. Or your readers may decide that you do not know much about one of your subjects. If indeed your knowledge about your subjects is limited, discuss only those points about which you are most confident, or consider changing subjects completely.

Sample Essay #1

BUDDHISM, HINDUISM, AND ZOROASTRANISM: PARALLELS TO CHRISTIANITY

Most Americans go to church each Sunday to meet and pray and serve our Supreme Being—the Lord Jesus Christ. To many of us who are Christians, Christianity is the only religion that we know, and our God is the only God that we serve. What many of us fail to realize is that there are millions of people around the world who are not Christians and who do not serve Christ. However, their basic religious beliefs and conduct are much the same as Christians'.

For instance, Buddhism, a religion practiced mostly in the Orient, has some doctrines that can be compared to those found in Christianity. Buddha, who parallels Jesus in origin and supremacy, is Buddhism's patron saint. There are millions of Buddhists who conduct themselves according to a moral code quite similar to the Ten Commandments. This code also dictates that believers should not kill, steal, lie, commit adultery, or give way to drunkenness. To Buddhists, reaching the epitome of peace and contentment is not going to heaven, but attaining Nirvana, which is not a place one goes after death, but is a state of absolute blessedness that a person may find while he still lives. However, like the Christian, the Buddhist must be virtuous to reach his utopia. He must be pure, patient, charitable, and courageous. All of these dictates were written down by Buddha's disciples in the *Canon of Buddhist Scriptures,* a book much like the Christian Bible.

Hinduism, whose extensive following is found mainly in India, is not without its similarities to Christianity. Although it has several gods, Brahman is its supreme soul. Hindus are quite devout in their beliefs and follow a very strict code of conduct in order to please their god, just as Christians order their lives to please God. Hindus' concept of heaven is called perfection, which is reached when a believer goes through various transmigrations. *The Vedas* is the Hindu Bible, and, like its Christian and Buddhist counterparts, it contains the laws by which believers should conduct themselves.

Although Zoroastrianism, a little known religion which claims only a small following, and is located mainly in Iran, cannot claim as many followers as Buddhism or Hinduism, it also bears some striking likenesses to Christianity. Zoroaster is the religion's benevolent force. His believers, much like Christians, hold that good thoughts and good deeds are the main order of life. Also, like Christians, they believe that good must triumph over evil and that man must live a life of piety and self-renunciation in order to be saved from the darker forces of the world. Zoroaster's believers' heaven is called paradise, a place like heaven where all good people go. Their belief is that the wicked will be punished forever in hell. The point should also be made that Zoroaster, like Jesus Christ, demanded the abandonment of false gods and the worship of one true god, who created all men. The dictates of Zoroastrianism can be found in the holy book called *Zen-Avesta*, which contains parables and laws that are strikingly similar to those found in the Christian Bible.

Christianity is indeed one of the dominant religions in the world, but it is not the only one. When Christians kneel to worship Jesus Christ, we should not be amazed that someone, someplace else in the world is worshiping Buddha, Brahman, Zoroaster, or some other god, perhaps at the same time, and often, with a similar concept in mind.

Sample Essay 2

BEAUTY IN THE 90'S

What is beauty? What makes a person beautiful? Is the supermodel who makes millions from walking down a runaway beautiful? Is the female Congresswoman who spends the majority of her time trying to solve the problems of her country beautiful? What about the housewife/mother who spends all of her day cooking, cleaning, and taking care of her children? Is she beautiful? The question of beauty has long mystified the general population, but the answer is really quite simple. Beauty is subjective. What may be beautiful to one person might seem quite plain and average to another. What one might find aesthetically pleasing could possibly give another an "eye-ache." There are different levels, or standards, of beauty. However, people generally tend to have the same views on what is beautiful and what isn't. These generalizations combine to form societal standards of beauty and self-image. They are the views of society as a whole, and the views of one individual do not affect society's standards. There are many different media methods that play a major role in determining what beauty really is. The television industry, and the magazine industry are just two media methods that influence society's views on beauty. Of the two, the magazine industry has a more direct role in contributing to society's opinion on what makes an individual beautiful. There are magazines aimed at male audiences, as well as magazines targeting females. There is quite a difference, though, between the two types of magazines, besides the most obvious gender discrepancy. *EM* (Ebony Man) and *Essence*, a male and female magazine (respectively) in the magazine industry contribute strongly, although differently, to societal standards of beauty and self-image through their photographs portraying the ideal male/female, the content of their respective articles, and advertisements aimed directly at the audience of the magazine.

While skimming through many popular magazines which focus on young men and women, one can rightly assume that society believes that thinner is better. *Essence*, a female magazine, further emphasizes the societal belief that a woman with a small waist and slender figure is beautiful. In the photographs within the magazine, there are no overweight models with disproportionate figures. Moreover, there is an abundance of rail-thin models sporting elegant clothes and ingenious hairstyles. These models are part of an era where "thin is in" and fat just does not cut it. Slender models appeal to the female audience of *Essence* because they give women a goal to aim for. Many women want to look like a model because they feel that looking like a model will make them beautiful. This belief can be attributed to society's strong influence on the ideals of beauty.

EM, a magazine created for the African-American male, is a very good example of how male magazines portray the ideal man. Male magazines depict the ideal man as tall, dark, and handsome. Not only must the ideal male possess these qualities, but he must also exhibit defined muscles and a body that contains a minimal amount of body fat. This image of the ideal man is what sends many a man into the weight room every week to tone up his body. It is what causes men of this day and age to place such a high value on physical appearance. This image of the ideal man further promotes the societal belief in beauty being proportional to weight.

It is easy to believe after perusing several magazines, that the magazine industry, as well as society, knows how important the content of the magazine is to the reader. In female magazines, a great deal of emphasis is placed upon beauty tips and health/beauty aids. In regard to articles, there are a great many stories dealing with real-life issues (such as AIDS and teenage pregnancy) and current events. Also, female magazines tend to contain articles centered around the fashion industry and what goes on in that industry. The emphasis on how to make yourself and keep yourself beautiful also advances the belief that society has of women and beauty.

Male magazines, however, do not target the same issues that female magazines target. Instead of health tips and health/beauty aids, *EM* contains information on current events and sports. There is less information on the fashion industry and much more on current events. There is hardly any written evidence in male magazines that can be compared to that in female magazines, besides the common link of current events. Male magazines tend to stress the issues of manliness and deal with technology and politics. This serves to enforce the belief that the male is the one who is more level-headed and serious-minded about life.

It is easy to determine which audience a particular magazine is aimed at through the examination of its advertisements. The ads in *Essence* tend to deal more with health/beauty aids more than anything else. There are ads for aspirin, maxi pads, tampons, cosmetics, and hygienic supplies. These ads make up the majority of the total ads placed in female magazines because females tend to place a greater emphasis upon personal care than males. There are also ads for cars and other technological appliances such as cellular phones, but the majority of space is allocated to personal care ads.

Male magazines, however, are the exact opposite. In *EM*, the ads tend to stress technology. There are a great deal of ads for automobiles, as well as for phones and such. There are a few cologne ads, but the main emphasis in male magazines seems to be on cars and other technological appliances. The fact that the ads in male magazines feature automobiles serves to further accentuate the societal belief among males that a car is a symbol of beauty. Many females today judge a man based on what he drives rather than who he is. Therefore, males believe that the bigger and better car they have, the more females they can attract. This tends to give credence to the idea that the ads in magazines contribute to societal standards of beauty.

In the magazine industry, *EM* and *Essence* contribute strongly, although somewhat differently, to societal standards of beauty and self-image through their photographs portraying the ideal male/female, the content of their respective articles, and advertisements aimed directly at the audience of the magazine. In the 90's, society has formed certain standards for what it views as beautiful. These standards are applied to all things, people and objects alike. The magazine industry has a major role to play in the development and promotion of these standards of beauty. Male and female magazines handle their roles differently. Although they share similar stances on certain issues, the gender barrier still remains. However, it is certain that they are both useful in the development of society's standards of beauty and that they both continue to contribute to such. Beauty may be only skin deep, but in this day, many people can't seem to see that far.

Activity 1

Essay Development
Directions: Complete the comparison-contrast essay that follows:

THE PEOPLE'S CHOICE

Despite their professed penchant for change and novelty, today's television audiences still long for the same picture show—the "shoot'em up, get the bad guy" formula. And their desires are fulfilled, for today's cop shows are replicas of yesterday's western series. While the setting has changed, much remains the same.

First Body Paragraph

Second Body Paragraph

Third Body Paragraph

The sitcoms may change from season to season. But the one constant in television programming is the western and its offspring.

Activity 2

MINI FIELD EXERCISES

1. The next time that you are sleepy, set your alarm clock for forty-five (45) minutes; then lie down. Write down what you recall from that sleeping period. Did you dream? Do you remember what you dreamed? How did you feel upon arising? On another day or later that same evening, set your clock for a five to eight hour period. Then lie down. After five to eight hours, record what happened during this period. Answer some of the same questions raised earlier. What is the difference between taking a nap and sleeping?

2. Think about your classes. Do you pay more attention in one than you do in another? Do you recall what the teacher in one class said more often than you do what the teacher in another said? Do you listen in one and hear in another? Think about it, and then in 250–300 words, discuss the differences between hearing and listening.

3. Visit your favorite restaurant. Compare romantic couples' behavior to that of non-romantic couples. Write your response in 250–300 words.

4. Visit three fine department stores and observe the sales personnel's reaction to a variety of customers. [Or visit three fine department stores on three consecutive days wearing different apparel and note the reactions of the sales personnel to you on each visit.] Record your findings in 250–300 words.

Assignment I
Choose one of the topics listed below and write an essay of 500 words.

1. Compare fate and destiny.
2. What is the difference between having a degree and being educated?
3. Compare one current athlete to one former athlete who played the same position in a professional sport.
4. Compare a female preacher to a male preacher.
5. What is the difference between being envious and being jealous?
6. Contrast viewing a movie at home and viewing one at the theater.
7. Compare adolescence to middle age.
8. What is the difference between being lonely and being alone?
9. What is the difference between having a job and having a career?
10. Compare shopping to buying.

Assignment II

Choose one of the topics listed below and write a 700–1000 word comparison essay.

1. Compare two different majors that might prepare you for the same professional career.
2. Compare unethical behavior to immoral behavior. Be sure to provide specific examples for each subject.
3. In the periodical section of your university or public library, review several current magazines aimed at female audiences and several aimed at male audiences. Consider how each magazine reaches its audience through its selection of articles and advertisements. Write an essay about how the magazine industry contributes to societal standards of success.
4. Read Andrew Marvell's poem, "To His Coy Mistress," and Christopher Marlowe's poem, "The Passionate Shepherd to His Love." Compare the subject and speaker's arguments.

Assignment III

1. Visit the electronics department of several major department stores in your city or town and gather data on brand models of appliances that college students usually purchase (computers, stereo systems, microwave ovens, for instance). Analyze your data and write the text for a brochure that will help most students make a wise purchasing decision about the appliances you have chosen.
2. Write a paper comparing the description of the treatment of children in Charles Dickens' novel *Oliver Twist* to the description of the treatment of children in a contemporary work (fiction or nonfiction).

CLASSIFICATION

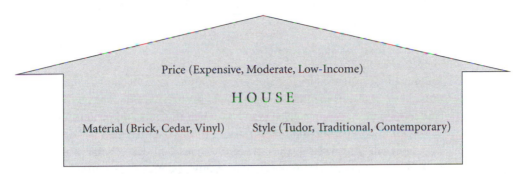

In this section we address *classification,* the strategy that requires you to group items according to their common qualities or characteristics. In this classification essay, you will sort items into categories or sub-categories in order to make some point about the larger group as a whole or about the individual divisions of that group. The point—the purpose—that you make is the thesis sentence that will appear in the introduction. In the example above, *house* has been classified according to *material, price,* and *style.* If you were to decide to write an essay classifying house, your thesis should indicate the purpose or significance of one kind of material, price, or style as opposed to the other two mentioned in each category.

Each classification is made on the basis of a *ruling principle,* a single criterion that is common to each member of each group. Strict adherence to your ruling principle ensures that your groupings will be consistent, logical, and complete. In the figure above, *style, material,* and *cost* are ruling principles used to classify. Throughout your essay you will discuss only one of these ruling principles. You should arrange these categories in some logical order befitting your thesis—your purpose; therefore, you would not choose to include *cul de sac* in a classification discussion that obviously uses *material* as its ruling principle. It would be illogical to do so. You should also adhere to a ruling principle as the basis of the grouping to avoid overlapping.

Make certain that your groupings are complete. When you attempt to classify an item or subject, make sure you can group it into at least three categories. If there are more than three categories for the ruling principle you choose, identify them. Otherwise your discussion will be incomplete. For example, in the classification of houses, the three styles mentioned do not represent the only styles of houses. If you were to write on only these three styles of houses, you would need to mention that they are the only styles in a particular area or provide some other principle.

This discussion of the groupings will be the body of the essay. Therefore, keep in mind that you are to provide a discussion—specific details, examples, commentary, and other strategies—some comparison-contrast in particular—not generalizations upon generalizations. Provide equal discussion of each category you identify. For instance, if you can provide ample details about expensive and moderate houses but have limited knowledge about low-income houses, perhaps you should consider another ruling principle for your classification or try classifying another subject.

For this assignment, you may need to spend more time planning than you may have spent in writing papers on the other modes to ensure that you choose the ruling principle and appropriate groupings for your classification paper. As usual, write an introduction that will excite readers and a conclusion that clinches your point.

Sample Essay #1

TYPES OF COLLEGE STUDENTS

On any modern-day college or university campus, students and professors alike can readily identify the many types of students who register for undergraduate classes in a given year. Also, such students and professors are adept in comparing and/or contrasting those students, the majority of whom fall into three distinct types: the conscientious scholar who takes all class meetings, lessons, activities, requirements, and assignments seriously; the **crafty "would-be, could-be" student scholar** who uses the "hit and miss" or "snow-job" approach to an education that currently he/she is too busy to pursue but smart enough to snare a high grade; and the **anonymous, transparent, slide through** student who feels a "C is tantamount to his/her just "showing up" regularly.

The answer to any classmate or professor's dream in the college or university classroom is the **conscientious scholar** who takes all class meetings, lessons, activities, requirements, and assignments seriously. In comparison/contrast to the latter two students, the conscientious student-scholar completes activities as listed. He/She recognizes both the present and future value of serious learning, the kind that prepares one for a world marketplace.

The scholar prepares for classes ahead of time, attends classes as scheduled, confers with the professors for appropriate clarification, studies and researches carefully and regularly, takes thorough notes, evaluates ideas, issues, and conclusions, raises questions and formulates his/her own responses. Further, the conscientious scholar arrives for instruction on time, listens to class instruction attentively, participates in learning activities fully, fulfills all class requirements, and remains in class the entire period. Further, the scholar volunteers for extra assignments, seeks related information both from the professor and from independent sources, shares his findings, and takes delight in the challenge of personal growth and development. In short, the conscientious scholar takes his education seriously and is careful not to shortchange himself/herself, academically.

In contrast to the conscientious scholar at the college or university level is the crafty **"would-be, could-be" student scholar** who uses a self-styled, well-oiled, well-used "hit and miss" or "snow-job" approach to an education that currently he/she is too busy to pursue but smart enough to snare a high grade (or so he/she thinks). The crafty "would-be, could-be" student scholar has the ability, the stamina, and the backing to be a successful scholar, but for many reasons, he/she does not feel the need to meet the rigors of academic pursuit in traditional fashion as outlined above. Rather than utilizing unique communication skills in a similar manner, he/she prefers to fine tune his/her skills by practicing the "hit and miss" or "snow-job" approach to academic excellence.

The "would-be, could-be" "drop-in, drop-out" scholar perfects the drop-in/drop-out approach, dropping in for a day or two and dropping out for more, dropping in an early class but dropping out before the late class meets (or vice versa), and dropping in a class late and slipping out early or coming on time, signing the roll or making a presentation before dropping out. Since the snow banks in Florida are so high and the snow capped walls are so long, the professor cannot see the various entrances and exits, he/she seems to think. Likewise, the professor will not recognize the verbal, non-verbal, and written "snow-jobs" that are so craftily perfected from one instance to another. In addition to other crafty skills, this "scholar" can prepare other teachers' homework in class, visit with classmates, share pictures, take a nap, or just ignore class instruction. Of course, if one method fails, the crafty student can always assume that indeed the professor must of necessity be either blind, naive, or stupid. Thus, prior to the chat with the professor, the crafty "would-be, could-be" "scholar" remembers to don a serious face, take a professional stance, and use an educated voice as he/she "snows" the professor into belief, empathy, and cooperation. Of course, if all of this craftiness fails, as a last resort, the "scholar" can take offense and "find" reasons why it is the professor who is at fault. After all, the "scholar" can always seek assistance from at least one administrator whom he/she has successfully snowed into categorizing him/her as a scholar of the highest order.

In further contrast to the conscientious scholar as well as to the crafty student "scholar" at the college or university level is a third student, the **anonymous, transparent, slide through** student. Not letting the professor know who he/she is, what he/she is doing, what his/her purpose or mission is, or whether he/she is a part of the class seems to be the trademark of this student. Unlike the scholar, he/she does not take a conscientious approach to education but like the student "would-be, could-be" "scholar," he/she plays the "do-drop-in, now you see me, now you don't" game. He/She will not officially drop the class but will not attend or participate in class activities or submit assignments regularly. He/She offers no explanations and submits no excused absences, believing that since he/she is not in class enough for his/her classmates or the professor to know him/her, the teacher cannot see right through his/her attempts to beat the system. Thus, the "would-be, could-be" "scholar" thinks that if he shows up periodically, he should be given no less than a "C" grade. Thus, he shows up at exam time, for in-class writing activity, or at presentation time—sometimes. Characteristically, on the last day, he/she brings mounds of excuses and several excused absence forms, to make everything all right.

Most students and professors concur that as long as there are colleges and universities, the three types of students mentioned above are easily discernible. New types of students will enter America's classrooms, but the three typical ones discussed here will still be visible.

Sample Essay #2

TEACHERS: DEDICATION TO THEIR PROFESSION

Have you ever been in a classroom where the teacher lectured the entire time? Have you ever been in a class where the teacher attended the class only occasionally? Have you ever been in a classroom where the teacher did nothing but show movies or assign in-class reading assignments? Most students have had experiences with these types of teachers. These actions illustrate that teachers vary in their dedication to their profession.

Teachers who are dedicated to their profession usually do a good job of fulfilling the course objectives. These teachers never miss a day of class unless it is absolutely necessary. Dedicated teachers are always willing and able to answer questions. These teachers often go out of their way to find an effective method of presenting information to the class so that more students will understand. Dedicated teachers rarely waste any class time in their effort to ensure that they teach material that is designated for that particular class. In general, these teachers are hard-working, effective, efficient, responsible, and reliable.

Teachers who are not completely dedicated to their profession can be classified as half-hearted teachers. These teachers occasionally miss class and are almost five or ten minutes late everyday. Half-hearted teachers do not always present material in a clear manner and often have trouble answering questions. These teachers rarely relate any discussions to current events or use personal experiences or stories to help clarify a point. Class assignments and tests are also returned several days after the due date instead of the next day. In general, these teachers are somewhat carefree, partially interested in what they do, occasionally reliable, and helpful only to an extent.

The sole interest of teachers who are not dedicated to teaching at all is a summer free of job-related responsibilities. These teachers hardly ever come to class on time and are usually unprepared. They do not give examples in class, answer questions, or discuss assignments. They do not give the class a chance to ask questions or the opportunity to come in for help. These teachers never return homework assignments or tests. Their negligence makes it impossible for the students to have any idea of how they are performing in class. The only thing these teachers do well is count the number of days until the next holiday or break. In general, these teachers are unhelpful, unorganized, insufficient, and incapable.

Believe it or not, the teachers of today fall into all of the three categories. As important as education is, something should definitely be done to make more teachers completely dedicated to their profession.

Activity 1

Essay Development

The introductory paragraph and concluding paragraph have been provided for you. Now develop body paragraphs to complete the essay.

ATTITUDES TOWARD THE ELDERLY

Society seems to be indifferent toward the elderly. Society doesn't have time to be bothered with looking after a world of "useless babies." The elderly worry others about places they need to go; they annoy people with how they think children should be raised; they cause anxiety when they drive, and they can be a menace lying around on the streets. I have noticed that different classes of elderly people receive different types of treatment from society. The attitudes of society toward the elderly differ based on the social status of the elderly person.

First Body Paragraph

Second Body Paragraph

Third Body Paragraph

From their actions or inaction, people today are not interested in the elderly. They appear to be saying, "You are in the way, old people. You are too slow; you are not with it. If you can help, please do. If not, move out of the way!"

Activity 2

MINI FIELD EXERCISES

1. Read the comics section of the Sunday issue of your local paper. What types of situations are addressed? What are the subjects of these comic strips? What are the themes? In 200–300 words classify Sunday comics.

2. Visit the campus library two times; spend at least an hour each trip. Observe the library patrons. Construct a chart or draw a diagram of three common types of library patrons. Where do they sit? Do like groups sit together, or are they scattered throughout the library? Classify these patrons pictorially.

3. For two days, pay special attention to people when they smile. Do all smiles convey the same thing? Do people smile the same way or to the same extent? What messages do smiles convey? In 200-300 words, write a paragraph classifying smiles.

4. Interview five to seven friends and/or associates to see how they classify a particular subject. Think of a subject that people feel strongly about—a subject that may cause them to have certain prejudices or cause them to exhibit certain behavior toward others—a subject such as race (a particular race), religion (a certain religious denomination), or gender (attitudes about men or women). Why do people have the opinions or reactions to one

topic or a similar topic? Are their assumptions based on one single principle? If so, what impact does classification have on views? Share your results in a 200–300 word paragraph.

Assignment I

Choose one of the topics listed below and write an essay of 500 words. Brainstorm for principles or categories of that subject. Then select the principle that most interests you and write a classification essay.

1. sports fans/athletes
2. funerals/parties/weddings
3. love songs
4. game or talk show hosts/comedians
5. beaches/theme parks/public parks
6. home peddlers/telemarketers
7. hair salon patrons/hairstylists/barbers
8. Colognes/lingerie/footwear
9. con artists/leeches/human parasites
10. teachers' offices/doctor's offices/pastors' offices

Assignment II

Choose one of the topics listed below and write a 700-1000 word classification essay.

1. Listen to at least three recordings of blues, jazz, or classical music. Write an essay classifying the genre or sub-genre of one of these musical forms.
2. Visit malls, bookstores, art shops, gift stores, and/or museums to study art figurines and keepsakes of a particular ethnic group. Write a paper classifying some artistic feature of one of these cultures.
3. Classify the residential lifestyles of your peers.
4. Peruse the inspirational verse written in greeting cards, essays, or articles. Aside from genre, identify a ruling principle for these inspirational writings.

Assignment III

1. Read editorials written by a syndicated columnist over a two year period. Discuss the type of editorials this renown columnist writes.
2. Listen to satirical commentators such as Mickey Rooney, Dennis Miller, and Chris Rock for two of their commentaries. Classify them according to style of delivery.

CAUSE AND EFFECT

Why? What happens if? These are commonplace questions raised by all people from their earliest years of life throughout their life cycle. And someone—usually a loved one—raises the same question—why?—after each person's life cycle ends. "Why" and "what effect" type questions play the decisive role in structuring the cause and effect or causal analysis paper. And the responses provided for these questions play an even more critical role because they substantiate your *argument*—one of the more difficult, if not the most difficult, exposition essays you will have to write.

The cause and effect essay analyzes the reasons that an event occurred (causes) or the results (effects) of that occurrence. Because there are usually several causes or effects involved in any single occurrence, you must be careful to avoid oversimplifying causes and effects in your essays. In that effort, you should consider both *major* and *minor* causes if your aim is to prove *why* some phenomenon happened.

The major cause is one which is sufficient, by itself, to cause a particular effect. The minor cause may be one of many causes, but cannot *by itself* produce a particular effect. To illustrate, infidelity may be the cause of or a major contributing factor in a divorce, whereas an annoying habit such as squeezing the toothpaste from the middle of the tube may be one of several minor causes that leads to squabbles between spouses, and, of course, frequent squabbles sometimes lead to divorce. However, seldom does a disagreement about something as minor as toothpaste lead people to divorce court.

Also, you should be aware of the distinction between an *immediate* and an *ultimate* effect. An immediate effect is one that becomes obvious before the interposition of another effect, while an ultimate effect is one that may take longer to occur and may be of far greater significance. Too often in writing causal analysis, some writers hastily select and discuss immediate occurrences as definitive effects when the ultimate effects may be more far-reaching and more problematic. For example, a parent's failure to chastise a child for being dishonest or disobeying some parental rule may contribute to the child's becoming a spoiled brat. Anyone aware of the parent-child relationship in this case, as well as the child's "devil may care" attitude, may conclude that the child is indeed spoiled. This, however, is an obvious or immediate effect. But a more consequential effect may be that the child later becomes an adult who is irresponsible on the job, in a marriage, or as a parent; or the child becomes an adult who may commit a crime, unfearful of retribution.

Snap judgments based on obvious results can prove as unreliable as judgments formed because of illogical thinking. It would be a mistake to assume that a spoiled child undoubtedly will become a criminal, just as it is illogical to assume that the fact that it rains immediately after you have washed your car indicates that rain is an effect of your having washed your car. Clearly, both conclusions here are examples of illogical reasoning or the *post hoc ergo propter hoc* fallacy (which in Latin means "after this, therefore, because of this").

To avoid making this kind of error in judgment and thus a poor argument for your essay, you must spend enough time planning the paper. Make sure that the thesis and plan of development will adequately address the question raised. Just as you should avoid confusing immediate and ultimate effects, you must be certain to avoid making absolute statements about causes and effects in your thesis. It would be an error to say that eating pork causes one to develop hypertension, suggesting that anyone who eats pork at any time, for any length of time, will automatically develop hypertension. In writing a cause and effect essay, consider the same potential exceptions that are likely to exist with other matters of life. Modify your thesis to reflect that perhaps *excessive* consumption of pork for a *lengthy* period of time *increases* one's chance of developing hypertension. Learn to *qualify* your assertion.

Another point to consider is the development of your idea. If you can offer virtually no discussion for the cause or effect that you identify, you cannot write an effective analysis. In other words, do not write about a cause or effect that is circular, such as this statement: Fatigue is the result of people tiring themselves out." What else can be said here? Make certain that whatever causes or results you identify, you can provide strong support—a good *argument*—for your view. You may need to provide specific examples—not just one, but several case studies—or you may wish to provide a detailed narrative (anecdote) identifying a cause or effect. You may need to use descriptions or make comparisons to prove your point.

In writing the causal analysis essay, you will use more *critical thinking* than you may have had to use in developing the previous rhetorical patterns. For instance, you will need to consider what your reader may say about one of your causes or effects and make sure that you provide a counterstatement to give your argument more credibility. For inexperienced writers, it is usually a good practice to avoid attempting to write on both causes and effects in an essay—especially a timed-writing essay. Too often these writers spend too much time on causes and almost none on the effects or vice versa. Thus, it is better to discuss one of these and give equal treatment to each of the causes or effects that you identify for your plan of development. With this essay, as with all of the others discussed, you will need to write an emphatic conclusion. Depending on the subject of your causal analysis essay, you may need to make a recommendation or a prediction in your conclusion.

Sample Essay #1

WOE IS MY WRITING

Although I was glad to be able to come to college, I must admit that I was a bit apprehensive about my ability to do college-level work. I have now been at the university for almost a semester, and I am happy to say that I am doing well in my courses—at least in all but one. My Freshman Composition 101 class is a problem for me, not because of the grammar exercises that I must study and complete, but because of the great number of essays that I must write. Because I did not write much in high school, I often suffer from writer's block, and usually, rather than writing, I would rather be having a good time. Writing essays for my English class is almost impossible for me.

I did not write very extensively in high school. For example, in the tenth grade, the class was required to write only a few paragraphs—five or six at the most. Some paragraphs required us to write briefly about a literary work like "A Cask of Amontillado", "The Raven", or "God's Trombone". With other paragraphs we wrote from personal experience. These little pieces of written communication usually encompassed such subjects as "my summer vacation," "my aspirations for the future," or "why I want to attend college." In the eleventh grade, we wrote two or three book reports. In them we gave only plot summaries. We were never asked to study and develop an idea on a specific character, event, or literary element within a story. In the twelfth grade the class was required to construct a research paper; however, the teacher, for whatever reason, restricted us to five pages and never really drilled us on any formal format. She never, in fact, mentioned a thesis statement or even an introduction, body, or conclusion. Thus, my high school writing experience was very limited, and this limitation most definitely contributes to my writing woes in Comp 101.

Writer's block serves only to aggravate my lack of writing experience. Even after I read the assignment very closely and have chosen a topic that I think that I can write about, I too often draw a blank. It seems as if all thoughts simply jump ship and dessert me. I can sit in my chair and doodle for an hour, but nothing seems to come. Although my mind is blocked from writing a single sensible word, it has no qualms about my scribbling down a multitude of dribble. For example, I might sit at my desk and write down the names of all of the guys that I have dated, placing each in a category according to his spending inclination—"big spender", "so-so spender", and "down right cheap". Then my mind wonders to what I want to wear to the Moon on Friday night. "Do I want to wear my beige mini-skirt and my tall brown suede boots? Or do I want to wear my 'hug-me-tight-in-all-the-right-places' fuchsia jumpsuit that Auntie Jackie bought me for Christmas?" In this process of thinking about everything but my essay, my eyes inevitably land on the television set, and I realize that one of my favorite sitcoms is coming on in about five minutes. I get up from my desk and find myself a comfortable chair and an economy-size bag of corn chips. My mind is then occupied with watching the antics of Kelsey Grammar, Martin, or Bill Cosby. It is needless to say that by this time, my essay is blocked out altogether.

I must admit that the main contributor to my writing problem is the fact that instead of sitting in my dorm room writing an essay about "Teenagers in the Nineties", I would rather be one of those nineties teenagers who are having a jolly old time. For example, I would much rather be on the basketball court playing a pick-up game with Christie, Laura, and some of the others who love to play the game. Shooting a few hoops would beat drafting a three-pronged theses sentence any day. Also, going to a movie would be far more pleasant than conjuring up a topic sentence and trying to decide what its primary and secondary sentences would be. At the movies, I could be looking at a suspense thriller such as "Scream", and yelling by head off. Or, I could be snuggled up to my significant other watching "Titanic". Transitions and the placement of modifiers would be far my mind. In addition, dancing to a little rap, rock 'n' roll, or country western music at my favorite club would satisfy me much more at the end of the day than trying to put an effective conclusion to a five paragraph theme. Evidently, my desire to enjoy myself is going to be the main factor in my having to repeat my English class.

Obviously, writing essays is not easy for me. I know that I must overcome my weak writing background, my tendency to have writer's block, and my overwhelming inclination to have fun, if I intend to "C" myself out of this course.

Sample Essay #2

SOMETHING MISSING

In America, people are in hot pursuit of the "good ole American dollar." Though many people would like to make life more comfortable for their offspring than it was for themselves, they are doing so at a big sacrifice. Too many parents today are neglecting their children.

To be successful in life, people often make their jobs a top priority. When parents' jobs become top priority, their devotion to other areas in their life decreases. To get ahead, parents may have to work long hours or travel long distances to get to and from their jobs. These factors reduce the amount of time that parents can spend with their children. While seeking to climb the stairs of success on a job is demanding work, the same is true of rearing children. If parents' most concentrated energy is spent at work, when they get home, they are weary and their patience may be short. Since they are aware of this, they often try to find someone else to take care of their children.

Many grandmothers, aunts, babysitters, and friends keep children for people who cannot devote the proper time to them. While in some cases it may be necessary for parents to take this kind of action, children may not understand that necessity. They may begin to doubt their self-worth. They do not seem to understand why "mommy and/or daddy" cannot take care of them or why they do not see their parents all day. When children are being nurtured by someone else, a relationship of love and caring develops between the children and the nurturers. As a result, children may associate time spent with them talking, reading, and laughing as signs of affection. Because there is little time spent this way between children and working parents, that loving parent-children relationship may never be established.

Worst of all, guilt-ridden parents may try to buy the adoration of their children. They can clearly see the distance between them and their offspring, and consequently, may try to close that gap by showering the children with material things. The parents may buy the children loads of toys, racks of clothes, or piles of entertainment software. However, children understand how easy it is and how little time it takes to charge an item at a store. These unimaginative acts by parents may stir bitterness in children's hearts which they may cling to for a long period of time.

Although earning high salaries can enable parents to provide their families with beautiful, comfortable homes and elegant or sporty cars, the adage holds true that money cannot buy love or happiness. In order to receive the love of their children, parents must show the children that they are the most important concern of theirs.

Activity 1

Essay Completion

The cause and effect essay below has been started for you. Develop the body of the essay, using the thesis statement provided in the introductory paragraph.

THE GREAT OBSESSION

We see it every day. Turn on the television, look in a book, visit the nearest department store, or look as you drive down the street. You will see evidence that people are concerned about how their hair, skin, body, and clothes look. And this is great; everyone enjoys looking at attractive people, but sometimes people go too far in their effort to look attractive. *Clearly, some of the measures many Americans take in their attempt to improve their appearance demonstrate that they have become obsessed with their appearance.*

First Supporting Paragraph

Second Supporting Paragraph

Third Supporting Paragraph

In our age of advanced technology people do not have to worry about some of the concerns that used to plague them. Thus, they have more time to think about how they look than how they will survive. But there are too many other problems that still need addressing for people to spend as much time as they do looking in the mirror, worrying about something as superficial as good looks.

Activity 2

MINI FIELD EXERCISES
Respond to one of the exercises below.

1. Jot down a list of things that cause you to become angry. Now analyze each of these things. Are all of them major? Organize your causes according to minor reasons, then major ones. Write a paragraph substantiating your argument. Indicate what you do when you become angry. Give your paragraph to one of your classmates to analyze for causal analysis.

2. Spend one day smiling at people as you go about your routine; notice the reaction or effect that your smile has on other people. Do they smile back, frown at you, or ignore you completely? Then, on another day, go through your routines pleasantly but, when possible, avoid smiling. Record the reaction or effect that your smiling or not smiling has on others you meet. Then prepare a 250-300 word written response on the effects of smiles on people.

3. What causes a person to be romantically attracted to another? Most people assume it is only physical attraction. Is it? Poll a dozen or more young people, half of whom are currently in a relationship, to discover what causes them to be romantically attracted to others.

4. Some people believe that manners belong to a bygone era. Is this true? Do people say "thank you" when you hold the door for them or do some other courteous act? Do drivers wave, indicating their appreciation when you allow them access when they want to get in front of you in your lane? Do you notice whether people say "excuse me" when they accidentally bump into you? In 200–300 words, briefly discuss the effect(s) that bad manners have on you.

Assignment I
Choose one of the topics listed below and write an essay of 500 words.

1. What causes people to end romantic relationships?

2. Why do people join gangs (or cults)?

3. Why did you choose the particular major you have chosen to study?

4. There are an increasing number of young men wearing their hair long today. What accounts for this new trend?

5. Granting college students inter-room visitation rights can have only positive results.

6. Raising the national speed limit to 65 miles per hour (mph) will have _____ effects.

7. The internet is one of the most advantageous/disadvantageous technological advances of our century.

8. Why do many people still participate in unprotected sex and/or have multiple sexual partners, despite warnings of the imminent dangers of such actions ?

9. A number of films today address real social issues of the present or past. What effect(s) does this type of film have on you or the public?

10. What causes a student to admire his/her teacher?

Assignment II
Choose one of the topics listed below and write a 700–1000 word causal analysis essay.

1. Certainly, community plays a role in the development of its inhabitants, but who or what plays the larger role? In essence, does environment play the most definitive role in the kind of person one becomes, or is there a more significant factor(s) than environment involved?

2. Today, many people have very different values and beliefs from their parents. Yet, in this age of constant change, this age of skepticism, this age of shocking fads and what some perceive as immoral, or even amoral, conduct, what accounts for the popularity of religious music? How does it differ from other music? What causes many people of different races to still love religious music?

3. With access to the Internet Superhighways, more people have access to confidential information than ever before. What has been the effect of this accessibility? What is likely to be the long term effect(s)?

4. We live in a society that spends millions of dollars a year on cosmetics, cologne, and wearing apparel that supposedly give us sex appeal; a society in which people have waged verbal war and won their battle to keep prayer out of schools; a society that was founded on principles of freedom and justice for all; and a society that prides itself on being *modern*. Yet, why does this same society quickly condemn others' sexual lifestyles and behavior when it in any way deviates from Biblical laws, the same source that emphasizes prayer? Why, especially, does this same society quickly expose, ridicule, and sometimes terminate people in high profile positions when their sexual lives or lifestyles in general differ from Biblical or moral teachings? In responding to these questions, consider figures like politicians, famous singers and stars, teachers, and clergymen.

Assignment III

1. Consider these questions: Is there a thin line between love and hate? If love leaves, was it love in the first place? Exactly what causes love to turn to hate? Now read the Biblical story of Joseph and his brothers (Genesis 37), look at a video of the movie *War of the Roses*, listen to a song that describes love that changed to hate. Write a paper explaining what causes love to turn to hate.

2. Excluding ethnic stereotypes, discuss the psychological and sociological effects of stereotyping. What kind of effect does the stereotyping have on self-image? On behavior? What are the occupational ramifications of stereotyping?

DEFINITION

As we go about our daily lives, we sometimes encounter words or concepts that cause us to pause to consider exactly what they mean. We have a "sense" of the meaning but are insecure in our complete understanding. Sometimes a simple trip to the dictionary is sufficient to define the term for us. At least we can find its denotation and gain some confidence in or knowledge of what the term means. However, often, the dictionary is insufficient in satisfying our curiosity about meaning. At those times we find ourselves explaining what a "thing" is not. Or we identify something similar to it. Also we may explain how it works or functions.

Each of these techniques is an appropriate manner of defining a "thing" or a "concept" when the dictionary definition (denotation) is not quite enough. We often use a combination of such techniques because we realize that a single technique may not adequately define a term. This combination represents the *extended definition*, which is a detailed explanation or clarification. Extended definition is useful and may even be necessary when you need to indicate nuances of abstract terms or concepts (freedom, honesty), slang (homeboy), trends (hip-hop culture), or when you wish to provide a subjective definition for a familiar or controversial term (affirmative action).

An essay which focuses on definition is necessarily an extended definition and requires you to employ many of the strategies mentioned above, as well as several other strategies. When you develop a definition essay, you must first determine your purpose. If your purpose is to provide information, you must provide details as objectively as you can so that your readers understand accurately the information you are providing. If, however, you wish to persuade your readers that a term has more meaning than is commonly offered, you might use techniques that allow you to be subjective in explaining what the term means to you. For instance, in the 80s and early 90s, the term "blue-eyed soul" was used to refer to singers like Michael Bolton and the duo Hall and Oates. If your purpose in defining this term is to inform, your main strategy of development might be illustration. If, however, you wish to convince your readers that "blue-eyed soul" is an imitation of "soul music" you might, in addition to providing examples, show negation or comparison and contrast. In most instances, your purpose will determine the strategies that will be most effective in defining the term or concept.

Whatever your purpose is, you should employ as many strategies as are effective in defining your term or concept. Make sure, however, that your strategies help to clarify rather than obscure the term. Some strategies that you may find effective are:

    a. negation (tell what the concept/thing is not)

    b. comparison/contrast (identify similarities or differences to like terms)

    c. function (explain the use)

    d. process analysis (explain how it works)

    e. description (provide physical detail)

    f. causal analysis (explain the causes or the effects)

    g. Illustration (give examples)

    h. narration (tell a brief story)

    i. history (provide historical data)

    j. synonyms (provide terms that may be familiar)

As you develop your essay, keep in mind that your goal is to explain or clarify a specific meaning for your audience. In that effort, you must be as detailed and as clear as you can. Avoid incomplete or circular definitions (e.g., comparison means to compare two subjects) that will send your readers elsewhere searching for further clarification. Even if your goal is to convince your readers that a term has meaning other than that with which they are familiar, clarity and specificity allow them to consider the plausibility of your argument.

Sample Essay #1

NO TIME FOR NO PRIDE

The quest for the true meaning of ethnic pride has divided the African American community. Without the lessons of their ancestors to guide them, many of today's generation of African Americans have resorted to superficial attempts to fill the void caused by the absence—often resulting in disaster—of ethnic pride. The irony of the situation is that ethnic pride is a simple concept. To have ethnic pride means to be aware of the history of one's ethnic group, to have no qualms about sharing that knowledge and experience with others, and to strive to live in a manner that would be commended by one's ancestors.

A wise man once said that "he who does not know his past is doomed to repeat it." The veracity of this statement has been proven through the degradation of black society over the last thirty years because that degradation is identical to the pattern of events that led to the ultimate downfall of many nations on the African continent. After being brought to America as slaves, Africans were sold to British colonists who used them to do manual labor which was considered too hard for white men. Finally, after a war which divided the United States, African Americans were given their freedom, but were afforded none of the privileges that men of no pigmentation received. In the 1950s and 1960s, African Americans rallied behind a handful of other African Americans who had a vision of a world which showed no favor to anyone on the basis of color. After multiple successes in having laws passed which would be of aid in the process of realizing that dream, many of the leaders were assassinated by those people who were too ignorant to understand that the leaders of the movement only wanted to make America a better place for all people. After the deaths of the leaders, a period of improvement for black people followed. More laws were passed which would ensure that a certain number of jobs, scholarships, and other programs would be set aside for African Americans each year, because otherwise white Americans would only give these things to other white Americans. This pattern would not continue for long, however.

The mid '80s produced a wayward generation of young African Americans. This generation took the education that it was being given for granted and turned its attention to less worthy pursuits. Larger and larger numbers of black males were convicted of felonies. More youths began to experiment with illegal drugs, and more were arrested for experimenting (or using drugs). The rate of increase of black-on-black crimes was alarmingly high. In effect, African Americans were proving to white Americans, who had just passed laws to give black people better chances to become successful in America, that black people were not worthy of the rights that they had just been given. African Americans were waging war on each other over petty things while white Americans signed contracts and passed laws which affected the world. But this was not the first time that black people had destroyed themselves by losing sight of the possible consequences of their actions. At the dawn of American slavery, warring African kingdoms would sell prisoners seized during battle to English and Dutch merchants as slaves. The prisoners were warriors, the brightest and strongest of their nations. In truth, the kingdoms were stripping each other of the ability to survive and selling it to the white men who grew rich from it. African Americans today are doing the same thing, except the slave owners are prisons and graves.

To be a paragon of ethnic pride, one must be willing to share knowledge not only with people of one's own ethnic group, but also with people of other ethnic groups as well. The man who became known as Malcolm X began his career as a Muslim preacher advocating the innate evil of all white men, and therefore sought only to enlighten African Americans. However, later in his life he learned that his message was meant for people of all colors. He also learned that all white people aren't evil, and he began to teach people of all colors. In Ralph Ellison's short story, "Flying Home," the "educated" young black man (Todd) believes himself to be above ordinary black people because he is a pilot for the army. His plane crashes, and he injures his ankle. An old black man (Jefferson) and his son find him lying in the middle of a field and attempt to help him. The old man sends his son after a white man who has been known to help black people on occasion. While his son is away, Jefferson tells Todd a story which was intended to convey how proud he was that Todd was a pilot, but Todd takes offense at the story and dismisses it as just the rambling of a stupid, country Negro. When the white man comes, Todd upsets him with his arrogant attitude. The white man loses his temper and is about to beat Todd, when Jefferson steps in and tactfully persuades the white man to let him and his son take Todd to the army base.

The old man had ethnic pride. He was proud of Todd's accomplishment and tried to help Todd even after Todd has been rude to him. Todd, on the other hand, had nothing even resembling pride in his heritage. During the entire story, Todd was continuously reminding himself that the reason that he had learned to fly was to get away from all of the ignorant black people. Instead of using his opportunity to help African Americans, he became a disgrace to his race. Despite all of his 'knowledge' Todd was ignorant of the true spiritual nature of African Americans. Paul Laurence Dunbar wrote a poem called "We Wear the Mask" which tells of how agonizing black life can be and how all black people wear masks to hide their true feelings from the rest of the world. Black people are able to suppress their emotions and smile. The first stanza of the poem says, "We smile, but O great Christ, our cries to thee from tortured souls arise,/ We sing, but O the clay is vile beneath our feet, and long the mile;/ But let the world dream otherwise,/ We wear the mask." This means that Christ feels all of "our" pain, and the mask has a purpose. One day the masks shall be taken off, and the world will be shocked to see what has been uncovered, but until then, "We wear the Mask." Jefferson wears the masks, but underneath it, he knows a lot more than Todd gives him credit for. It is this hidden knowledge that perhaps saves Todd's life.

Lifestyle is another important part of ethnic pride. If someone is proud of his ethnic heritage and understands the principles that were held dear to the hearts of his ancestors, then he must live a life that would both please his ancestors and show those who don't fully comprehend the meaning of ethnic pride how someone who does understand it should live. Maya Angelou's poem, "Still I Rise," describes the attitude of someone who is full of ethnic pride. She writes:

You may write me down in history
With your bitter, twisted lies,
You may trod me in the very dirt
But still, like dust, I'll rise.

. . . .

Out of the huts of history's shame
I rise
Up from a past that's rooted in pain
I rise
I'm a black ocean, leaping and wide,
Welling and swelling I bear in the tide.
Leaving behind nights of terror and fear
I rise
Into daybreak that's wondrously clear
I rise
Bringing the gifts that my ancestors gave,
I am the dream and the hope of the slave.
I rise
I rise
I rise

A person with an attitude like this embodies ethnic pride. Aware of the obstacles that he faces because of race, he is still proud to be black and would not choose any other color. No matter what bigots may do to hurt him, he will rise to complete his life's task, and on the way, he will help other African Americans. He truly is the "dream and hope of the slave" because he lives in a world where black people have been given the freedom to do anything that they put their minds to.

To have pride in his heritage, one must have knowledge, be able to apply it, and provide a good example for those around him. It is important that racial barriers fall, and they can begin to fall when each of us develops self-knowledge and self-love.

Sample Essay #2

FROM BOYS TO MEN

Theoretically, a man can be defined as an adult male that is homo sapien (human). However, in practice, being a man goes far beyond the theoretical definition. Being legally classified as a man goes far beyond the theoretical definition. One can be legally classified as a man without carrying himself as such. Specifically, being responsible, being humble, and being respectful are qualities which separate the men from the boys.

Being responsible is an extremely essential trait of a man. A man's responsibility is what determines whether he can take care of his various obligations (family, bills). For example, if one goes out and purchases an expensive stereo with most of his paycheck, which was to be used to pay the upcoming bills, then he is irresponsible and, therefore, not a man. Responsibility also requires that one does what is right in any situation. In "The Man Who Was Almost a Man," Dave is a prime example of one who doesn't do what is right. Dave is supposed to take the two dollars that he receives from his mother, buy a pistol for his dad, and take it to her to be concealed. When he buys the gun, he lies to his mother about where he put it and takes it to work with him the next morning. The end result is that Mr. Hawkins' (his employer's) mule is shot and killed by accident. Although Dave bought the gun because he thought that it would make him a man, his act of irresponsibility shows that he is still but an adolescent. This story is also a good example of why most good parents always emphasize responsibility. Without adequate responsibility, one cannot call himself a man, in the practical sense. Responsibility is only but one trait of a man, however.

Being humble is another characteristic that is a part of being a man. Being humble is not a characteristic that should be confused with being weak. It is actually a trait that should be associated with strength. Humbleness requires one to suppress his anger and use that energy in a more constructive manner. According to Rudyard Kipling, "If you can make one heap of all your winnings / And risk it on one turn of pitch and toss, / And lose, and start again at your beginnings / And never breathe a word about your loss," this makes one a man. Most people believe that complete expression of their anger makes them more of a man because it usually involves a demonstration of physical strength. However, this is the reason that many of them are either locked away in prison or dead. Had they remained humble and kept their anger under control, they wouldn't be in the predicament that they are in. As a result, each one of them could be considered more of a man.

Being respectful is the final characteristic of a real man. A real man is respectful to women, to his elders (his parents especially), and most of all, to himself. In "A Man That Was Almost A Man," Dave shows his disrespect for elders, including his parents, through his dishonesty. He lied to Mr. Hawkins about how his mule died, and he lied to his father concerning the final whereabouts of the pistol, saying that he threw it in the creek when he actually buried it next to a tree. This dishonesty is certainly disrespect toward these adults and their intelligence. Also, many consider themselves to be men; yet, they are the most guilty for disrespecting and degrading women. If a man feels that he has to disrespect women for whatever reason, then he is not really a man at all. He can be called an adolescent adult. However, for a man to respect women or his elders, he must first respect himself. If he doesn't respect himself, he can't truthfully respect anyone else and is, therefore, not a man.

Obviously, being a man is more than just being a human and a male that is at least twenty-one years of age. A man is not what one is but how he lives and carries himself. There are many adult male human beings. However, only a portion of them can be considered men.

Activity 1

Essay Development

A definition essay has been started for you below. Complete the thesis statement, develop the body paragraphs to support your thesis, and complete the concluding paragraph.

DEFINING FRIEND: A TRICKY TASK

"You just call out my name and you know wherever I am / I'll come running to see you again." "The good times, the bad times, I'll be on your side forever more,/ That's what friends are for . . .." We have heard them all, songs about friends; discussions about friends; and stories about friends; but we truly learn what a friend is through the relationships which we share with others over a period of time. Repeatedly, experience has proven that a friend is . . . .

First Body Paragraph

Second Body Paragraph

Third Body Paragraph

Some say you meet only one in a lifetime. And still others with a series of bad relationships with others may have resolved that there is no such thing. But experiences I have had have proven to me that there is such a jewel as a friend.

Activity 2

MINI-FIELD EXERCISES

1. Think about a special experience or event that occurred with you and your mother or father. Now write a 250–300 word narrative of that experience or event that will define what a "mother" or a "father" is.

2. Sometimes people use a pejorative term to define or describe someone whose behavior appears to be different from theirs or that of most people whom they know. Think about a personality from the music or film industry whose behavior or personality has been misunderstood/misperceived. What are some of the terms that have been used to define this person or his/her behavior? Cite them and then choose a term that better defines the person or his/her behavior and explain the appropriateness of your word choice for the person.

3. Poll at least fifteen people of different age groups and different ethnicities to discover how they define "life." Do they define "life" in the same way? Synthesize what your respondents have to say and in 250–300 words define "life," using illustration as the major strategy for development.

4. Freewrite about yourself for about fifteen minutes. Then stop and stare into a mirror. What do you see? Take five minutes and freewrite about yourself. Compare the two pieces of writing. How did you define yourself? Briefly (150–200 words) explain your perception of self.

Assignment I

Choose one of the topics listed below and write an essay of 500 words. Remember to employ as many defining techniques as necessary to ensure that your definition is comprehensive enough that your audience will know what the term means from your point of view.

1. Hip-hop Culture
2. Common Sense
3. Trash TV
4. Big Mama
5. Depressed
6. Baby Boomer
7. Lady
8. Decency
9. Rebel
10. Wanna-Be

Assignment II

Choose one of the topics listed below and write a 700–1000 word definition essay.

1. Using a fictional character, historical figure, contemporary person, define the term "hero."

2. Using a poem, song lyrics, and a movie, write a paper defining "love."

3. Using the elements (air, water, fire, earth) and some other product of nature, such as a plant or flower, insect, or mineral, write a paper defining yourself.

4. Choose a professional from three different sports and write an essay defining the superstar athlete.

Assignment III

1. Survey a representative number of your classmates or dorm mates to determine their definition of the ideal relationship/perfect date. Use as many of the techniques for defining as you find appropriate in your queries. For example, encourage your respondents, to provide *examples,* or *anecdotes,* to make *comparisons* or to explain what makes a date perfect or a relationship ideal. Analyze your responses to determine what represents for most of your peers the "perfect date" or the "ideal relationship." Write an essay which might appear in the feature section of your college newspaper.

2. In an era in which the media provides immediate access to nudity, profanity, and obscenity and therefore makes us less sensitive to that which once was considered socially taboo, what now defines "indecent"?

ARGUMENTATION

Throughout the text we have indicated that strategies used in writing essays are the same strategies that are used every day in oral communication and in performing various life tasks. We make descriptions, recant happenings or chronicle events, clarify through specific examples, provide instructions, point out similarities and differences, show causal relationships, and define and redefine everything. Now we address *argumentation* or *persuasion*—the fourth type of written discourse.

Of course, all of the writing strategies discussed are persuasive to a certain extent in that you as the writer want your audience to recognize that you can substantiate your thesis. This is why you use numerous specific details to support topic sentences or give equal analysis to points in comparison. In these, argument alone is not the sole purpose as it is in this fourth type of discourse. With argumentative discourse, you, as the writer, write for the sole purpose of persuading your audience to take your side, adopt your view or take some suggested action, trust your judgment, or, if nothing else, confirm that you have a very valid view. Unlike the arguments that you may sometimes engage in with friends or associates, wherein you often allow subjectivity to rule your reasoning and judgment, in writing arguments you must always be objective, provide concrete detail, and remain focused. The following two types of argumentation will be discussed in this section: the *position paper* and the *proposal*.

THE POSITION PAPER

In any argument, people usually take one position—one stand—on something that another or others oppose. The same is true of the written argument. In the position paper you will agree or disagree about a subject or issue—a controversial subject, such as living together without marriage, capital punishment, or pornography. Since you must discuss a debatable subject in the position paper, you *must* take a position *for* or *against*, or you must *agree* or *disagree*. There can be no "middle of the road" position or "maybe" stance. Therefore, when you write your position essay, be certain to choose a subject with which you are very familiar or one about which you have a strong opinion. You might wish to spend sufficient time brainstorming or writing a jot list to determine your true position on the topic(s) at hand before you begin your draft. Sometimes, people believe they hold one view about a controversial issue but discover that they cannot write 500 words or more about their position because they have only *one* reason for believing what they believe. You must be able to provide several strong points to support your position, points that are not subjective or overlapping. On occasion you might be able to provide more specific points to support a side of an issue (Side A) that you oppose than the one you hold dear (Side B). If time is an issue, you might wish to write in support of Side A rather than repeat the same point about Side B, resulting in a weak argument and consequently a grade that does not reflect your writing ability. Your other obvious option is to choose a different topic. In either case, make certain that your thesis statement explicitly reflects your position on the topic.

In some instances, you will need to provide limited background on the subject, if you are writing about an issue that may not be as global as debatable issues such as abortion or euthanasia. In a short essay (500 words) this brief information would appear in the introductory paragraph, or in a longer essay (750 words or more), a short transitional paragraph after the introduction should suffice.

Then you are ready to write the body of the essay. Here you defend your position by providing unbiased, accurate details. You may provide a few personal experiences, but in your attempt to remain as objective as possible, keep these to a minimum as you cite illustrations about acquaintances' experiences, case studies, statistics, and similar details. Draw upon other writing strategies discussed, if necessary, to prove your point—strategies such as narration, definition, description. The point to remember is that you must present a strong case, and you cannot achieve this end by piling generalization upon generalization.

Show that you are thoroughly knowledgeable about your topic, the pros and the cons. To make an informed decision you must know and let your audience know that you have thought about your subject thoroughly before forming your opinion; however, you should not write "I believe," "I think," or "I feel" in the paper itself. You must indicate that you are a logical thinker, and as such, you anticipate the opponent's objections to your arguments, conceding when your opponent may have a valid or worthwhile question or criticism, but countering that question or criticism with some reasonable explanation or possibility that will show the merit of your position.

As a logical thinker you want to show that you exercise reason over emotion in defining your position, but some emotional appeal will influence your audience to adopt your belief or take the action that you wish them to take. Although most position papers address philosophical issues, some also seek to rouse audiences to action to vote for or against something, such as the right to life bill or the proposition to require the homeless to go to shelters or face imprisonment. In the former case, you might write a graphic description of an abused child who was abandoned at two years of age by a parent who was forced to have the child in the first place, thereby causing someone to question whether women should be forced to have children whom they conceive. Or in the latter situation, you might admonish your audience to force the homeless into shelters as an act of obedience to the Christian challenge to remember the poor. Surely, some of your audience will share sentiments after such comments. But piling a series of similar statements into your paper might defeat your effort as readers dismiss you as an overly sensitive "do-gooder." So, practice caution in using emotional appeals. Try to balance logic (reason) with emotion. When in doubt, rely on logic.

Of utmost importance in writing the position paper is the organization of your supporting points. While a few teachers may encourage you to place your most important supporting point first, most agree that presenting the most crucial point last is a more emphatic means of organizing the position paper. Readers are more likely to be affected by what they see last than what they see initially. Of course, that also means that an effective conclusion is a crucial requirement of this essay.

Sample Essay #1

THE VOICE OF A NEW GENERATION

It is no secret that many rap songs have explicit lyrics implying violence. To many, rap is viewed as an unneeded advocate of violence and should be thoroughly censored, if not banned altogether. Surprisingly, television and the movies are not under as much scrutiny as rap is. This new age form of music is, like most other forms of music, an artistic expression. Being a form of expression, rap music explains and describes how life in America is, as the rapper perceives it, for himself (or herself) as a black person and for black people in general, and for the black male in particular. Therefore, this form of "cultural" expression should not be subjected to any form of censorship.

On practically every rap album there is usually some form of anger or, as some might put it, some type of "violence" expressed. This expression is nothing more than a reaction to a sometimes violent environment. Most rap artists profess contempt toward the American government (i.e., the police and the justice system) and government officials and representatives for the unequal oppressive status that the majority of black people are in, socially, economically, and/or politically. In this sense, rap music becomes a powerful medium by which America is continuously made aware of the feelings of those black people who suffer any injustices. An example of this continuous awareness is expressed in the rap group Ghetto Boyz/s hit, "Crooked Officer." In this song one of the members of the group explains what he is going to do (or at least attempt to do) to any police officer who "tries" him like those officers who "tried" Rodney King. He explains:

> . . . just like Rodney King
> But if you try that sh.. With me its gonna
> be a different scene,
> . . . .
> . . . .
> Cause I'm comin' after yo' a.. Crooked
> officer!

It is indeed logical to conclude that broadcasting this kind of violence is doing nothing but encouraging it. However, the same could be and has been said about television, which has yet to be banned or censored.

Most rap music expresses a concern for the plighted position that black people in America are in. No longer is it just an expression (good or bad), but it becomes one of numerous political devices that seek to unite the black community. One might argue that rap music does the antithesis, and prior to the 1990s this may have been a good argument. However, if one is a true listener of (old school) rap, he/she will find that the big name rappers promote unity within the black community. Two good examples of rappers whose lyrics promote unity are Queen Latifah and Tupac Shakur. In her song "U.N.I.T.Y.," Queen Latifah calls for complete unity of the black community, and she strongly criticizes brothers that refer to sisters as "bitch" or "ho." In "Keep Your Head Up" Tupac expresses his sympathy for black women, especially those in the ghetto who have been abandoned, with their children, by black men. He strongly condemns the black man for his action and implores him to stop deserting his woman and unite with her. These are the typical strategies of most of the contemporary rap artists.

Rap music has become a strong voice throughout America. Just like television and the movies, rap has been accused of instigating violence in an already volatile society. But censoring rap without censoring television and movies is hardly a solution. Unlike television and the movies, which seek to entertain, rap ultimately seeks to educate and effect change.

Sample Essay #2

THE CHRISTIAN CHURCH

It is said that God made man in His own image. If the New Testament instructs us to live our life as Jesus lived His, why is there so much corruption in our communities? Worst, why is there so much corruption in our churches? Has the modern day Christian church failed the flock of God? Apparently so.

A religion, as defined by anthropologists, is a spiritual belief shared by a group of people. The icon of that religion answers the unbelievable. Today, throughout America, religion has become a business, often an unscrupulous business seen and heard on the television and the radio. But what happened to cause the church to go corrupt? One can trace one of the problems of the church back to Europe during the mid-18th century. During this time, the Pope was the highest religious figure. Below the Pope were the archbishops who were noblemen. What happened was that a son of a nobleman would assume high positions under the Pope. It's important to note that these appointments weren't always a result of a nobleman receiving his calling. Many appointments were made as a result of political and business transactions. Under the noblemen was the peasant; the peasants would become monks, the lowest religious figures. Historians cite the fact that many of the laws passed were to benefit the clergy and the noblemen. The peasants were charged for taxes by the local government. They were charged rent for untaxed land owned by the church. They were forced to pay ten percent of their income. We know this today as paying tithes. The church during this time was exempt from paying taxes. So, it's safe to say that the church was powerful and had much influence on the people and government.

Today, churches ask that their members pay a tithe, a penny collection, a love offering, and sometimes a collection to pay the minister on his anniversary. All of the money received from the various offerings, as well as the land owned by the church, is exempt from taxes. Now the preacher is quick to say that when a man robs God he adds to his damnation. Where does all of this money go? If God is the creator of life and everything that surrounds that life, why are men and women using His name to benefit themselves? Perhaps the church today is a business that makes some individuals rich.

The church has programmed its members to hate instead of love. In St. Matthew 7:1, Jesus tells us "to judge ye not." He even leaves us two commandments. The first is to love Him. The second is to love one another as He loved us. These aren't the only scriptures in the Bible that instruct us to love everyone. Yet, Christians argue with one another on who's in the right denomination: which is more correct, the Holiness preacher or the Baptist preacher; why can't my sister be a Methodist even though my mom is a Presbyterian? God is not the author of destruction. He is the author of peace. It is not the Bible that leads its readers to hate; often it is the teacher of the Bible that leads the followers of Christ to hate. The concept that one's religion is better than another's is based on the same ethnocentric view that says one's race and culture is better than that of others.

Another program that is killing the heart of loving people is the childish conversation that deals with the color of Jesus. Now Michelangelo was commissioned by the Pope to paint a picture of Jesus, Mary, and Joseph. For his models, it is said he used his aunt, uncle, and cousin. They, of course, were blond headed with blue eyes. The Bible says Jesus had hair of wool. His skin was like burned brass. His eyes were red like fire. His voice was like the roar of the ocean. Now these are descriptions that supposedly give one the identity of Jesus. But Jesus did not say only black people are my children; nor did he say only white people are my children. Why do we spend our time discussing the color of Jesus? We should be investing our time in what He said and what He did.

The preacher begins to preach. He starts off singing a hymn. Then he reads a scripture. After doing this, he elaborates on the scripture he read. At a certain time the preacher begins to emphasize certain words. He begins to move around in the pulpit. He looks a man in the eye and tells him he's going to hell unless he repents of all of his sins. The preacher begins to give a vivid description of how hot hell is. Then he turns to a sister and shouts, "Have mercy on me!" By now the pianist has begun to play different songs that complement the preacher's voice. Meanwhile, an elderly woman jumps up and down, with her hands in the air, face upward, tears running down her face as she shouts, "Thank you, Jesus."

After all the music and shouting have reached a climax, the preacher "opens the doors of the church." No one joins this Sunday. After church, the preacher asks one of the members how much she enjoyed his sermon. She replies by saying that she loved it. But in her heart and in her mind, she loves the drama of his sermon. She could not tell you what he said to save her life. For once, I would like to attend a church and *hear* a sermon, not just listen. You can listen and not hear. Many people go to church and receive emotional rhetoric. Their energy reaches a high. But their knowledge remains the same. There has to be a balance that allows one to receive knowledge as well as an emotional high from a sermon.

The church is an institution that dates back before Christ. When used in ways that hinder the spiritual growth of a person, the church ceases to be needed. This belief holds true for any faith that fails to deliver as it should.

Assignment I

Choose one of the topics listed below and write a position paper.

1. Interracial adoptions should/should not be allowed.

2. Former sexual offenders do/do not deserve anonymity.

3. A criminal sentenced to death should/should not be given a specified number of appeals.

4. In light of the increased use of hazardous homemade hallucinogens, marijuana should/should not be legalized.

5. In professional sports tougher penalties should/should not be imposed for unsportsmanlike conduct that causes personal injury or property damage.

6. As we approach the twenty-first century, Affirmative Action is/is not needed.

7. Same-sex marriages should/should not be acceptable (legal).

8   Professionals, minorities in particular, who have creative control in movies or T.V. series have/do not have a responsibility to present positive images.

9. Teenagers who commit violent crimes should/should not be given the same judicial treatment as that given to adults.

10. Tobacco companies should/should not be held responsible for health problems or death resulting from illness(es) contracted through smoking.

Assignment II

Divide the class into three groups and choose a controversial subject to debate. One-third of the class will present the pros of the issue; one-third will present the cons; and the other third will evaluate both groups for effective argumentation. The topic choices for your debate follow.

1. Women and men should undergo the same training at military schools and basic training installations.

2. There is a time to hate. There is a time to kill.

THE PROPOSAL

In the previous discussion you learned about presenting the written philosophical argument—the position paper—the most common argumentative essay. Now you will learn about the second most common type of written argument—the proposal—the problem solving feature of writing, arguing for some action to occur.

In writing the proposal you offer a solution for some existing or potential problem—not just an annoyance but some problem that is threatening to the welfare of someone or the productivity or survival of some institution or entity.

Provide background information about your situation (define the problem), unless you know that the audience is very familiar with the situation at hand. For example, if you are proposing a solution to the parking problem on your campus and you know that your audience consists of faculty, students, and staff, you will not need to provide as many specific details as you would provide for an audience unfamiliar with your campus. The summary of the definition of the problem should be no more than one-fourth of the proposal itself.

The body of the proposal will be a series of significant steps involved in the implementation of your solution to the problem which you identify in the introduction. Your plan must indicate that you have given the problem and solution much thought, critical thought, weighing the pros against the cons. You acknowledge this in the essay by citing what has already been done to solve the problem and indicating why this solution has proven ineffectual. As an objective thinker, you do not use this opportunity to make personal attacks on another person, organization, or company. Simply explain that whatever solution currently attempted has had little positive change or effect, has made the situation at hand worse, or created a new set of problems. In some cases, the previous theorized solution may, in fact, have yielded some measure of improvement. If it has, concede that advantage but stress the fact that the solution that you have in mind will resolve the existing problem more quickly and more effectively. Your audience will respect you and pay more attention to your plan.

In providing your solution, be certain to state all significant details about how the problem should be resolved. Provide answers to questions like these: Who will be responsible for executing the task? What preliminary work, if any, must be done? For instance, will there be a petition to sign? Letters to write? What, if any, materials will be needed? How much money will be needed? Where will the money come from? How will it be disbursed? Who will disburse it? What other resources will be needed? What timeline is involved for completion of said task? What other outcomes other than the obvious—that stipulated in the thesis—will come out of this? Responses to these questions may be addressed in general body narrative without subheadings to identify problem, plan implementation, results and so forth, or you may use these or other headings that you desire.

These and/or similar questions must be addressed in a logical order. And since proposals are *always* read, but not always presented orally as well, you need to provide all data necessary to persuade your audience, who will approve by voting for it or funding the proposal and/or executing it. You will do a more effective job if you consider your opponents' objections, so raise them and refute them. For instance, proposing that your school hire more personnel to help at a time when the school is experiencing financial difficulties might well add to the existing financial problem;

nevertheless, you would counter that objection to your proposal for hiring the additional staff by pointing out how these additional workers would enhance the school's image that has been hurt by the yearly criticism of the registration process at the school, causing student and staff frustration and possibly deter someone from attending the school. And you might also indicate that these additional staff members who work with registration once or twice a semester can be given some other assignments during non-registration periods, perhaps in administration, thereby increasing efficiency in the workplace.

Be certain to clarify any terminology that others might not readily understand. Most proposals are written in a businesslike tone, but some are humorous or satiric, depending upon the subject, or your objective. In Jonathan Swift's plan, *A Modest Proposal*, the author proposes cannibalism as a means of shocking and shaming those with power to do so to enact laws or take action to help feed the starving Irish population in the eighteenth century. You also might wish to provide a satirical proposal to some serious problem. Always think carefully about your complaint or problem and the most *feasible* solution to that problem. Then argue your case, always aware that the best argument—the best sales pitch, in this case—for your proposal is the expressed need, implementation plan, clarity of your strengths and possible drawbacks and feasibility of your proposal itself.

Sample Essay #1

BACK TO THE COMMUNITY

One of the ongoing contemporary problems plaguing our country is juvenile crime. There is a constant state of fear in which American cities find themselves where the juvenile is concerned, and as he/she continues wreaking havoc across this country, that constant state of fear will remain in the hearts of the "good" citizens here. So what do we do about it?

The first thing we can do is to stop focusing on intervention and dedicate ourselves to prevention. Once youth begin committing crimes, intervention programs have proven to be, for the most part, futile. If government is truly concerned about crime, preventive measures must be devised and implemented. One of these measures would require local government to give parents the right to discipline their children in a way that is consistent with their particular culture. Putting the millions of dollars that are being wasted on some juvenile intervention programs, such as boot camps, into communities would be the other contributing factor in alleviating the juvenile crime problem.

The fundamental problem with juveniles is discipline. It seems that whenever a discussion of juvenile crime occurs, there is always mention made of the legal liabilities for disciplining one's children. Many adults recount stories of how they were "beaten" by their parents (or grandparents, aunts, uncles, neighbors) whenever they *needed* it. If a child got out of his/her place, then that child was instantaneously "tended" to. Now the local HRS department is, to a great extent, an overseer of the family. HRS can legally punish parents who they perceive as "abusive" to their children, and at the same time critics accuse parents of permissiveness. It is as though parents are in a "damned-if-you-do, damned-if-you-don't" situation. With so many youths finding themselves caught up in the criminal justice system—if they are lucky—or dead (if they are not), America's future seems endangered.

The trend in many cities now is the boot camp. This plan typically consists of four phases which, respectively, include four months of intensive miliary drills and exercise; focus on education and reintroduction into the community; three month follow up care, with continued visits to the camps; and total reintegration into the community. This plan seems to give the local government control and authority over the child and renders the parents and community powerless. This form of "child rearing" is insensitive. The power must be given back to the parents.

The money that cities put into boot camps can truly save our community and the cities from inevitable social disaster. Half of the money spent annually could generate enough jobs in urban areas around the country to significantly lower unemployment rates, especially among youth. In a matter of years run-down communities would be filled with life and could become economically viable. Unfortunately, there is no doubt that there would be individuals who would continue to commit crimes, as there have always been, but the re-established integrity of the urban community would make those individuals the minority.

A genuine interest in the lives of youth would mandate the implementation of preventive measures to stop juvenile crime. The continued focus on the victims, the offenders themselves, and parents (in addition to the citizens who are victimized), will give only a partial picture of the problem. When officials begin to analyze the problems that cause youth to resort to criminal alternatives such as those mentioned above, then and only then can we begin to resolve the problems in our communities. This pragmatic approach can do more harm than building more institutions to house criminals does. Anything short of this preventive approach would continue to cost us our young and ultimately our future.

Sample Essay #2

A PROPOSAL FOR HELPING THE HOMELESS

Each year millions of people are forced to live a life of wandering through streets and down dark alleys seeking shelter beneath cardboard boxes and satisfying their hunger with whatever leftovers they are able to find. The irony is that many of these downtrodden souls—homeless people, which include children—are citizens of one of the wealthiest nations in the world—America. Of course, different organizations accept donations, food, and clothing to aid this ever increasingly homeless population. However, shouldn't our government play a role in solving this crisis? Should the American people be held responsible for people who eat out of trash cans? Unfortunately, federal assistance is only given to those who qualify for it, so many homeless people starve. It stands to reason that there will always be a homeless population, but what if Congress were to pass laws to help vagabonds improve their lot in life? Would new legislation serve to remedy some of the problems faced by many of America's homeless population?

To make any significant improvements in policy, one has to recognize the possible economic impact that such policy will have on each citizen. Therefore, the American public has to understand that everyone must be willing to provide some type of financial assistance to offset many of the expenses that will accrue to implement many of the programs that will be created. Naturally, one would suggest that if a family earns over two hundred thousand dollars a year, it should be taxed more than a family that earns twenty-four thousand dollars a year. However, taxing one portion of the population still is not going to remedy many of the ailments of the homeless. What if Congress were to pass a bill that required that a small percentage of each customer's utility bill or any such household bill were to provide assistance to those new programs? The money generated could go to building more advanced shelters that could provide resources that may help the homeless help themselves. Also, the money received could be used to prevent would-be vagrants from entering a life of begging by providing them with employable skills.

At many corners, men hold signs that read, "Disabled Vet. Will Work for Food." A man or woman who has risked his or her life for his country should not have to beg. Contrary to many stereotypes, many homeless people never served in the military. Some were teachers who for 8-9 hours a day were expected to prepare students for the challenges of tomorrow, and some were business people whose every move determined the fate of hundreds of employees. Many of these same people were mothers and fathers who were affected by downsizing or false litigation. Having served their country well, they should now be served. One feasible solution would be for Congress to set up a system that would allow for a portion of an employee's pay to go to some type of emergency relief fund. In the case of the soldier, instead of making the soldier pay taxes, take that taxable percentage and establish colleges for veterans using old military bases for educational facilities. This plan would make the transition from being a paid, secured soldier to being a working blue or white collar worker much easier. What happens in many cases is that the military prepares most soldiers to serve the government instead of preparing them to serve the people. A similar proposal could be made for all other employees. The closest thing that resembles such a notion is the present social security system, which is forever being scrutinized for its lack of "security." Most employees may oppose such a bill, but one never knows when he or she will be forced to rely on such a program.

Every night in America, restaurants throw food away that was not sold nor eaten that evening. Grocery stores send damaged merchandise back to the warehouse; in many cases, the merchandise ends up in the trash can. Congress should pass a bill that would fine restaurants and grocery stores for throwing away food and nonperishable items. As Americans, most are privileged to enjoy many of the finer things in life. Unfortunately, many tend to place less value on extensive consumption because they have been taught to live in excess. Therefore, one can understand how restaurants and grocery stores are able to discard with many vital resources because the consumer is taught to throw excess products away. Subsequently, many homeless people who would benefit from this excess never fully reap any assistance until they wander at night and discover much of the "waste" that has been created by many American's obsession with excess. Also, Congress should compensate those very same entities for donating groceries which would otherwise be discarded. Congress could give restaurants and grocery stores some type of allowance (subsidy) from the government. With this allowance the business would be able to employ people that can cook that restaurant's food for homeless people at shelters. Grocery stores would be able to donate food as write-offs on their taxes.

The knowledge that millions of people walk the streets day and night should make those fortunate Americans appreciate what they have. In a time when a man can be sent to explore the never ending universe, it is absurd to think that America cannot solve a problem that definitely affects the very fabric of its culture. The suggestions proposed in this essay will not alleviate homelessness. But the writer hopes that as America continues to strive for greatness, many of its citizens' basic needs will be met. Each citizen should take it upon himself to improve the well being of at least one homeless person—if not by considering the aforementioned suggestions, then by resorting to any means necessary.

Assignment I

Choose one of the topics below and write a proposal.

1. A plan to handle crowd control at social events sponsored by your school (or fraternity/sorority/organization).
2. An effective way to punish and rehabilitate child offenders.
3. A plan to improve student-teacher relations in your department.
4. A plan to improve dissemination of student news (deadlines, registration, graduation, career placement, social/cultural activities) at your school.
5. A plan to secure funding for a student-run business.
6. A plan to solve the drug problem in your community.
7. A plan to get funding for a park, recreation center, or gym near your community.
8. The method(s) to revitalize some floundering business.
9. A plan to develop an arts program.

10. A plan to end feuding between two friends (neighbors or relatives) of yours.

Assignment II

Divide the class into four groups and write a proposal on one of the topics listed below. Each group will have to present its proposal to the class and will be evaluated by the class.

1. A proposal for retooling Affirmative Action laws.

2. A proposal to outlaw Freshman Composition.

7

Using Literature as a Source in Writing

SELECTED LITERARY ANALYSIS

You have already studied basic essay organization and development. You have learned about the thesis statement and its function, the topic sentence and its relationship to the rest of the body paragraph, and the makeup and function of the introduction, body, and conclusion. You have also become acquainted with the various rhetorical patterns—classification, comparison/contrast, process analysis and the like. When writing about literature, you will find yourself employing the same writing skills and applying the same knowledge you acquired in studying the rudiments of the essay. However, writing about literature takes you a few steps further than just organizing and developing ideas based solely upon your own observations, experiences, opinions, or beliefs.

Writing an essay about literature compels you to focus on an author's work and formulate a response to the entire work or analyze various elements within a literary work. You may want to extend your observations beyond a single work and compare and/or contrast specific elements of two or more works by an author or compare and/or contrast the themes, use of symbols, or the choice of meter used in the works of two or more authors. On the other hand, you may want to analyze the process that a poet uses to construct a sonnet, or you may choose to classify certain novels according to theme, characterization, or point of view. Remember, although you are now writing about literature, you will still need to use your previously acquired knowledge and writing skills.

Also remember, however, that constructing the literary essay does require some special considerations. Before you undertake this somewhat new endeavor, there are some aspects of literature with which you need to be familiar. First of all, you should need to have a clear understanding of the four basic genres of literature: prose fiction, drama, poetry, and non-fiction. In addition, you need to recognize various literary elements—at least the major ones. The capsuled definitions below and their accompanying brief discussions will help you to get started in understanding literature and then writing about it.

Genres

Critical discussion of literature classifies it into four major genres (kinds or types), which include prose fiction, drama, poetry, and non-fiction. These major genres are subdivided into less broad categories which include short stories and novels (prose fiction), tragedies and comedies (drama), lyrics, odes, ballads (poetry), and non-fiction prose (essays).

Prose Fiction

Novels and short stories, usually written in prose, present a set of circumstances in which the writer manipulates characters, actions, dialogue, and setting. Sometimes symbolism and imagery are dominant features in novels and short stories. However, plot and character development are the essentials of fiction and are often grounded in conflict, the resolution (or non resolution) of which enables the writer to express a point of view about humanity and about life. Novels may be further sub-divided into types such as romance, detective, or epistolary because of features exclusive to these types.

Poetry

The features of poetry include rhyme, versification, and rhythm (meter). Like fiction and drama, most poetry tries to express some point about humans or the things with which humans are concerned—love, nature, life, death—but unlike fiction or drama, poems make those points concisely by using figurative language and imagery. Not all poems rhyme or have rhythm. Blank verse, for instance, employs/uses no rhyme; free verse uses neither rhythm nor rhyme. Poetry is further categorized according to form (sonnet, *haiku*), content (ballads, dramatic monologue), and language (elegy, ode).

Drama

Like fiction, drama focuses on character and dialogue as elements that enable the dramatist to espouse his or her point of view about humanity and life issues. Dialogue is usually the most dominant feature in a drama, although other elements like setting and stage directions combine to help the writer convey his or her main point. Most dramas are written to be performed; so the ability to *see* characters—their facial expressions, their dress, their movements—is an added feature of the drama. Dramas are often categorized as tragedy, comedy, historical, absurd, and others.

Non-fiction Prose

Non-fiction prose includes essays, biographies, and speeches as well as textbooks and historical and scientific data. This type of prose usually explains or clarifies some idea, principle, or position. It can be instructive and/or persuasive.

Literary Analysis

To write effective essays using literature as your source or to write effective literary analyses, you must have an understanding of salient features that are found in fiction, drama, and poetry. The following is an explanation of the most common features that appear in these groups: plot, structure, setting, foreshadowing, climax, character, conflict, theme, point of view, imagery, symbol, irony, satire, figurative language, meter, rhyme, and alliteration.

Plot: the sequence of actions or events that occur in a literary work. There may be subplots within the larger storyline. Only occasionally will poems, however, have plots. Robert Browning's "Porphyria's Lover" is such a poem.

Structure: the arrangement or outline of the plot development, such as rhyme and meter in poems, acts and scenes in drama, letters (epistolary) in novels.

Setting: time, place, and atmosphere of a literary work. A drama may be set in Tallahassee, Florida, in 1930, in a log cabin on a rural road.

Foreshadowing: comments or clues about an occurrence(s) in a work prior to the actual occurrence(s) itself.

Conflict: confrontation or strife between two opposing forces.

Climax: the point in which conflict or strife reaches its most intense point, leading to the resolution of the conflict.

Character: fictional person or persons who play a role in the work. A character does not have to be human. Sometimes institutions, nature, or inanimate creatures may be the character(s). The major character in a work is called the protagonist, and the antagonist is the character or thing that opposes the protagonist.

Theme: a main point or central idea in literary works.

Point of View: how the story is told. The person who actually tells the story is called the narrator. Usually, the narrator is not the author. When told from the first-person perspective, the narrator is a participant in the events in the story or has close observation of them. If the story is told from a third person perspective, the narrator is a reporter, an observer. He tells what the characters say or do, sometimes giving an assessment of their behavior. The third-person narrator may tell what the characters think as well. In the latter case, the narrator is called *omniscient* (all-knowing); when he provides limited knowledge, he is *limited.*

Imagery: sensory impressions that are produced by certain descriptions in the work, i. e., what can be seen, heard, smelled, tasted, or touched simply by the reading of the work.

Symbol: any object, person, or place that represents itself while suggesting one thing or several, quite often an abstraction, such as peace.

Irony: incongruence between what is and what is believed. The three types of irony are verbal, situational, and dramatic. With *verbal* irony, what the character says differs from what he/she means. With *situational* irony, what occurs differs from what was expected; and finally, with *dramatic* irony, the character's understanding or perception of what occurs differs from the audience's knowledge of it or what the author intends.

Satire: use of ridicule to condemn some type of action or the lack thereof, usually written with the intent to effect some action or improvement.

Figurative Language: language that compares either through implication or direct expression. For instance, a *simile* compares using *like* or *as*; a metaphor implies that something *is* something else.

Meter: various stress alterations of a line (primarily found in poetry).

Rhyme: a similarity in sound, usually heard in line endings of poems.

Alliteration: the repetition of initial consonant sounds.

WRITING ABOUT CHARACTER

In literature classes or during class discussions of literature as the source for writing, students are often asked to write a character analysis or characterization paper. In writing the character analysis essay, you will tell what kind of person the character(s) in a work is. Is the character kind, mean-spirited, gifted, evil, or innately good? Does the character remain the same or change? In writing the characterization essay, you consider how the author creates the character. More specifically, in writing about character and/or characterization, you should read the literary work and consider the following:

1. what the character says
2. what the character means
3. whether the character is believable
4. what the narrator says about the character
5. what the other characters say about the character
6. what the other characters say to the character
7. what the character does.

Sample Essay #1

BENEATH THE COSTUME

It is carnival time in the town, and both Montresor and Fortunato, the only two characters in Edgar Allen Poe's "The Cask of Amontillado," are dressed for the occasion. In fact, their wearing apparel does more than just fit the occasion—it also fits the nature of each man. In this short story, Poe uses costuming in an almost allegorical fashion to allow the audience to readily discern the true character of Fortunato and Montresor.

Fortunato, the object of Montresor's revenge, is dressed in a costume that represents his gay, but foolish, nature. "The man wore motley [a fabric that has many bright colors]. He had on a tight-fitting parti striped dress, and his head was surmounted by the conical cap and bells."

Fortunato, in essence, is dressed like a court jester—a fool or buffoon. Throughout Montresor's execution of his plot to take Fortunato's life, he, Fortunato, laughs and makes merry, totally unaware of his impending demise, in spite of the many indications and references that Montresor makes to vengeance and to the past. Even after he has been physically seized by Montresor in the catacombs, he continues to laugh, and the bells on his conical cap continue to jingle. Even when he is bound with shackles, he says to Montresor, "Ha! ha! ha!—he! he! he!—a very good joke indeed—an excellent jest." Fortunato is obviously a person who is deficient in judgement and understanding. His costume does not belie his true character.

Like Fortunato, Montresor is appropriately costumed. He is a man who wishes to hide deceit. In fact, Montresor recounts, "It must be understood that neither by word nor by deed had I caused Fortunato to doubt my good will." Thus, he dons a mask of black silk and draws a roguelaire (a short cloak) about him. With a smile and words of friendship, he lures an unsuspecting Fortunato to his death. Montresor, always careful to disguise the blackness of his heart and intentions, does not dare to allow his bent toward "vengeance without impunity" to be seen. Therefore, he wears a black mask to cover his face and a cloak to cover his body. Both are used figuratively to cover that which is underneath; Montresor is dressed to conceal his intentions, as well as his true character.

The essence of each man's character is a story of contrasts and costumes. Fortunato is a foolish, but likeable, character, who is out to enjoy the festivities of the carnival and of life. He is a colorful character filled with mirth. His costume of bright colors and jingling bells attests to who he is. Montresor, on the other hand, is a man hardened by the desire for vengeance. He is a cold, calculating individual who has a definite dark and deceitful side. What would be more fitting apparel for him than a cloak and a black mask? In each case, the costume for the carnival depicts the character of the man.

What's behind a costume? Could it merely be the desire to dress for a special occasion? Could it be an attempt to cover true feelings? Or could it be used to highlight the character of the man who wears it?

Sample Essay #2

MR. AND MRS. WRIGHT: A STILL LIFE SKETCH

"A Jury of Her Peers" is a narrative of a woman who used to be happy singing in the choir and wearing pretty dresses. Now, she is married to a man who is almost the total opposite of herself—quiet and introverted. He is so used to peace and quiet that he wants it at all times, so he makes his home in an out of the way place where he will not be disturbed much, does not install a telephone because he does not want people to call him, and discourages visitors from coming to their home. Minnie needs companionship, so she buys a canary. The bird's singing disturbs Mr. Wright so much that in his rage he breaks the bird cage and strangles the bird. The strangled bird provides insight into the characters of Minnie Wright and her husband.

Minnie Wright lived an isolated and lonely life. The Wright house is far away from other houses in the town. The house is described as "a lonesome-looking place. It was down in a hollow, and the popular trees around it were lonesome looking trees" (293). Mr Wright is used to peace and quiet, and when he marries Minnie, he continues his ways. He refuses to install a telephone in their home because he does not want people to have such easy access to him. He does not want to be bothered by people in the town. The people of the town know that Mr. Wright enjoys quiet and do not disturb him. Mrs. Hale, one of the main characters in the story, never visited her friend, Minnie, because of John Wright.

Mr. Wright was a very controlled man, except when his peace and quiet were disturbed. Mrs. Hale describes him: "He didn't drink, and kept his word as well as most, I guess, and paid his debts. But he was a hard man, Mrs, Peters. Just to pass the time of day with him—." At this Mrs. Hale shivers "a little" to suggest displeasure at the thought (303). Mr. Hale adds, "I'd spoke to Mr. Wright about it [getting a telephone] once before; but he put me off, saying folks talked too much anyway, all he asked was peace and quiet—guess you know about how much he talked himself" (295).

Minnie Wright changes drastically over the twenty years she is married to Mr. Wright. Before she married him she wore dresses and sang in the church choir. Mrs. Hale remembers, "She used to wear pretty clothes and be lively—when she was Minnie Foster, one of the town girls, singing in the choir" (299). She also describes Minnie Foster as "kind of like a bird herself. Real sweet and pretty, but kind of timid and fluttery" (303). But now Minnie wears shabby clothes and no longer sings. In fact, she is quiet like her husband. Her only real joy came from her canary, which sang in its cage. Mr Wright, however, does not like singing and the noise the bird makes. He kills the bird. Mrs. Hale comments on Minnie's probable reaction, "If there had been years of—nothing, then a bird sang to you, it would be awful—still—after the bird was still" (305).

Minnie Foster became, over her twenty years of marriage to John Wright, quiet and "still." Yet, she retained a part of herself in her singing, fluttering canary.

Topics for Character Analysis

1. Read Nathaniel Hawthorne's short story "Rapuccini's Daughter." Write a paper characterizing the main characters.

2. Discuss the major conflict in Chinua Achebe's novel *Things Fall Apart* by focusing on the main character.

3. Study the character Troy, in August Wilson's play, *Fences*. Discuss his basic character and how it affects his relationship with his family.

4. Define the Shakesperian villain using *MacBeth*, *Julius Caesar*, and *Othello* as sources.

WRITING ABOUT THEME

What is the difference between these two questions: "What is the work about?" "What does it mean?" The difference is simple. The first question requires you to tell the subject and what happens in a literary work, whereas the second requires you to tell or explain the significance of what happens in the story. To say that the theme of a work is "revenge" is insufficient. To indicate what the work suggests about revenge leads you to an effective theme to develop in an essay. In writing about theme, you will study the title, characters, the setting, the imagery, and other features to determine what they mean, not only in the work, but also to determine whether they make a statement about life in general. You seek to find the message, the lesson, and/or often the major reason underlying the writing of the literary selection. In considering the theme of a work, ask yourself the following questions:

1. What does the work say about people—their behavior or attitudes?

2. What does it say about the human condition?

3. What does it say about human beings and their interaction with one another?

4. What does it say about their interaction with God?

5. What does it say about their response to nature or the environment?

6. Is there one central idea, or are there several presented?

7. Are the ideas presented here novel, provocative, or archetypal?

8. Is there a theme at all?

9. Who or which literary element best conveys the theme?

10. Is the theme only partially developed, and, if so, is that the author's intent?

In writing about theme, you must accept the fact that in literary analysis, unlike in science or mathematics, there is no "one" or "exact" answer. Most importantly, however, you must be able to substantiate your assertion about theme or whatever you are discussing.

Sample Essay #1

WHEN TWO WORLDS COLLIDE

Bessie Head's *Life* is a short story in which "murder" is the focus. The author describes a marriage in which one of the partners, the wife in this case, is forced to relinquish a part of her identity, a loss which results in murder. Head's story suggests that retaining one's "self" in a marriage is crucial if the marriage and, especially, the *people* in it are to survive.

Life, set in a village in Botswana, is the story of a former prostitute, Life Morapedi, who returns to her village after having lived many years in Johannesburg. Life is described as being "bright and vivacious," a girl who has a "friendly manner" and who "laughs freely and loudly." She is often referred to as being "hysterical." She spends her time at a recently opened bar drinking and playing her transistor radio loudly. Her companions are the beer-brewing women who say, "Boyfriends, yes. Husbands, uh, uh, no. . . . We want to rule ourselves." Life's own motto is "Live fast, die young, and have a good-looking corpse." Lifestyle in the village is a stark contrast to that in Johannesburg. The villagers live ordinary, perfunctory, and dull lives until Life returns. She brings laughter and fun to the villagers who love her spirit. When she meets and marries Lesego, the leading citizen in the village, she becomes a "changed" woman.

Lesego is introduced thusly: ". . . one evening death walked quietly into the bar. It was Lesego, the cattleman . . ." Lesego is the richest and most respected man in the village; he is honest, wise, and generous. Accustomed to having his counsel sought, he makes quiet and rational judgement on the lives of his fellow villagers. His meeting with Life is described:

> Whereas all the other men had to approach her, ... he stood his ground, turned his head slowly, and then jerked it back slowly in a silent command: "Come here." She moved immediately to his end of the bar. "Hullo," he said, in an astonishing tender voice and a smile flickered across his dark reserved face. . . . Basically he was a kind and tender man, . . . he took his dominance and success for granted. But they looked at each other from their own worlds and came to fatal conclusions—she saw in him the power and maleness of the gangsters; . . . he was attracted to the undertone of hysteria in her. (439)

At this point the narration foreshadows its outcome. Lesego's description as dominance indicates that he is traditional in his views, despite his attraction to "an entirely new kind of woman"; that he is an honored and respected man in his village suggests that he is unlikely to change. In fact, after their marriage it is Life who announces, "All my old ways are over, ... I have now become a woman." She is described as "still happy and hysterical." However, Lesego's dominant nature surfaces when he informs her that he will control all the money and that she will stop playing her transistor radio all day. He also quietly tells her, "If you go with those men again, I'll kill you."

Although Life makes an effort to adjust to her new life, she "rapidly began to fall apart." The narrator explains, "When the hysteria and cheap rowdiness were taken away, Life fell into the yawn; she had nothing inside herself to cope with this way of life that had finally caught up with her." Life tells the beer-brewing women, "I think I have made a mistake. Married life doesn't suit me." She realizes that she cannot remain in a marriage that is "like death" to her. After having had independence to control her money and to decide her entertainment, Life has that independence stripped from her because Lesego needs to maintain his own status in his village. The "hysteria" which describes Life is simply her joy for life. Her marriage to Lesego has "killed" that joy. Life then "chooses" death when she disobeys Lesego by selling her body again.

Lesego loses that which he tried to protect—his honor and respectability—when he is jailed for his wife's murder. Life is forced to lose her identity in her marriage and orchestrates her own death rather than live with her loss. Life and Lesego are symbolic of the song sang by the beer-brewing women, "That's What Happens When Two Worlds Collide."

Sample Essay #2

THE FLEETINGNESS OF GLORY AND SUCCESS

Glory and success are two recurring subjects discussed in literature, and they are two objectives men and women have sought to achieve in everyday life. Glory and success are means of establishing social position and are often used to describe the wealthy or the powerful (who are many times the same). Those who achieve the status of being successful or glorified are often the recipients of society's greatest accolades. These are the elite few who we proclaim to be our heroes and role models. However, A. E. Housman's poem "To an Athlete Dying Young" reminds us that glory and success achieved in life are soon forgotten after death.

Housman, in the first stanza, calls to mind the vivid images of glory and success that so many of us envision when we think of a hero's welcome:

The time you won your town the race
We cheered you through the market place
man and boy stood cheering by
And home we brought you shoulder-high.

The cheering crowds, adoring fans, and the triumphant parade through town upon the shoulders of supporters confirm the good ol' hometown boy's new found fame and the pride his community feels because he has put their hamlet on the map. But one must wonder what the fate is of such a group of people that allows their hopes and dreams to become embodied in one man or woman. Does the entire populace fall into despair when the glory of their champion ends? Should not they desire to seek their own satisfaction rather than allow someone to find it for them?

In the third stanza, Housman speaks directly to the young athlete:

Smart lad, to slip betimes away
From fields where glory does not stay
And early though the laurel grows
It withers quicker than the rose.

His message is one that encourages this young athlete to find worth in more than just athletic endeavors. Housman describes the smart lad as one who should not become locked into but one who should even move away "From fields where glory does not stay." He makes a fitting reference to the laurel, long time symbol of victory and achievement. It is a crown which adorned mythological Greek and Roman gods as well as the true to life Roman emperors and Greek conquerors, but like glory and success, this symbol withers quicker than the rose.

Many think fame can long outlive the individual who earned it, but Housman is quick to tell us that this is not always the case. In fact, he says there are "Runners who renown outran and the name died before the man," suggesting that many times the fame of the famous is forgotten even as they go on living. The achievements of the past are not always long remembered into the future. Housman refers to the fading echoes which suggest the short amount of time glory will last.

Most certainly, the themes of Housman's poem apply to our world, that is, a world in which the quest for power and status becomes a driving force in many people's lives—also a world in which those with athletic prowess are rewarded top dollar over presidents of nations whose decisions can affect the lives of hundreds of millions. It would seem that some reassessment of our value structure is in order.

Topics for the Theme Paper

1. Read Ralph Ellison's short story "King of the Bingo Game." Then discuss Ellison's treatment of the theme of man's inability to find his place in the world.

2. Read Aristophane's play *Lysistrata* and discuss what this play says about war or the battle between the sexes.

3. Read e.e. cummings "Pity This Busy Monster, Mankind" and Wordsworth's "The World Is Too Much With Us." Compare the themes of these poems.

4. Read Toni Morrison's *Song of Solomon* and discuss one of its themes.

WRITING ABOUT SYMBOLISM

How often have you bought or picked red roses for someone very dear or special to you? How many times have you given heart-shaped boxes of chocolates to a favorite friend? You probably already know that red roses and heart-shaped boxes of chocolates symbolize, represent, or, as is commonly said, "stand for" romance. Simply, this means that like the general population, you use symbolism as a regular part of everyday life.

Symbols appear in short stories, poems, and plays that you read, discuss, and write about in composition classes. Often, in your readings and discussions you will find that symbols occur in various places, such as in specific characters' names, in their language, or in their residence. Likewise, you will discover symbols or symbolism in beliefs and customs described in various works. You will find that some things at first glance may merely seem to be ends within themselves but actually do mean or represent something more—something deeper, more significant. Recognizing symbols within a literary work can be a painstaking job. They are not labeled, and sometimes they do not represent anything significant. Your job is to examine the text and draw, and support, your conclusions.

In writing the paper on symbolism in a work, you should respond to the following questions:

1. Is reference made to an object, person, or place *repeatedly*?

2. How is the reference to this object, person, or place used?

3. Is there a relationship between this symbol and some feature of the literary work, some connection between it and the plot or character(s) or setting or theme?

4. Where exactly does the symbol appear? At the beginning of the work? In the middle? At the end? At the crucial points in the plot? Does it recur throughout the work? What effect does the placement of the symbol have on the meaning of the work or on the reader's perception, if any?

5. What does the symbol mean?

6. Does it have only one meaning?

7. Is there more than one symbol? If so, are they somehow related?

8. What is the overall impact of the symbol(s) on the literary work?

Sample Essay #1

THE MULTI-FACETED MASK

The poet—the one who is gifted in the perception and expression of the beautiful or the lyrical—employs many vehicles to craft his memorable lines. Personification, alliteration, onomatopoeia—a host of poetic elements can be manipulated in a way that brings life to mere words. One especially functional literary entity is the symbol, that which embodies more than its literal, concrete meaning. Paul Lawrence Dunbar is a poet who is very adept at handling such representations to impart both meaning and feeling in his work. In "We Wear the Mask," Dunbar uses the mask to represent not one, but several aspects of the black man's measures to deal with a world that is indifferent to his pain.

Dunbar's mask first represents the black man's—especially the slave's—use of physical means to cover the evidence of his suffering. The poem opens with the mask that " . . . grins and lies/ It hides [his] cheeks and shades [his] eyes." Only a brief look in the history books, a fleeting perusal of pre-Civil Rights era news clips, or a first-hand account from an elderly black person will testify to the fact that the black man, only a few years ago, could not express his true feelings. He had to grin and act merry—"skin and grin" and "bow and scrape"—regardless of the pain that he felt within. The few blacks who ventured to express themselves through words, or even facial expressions, would usually wound up at the end of a rope. Thus, for mere physical survival, the "grinning, lying" mask was needed.

Dunbar's mask also stands for the black man's attempt to disguise his emotional agony. The second stanza opens with the black man "counting his tears and sighs." Here he takes an account of his feelings, but he dares not give voice to his tears and sighs; they are only a means of helping him to ventilate in secret—a means of helping him to cope with the fact that he is treated like a piece of property, not like a man. Because he wears this emotional mask, the world is oblivious to his suffering—or feigns to be. The black man pretends to be a happy creature, and, as Dunbar asks, "Why should the world know otherwise?" Thus, the mask does its job; it allows the black man to maintain emotional stability.

Finally, the mask represents spiritual coverage. " . . . O great Christ, our cries/To Thee from tortured souls arise." These lines epitomize the heart-felt sorrow of the enslaved soul. However, these lines also embody the coverage of hope that Christ provides—especially to the downtrodden, those who must wear masks. The black man is looked upon as an animal—a creature without a soul—by the society in which he exists. But he has a definite relationship with God. He must, however, " . . . let the world dream otherwise." This mask, the spiritual one, serves to veil the pain and anguish and to give solace and hope for tomorrow.

The multi-faceted mask gives the black man a means of dealing with his plight—a means of physical, emotional, and spiritual survival in a world that spurns him.

Sample Essay

"THE LAMB" VS. "THE TYGER": THE AWESOMENESS OF GOD

In "The Lamb" and "The Tyger," two companion poems, William Blake depicts the phenomenal and majestic creative ability of God as well as the purposeful design and unifying significance of all things that He made. Using the lamb and tiger as symbols, he explains the concepts of innocence and experience, with the two animals respectively representing these two virtues.

The lamb is essentially childlike, pampered, and, in fact, mirrors the image of God Himself. This "little lamb" is described as having "such a tender voice" not unlike that of a child. The description of the lamb is almost that of an infant totally depending on a parent, in this case Father God. God pampers the lamb and takes care of it, giving it "clothing of delight," "bidding thee feed," and most importantly, giving "thee life." In addition, a direct parallel can be made between Christ and the lamb. "He is called by thy name, / For he calls himself a Lamb," Blake writes. Therefore, the characteristics the author uses to describe Christ can be used interchangeably to refer to the lamb. [Christ] "is meek, and he is mild"; and in turn so is this creature. All of these character traits work collectively to create this gentle image of the lamb. The human being, as a child, symbolizes this meekness, gentleness, innate goodness.

On the other hand, the tiger is fierce, wild, and nocturnal, yet at the same time he is created with the identical love as the lamb, and by the same creator. There are frequent references made to fire, indicating the animal's fierceness and wildness, the dangerous side of man's personality, perhaps, or his potential. The tiger is described as "burning bright" and dwelling "in the forests of the night." Fire even burns in the eyes of the beast, but really Blake here describes growth of the infant (man) referred to in "The Lamb." The softness has disappeared, and the helpless infant has become an experienced person, capable of attack or harm. This, Blake seems to say, is what happens when one grows up. Nevertheless, despite the animal's (or man's) "dreadful hand and [his] dreadful feet," God is still responsible for this lovely creation. No one other than God "dare frame thy fearful symmetry." This creature was created with love as God "smiled his work to see."

In both poems Blake masterfully characterizes each animal, illustrating the versatility of God. What appears to the human mind as strange and unrelated so often is just the opposite. The fierce yet innocent mind is just too powerless to perceive.

Topics for the Paper on Symbols or Symbolism

1. Read Toni Morrison's *The Bluest Eye*. Then write a paper discussing the significance of symbolism in the novel.

2. Read several Negro spirituals, such as "Deep River," "Go Down, Moses," and "Didn't My Lord Deliver Daniel." Write a paper discussing the use and/or meaning of symbols to African Americans during slavery and today (if applicable).

3. Read John Donne's work, "Meditation 17," and discuss the symbolism of this devotional piece of literature. Is there one major symbol discussed? What is it? Are there several symbols? Are they related?

4. Read Alice Childress's drama *Wine in the Wilderness*. Write an essay discussing the significance of the protagonist as a symbol of African American pride.

WRITING ABOUT IMAGERY

One of the most important elements in literature, imagery, reinforces meaning in a literary work. Imagery requires you to engage your senses—sight, touch, sound, taste, and smell—to connect emotionally with what the author provides in his or her work. To help you make this emotional connection, the author constructs the image by choosing words or phrases that encourage you to recall pictures or sensations related to what he or she is describing. Consider these lines from Wordsworth's poem, "I Wandered Lonely As A Cloud," which is dominated by images of sight and movement.

> I wandered lonely as a cloud
> That floats on high o'er vales and hills,
> When all at once I saw a crowd,
> A host, of golden daffodils; . . .
> Fluttering and dancing in the breeze.
> . . . . . . the stars that shine
> And twinkle on the milky way,
>
> . . . .
> Ten thousand saw I at a glance
> Tossing their heads in sprightly dance.

The mental picture produced by this description allows the reader to imagine himself in a spring of dancing daffodils on a breezy spring day. Very likely his imagination returns to a day in his past during which he had a similar experience. This recollection is the emotional connection Wordsworth is seeking.

In writing an essay on imagery, consider the following:

1. Look for words or phrases that appeal to the senses.
2. Identify what is being described or compared.
3. Check to see if one image is more dominant than others.
4. Analyze the relationship of one image to another or to several images.
5. Consider what effect, if any, the images have on you, the reader.
6. Explain how the imagery functions to help define theme, character, or setting.

Sample Essay #1

THE DEATH EXPERIENCE

The world is revealed to man through his senses. Imagery is the vehicle through which the poet conjures up ideas that stimulate the sensations of sight, sound, taste, touch and smell. It is evident that some poets use imagery with greater facility than do others. Whereas some writers use trite and staid expressions such as "golden sunset" and "shimmering streams," others such as Emily Dickinson use figurative language to achieve its fullest sensory effect. In fact, Dickinson is a master craftsman at appealing to the senses. In "I heard a Fly Buzz—When I Died," she employs sight, sound, and touch to paint a clearly delineated portrait of the dying process.

Sound imagery permeates the poem. The onomatopoetic buzz of the fly is unmistakably reminiscent of the death rattle—the raspy sound made by a dying person. The intermittent dashes between ideas add to the unceasing buzz or "rattle" effect and highlight the fact that life is ebbing away. At the end of both the poem and of life, the buzz that was a steady hum at the beginning of the poem becomes an "uncertain stumbling Buzz." Death, obviously, is at hand. Dickinson takes sound from a melodious, almost symphonic rendition, to a cacophonic dirge in an effort to broadcast the essence of dying.

Dickinson again titillates the senses when she focuses on that which can be seen. Such expressions as "The Eyes around" and " . . . The King/Be witnessed—in the Room—" are used to paint a picture of the death watch. Visions of loved ones sitting at the bedside of one who is dying are brought to the forefront of the mind, and the appearance of the King, for the Christian believer, makes the transition from life to death a peaceful, even royal one. The reference to the color blue signifies a state of lifelessness—a state in which there is no red color to represent the hue of life. At the end of the poem, it is only fitting that the reader finds these lines—"And then the Windows failed—and then I could not see to see." Sight, like sound, allows the reader to experience the dying process.

The function of the touch imagery is a bit more subtle. Yet, it is quite functional in relaying the death experience. Ironically, one of the key elements of touch that Dickinson uses is stillness. She writes, "The Stillness in the Room/ was like the Stillness in Air." Dickinson uses this lack of movement to create a palpable feeling of lifelessness—that unmistakable nothingness that occurs "Between the Heaves of Storm." Words such as *dry* and *firm* serve only to make death even more tactile. Dickinson's use of the sense of touch makes death, the intangible, tangible.

A good poet always remembers the sensory world, for it is through the senses that his or her reader is allowed to experience the poem. Emily Dickinson's "I Heard a Fly Buzz—When I Died" appeals to the senses and allows her audience to hear, see, and feel the death experience that she sets forth.

Sample Essay #2

LANGSTON HUGHES' "DAYBREAK IN ALABAMA"

Langston Hughes' "Daybreak in Alabama" reads like the voice of a child unaware of the reality of a "dream deferred." The speaker in the poem aspires to be a composer who will create music that will somehow bring racial harmony and peace to humanity. Hughes uses imagery to compare music to this new "dawn" of racial harmony.

Visual imagery dominates the poem, which begins with the speaker describing a serene forest in which "the purtiest songs" control the atmosphere"

> Rising out of the ground like a swamp mist
> And falling out of heaven like soft dew
> I'm gonna put tall trees in it.

The reader is drawn into this forest by

> . . . the scent of pine needles

And the smell of red clay after rain

These olfactory images recall natural elements of the South, thus enabling Hughes to progress to his forest and flower imagery to describe a universal brotherhood and sisterhood of people of all colors and ethnic backgrounds:

And long red necks
And poppy colored faces
And big brown arms
And the field daisy eyes
of black and white black white black people
And I'm gonna put white hands
And black hands and brown hands and yellow hands
And red clay earth hands in it . . .

The images suggest an infinite, ever-connecting chain of people who are bound innately in a fellowship of love.

"Daybreak in Alabama" holds in its "dawn" the premise of Martin Luther King, Jr.'s "I Have A Dream" speech, in which he proclaimed, "I have a dream that one day the state of Alabama . . . will be transformed into a situation where little black boys and little black girls will be able to join hands with little white boys and white girls and walk together as brother and sister."

Hughes uses imagery to echo that "dream" for society.

Topics for the Imagery Paper

1. Discuss the bird imagery in Kate Chopin's "The Awakening."
2. Discuss the imagery in Ellison's *The Invisible Man.*
3. Discuss the imagery in. T. S. Eliot's poem "The Love Song of J. Alfred Prufrock" or "The Wasteland."
4. Discuss the imagery in one of the books of *Gulliver's Travels.*

PREPARING THE LITERARY PAPER

Step One: First Reading

The first reading actually begins before you start to read the content of the play, poem, or piece of fiction. A prereading consideration of the title of the work, its genre, as well as its author could deepen your comprehension of the ideas within any body of writing, especially those within a literary selection. For example, the title of Ralph Ellison's *Invisible Man* gives you some idea that the work focuses on an identity crisis. The fact that the work is a novel prompts you to expect to find such features as conflict, plot development, climax, and the like. If you are already familiar with other works by Ellison, then more than likely you would anticipate uncovering a lot of symbolism and dramatic irony.

Prereading can lend a great deal to your understanding, but it is in the actual reading that you begin to focus and analyze. You should read through the entire work, getting general ideas and formulating questions about the plot, rhyme scheme, or the essence of an aside or soliloquy. As you read, you will notice that certain impressions will keep recurring. For example, in *Invisible Man*, the grandfather motif is prevalent and animal imagery permeates the novel. Soon you will focus on such repeated elements and even anticipate them. Even in your first reading, you may want to mark the spots of various ideas by highlighting or underlining them. After you finish reading, jot down questions about the various images, symbols, character features, or other elements in the work.

Leave your questions for a few hours or even a day, if possible. Then reread your questions. Those ideas which still impress you should be considered for closer investigation. Perhaps you will begin to suspect a relationship between a few ideas or elements. For instance, the grandfather motif and the battle imagery in *Invisible Man* could work together to focus on the internal and external conflicts that the protagonist has. Or you may speculate that Emily Dickinson's personification of death in her poem, "Because I Could Not Stop for Death," makes death seem less forbidding.

Step Two: Second Reading

Your second reading is far more streamlined than your first. This time you are reading with a different purpose—to verify some of your initial impressions. As you reread, you will continue to highlight or underscore certain passages. You may even find it useful to color code certain passages that you believe work together to develop particular ideas or support your idea that certain imagery is being used. At the same time, you will begin annotating these lines, words, or ideas. All of this is done in an effort to answer the questions generated from your first reading.

Step Three: Third Reading

The third reading is done to fine tune strong impressions—to verify relationships or trace a particular element more closely. You will *scan* the work this time, and you will continue to annotate. During this stage, you will toss out some ideas and start to analyze others even more. Your ideas are coming together and a prevailing idea is taking shape.

Step Four: Prewriting

Group your ideas together according to your color codes and/or special notes or annotations. Try to write a tentative thesis statement for each group. At this point ask yourself a few pointed questions.

1. Does every item in the group help to support the tentative thesis?
2. Are there items that need to be discarded?
3. Would an item in one group help to develop the thesis of another group better?

After you have tested your idea groups, you could be ready to choose an area of development. Thus, you will formulate your argument—decide what you want to say about your chosen combination of ideas—and then write your thesis statement, remembering it can be altered as you plan your methods of organization and development.

With your thesis sentence written, you can begin writing a tentative outline. Make sure that each main topic in your outline supports a particular aspect of your thesis. In addition, you should have an adequate number of passages from the work to support your main idea and give credibility to your argument.

Step Five: Writing

You are now in familiar territory. The rest of the process you have already learned in Chapter Three, "The Essay in Summation." As you would do in the writing of any essay, write at least two drafts so that your work will be polished enough to be easily understood and even enjoyed. However, there are a few special *Do's* and *Don'ts* you need to keep in mind.

Do's

1. Relate references to characters, narrators, speakers, and actions in a work in the present tense.
2. Introduce quotations properly. (See Chapter 8, the unit on research.)
3. Focus your analysis on the work itself. Extraneous ideas may be interesting but will do nothing to promote your argument.

Don'ts

1. Do not make your paper a mere summary of a work. Instead, give a brief synopsis of the plot (about two or three sentences), along with the title of the work and the author's name, in the introduction.
2. Do not assume that the author and the narrator or speaker in the work are the same.
3. Do not indicate whether you like a work. Your assessment more than likely will not be relevant to support your argument.
4. Do not give your essay the same title as the work that you are discussing.

8

The Research Process

OVERVIEW

As an intelligent and industrious student, you should view a research project as your opportunity to gain in-depth knowledge about an interesting topic and also as the opportunity to practice skills that are necessary for competence in higher education and responsible careers. The knowledge gained from this activity could be the beginning of your expertise in the topic you research, and the research skills learned could be the initiation of a career in research. You can be assured, however, that the research procedure is not difficult, and that you can master it with earnest effort. With the promise that research skills could provide you with exciting career opportunities and/or gratifying higher learning, all you will need is a sincere desire to understand the research procedure and to practice each step thoroughly.

A short research paper is usually five to ten pages, but the length of a paper should not daunt anyone's ambitions. In the case of a five-hundred-word essay that you have been accustomed to, you have only stored knowledge or your creativity to rely on, but in the case of a research paper, you will have as many sources as you can consult on your topic, so you will find that it is quite often easier to write a research paper, even one of considerable length, than it is to write an impromptu essay. The research papers that will be assigned to you in your freshman year will be short, probably not more than ten pages, but as you become skilled in undergraduate studies, you may be expected to write longer research papers. If you learn the skills well, you will be prepared to grasp the challenge of longer and more intense research. In addition, with the computer and several online services, such as America Online; Freenet; and Internet, the Information Superhighway, research may be only a few clicks of a computer mouse away. To be ready for a career in the twenty-first century, you must be computer literate. On most campuses today, there are computer centers that are open to students.

The following instructions are designed to provide you with a clear and streamlined understanding of the Modern Language Association (MLA) research process. Even though research is flexible and does not always follow a linear pattern, it is helpful to think of the process in terms of steps. If you seem unable to progress from one step to the other, you will need to return to a previous step that will untangle the procedure, and then you will need to repeat the steps. You will usually know when the process cannot move forward, and you will realize that you must return to a previous step. For instance, if you cannot find sources about your research topic, as instructed in Step 2, you will know that you must pick a different topic, so you will need to return to Step 1 to choose another topic. Other modifications may include altering an outline or changing some of the content as you read more about your subject. If such changes are necessary, make them as soon as possible, so that you may begin to move forward again.

For a clear understanding of the following steps, you may need to refer to the glossary which provides definitions of terms that may be new to you.

Step l: Choose Your Subject and Limit It

If you were not assigned a subject or a topic, the most logical first step is to choose a subject that you would like to learn more about. A subject is usually a broad area of study that needs refinement or limiting. For example, "Fiction Writers" is a broad subject that may need several limitations. Skim through journals, books, newspapers, or ask friends or teachers and others for suggestions, and most of all, think of your preferences before you decide on a subject.

To move closer to a subject that you can cover in the five or ten pages of your research, think of limiting your subject to a specific period, a geographic boundary, one literary element, or to a combination of a few related aspects. For instance, if you apply these suggestions for limiting topics, and you choose to write about "Twentieth Century American Fiction Writers," this topic will obviously restrict your paper to the twentieth century and to American fiction writers. However, even these limitations are insufficient for a ten-page paper, because of the many volumes that twentieth century American fiction has filled, so more pruning will be necessary for high quality. Some of the best papers focus on a single problem; they cover a small subject area in great depth.

Let's say you decide, after you have read "The Storm" by Kate Chopin, that you would like to learn more about the themes that this writer delves into, so you also read *The Awakening,* "The Cadian Ball," and "The Story of an Hour." You uncover, story by story, that a common theme is the sexuality of wives at a time when such sensuality was considered unwomanly. You may then decide to explore how Chopin presents that theme in the works you read, which is how you arrive at your thesis statement. If you are writing a long paper (over ten pages), you may want to discuss each of the four stories. For a short paper (five to ten pages), however, one or two of the works will be sufficient. In the example of a short research paper that follows this discussion, the student chose to study two works she read. Her thesis statement, as yours should be, is a conclusion of findings or a hypothesis that is based on preliminary study. The thesis statement must be precise, concise, and a complete, unambiguous sentence that avoids figurative and technical language.

For a scholarly paper, a paper worth the research, you should not discuss a topic of little merit. Topics based on personal taste or preference, gossip, or hearsay are not worth anyone's time, especially in academia. The most successful research papers are those that discuss an aspect that has never been written about or one that discusses an old topic in a new way.

Write down your thoughts as you zero in on your topic. At first, your ideas may be scattered without organization, but after you evaluate and select those ideas you want to use, you will find some logical organization for them. Logical thinking might begin with a generalization and move to a specific idea, or it might begin with a specific idea and move to a generalization. The student's essay about Kate Chopin begins with a generalization and moves to specifics. The diagram below reflects one possible pattern of thinking for this essay.

Note that the arrows identify the directions that the student's thinking takes in limiting her subject. This thinking will lead to an organized outline.

It is important for you to be enthusiastic about your subject because you will live with it for at least a few weeks. As soon as you find your limited subject, it will be wise to form a working thesis statement (also known as a working hypothesis in scientific research) so that you can begin to search for valuable sources of information.

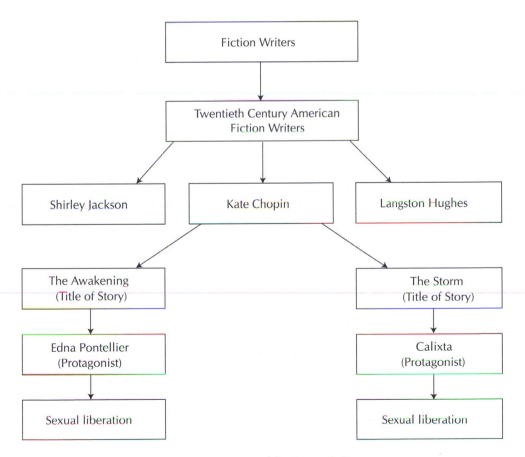

Figure 8-1. Diagram of the Research Process

Step 2: Compile a Working Works Cited List

A working works cited list (also called a working bibliography) is a compilation of sources that contain information about your subject or topic. Sources are books, journals, magazines, newspapers, all types of printed materials, personal interviews, online computer services, videos, movies, microfiche, microfilm, experiments, and a host of other media where information is found. You want to choose the best sources, which are the ones that are most authoritative, on your subject. To check the authority of an author, read about what the author has accomplished in the field you are studying. You may gather that information from the source itself or from the *Index of Authors* in your school library.

All sources can be divided into one of three types: Primary, Secondary, and Tertiary.

Primary sources are those sources which you investigate or research. The primary or the first research sample papers in this chapter are the *The Awakening* and "The Storm."

Secondary sources are the books, magazines, journals, and documentaries that experts and others have written about primary sources.

Tertiary sources, as the word "tertiary" suggests, are the sources that are third in rank. Tertiary sources are reviews of secondary works and are sometimes considered inferior to primary and secondary sources.

The working works cited list is best compiled on cards, one card for each potential source you may consult about your topic. This list is often made in the library or on a computer. As you discover additional sources that you may want to use, make cards for them, and add them to your stack, which in the final works cited page will become a list. Variations in format and information exist for different types of sources. Following is the required information and form for a work cited card for a book and examples of actual cards. Additional information on Works Cited appears in the reference sections at the end of this chapter.

1. Write the last name of the author of the source, followed by a comma, and his or her first name and/or initial. In the case of more than one author, other names (always list names in the order given on the title page of the book) may be written as they appear. If more than three authors' names appear, then list only the first author, followed by *et al* and a period.

2. Underline the title of the book, followed by a period. The titles of works that are published as separate entities are underlined. Shorter works such as magazine articles, chapters from books, and song titles are enclosed in quotation marks.

3. Copy the city of publication, followed by a colon.

4. Abbreviate the name of the publishers, followed by a comma.

5. Write down the copyright date, followed by a period.

P 107 *(Call Number)*   *(Subject) Edna's Awakening*

Ziff, Larzer. The American 1890's. New York: West Publishing Company, 1971.

LEAVE SPACE IN CASE YOU WANT TO WRITE A NOTE.

Figure 8-2. Example of a "Works Cited" Card

6. Jot down a note about the subject the source covers.

The example below follows the above instructions, because the source is a book.

PS 917 *(Call Number)*   *(Subject) Edna's Awakening*

Bogard, Carley. "The Awakening: A Refusal to Compromise." University of Michigan Papers in Women's Studies. Ann Arbor: The University of Michigan Press, 1977.

LEAVE SPACE IN CASE YOU WANT TO WRITE A NOTE.

Figure 8-3. Bibliography for an article in a book

Figure 8-3 is an example of a works cited card for an *article* taken from a book. Note that the title of the article appears after the name and is identified with quotation marks.

J 123 *(Call no.)*   *(Subject) Sex Education*

Sheehan, Sharon. "Another Kind of Sex Ed." Newsweek *13 July 1992: 10–11.*

Leave plenty of space for notes.

Figure 8-4. Bibliography for article

Figure 8-4 illustrates bibliographical information for an article taken from a weekly magazine. The title is in quotation marks, the magazine is underlined, and the publishing date of the magazine is given.

Notes may also be entered into your portable lap top computer, your personal computer, or a public computer that you may use at the library. However, it is good to remember that a computer that is available to the public does not guarantee privacy unless you transfer the information to a personal disk.

A works cited card for an electronic source should include the following: author's name, publication information for print source (title, date, etc.), title of the database (underlined), publication medium (CD-ROM), name of vendor, and the electronic publication date. An example of an Internet entry is shown in Figure 8-5.

Internet   Subject: *Sex Ed.*

*Kappel-Smith, Diana. "Fickle Desert Blooms: Opulent
One Year, No-Shows the Next." <u>Smithsonian
Magazine</u> (Mar. 1995): 9pp. Online. America
Online. Internet. 18 Apr. 1995.*

LEAVE SPACE FOR A NOTE.

Figure 8-5. Bibliography for Internet Entry

You may also check the reference section at the end of this chapter for more information on citations for electronic publications.

It is important to acquire a list of sources early in your research so that you will know if your topic is researchable with the available resources. If at Step 2 you cannot find sources and have to return to Step 1 to pick another topic, your browsing for sources may not have been wasted. You may have already discovered a topic that is researchable.

Accessing Sources

To write a thorough research paper you should fully utilize all sources available to you.

Library Sources

Libraries now store information about their holdings in a computer system called LUIS (Library User Information Services) instead of in card files. This new method is more efficient than card files. However, you may find card files still active at some libraries. A computer search system will guide you, step by step, when you are looking for information on your topic. You may request a source by typing in a command on the computer screen. For instance, if you want to find a particular work, type in its title (a command) such as:

The Storm (underlining and quotation marks are unnecessary)

The computer will indicate whether such a title is stored in the library. If several works with the same title are in the library, the computer will provide a list of those works and their authors. The list may appear with the following information:

1. The Storm by Jake Bake
2. The Storm by Katherine Chopin
3. The Storm by John Doe

You should type the number (such as "2") of the item you wish to view. The computer, on a second frame, will provide you with additional bibliographic information and a call number for the work you request. If the library where you are conducting your research has ties to surrounding libraries, the computer screen may indicate that the source you are looking for is located at one of its branches. In some libraries, such as university libraries, several campus branches or other universities in proximity may be tied to one central system.

If you wanted to find a list of the sources that discuss your topic, type in a subject or some key words, as in the following command:

Sexuality in early nineteenth century authors

If much has been written about this subject, you may get a list of thousands of books or other media such as microfiche or microfilm and their authors. Search the list and find the works that seem most pertinent and useful to you. Sources are numbered consecutively, so you may request to see the full bibliographical reference to a source, at any time while viewing the list. Type in the number that corresponds with the work you wish to view, and the bibliographic information, plus a call number will appear on a second frame. You can always return to the list with a command, which the computer will provide for you.

It is important to remember that you may not find a source on your particular topic, so you may have to look for information through key words and in subjects that include yours as a subdivision of the broader subject. For instance, if you want to find out critics' views on sex, you may need to consult a broader area, such as "Nineteenth Century Views on Sexuality."

When you search the computer for information about a selected work, you will need to note whether it is currently in the library stacks; whether it has been checked out, and if it has been checked out, its due date; or whether it has been ordered, but not yet received. You may be able to request the work from another university system, or reserve the work when it is returned. You will also need to note at which library the work may be shelved and write down its call number, if it is available. In addition, you will need to acquaint yourself with the numbering (filing) system that the library uses so that you can find the item easily. Most libraries post guides to their numbering systems in conspicuous places and have librarians that can answer your questions or orient you to a service.

The Computer

Among the many advantages of the computer, one advantage that has proven invaluable to researchers is its accessibility to worldwide research through the Internet. To access this information, all you will need is an understanding of some common computer rules. Application of those rules to the Internet provide you with information from around the world in much less time than it will take to conduct a similar library research.

Professors and Community Personnel

Sometimes, your university professor or people who work in the community may be knowledgeable about your topic. Ask professors and/or community people for leads on experts who may have researched your topic or related areas, or who may have practical knowledge about your topic.

Step 3: Take Copious Notes

If you have been worrying about where you will get information to s-t-r-e-t-c-h your paper to ten pages, worry no more. Extensive reading, and the resulting note-taking, will provide you with sufficient ideas to write a strong paper. Write as many notes as possible that pertain to your topic. As you read and gain more ideas, you may have to change a working outline, change some information, or adjust your working thesis statement to accommodate the new ideas. However, if changes to the thesis statement must be made, they should be made as early as possible into the research procedure. A refined and unambiguous thesis statement will provide focus for efficient notetaking, because all notes must be related to the thesis statement and its parts.

Notetaking may be done by lap top computer, an accessible library computer at a local computer site, your personal computer, or on 6" by 4" notecards. Even though hand written notecards may sound outmoded, notecards have served renowned researchers throughout history. Notecards provide you with the convenience of being able to arrange them according to the subtopics that you will have in your outline. For instance, let's say you are writing the part of your paper on Kate Chopin's *The Awakening* (as the student did in the first sample research paper) and the first subdivision of your outline deals with the sexual liberation of the protagonist, Edna Pontellier. Group all your notes on Edna's sexual liberation into one stack. However, if you have subdivisions under "sexual liberation," such as "sexual liberation in marriage" and "sexual liberation out of marriage," then you will want to break that larger stack into smaller ones according to those subdivisions. In other words, create a filing system for easy reference. It is simple to see that when you write about "The Storm," you could duplicate the system you followed for *The Awakening*. As you write from one division in your outline to another, your notes will be in place for each portion of the writing task. This may be illustrated as follows if we use Roman numeral I and its two main divisions in the sentence outline:

> I. All notecards on Edna Pontellier's revolutionary ideas about sex after marriage.

Use your notes to write on this section.

> A. All notes demonstrating how Edna is trying to find her identity.

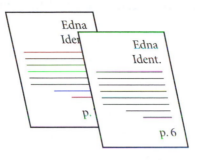

Use your notes to write on this section.

    B. All notes on Edna discovering her feelings about marriage
       while trying to find her identity.

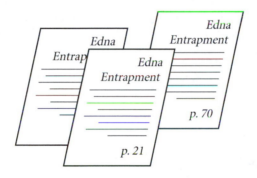

Use your notes to write on this section.

Follow this procedure until all sections have been written. The computer has its advantages in this area also. It allows you to "cut" ideas from one place and "paste" them in more appropriate places, but you will not be able to view all of your notes on the same frame of the screen. You may want to print your notes, divide each with scissors, write in divisions or subdivisions if they have not been previously written in, and then group them as you did with the notecards. Notecards or divided notes may be spread out for easier viewing and organizing. A significant advantage with the computer is the speed with which notes can be written and the speed with which they can be moved from one place to the other.

Notes should contain complete ideas that pertain to your research, so you should write complete sentences to avoid misunderstanding what you meant when you read your notes later. There are three basic ways to write notes: (1) *Verbatim*— word for word reproduction of the source; (2) *Paraphrased*—restatement in your own vocabulary; and (3) *Summarized*—a synopsis of the idea. Of the three types of notes, paraphrased ones are used most frequently. Verbatim notes are used when you want to recreate the special effects that the original source created. Summarized notes are used when you do not need to restate all the details of the original source.

For short research, you may use your "working" works cited cards as notecards also; but for longer research, it will be more convenient to make separate cards for the works cited and for your notes to make it easier to create different filing systems for each. For short research, since you already have all of the bibliographical information on cards, you may simply add notes to the cards of sources you use. In fact, you might already have some notes on those cards from Step 2. Here is an example of a note on a works cited card:

PS 917 (Call Number)   *(Subject) Edna's Awakening*

Bogard, Carley. "The Awakening: A Refusal to Compromise."
<u>University of Michigan Papers in Women's Studies.</u>
Ann Arbor: The University of Michigan Press, 1977.

Edna will awaken in the novel and discover that she is caged
in a marriage that does not allow her to grow or to become a
mature, self-assured woman with a mind of her own and a
sexual body of her own. p. 15

Figure 8-6. Works Cited Card With Note

Step 4: Prepare an Outline

Any research paper should have an outline. The three most common types of outlines are scratch, topic, and sentence. A simple scratch outline will work for a short essay in class, but a more formal topic or sentence outline is necessary for a research paper. The outline should be typed, edited, and proofread along with the rest of the paper and should be attached after the title page.

You may begin planning early in your research by writing a working outline of the points you want to cover. Even though the working outline will be tentative, it will provide you with early focus, which is necessary to start the paper. When you have read more about your topic, you may want to alter your outline in some ways to reflect what your research has uncovered.

The *scratch outline* is informal and usually takes the form of a list of the main points you plan to cover. A sample of a scratch outline for the paper on Kate Chopin's works follows:

1. Edna Pontellier in *The Awakening*
   a. Identity
   b. Sentiments about marriage
2. Calixta in "The Storm"
   a. Identity
   b. Sentiments about marriage

The *topic outline* is more formal than the scratch outline and uses parallel constructions and key words, phrases, or clauses to suggest divisions and subdivisions of ideas. There are several conventions that you must be aware of to write an effective one. For further discussion on outlining, see Chapter Three.

The entire outline should demonstrate logical or carefully reasoned thinking. You will begin with a thesis statement; from that thesis statement must flow several major ideas, and from those major ideas must flow minor ones. Those major divisions (parts) will evolve directly from the thesis statement and should be arranged in logical chronological, emphatic, or spatial order. Those major evolving ideas should be noted with Roman numerals and should be placed closest to the left hand margin to show their primary rank.

Subdivided, secondary ideas should always result in at least two parts. The logic is that you have taken the lesser idea from the greater one, and divided it, or broken it into smaller, more manageable portions, so you must have at least two parts, because anything that is broken is always fragmented into at least two pieces. Break a stick of chalk, for example; you will always get at least two pieces. It means, then, that if you subdivide Roman numeral I (the first level), the result must be at least an A. and a B. of the second level, but, of course, more than two subdivisions are possible. A topic outline for the research paper on Kate Chopin's works follows:

TOPIC OUTLINE

Thesis Statement: Kate Chopin's protagonists, Edna Pontellier in *The Awakening* and Calixta in "The Storm" dared to express sexual ideas that were revolutionary to married women in the early twentieth century.

I. Edna Pontellier in *The Awakening*
   A. Tries to find her identity
   B. Discovers her feelings about marriage
      1. Thinks sensuality should not end after marriage
      2. Finds that her marriage is an entrapment
      3. Explores an extramarital affair
         a. Leads to depression
         b. Ends with suicide

II. Calixta in "The Storm"
   A. Entangles herself in an extramarital affair
   B. Shows no remorse for the affair

The *sentence outline* is the most formal outline. You must follow all of the leveling and paralleling rules given for the topic outline, but each idea must be expressed in a complete sentence instead of in key words, phrases, or clauses. The following is a sentence outline for the paper on Kate Chopin's works:

SENTENCE OUTLINE

Thesis Statement: Kate Chopin's protagonists, Edna Pontellier in *The Awakening* and Calixta in "The Storm" dared to express sexual ideas that were revolutionary to married women in the early twentieth century.

I. In *The Awakening,* Edna Pontellier expresses some revolutionary ideas about sexual sensuality after marriage.

    A. Edna tries to find her identity.

    B. In trying to find her identity, Edna discovers her feelings about marriage.

        1. Edna finds that sexual sensuality should not end after marriage.

        2. Edna feels that her marriage is an entrapment.

II. Calixta in "The Storm" also expresses the idea of sexual liberation.

    A. Calixta entangles herself in an extramarital love affair.

    B. Calixta is not ashamed of her infidelity.

Step 5: Write a Rough Draft

A rough draft of a paper is the first attempt that you will make at writing the paper. If you have typed your paper on the word processor, then you will need to make a copy of your unedited paper and turn it in with your final copy.

To begin a rough draft, arrange your computer notes or notecards according to the various levels in your outline. Study the information that your notes provide under your first major point. Compare/contrast what each source has said about your topic. Do your sources concur? If all of your sources concur, then you may comment on their agreement on that point. If you agree or disagree with the experts, then you will need to say so and offer proof for your stance.

Your rough draft does not have to be perfect, but it should be as complete as possible so that after writing the rough draft your job will be to type, edit, and proofread. It is advisable that you write your rough draft in installments and let each part incubate. Incubation involves pondering over what you have written. Debating ideas in your mind or with others will help you to strengthen your paper.

Introductions to papers are usually difficult to write. Some writers may write them last, but if you can write yours first, then that introduction may provide you with valuable context and will lead you to a smooth link to your thesis statement. When you do write the introduction, however, it should stimulate your reader to want to read more. This means that you will have to display some of your most careful thinking. You may even want to be a bit dramatic to draw your reader into your discussion, but you should not commit the sin of embellishing to the point of sounding insincere, or you may lose your reader. The same techniques used in writing introductions for short essays may also be used in writing introductions for research papers.

The thesis statement will provide focus for each sentence and paragraph. Write a topic sentence that expresses the first main idea of your outline and that will be the controlling idea for the first body paragraph. For example, the first main idea for the first body paragraph of the paper on Kate Chopin, as taken from Lavonne Cliff's (the student writer) sentence outline is "In *The Awakening,* Edna Pontellier expresses some revolutionary ideas about sexual sensuality after marriage." The topic sentence of her second paragraph is "Chopin's novel, *The Awakening,* has been considered one of the most important pieces of fiction about the sexual life of a woman, and the first to fully face the fact that marriage did not end a woman's sensuality, but was instead an episode in her continuous growth."

Your job should follow that pattern of providing adequate support for the topic sentence of each paragraph. You may decide to use one expository pattern of development, such as illustration, comparison/contrast, cause/effect, division/classification, definition, process analysis, or argumentation, narration and description. Most researchers use a variety of modes. Detailed elements such as examples, statistics, expert opinions, experiments, experiences, facts, and anecdotes are used for supporting and elaborating points.

Transitions show relationships between ideas and create smooth flow between sentences and paragraphs. You may think of the transitions between sentences as the cement (mortar) that holds bricks together in the walls of a building, and transitions between paragraphs as the pillars that hold the walls together. Transitions are necessary to hold all the parts together and to maintain coherence.

Every manuscript should be double spaced. If the manuscript is a rough draft, you will need the space between the lines and the wide margins to write notes about what needs to be edited in your final paper. If the double spaced manuscript is the final draft, your instructor will also need the space for comments.

A successful paper must be read and re-read, edited and re-edited. Your time must therefore be budgeted so that each step of the paper can be proofread and edited. In addition, it will be smart to begin paginating from your first draft for quick reference when editing. Numbered pages will also help the typist not to omit a page(s) when working on the final draft.

Step 6: Document Your Sources

Proper documentation of each source must be made. This ensures that you give credit to your sources and that you protect yourself from being accused of plagiarism. Even if you paraphrase the source's idea(s), you must give credit to the source by documenting. Documentation of an idea that is fewer than four manuscript lines and that is written as part of the text follows the form below:

> "Mrs. Chopin displays the gradual arousal of a woman to the gratification and the peril of extramarital sexual satisfaction" (Arms 215).

The quotation marks signal that this sentence was copied verbatim and is fewer than four lines of normal text. Four lines or more of text are indented ten spaces and blocked without quotation marks. Credit is given to the author of the quotation by writing, in parentheses, his or her last name and the page from which the quotation was taken. One space separates the last name from the page number and a period is put outside of the closing parenthesis because it is written within a paragraph.

You might contend that you will need to document every sentence, since you are a student just learning about your topic; however, you are expected to do more than copy information. A compilation of excerpted material is not research. You are expected to show that your mind has been evaluating, analyzing, and responding to the notes as you read them. You need not, however, use first person phrases such as "in my opinion" or "I am certain" to show that you are thinking, because such phrases suggest insecurity about your discussion. If, as skillful researchers do, you signal where your sources' ideas begin and end, the reader will know which are your ideas and which are your sources'. To indicate the beginnings of your sources' ideas, you will need attributions (signaling phrases) such as the following:

- The literary critic, Carley Bogard stated . . . . (124)
- Information taken at that time reveals . . . . (Ziff 22)
- Another expert pointed out that . . . . (Eble 89)

The documentation (author's last name and page number) in parentheses will show where the expert's ideas end. If you name the author in the attribution, as is demonstrated in the first example above, you need not name him or her in the parenthetical documentation.

Step 7: Write the Final Works Cited Page

The final Works Cited page is an alphabetically arranged list of all of the sources (according to last name). In step 2, you began compiling a working works cited list (also called the working bibliography) and added to it as you found additional sources for your paper. You may have also made those same cards into notecards, adding notes to them. The cards that contain the notes you used for your paper need to be alphabetized according to authors' last names. Check those sources that you used to make sure that they correspond with the documentation that is contained in your paper. For each work you have cited, you must have at least one documentation.

If you followed the conventions of mechanics and punctuation for writing note cards, the works cited list will not be difficult to compile. This page should also be double-spaced, and the first line of each entry should be typed flush with the left hand margin; subsequent lines under each entry must be indented five spaces. See section on Documenting Research.

Step 8: Prepare the Final Draft

If you carefully revised your rough draft, then typing the final paper should be easy. For easy reference, the procedure for typing the paper has been arranged into the following steps:

1. Type your title page, using similar information as that provided in the sample research paper in this chapter.

2. Pagination should begin with your title page which should be considered page i, but is numbered "in the blind" with no number appearing on it. Lower case Roman numerals (i, ii, iii, iv, v, etc.) should be used for pagination of your outline and any other material that appears before your first page of text. Your first page of text and successive pages should be numbered with Arabic numbers (1, 2, 3, etc.). In addition to page numbers, use your last name as a running head (as is illustrated in the sample by Cliff). Page numbers

should appear with running heads, one inch from the top right hand corner.

3. Follow the outline format as given in the instructions under topic and sentence outlines.

4. Start the first page of the paper with the title of your paper centered about two inches from the top.

5. Type subsequent pages with page numbers, one inch from the top, and all other margins as the first page.

6. Type the works cited page with the words "Works Cited" centered two inches from the top and other margins as for page one. Alphabetize works according to authors' last names and type the first line of each entry flush with the left hand margin. Subsequent lines in entries must be indented five spaces under the first line. All the punctuation directions given for writing the "working works cited" cards must also be followed when typing the final works cited list.

The research paper must look very neat and as error free as possible. You have been working on it for at least a few weeks, so the expectation of any professor is that you have edited and proofread your paper very carefully and rendered your best ideas effectively. (See sample research essays at end of this chapter.)

Research Activities

Activity 1
Limit the following broad subjects to a topic you can research in ten pages: Education, Pollution, Medicine, Business, Politics, Religion, Athletics, Psychology, Modern Technology. Diagram the procedure that you followed (an example is given in Figure 8-1) in limiting the topic and then exchange your diagram with classmates. After you have critiqued your classmates' diagrams and they have critiqued yours, select a topic (not discussed with your classmates) and diagram your thinking. Submit the completed diagram to your teacher for approval.

Activity 2
If you do not know how to use a computer to find working sources (printed and electronic) at your school library, go to the library, pick a subject in whatever discipline your interests lie, and then try to find call numbers for at least three specific works on the computer. Locate the works by their call numbers. If you have difficulties finding materials, consult a librarian and ask him or her to explain the system to you.

Activity 3
Go to your school's media/computer center and inquire about computer facilities for students. Learn how to conduct research on the computer, and make a printout of information you gathered on a particular topic.

Activity 4

Write a scratch outline for two of the following topics:

1. An animal you would like to be or learn more about.
2. A business you would like to open.
3. Worldwide or national problems that need immediate solutions.
4. Political games that are played in the workplace.

Activity 5

Write topic outlines for the topics you wrote about in Activity 4.

Activity 6

Write sentence outlines for one of the topics suggested for the scratch outline exercise.

DOCUMENTING RESEARCH

Any time you use material derived from specific sources, whether quoted passages or summaries or paraphrases of fact, opinion, explanation, or idea, you are ethically obligated to let your reader know who deserves the credit. Further, you must tell your readers precisely where the material came from so that they can locate it for themselves. Often readers will want to trace the facts on which a conclusion is based, or to verify that a passage was quoted or paraphrased accurately. Sometimes readers will simply want to follow up and learn more about your subject.

There are basically two ways for a writer to show a "paper trail" to sources. The most widely used format today is the parenthetical reference, also called an *in-text citation*. This is a telegraphic, short-hand approach to identifying the source of a statement or quotation. It assumes that a complete list of references appears at the end of the paper. Each entry in the list of references includes three essential elements: authorship, full title of the work, and publication information. In the references, entries are arranged, punctuated, and typed to conform to the bibliographic style requirements of the particular discipline or of the instructor. With this list in place, the writer is able to supply the briefest of references—a page number or an author's name—in parentheses right in the text, knowing that the reader will be able to locate the rest of the reference information easily in the list of references. The second method for showing a paper trail is the footnote style—which is less often used today than the parenthetical system.

For more detailed information on the conventions of style in the humanities, social sciences, business disciplines, and sciences, refer to these style manuals:

- Gibaldi, Joseph, *MLA Handbook for Writers of Research Papers*. 4th ed. New York: MLA, 1995.
- *Publication Manual* (of the American Psychological Association). 4th ed. Washington, DC: APA, 1994.
- *Chicago Manual of Style*. 14th ed. Chicago: University of Chicago Press, 1993.
- *CBE Style Manual*. 5th ed. Bethesda, MD: CBE, 1983.
- Li, Xia, and Nancy B. Crane. *Electronic Styles: An Expanded Guide to Citing Electronic Information*. Westport: Meckler, 1996.

In a research paper, either of these systems of source citation is followed at the end by a list of references. In the MLA system, the list of references is called "Works Cited." Keep in mind that the complete information provided in the list of references will be the basis of your in-text citations. The parenthetical form provides minimal information and sends the reader to the list of references to find the rest. By contrast, the footnote or endnote system virtually duplicates the information in the list of references but uses a slightly different arrangement of the elements in the entry. Following is an index to this section on the MLA system of documentation.

Making in-text citations in the MLA format

When you make a parenthetical in-text citation, you assume that your reader will look to the list of "Works Cited" for complete references. The list of references at the end of your paper will provide three essential pieces of information for each of your sources: author, title, and facts of publication. Within your paper, a parenthetical citation may point to a source considered as a whole or to a specific page location in a source. Here is an example of an MLA in-text citation referring to a story as a whole.

> In "Escapes," the title story of one contemporary author's book of short stories, the narrator's alcoholic mother makes a public spectacle of herself (Williams).

The next example refers to a specific page in the story. In the MLA system, no punctuation is placed between a writer's last name and a page reference.

> In "Escapes," a story about an alcoholic household, a key moment occurs when the child sees her mother suddenly appear on stage at the magic show (Williams 11).

Here is how the references to the Williams story would appear as described in the list of references or "Works Cited."

> Williams, Joy. "Escapes." <u>Escapes: Stories</u>. New York: Vintage, 1990. 1–14.

Deciding when to insert a source citation and what information to include is often a judgment call rather than the execution of a mechanical system. Use common sense. Where feasible, incorporate citations smoothly into the text. Introduce the parenthetical reference at a pause in your sentence, at the end if possible. Place it as close to the documented point as possible, making sure that the reader can tell exactly which point is being documented. When the in-text reference is incorporated into a sentence of your own, always place the parenthetical reference *before* any enclosing or end punctuation.

> In Central Africa in the 1930s, a young girl who comes to town drinks beer with her date because that's what everyone does (Lessing 105).

> In a realistic portrayal of Central African city life in the 1930s (Lessing), young people gather daily to drink.

When a quotation from a work is incorporated into a sentence of your own, the parenthetical reference *follows* the quotation marks, yet precedes the enclosing or end punctuation.

> At the popular Sports Club, Lessing's heroine finds the "ubiquitous glass mugs of golden beer" (135).

Exception: When your quotation ends with a question mark or exclamation point, keep these punctuation marks inside the end quotation marks, then give the parenthetical reference, and end with a period.

> Martha's new attempts at sophistication in town prompted her to retort, "Children are a nuisance, aren't they?" (Lessing 115).

Naming an author in the text

When you want to emphasize the author of a source you are citing, incorporate that author's name in your sentence. Unless you are referring to a particular place in that source, no parenthetical reference is necessary in the text.

Biographer Paul Mariani understands Berryman's alcoholism as one form of his drive toward self-destruction.

Naming an author in the parenthetical reference

When you want to emphasize information in a source but not especially the author, omit the author's name in the sentence and place it in the parenthetical reference.

Biographers have documented alcohol-related upheavals in John Berryman's life. Aware, for example, that Dylan Thomas was in an alcohol-induced coma, dying, Berryman himself drank to escape his pain (Mariani 273).

When you are referring to a particular place in your source and have already incorporated the author's name into your sentence, place only the page number in parentheses.

Biographer Paul Mariani describes how Berryman, knowing that his friend Dylan Thomas was dying in an alcohol-induced coma, himself began drinking to escape his pain (273).

Documenting a block quotation

For block quotations, set the parenthetical reference—with or without an author's name—*outside* of the end punctuation mark.

The story graphically portrays the behavior of Central African young people gathering daily to drink:

> Perry sat stiffly in a shallow chair which looked as if it would splay out under the weight of his big body . . . while from time to time—at those moments when laughter was jerked out of him by Stella—he threw back his head with a sudden dismayed movement, and flung half a glass of liquor down his throat. (Lessing 163)

A work by two or three authors

If your source has two or three authors, name them all, either in your text or in a parenthetical reference. Use last names, in the order they are given in the source, connected by *and*.

Critics have addressed the question of whether literary artists discover new truths (Wellek and Warren 33–36).

One theory claims that the alcoholic wants to "drink his environment in" (Perls, Hefferline, and Goodman 193–94).

A work by four or more authors

For a work with four or more authors, name all the authors, or use the following abbreviated format with *et al.* to signify "and others."

Some researchers trace the causes of alcohol dependence to "flawed family structures" (Stein, Luber, Koman, and Kelly 318).

Some researchers trace the causes of alcohol dependence to "flawed family structures" (Stein et al. 318).

Stein and his coeditors trace the causes of alcohol dependence to "flawed family structures" (318).

Reference to two or more sources with the same authorship

When you are referring to two or more sources written by the same author, include in your in-text citation a shortened form of each title so that references to each text will be clear. The following example discusses how author Joy Williams portrays the drinking scene in her fiction. Note that a comma appears between the author's name and the shortened title.

> She shows drinking at parties as a way of life in such stories as "Escapes" and "White Like Midnight." Thus it is matter of course that Joan pours herself a drink while people talk about whether or not they want to survive nuclear war (Williams, "White" 129).

Distinguishing two authors with the same last name

Use one or more initials to supplement references to authors with the same last name.

> It is no coincidence that a new translation of Euripides' The Bacchae should appear in the United States (C. K. Williams) at a time when fiction writers portray the use of alcohol as a means of escape from mundane existence (J. Williams).

Two or more sources in a single reference

Particularly in an introductory summary, you may want to group together a number of works that cover one or more aspects of your research topic. Separate one source from another by a semicolon.

> Studies that confront the alcoholism of literary figures directly are on the increase (Mariani; Dardis; Gilmore).

A corporate author

A work may be issued by an organization or government agency with no author named. Cite the work as if the name given is the author's. Since the name of a corporate author is often long, try incorporating it into your text rather than using a parenthetical note. In this example the corporate author of the book is Alcoholics Anonymous. The book will be listed alphabetically under "Alcoholics" in Works Cited.

> Among publications that discuss how to help young people cope with family problems, Al-Anon Faces Alcoholism, put out by Alcoholics Anonymous, has been reissued frequently since 1974 (117–24).

A multivolume work

When citing a page reference to a multivolume work, specify the volume by an arabic numeral followed by a colon, a space, and the page number. The Trevelyan history is in four volumes.

> Drunkenness was such a problem in the first decades of the eighteenth century that it was termed "the acknowledged national vice of Englishmen of all classes" (Trevelyan 3:46).

A literary work

Well-known literary works, particularly older ones now in the public domain, may appear in numerous editions. When referring to such a work or a part of one, give information for the work itself rather than for the particular edition you are using, unless you are highlighting a special feature or contribution of the edition.

For a play, supply act, scene, and line number in arabic numerals, unless your instructor specifies using Roman numerals for act and scene (II.iv. 118–19). In the following example, the title of the literary work includes numerals referring to the first of two plays that Shakespeare wrote about Henry IV, known as parts 1 and 2.

> Shakespeare's Falstaff bellows, "Give me a cup of sack, rogue. Is there no virtue extant?" (1 Henry IV 2.4. 118–19).

To cite a modern editor's contribution to the publication of a literary work, adjust the emphasis of your reference. The abbreviation *n* stands for *note.*

> Without the editor's footnote in the Riverside Shakespeare explaining that lime was sometimes used as an additive to make wine sparkle, modern readers would be unlikely to understand Falstaff's ranting: "[Y]et a coward is worse than a cup of sack with lime in it. A villainous coward!" (1 Henry IV 2.4. 125–26n).

Material quoted in your source

Often you will want to quote and cite material that you are reading at second hand—in a work by an intermediate author. Quote the original material and refer to the place where you found it.

> Psychoanalyst Otto Fenichel included alcoholics within a general grouping of addictive personalities, all of whom use addictive substances "to satisfy the archaic oral longing, a need for security, and a need for the maintenance of self-esteem simultaneously" (qtd. in Roebuck and Kessler 86).

An anonymous work

A work with no acknowledge author will be alphabetized in a list of references by the first word of its title. Therefore cite the anonymous work in the same way in your parenthetical reference. The title in this example is *The Hidden Alcoholic in Your Midst.*

> People who do not suffer from addiction often can be thoughtless and insensitive to the problems of those around them. That is the message of an emotional and

thought-provoking pamphlet (<u>Hidden</u>), whose author writes anonymously about the pain of keeping his alcoholism secret.

Page locations for electronic sources

You will find that some electronic sources and documents from the Internet have page numbers; others have paragraph numbers; many have neither. Since you need to provide specific information to show readers where to locate and examine sources, you can follow these general guidelines—an extension of those developed by the Modern Language Association for print sources. Examples are hypothetical.

- Begin the parenthetical citation by referring to the author or title of the source, as you would with any other in-text citation (provided these are not previously mentioned in your sentence).

- Refer to a page number in the electronic source, if provided.

  leading scientists have called for a moratorium on the release of genetically engineered organisms into the environment (Weiss 12).

- If the electronic source has no page numbers, refer to paragraph numbers (if provided). If your citation begins with the author's name or a title, place a comma and follow with the abbreviation *par.* or *pars.*, and indicate the paragraph(s) used.

  Hardy reports that many geneticists object to the idea of a moratorium and have formed their own lobbying groups to fight such moves (par. 14).

- If no pagination or paragraph numbering is provided, you can use abbreviations like those used for classic literary works to refer to a structural division within the source: "pt." for part; "sec." for section; "ch." for chapter; "vol." for volume.

  In the absence of agreement within the scientific community, Norman Stein, director of Genetics Watch, has called for a "sensible government policy" (qtd. in Lubber sec. 5).

- If the electronic source provides no pagination, no paragraph numbering, and no internal structural divisions, cite the source by name only. At the Works Cited page, readers will see that the electronic source was not paginated.

  Scientists prefer to govern themselves; historically, the threat of government intervention has prompted voluntary restraints from scientific organizations (Wesley).

- Finally, when you are citing a one-page electronic source or an electronic source in which entries are arranged alphabetically (such as a CD-based or online encyclopedia), no in-text reference to a page or paragraph is needed. The following reference is to a "Works Cited" list that names an anonymously written article in an online encyclopedia.

> For centuries, farmers have manipulated "genetic materials to achieve desired changes in plants and animals" ("Genetic Engineering").

Following MLA parenthetical style, these in-text citations of electronic sources refer readers to detailed entries in the Works Cited list.

INTEGRATION OF QUOTATIONS

Integrate quotations smoothly

Using signal phrases and appropriate verbs.

When you refer to borrowed material in your research paper, whether by summary, paraphrase, or direct quotation, it is best to introduce the material with a signal phrase, which alerts the reader that the borrowed information is about to be stated. Signal phrases (such as, *according to Leslie Pardue*) help the reader follow your train of thought. They also tell the reader who is speaking and, in the case of summaries and paraphrases, signal phrases indicate exactly where your ideas end and someone else's begin. Without a signal phrase to integrate a quotation into the flow of your paper, the quotation seems to come from nowhere and jars the reader. Consider the following examples:

Unannounced Quotation

Most Americans think, that we are producing more trash per person than ever, that plastic is a huge problem, and that paper biodegrades quickly in landfills. "The biggest challenge we will face is to recognize that the conventional wisdom about garbage is often wrong" (Rathje 99).

Integrated Quotation

Most Americans think that we are producing more trash per person than ever, that plastic is a huge problem, and that paper biodegrades quickly in landfills. William L. Rathje, director of the Garbage Project at the University of Arizona, views the issue differently; he believes that "the biggest challenge we will face is to recognize that the conventional wisdom about garbage is often wrong" (99).

The quotation in the second example is integrated into the text not only by means of a signal phrase, but in two other ways as well. By mentioning the speaker's authority and that he "views the issue differently," LaRose provides even more of a context for the reader to understand how the quotation fits into the discussion.

How well you integrate a quotation, paraphrase, or summary into your paper also depends partly on your choice of signal phrase, in particular, the verb in the signal phrase. It is the verb that conveys the tone and intent of the writer being cited. If a source is arguing, use the verb *argue* (or *asserts*, *claims*, or *contends*); if a source contests a particular position or fact, use *contests* (or *denies*, *disputes*, *refutes*, or *rejects*). By using verbs that are specific to the situation in your paper, you help the reader process and organize the information you are presenting and thereby justify your use of the quotation. Also, by choosing verbs carefully, you avoid the monotony of repeating the overworked *notes*, *says*, *states*, or *writes*.

Quoting literary texts

When writing a paper based on a literary text, quote selectively and provide adequate context for quotations. Also be sure to integrate literary quotations gracefully and in such a way that they clearly support your point. Consider the following examples from a student paper on the short stories of Edgar Allan Poe.

> *WEAK*
>
> Poe often uses specific details from the setting of his stories to suggest the psychological states of his characters. For example, in describing the "barely perceptible fissure" (237), he prefigures Roderick's mental disintegration.

> *EFFECTIVE*
>
> Poe often uses specific details from the setting of his stories to suggest the psychological states of his characters. In "The Fall of the House of Usher," for example, the narrator's description of the "barely perceptible fissure" (237) in the Usher mansion prefigures Roderick's own mental disintegration.

Naming the short story provides more of a context for the quotation, and explicitly stating that the fissure was in the front of the Usher mansion nails down the comparison between setting and psychological state.

Set off long quotations

Set off or block prose quotations that are longer than four lines to help your reader more clearly see the quotation as a whole. Verse quotations are set off when longer than three lines. Set-off quotations are indented ten spaces from the left margin and double-spaced; no quotation marks are necessary because the format itself indicates the passage in a quotation.

Use long quotations sparingly so your paper does not appear to be mostly other people's words. Before deciding whether to include a long quotation, ask yourself, "What is my purpose in choosing this form rather than summary or paraphrase?"

The following example is taken from student Karen Bellitto's library research paper on John Updike's story "A Sense of Shelter." Here Bellitto is discussing the story's main character, William, as he relates to other characters.

> Fearing rejection from his fellow high school seniors, William chooses to sit with the more accepting juniors, who tend to look up to him as an older student. In addition, Updike sharply contrasts William's behavior with that of the character he loves, Mary, who is more adventurous. Critic A.S.G. Edwards explains this contrast:
>
> > On each of the three occasions she appears, Updike presents her going away from William's world, away from the classroom, out of the soda bar, and finally out of the school itself. This final encounter effectively dramatizes the nature of the contrasting characters: Mary's steady progression through and finally away from the school out into the cold world more appropriate to her greater experience and maturity is set

against William's hurried retreat into the womb-like warmth of the school. (467)

The colon following Bellitto's sentence introducing the quotation indicates that the quotation is closely related to what precedes it. Note that, unlike an integrated quotation in which the parenthetical citation is inside the end punctuation, with a long quotation the parenthetical citation goes outside the final punctuation, according to MLA style.

On occasion, long quotations contain more information than you need to use. In such situations you can use an ellipsis mark to show that you omitted material from the original text, in this way keeping the quotation to the point and as short as possible.

Another mark of punctuation that is useful when working with quotations in brackets. These squared parentheses allow you to insert your own words into a quotation to explain a profound reference, for example, or to change a verb tense to fit your text.

According to Rathje, "There are no ways of dealing with it [garbage] that haven't been known for many thousands of years" (100).

Avoid plagiarism

The importance of honesty and accuracy in doing library research cannot be stressed enough. Any material borrowed word-for-word must be placed within quotation marks and properly cited; any idea, explanation, or argument you borrow in a summary or paraphrase must be documented, and it must be clear where the borrowed material begins and ends. In short, to use someone else's ideas in their original form or in an altered form without proper acknowledgment is **plagiarism**. And plagiarism is a serious offense regardless of whether it occurs intentionally or accidentally.

A little attention and effort at certain stages in the research process can go a long way in eliminating the possibility of inadvertent plagiarism. At the note-taking stage, check what you record on your note card against the original, paying particular attention to word choice and word order, especially if you are paraphrasing. It is not enough simply to use a synonym here or there and think it is a paraphrase; you must restate the idea in your own words, using your own style. At the drafting stage, check whenever you incorporate a source into your paper, be careful to put quotation marks around material taken verbatim, and double-check your text against your note card— or better yet, against the original source if you have it on hand. Remember, a quotation is a quotation; it is not enough to cite one as if it were a paraphrase.

PREPARING A LIST OF REFERENCES IN THE MLA FORMAT

In research papers following MLA format, the list of references is called "Works Cited" when it includes those sources you have referred to in your paper. Be aware that some instructors request a more comprehensive list of references—one that includes every source you consulted in preparing the paper. That list would be titled "Bibliography."

The examples in this section show how entries in the "Works Cited" list consist of three elements essential for a list of references: authorship, full title of the work, and publication information. In addition, if the work is taken from an electronic (online) source, consult 36a-3. The basic format for each entry requires the first line to start at the left margin, with each subsequent line to be indented five typed spaces from the left margin.

Not every possible variation is represented here. In formatting a complicated entry for your own list, you may need to combine features from two or more of the examples.

The MLA "Works Cited" list begins on a new page, after the last page of your paper, and continues the pagination of your paper. Entries in the list are alphabetized by the author's last name. An anonymous work is alphabetized by the first word in its title (but disregard *A, An,* and *The*).

Listing books in the MLA "Works Cited" format

The MLA "Works Cited" list presents book references in the following order:

1. Author's name: Put the last name first, followed by a comma and the first name (and middle name or initial) and a period. Omit the author's titles and degrees, whether one that precedes a name (Dr.) or one that follows (Ph.D.). Leave two types spaces after the period.

2. Title of the book: Underline the complete title. If there is a subtitle, separate it from the main title by a colon and one typed space. Capitalize all important words, including the first word of any subtitle. The complete title is followed by a period and two typed spaces.

3. Publication information: Name the city of publication, followed by a colon and one typed space; the name of the publisher followed by a comma; the date of publication followed by a period. This information appears on the title page of the book and the copyright page, on the reverse side of the title page.

If the city of publication is not well known, add the name of the state, abbreviated as in the zip code system. Shorten the name of the publisher in a way that is recognizable. "G. P. Putnam's Sons" is shortened to "Putnam's." For university presses use "UP" as in the example "U of Georgia P." Many large publishing companies issue books under imprints that represent particular groups of books. Give the imprint name first, followed by a hyphen and the name of the publisher: Bullseye-Knopf.

Any additional information about the book goes between the author and title or between title and publication data. Observe details of how to organize, abbreviate, and punctuate this information in the examples below.

A book with one author

The basic format for a single-author book is as follows:

Mariani, Paul. <u>Dream Song: The Life of John Berryman</u>. New York: Morrow, 1990.

A book with two or three authors

For a book with two or three authors, follow the order of the names on the title page. Notice that first and last name are reversed only for the lead author. Notice also the use of a comma after the first author.

Roebuck, Julian B., and Raymond G. Kessler. The Etiology of Alcoholism: Constitutional, Psychological and Sociological Approaches. Springfield: Thomas, 1972.

A book with four or more authors

As in the example under in-text citations (see 36a-1), you may choose to name all the authors or to use the abbreviated format with *et al.*

Stein, Norman, Mindy Lubber, Stuart L. Koman, and Kathy Kelly. Family Therapy: A Systems Approach. Boston: Allyn, 1990.

Stein, Normal, et al. Family Therapy: A Systems Approach. Boston: Allyn, 1990.

A book that has been reprinted or reissued

In the following entry, the date 1951 is the original publication date of the book, which was reprinted in 1965.

Perls, Frederick, Ralph F. Hefferline, and Paul Goodman. Gestalt Therapy: Excitement and Growth in the Human Personality. 1951. New York: Delta-Dell, 1965.

A dictionary or encyclopedia

If an article in a reference work is signed (usually by initials), include the name of the author, which is spelled out elsewhere in the reference work (usually at the beginning). The first example is unsigned. The second article is signed (F.G.H.T.).

"Alcoholics Anonymous," Encyclopedia Britannica: Micropaedia. 1991 ed.

Tate, Frances G. H. "Rum." Encyclopedia Britannica. 1950 ed.

A selection from an edited book or anthology

For a selection from an edited work, name the author of the selection and enclose the selection title in quotation marks. Underline the title of the book containing the selection, and name its editor(s). Give the page numbers for the selection at the end of your entry.

Davies, Phil. "Does Treatment Work? A Sociological Perspective." The Misuse of Alcohol. Ed. Nick Heather et al. New York: New York UP, 1985. 158–77.

When a selection has been reprinted from another source, include that information too, as in the following example. State the facts of original publication first, then describe the book in which it has been reprinted.

Bendiner, Emil. "The Bowery Man on the Couch." The Bowery Man. New York: Nelson, 1961. Rpt. in Man Alone: Alienation in Modern Society. Ed. Eric Josephson and Mary Josephson. New York: Dell, 1962. 401–10.

Two or more works by the same author(s)

When you cite two or more works by the same author(s), you should write the author's full name only once, at first mention, in the reference list. In subsequent entries immediately following, substitute three hyphens and a period in place of the author's name.

Heilbroner, Robert L. The Future as History. New York: Harper Torchbooks-Harper, 1960.

---. An Inquiry into the Human Prospect[u]. New York: Norton, 1974.

A translation

When a work has been translated, acknowledge the translator's name after giving the title.

Kufner, Heinrich, and Wilhelm Feuerlein. In-Patient Treatment for Alcoholism: A Multi-Centre Evaluation Study. Trans. F. K. H. Wagstaff. Berlin: Springer, 1989.

A corporate author

If authorship is not individual but corporate, treat the name of the organization as you would the author. This listing would be alphabetized under "National Center."

National Center for Alcohol Education. The Community Health Nurse and Alcohol-Related Problems: Instructor's Curriculum Planning Guide. Rockville: National Institute of Alcohol Abuse and Alcoholism, 1978.

Signaling publication information that is unknown

If a document fails to state place or date of publication or the name of the publisher, indicate this lack of information in your entry by using the appropriate abbreviation.

Missing, Andrew. Things I Forgot or Never Knew. N.p.: n.p., n.d.

In the above example, the first *n.p.* stands for "no place of publication." The second *n.p.* means "no publisher given," and *n.d.* stands for "no date."

An edition subsequent to the first

Books of continuing importance may be revised substantially before reissue. Cite the edition you have consulted just after giving the title.

Scrignar, C. B. Post-Traumatic Stress Disorder: Diagnosis, Treatment, and Legal Issues. 2nd ed. New Orleans: Bruno, 1988.

A book in a series

If the book you are citing is one in a series, include the series name (no quotation marks or underline) followed by the series number and a period before the publication information. You need not give the name of the series editor.

Schuckit, Marc A., ed. <u>Alcohol</u> <u>Patterns</u> <u>and</u> <u>Problems</u>. Series in Psychological Epidemiology 5. New Brunswick: Rutgers UP, 1985.

An introduction, preface, foreword, or afterword

When citing an introductory or concluding essay by a "guest author" or commentator, begin with the name of that author. Give the type of piece—Introduction, Preface—without quotation marks or underline. Name the author of the book after giving the book title. At the end of the listing, give the page numbers for the essay you are citing. If the author of the separate essay is also the author of the complete work, repeat the author's last name, preceded by *By*, after the book title.

Fromm, Erich. Foreword. <u>Summerhill</u>: <u>A</u> <u>Radical</u> <u>Approach</u> <u>to</u> <u>Child</u> <u>Rearing</u>. By A. S. Neill. New York: Hart, 1960. ix–xiv.

In this book, the editors also wrote the introduction to their anthology.

Josephson, Eric, and Mary Josephson. Introduction. <u>Man</u> <u>Alone</u>: <u>Alienation</u> <u>in</u> <u>Modern</u> <u>Society</u>. Ed. Josephson and Josephson. New York: Dell, 1962. 9–53.

An unpublished dissertation or essay

An unpublished dissertation, even of book length, has its title in quotation marks. Label it as a dissertation in your entry. Naming the university and year will provide the necessary publication facts.

Reiskin, Helen R. "Patterns of Alcohol Usage in a Help-Seeking University Population." Diss. Boston U, 1980.

Listing periodicals in the MLA "Works Cited" format

A *periodical* is any publication that appears regularly over time. A periodical can be a daily or weekly newspaper, a magazine, or a scholarly or professional journal. As with listings for books, a bibliographical listing for a periodical article includes information about authorship, title, and facts of publication. Authorship is treated just as for books, with the author's first and last names reversed. Citation of a title differs in that the title of an article is always enclosed in quotation marks rather than underlined; the title of the periodical in which it appears is always underlined. Notice that the articles *a, an,* and *the,* which often begin the name of a periodical, are omitted from the bibliographical listing.

The facts of publication are the trickiest of the three elements because of the wide variation in how periodicals are date, paginated, and published. For journals, for example, the publication information generally consists of journal title, the volume number, the year of publication, and the page numbering for the article cited. For newspapers, the listing includes name of the newspaper, full date of publication, and full page numbering by both section and page number(s) if necessary. The following examples show details of how to list different types of periodicals. With the exception of May, June, and July, you should abbreviate the names of months in each "Works Cited" entry (see 31d).

A journal with continuous pagination through the annual volume

A continuously paginated journal is one that numbers pages consecutively throughout all the issues in a volume instead of beginning with page 1 in each issue. After the author's name (reversed and followed by a period and two typed spaces), give the name of the article in quotation marks. Give the title of the journal, underlined and followed by two typed spaces. Give the volume number, in arabic numerals, after a typed space, give the year, in parentheses, followed by a colon. After one more space, give the page number(s) for the article, including the first and last pages on which it appears.

Kling, William. "Measurement of Ethanol Consumed in Distilled Spirits." Journal of Studies on Alcohol 50 (1989): 456–60.

In a continuously paginated journal, the issue number within the volume and the month of publication are not included in the bibliographical listing.

A journal paginated by issue

Latessa, Edward J., and Susan Goodman. "Alcoholic Offenders: Intensive Probation Program Show Promise." Corrections Today 51.3 (1989): 38–39+.

This journal numbers the pages in each issue separately, so it is important to identify which issue in volume 51 has this article beginning on page 38. The plus sign following a page number indicates that the article continues after the last-named page, but after intervening pages.

A monthly magazine

This kind of periodical is identified by month and year of issue. Even if the magazine indicates a volume number, omit it from your listing.

Waggoner, Glen. "Gin as Tonic." Esquire Feb. 1990: 30.

Some magazines vary in their publication schedule. *Restaurant Business* publishes once a month or bimonthly. Include the full date of publication in your listing. Give the day first, followed by an abbreviation for the month.

Whelan, Elizabeth M. "Alcohol and Health." Restaurant Business 20 Mar. 1989: 66+.

A daily newspaper

In the following examples, you see that the name of the newspaper is underlined. Any introductory article (*a, an,* and *the*) is omitted. The complete date of publication is given—day, month (abbreviated), year. Specify the edition if one appears on the masthead, since even in one day an article may be located differently in different editions. Precede the page number(s) by a colon and one typed space. If the paper has sections designated by letter (A, B, C), include the section before the page number.

If the article is unsigned, begin your entry with the title, as in the second example ("Alcohol Can Worsen . . . ").

Welch, Patrick. "Kids and Booze: It's 10 O'Clock—Do You Know How Drunk Your Kids Are?" Washington Post 31 Dec. 1989: C1.

The following entry illustrates the importance of including the particular edition of a newspaper.

"Alcohol Can Worsen Ills of Aging, Study Says." New York Times 13 June 1989, natl. ed.: 89.

"Alcohol Can Worsen Ills of Aging, Study Says." New York Times 13 June 1989, late ed.: C5.

A weekly magazine or newspaper

An unsigned article listing would include title, name of the publication, complete date, and page number(s). Even if you know a volume or issue number, omit it.

"A Direct Approach to Alcoholism." Science News 9 Jan. 1988: 25.

A signed editorial, letter to the editor, review

For these entries, first give the name of the author. If the piece has a title, put it within quotation marks. Then name the category of the piece—Letter, Rev. of (for Review), Editorial—without quotation marks or underline. If the reference is to a review, give the name of the work being reviewed with underline or quotation marks as appropriate.

Fraser, Kennedy. Rev. of Stones of His House: A Biography of Paul Scott, by Hilary Spurling. New Yorker 13 May 1991: 103–10.

James, Albert. Letter. Boston Globe 14 Jan. 1992: 61.

Stein, Norman. "Traveling for Work." Editorial. Baltimore Sun 12 Dec. 1991: 82.

Listing other sources in the MLA "Works Cited" format

An abstract of an article

Libraries contain many volumes of abstracts of recent articles in many disciplines. If you are referring to an abstract you have read rather than to the complete article, list it as follows.

Corcoran, K. J., and M. D. Carney. "Alcohol Consumption and Looking for Alternatives to Drinking in College Students." Journal of Cognitive Psychotherapy 3 (1989): 69–78. Abstract. Excerpta Medica Sec. 32 Vol. 60 (1989): 40.

A government publication

Often, a government publication will have group authorship. Be sure to name the agency or committee responsible for writing a document.

United States. Cong. Senate. Subcommittee to Investigate Juvenile Delinquency of the Committee on the Judiciary. Juvenile Alcohol Abuse: Hearing. 95th Cong., 2nd sess. Washington: GPO, 1978.

An unpublished interview

A listing for an unpublished interview begins with the name of the person interviewed. If the interview is untitled, label it as such, without quotation marks or underlining. Name the person doing the interviewing only if that information is relevant. An interview by telephone or e-mail can be noted as part of the interview citation.

Bishop, Robert R. Personal interview. 5 Nov. 1987.

Bly, Robert. Telephone interview. 10 Dec. 1993.

An unpublished letter

Treat an unpublished letter much as you would an unpublished interview. Designate the recipient of the letter. If you as the writer of the paper were the recipient, refer to yourself as "the author."

Bishop, Robert R. Letter to the author. 8 June 1964.

If a letter is housed in a library collection or archive, provide full archival information.

Bishop, Robert R. Letter to Jonathan Morton. 8 June 1964. Carol K. Morton papers, Smith College, Northampton.

A film or videotape

Underline the title, and then name the medium, the distributor, and the year. Supply any information that you think is useful about the performers, director, producer, or physical characteristics of the film or tape.

Alcoholism: The Pit of Despair. Videocassette. Gordon Jump. AIMS Media, 1983. VHS. 20 min.

A television or radio program

If the program you are citing is a single episode with its own title, supply the title in quotation marks. State the name and role of the foremost participant(s). Underline the title of the program, identify the producer and list the station on which it first appeared, the city, and the date.

"Voices of Memory." Li-Young Lee, Gerald Stern, and Bill Moyers. The Power of the Word with Bill Moyers. Exec. prod. Judith Davidson Moyers and Bill Moyers. Public Affairs TV. WNET, New York. 13 June 1989.

An interview that is broadcast, taped, or published

Treat a published interview as you would any print source. A broadcast or taped interview can be treated as a broadcast program.

"The Broken Cord." Interview with Louise Erdrich and Michael Dorris. Dir. and prod. Catherine Tatge. A World of Ideas with Bill Moyers. Exec. prod. Judith Davidson Moyers and Bill Moyers. Public Affairs TV. WNET, New York. 27 May 1990.

A live performance, lecture

Identify the "who, what, and where" of a live performance. If the "what" is more important than the "who," as in a performance of an opera, give the name of the work before the name of the performers or director. In the following example, the name of the speaker, a cofounder of AA, comes first.

Wilson, Bill. "Alcoholics Anonymous: Beginnings and Growth." presented to the NYC Medical Society. New York, 8 Apr. 1958.

A work of art

Underline the title of a work of art referred to, and tell the location of the work. The name of the museum or collection is separated from the name of the city by a comma.

Manet, Edouard. The Absinthe Drinker. Ny Carlsberg Glyptotek, Copenhagen.

Computer software

Like a printed book, computer software has authorship, a title, and a publication history. Include this in any bibliographical listing, along with relevant information for your reader about the software and any hardware it requires. Underline the title of the program. Identify the title as computer software. In the example, the name of the author and the location of the company would be added if they were known.

Alcohol and Pregnancy: Protecting the Unborn Child. Computer software. Student Awareness Software, 1988. 48K Apple II and 256K IBM PC.

A separately issued map, chart, or graph

Even a freestanding map or poster generally tells something about who published it, where, and when. Give the title, underlined, and any identifying information available. Use the abbreviation *n.d.* any time a date is lacking in publication information.

Roads in France. Map. Paris: National Tourist Information Agency, n.d.

Listing electronic sources in the MLA "Works Cited" format

Electronic source materials are available to writers in a variety of delivery systems; the Modern Language Association (MLA) system for citing electronic sources varies slightly, depending on whether the material is delivered via

- a CD-ROM that is published periodically (like a journal);
- a CD-Rom that is published once (like a book);
- a diskette;
- a computer service (such as AOL or Prodigy); or
- the Internet.

The guidelines here are presented in sections that correspond to these delivery system—a presentation derived from the *MLA Handbook for Writers of Research Papers*, fourth edition. As electronic media evolve, conventions for listing digital sources in a "Works Cited" list will also change. However the details of citation may evolve, researchers will always need to give clear, consistent, and specific directions for locating every source used in a paper.

Electronic sources delivered via CD-ROM

When citing a source located on a CD-ROM, you will need to determine if the CD-ROM was published once (like a book) or is updated periodically (like a journal).

CD-ROMs updated periodically *with* a print equivalent

Present the following information in the order listed. Note that some information may be unavailable or not relevant to the Works Cited entry you are preparing: (1) author's name; (2) information for print equivalent (article title in quotation marks, journal or magazine underlined, volume and page, date printed). Following this information, list (3) the database name (underlined), (4) CD-ROM, (5) database provider or "vendor" (if given), and (6) date of CD-ROM publication.

Bureau of the Census. "Exports to Germany, East: Merchandise Trade-Exports by Country." National Trade Statistics (1995): 85–96. National Trade Databank. CD-ROM. U.S. Bur. of Census. 1 Aug. 1995.

CD-ROMs updated periodically with no print equivalent

Present the following information in the order listed. Note that some information may be unavailable or not relevant to the Works Cited entry you are preparing: (1) author's name; (2) article title in quotation marks, as well as the article's original date. Following this information, list (3) the database name (underlined), (4) CD-ROM, (5) database provider or "vendor" and (6) date of CD-ROM publication.

Gillette. "Gillette Co.: Balance Sheet, 12/31/93–9/30/95." Compact Disclosure. CD-ROM. Digital Library Systems, Inc. Oct. 1995.

**CD-ROMs or diskettes issued as a
single publication (analogous to publication of a book)**
Present the following information in the order listed. Note that some
information may be unavailable or not relevant to the Works Cited
entry you are preparing: (1) author's name; (2) title underlined or in
quotation marks. Follow with (3) product title (underlined); (4) ver-
sion/release information; (5)CD-ROM *or* diskette; (6) publication
information—city, publisher's name, year.

"Industrial Revolution." Concise Columbia Encyclopedia. Microsoft
 Bookshelf. 1994 ed. CD-ROM. Redmond: Microsoft, 1994.

Miller, Arthur. The Crucible. CD-ROM. New York: Penguin, 1994.

Pirsig, Robert M. Zen and the Art of Motorcycle Maintenance and Lila: An
 Inquiry into Morals. Voyager Expanded Book. Diskette. New York: Voyager, 1992.

Online sources: Computer services (AOL, Nexis, etc.)

The development of commercial, online providers such as America Online,
Prodigy, New York Times Online, Nexis, and Lexis has provided researchers with a
wealth of electronic sources. For citing commercial online services, follow these conventions:

Online sources *with* a print equivalent
Present the following information in the order listed. Note that some
information may be unavailable or not relevant to the Works Cited
entry you are preparing: (1) author's name; (2) information for print
equivalent, including the article title in quotation marks; journal, newspaper, or magazine underlined; the date originally printed. Following
this information, list (3) the database name (underlined), (4) Online,
(5) computer service (Nexis, AOL, etc.), and (6) date of your electronic
access.

Tyler, Patrick E. "Taiwan's Leader Wins Its Election and a Mandate." New
 York Times 24 Mar. 1996: A1. New York Times Online. Online. AOL. 27
 Mar. 1996.

Jager, Peter de. "Communicating in Times of Change; Communication in
 Management." Journal of Systems Management 45.6 (1944): 28l. Online.
 Nexis. 26 Mar. 1996.

Online sources with *no* print equivalent
Present the following information in the order listed. Note that some
information may be unavailable or not relevant to the Works Cited
entry you are preparing: (1) author's name; (2) information for electronic posting—title of article in quotation marks, and the date of posting if available. Following this information, list (3) the database name

(underlined), (4) Online, (5) computer service (Nexis, AOL, etc.), and (6) date of your electronic access.

> Mallory, Jim. "Senior Citizens Need Computing Too." 18 Mar. 1996. <u>Newsbytes</u>. Online. AOL. 24 Mar. 1996.

Online sources: Internet

The citation forms presented here follow specifications set out in the *MLA Handbook for Writers of Research Papers*, fourth edition. The *MLA Handbook* advises that listing an Internet source's electronic address is optional. Because an electronic address enables researchers to revisit any source that is still available on Internet servers, we have provided the electronic address for the examples below, following conventions recommended by the Alliance for Computers and Writing (its home page is http://english.ttu.edu/acw/). See the ACW page for a slight variation from MLA on citing Internet sources.

Preparing Works Cited entries

Present the following information in the order listed. Again, note that for any given source, not all of the information listed below will be available or will be relevant. Provide what information you can: (1) author's name; (2) print information or, if the material accessed has been posted electronically only, information on the posting:

- the underlined title of the larger work area—e.g., electronic journal, newsletter, or conference:
- any identifying reference numbers (e.g., volume or issue);
- in parentheses, date of electronic posting;
- number of pages or paragraphs (if provided, or n. pag. for no pagination). Use the abbreviations "pp." for "pages" and "par." or "pars." for "paragraph(s)."

Continue the entry with (3) Online; (4) the electronic database or "repository" holding the information, if relevant; (5) computer network; and (6) date of your access. Most Internet users consider it necessary to provide an electronic address of a source, introduced with the word *Available*. Follow with (7) the Internet address with protocol, plus (8) the path locators used for access.

FTP (File Transfer Protocol) sites

> Tompkins, David P. "Thucydides Constructs His Speakers: The Case of Diodotus." <u>Electronic</u> <u>Antiquity</u> 1.1 (1993): 5 pp. Online. Internet. 4 Nov. 1995. Available FTP: into.utas.edu.au departments/classics/antiquity/1, 1-June 1993/ (4) Articles/Tompkins-Thucydides

Gopher sites

> Cooper, Wendy. "Virtual Reality and the Metaphysics of Self, Community, and Nature." (14 Mar. 95): n. pag. Online. Internet. 26 May 1996. Avail-

able Gopher: apa.oxy.edu 12.International Philosophy Preprint Exchange
5. Preprints 6. Metaphysics 1. Cooper VR_and_the_Metaphysics_of_Self
5. VR_MUD._TXT

WWW (World Wide Web) sites

Welty, Eudora. "Place in Fiction." <u>Collected</u> <u>Essays</u>. New York: Harcourt,
1994. Online. Electronic Text Center. Internet. 24 Mar. 1996. Available
http://darwin.clas.virginia.edu/%7etsawyer/DRBR/welty.txt

Telnet sites

Cohen, Linda. "Wafer Production: Data Gathering and Analysis." <u>Semicon-</u>
<u>ductors</u> <u>Today</u> (9 Feb. 1996): n. pag. Online. Internet. 16 Aug. 1996.
Available Telnet: semi.ceres.freq.nit.com_73412

Synchronous communications (MOOs, MUDs, IRCs)

Jan D-Guest. Online synchronous interview. Online. Internet. 15 May 1996.
Available Telnet: wisdom.sensimedia 4567

E-mail and listserv citations

Andrews, Tamsey. "Remote Teachers and Engaged Learners." Personal e-mail.
Online. Internet. 6 Feb. 1996.

Nostroni, Eric. "Collaborative Learning in a Networked Environment." <u>Elec-</u>
<u>tronic</u> <u>Forum</u> (8 Sept. 95): n. pag. Online. Internet. 12 Apr. 1996. Avail-
able: eforum@cgu.edu

APA DOCUMENTATION

In writing a library research paper—or any other kind of research report, for that
matter—you are using the information and ideas of others. Whenever you directly
quote, summarize, or paraphrase another person's thoughts and ideas, or use facts
and statistics that are not commonly known or believed, you must properly acknowledge your source.

APA In-Text Citations

Like the Modern Language Association (MLA) style of documentation (see next section), the American Psychological Association (APA) style uses brief in-text citations
to refer the reader to full bibliographic information in a list of references at the end
of the paper. However, there are several format differences between MLA and APA.
The following format recommendations are based on the *Publication Manual of the
American Psychological Association*, 4th edition (1994).

An APA in-text citation gives the author's last name and the year of publication.
In the case of a quotation, include the page number (a page number for a paraphrase
or summary is optional). Use commas to separate items in the parentheses. The following examples illustrate correct form for APA in-text citations:

Paraphrase or summary with author's name in signal phrase

Give the year of publication in parentheses immediately after the author's name.

Milstein (1990) believes that such animals as the grizzly bear, Dall sheep, and golden eagle are in danger if measures are not taken to curb poaching in our national parks.

Paraphrase or summary without author's name in signal phrase

Give the author and year of publication in parentheses at the end of the cited material.

Such animals as the grizzly bear, Dall sheep, and golden eagles are in danger if measures are not taken to curb poaching in our national parks (Milstein, 1990).

Quotation with author's name in signal phrase

Give the year of publication in parentheses immediately after the author's name, and put the page number at the end of the quotation.

According to Milstein (1990), "As part of a recent Washington State wilderness bill, Congress upped the maximum fine for wildlife crimes at Olympic National Park from $500 to $25,000" (p. 125).

Quotation without author's name in signal phrase

Give the author, year of publication, and page number in parentheses at the end of the citation.

During one federal sting operation in North Carolina, "agents bought about 1,200 bear claws, on their way to becoming jewelry; 102 feet, an exotic delicacy; 320 gallbladders, considered a panacea in the Orient; 18 heads; and one live bear cub" (Milstein, 1990, p. 122).

A work with two authors

List both authors' names in the signal phrase with the year of publication immediately following, or put both names in a parenthetical citation. In this case, note that the ampersand (&) is used instead of *and*.

The resurgence of recycling in the 1980s can be traced to the confrontations between incineration and landfill projects (Blumberg & Gottlieb, 1989).

A work with three to five authors

Give all authors' last names in a signal phrase or parentheses in your *first* citation only; use an ampersand (&) instead of *and* in the parenthetical citation.

Liberation begins with an awareness that we all are to some degree prisoners of our own language (Clark, Eschholz, & Rosa, 1994).

In subsequent citations, use only the first author's name and *et al.* (Latin for "and others").

Clark et al. (1994) maintain that language is one of humankind's greatest achievements and most important resources.

A work with six or more authors

In all citations, use the first author's name followed by *et al.*

Cognitive behavior therapy is now recognized as an effective intervention for disturbed body image in young women (Rosen et al., 1989).

Author unknown

When the author is unknown, use the title of the piece in a signal phrase, or give a shortened title in a parenthetical citation.

In <u>Children of the Dragon: The Story of Tiananmen Square</u> (1990) the interconnections of the events leading up to the bloody massacre in June 1989 are presented in detail.

The interconnections of the events leading up to the bloody massacre in China in June 1989 (<u>Children of the Dragon</u>, 1990).

Corporate author

With corporate authorship, give the full name of the institution, agency, or organization in the signal phrase together with an abbreviation in brackets in the first citation.

According to Internal Revenue Service [IRS] (1987) regulations, deductions for interest paid on credit cards were phased out.

Under the new regulations, deductions for interest paid on credit cards were phased out (Internal Revenue Service [IRS], 1987).

In subsequent citations the abbreviation is sufficient both in a signal phrase and parenthetically.

Two or more authors with the same last name

When using references by two or more authors with the same last name, include initials with all references.

A survey completed by P. J. Babin (1995) showed that sales of cellular car phones tripled in the last five years.

More than one work in a parenthetical citation

When acknowledging more than one source in a parenthetical citation, present the sources in the order in which they appear in your list of references (i.e., alphabetically); separate the citations with a semicolon.

Environmentalists contend that solid waste disposal will be America's—if not the world's—most pressing problem in the decade of the 1990s (Blumberg & Gottlieb, 1989; Rathje, 1989).

Interviews, letters, memos, e-mail communications, and telephone conversations

Bennett and Ulrich (letter, July 19, 1995) are confident that their study on the effects of secondary smoke will be completed by the end of the year.

Do not include these items in your list of references.

APA-Style References

In APA style, the alphabetical list of works cited that appears at the end of a research paper is called *References*. Although each APA reference contains the same information that the corresponding MLA reference would, there are differences in the order of the information, indentation, punctuation, and mechanics. The following guidelines highlight those differences.

1. Start the first line of each entry at the left margin; indent subsequent lines three spaces.

2. Reverse *all* authors' names within each entry, and use initials, not first names.

3. Name all authors; do not use *et al.* Use an ampersand (&) instead of *and* in naming the second or last of several authors.

4. Give the date of publication in parentheses after the last author's name, followed by a period.

5. Underline the titles and subtitles of books and periodicals, but do not put quotation marks around titles of articles.

6. Capitalize only the first word of book and article titles and subtitles and any proper nouns. Capitalize the titles of periodicals according to standard rules (see MECH 1i).

7. Use the abbreviations *p.* or *pp.* for page numbers of all publications except scholarly journals.

Following are sample APA-style references for the types of sources you are most likely to encounter. For situations not covered here, consult the *Publication Manual of the American Psychological Association*, 4th edition, 1994.

Citing books

One Author
Katznelson, I. (1992). <u>Marxism and the city</u>. New York: Oxford University Press.

Two or More Authors
Davison, J., & Davison, L. (1994). <u>To make a house a home: Four generations of American women and the houses they lived in</u>. New York: Random House.

Debold, E., Wilson, M., & Malave, I. (1993). <u>Mother daughter revolution: From good girls to great women</u>. New York: Bantam Books.

Editors

Cohen, C. B. (Ed.). (1988). <u>Casebook on the termination of life-sustaining treatment and care of the dying</u>. Bloomington, IN: Indiana University Press.

Work in an Anthology

Pinderhughes, E. (1995). Biracial identity—Asset or handicap? In H. W. Harris, H. C. Blue, & E. E. H. Griffith (Eds.), <u>Racial and ethnic identity: Psychological development and creative expression</u> (pp. 163–179). New York: Routledge.

Corporate Author

National Association for the Advancement of Colored People. (1994). <u>Beyond the Rodney King story: An investigation of police conduct in minority communities</u>. Boston: Northeastern University Press.

Anonymous Book

<u>Children of the dragon: The story of Tianammen Square</u>. (1990). New York: Collier.

Edition Other Than First

Polsby, N. W., & Wildavsky, A. (1991). <u>Presidential elections: Contemporary strategies of American electoral politics</u> (2nd ed.). New York: Free Press.

Two or More Works By the Same Author

Sheehy, G. (1988). <u>Character: America's search for leadership</u>. New York: William Morrow.

Sheehy, G. (1992). <u>The silent passage: Menopause</u>. New York: Random House.

Sheehy, G. (1995). <u>Passages 2000: The revolution of second adulthood</u>. New York: Random House.

When listing two or more works by the same author, arrange them chronologically by year of publication, starting with the one published earliest. Repeat the author's name including any initials for all entries. If two or more works by the same author were published in the same year, use lowercase letters to differentiate them: (1992a), (1992b), (1992c).

Citing articles in periodicals

Article in a Monthly Magazine

Klingel, H. (1995, April). The South Bronx bounces back. <u>Smithsonian, 26</u>, 100–111.

Article in a Weekly Magazine

Como, J. (1995, April 17). Hero storyteller. <u>National Review, 47</u>. 53–56, 72.

Article in a Journal Paginated By Volume

Izraeli, D. N. (1993). They have eyes and see not: Gender politics in the Diaspora Museum. Psychology of Women Quarterly, 17, 515–523.

Article in a Journal Paginated By Issue

Lachman, S. J. (1993). Psychology and riots. Psychology: A Journal of Human Behavior, 30(3/4), 16–23.

Article in a Newspaper

Haverman, J. (1995, April 20). Indian tribes resist idea of state grants. The Washington Post, p. 19A.

Editorial

Cole E., & Rothblum, E. D. (1991). [Editorial]. Women and Therapy: A Feminist Quarterly, 11(2), 1–2.

Letter to the Editor

Seeley, D. S. (1991). "What's left?" is the wrong question [Letter to the editor]. Social Policy, 21(4), 60.

Book Review

Retish, P. (1992). [Review of the book The troubled adolescent]. Journal of Pediatric Psychology, 17, 245–246.

Citing electronic sources

Your goal with an electronic reference is to both credit the author and enable a reader to retrieve the source. APA recommends that you provide as much information as you can, including a specific retrieval path. For sources not covered in the following models, consult Li and Crane's (1996) *Electronic Style: A Guide to Citing Electronic Information* in the reference section of your library.

Periodically Updated CD-ROM Database

Waldron, A. (1989, March 14). Writers and alcohol [CD-ROM]. Washington Post. Available: 1994 SIRS, Inc./SIRS 1989 Alcohol—No. 4/48A

Nonperiodic CD-ROM Database

Randolph, J. (1992). Recycling of materials [CD-ROM]. The New Grolier Multimedia Encyclopedia. Available: Danbury, CT: Grolier Electronic Publishing

Online Database

James, C. (1994, September 16). An army family as strong as its weakest link.
New York Times [Online], Late Edition, p. C8. Available:
NEXIS/NEWS/NYT [1995, May 17]

Internet

Derian, J. D. (1994, September). Cyber-deterrence. Wired, [Online]2(9).
Available: Mosaic: http://www/wired.com/Etext/index.html File: Cyber-
deterrence: The US army fights tomorrow's war today

Online Electronic Text

Twain, M. (1993). The advance of Tom Sawyer [Online]. Available: HTTP:
http://www.cs.cmu.edu/Web/People/rgs/sawyr-table.html [1995, May 19]

Citing other sources

Government Publication

Internal Revenue Service. (1994). Your federal income tax (Publication 17).
Washington, DC: U.S. Government Printing Office.

Dissertation Abstract

Erwin, L. K. (1990). The politics of anti-feminism: The pro-family movement
in Canada (Doctoral dissertation, York University, 1990). Dissertation
Abstracts International, 51, 3237-A.

Computer Software

File f/x [Computer software]. (1990). Redmond, WA: Metz Software.

Video

Schmiechen, B. (Producer), & Adelman, L. (Director). (1978). Controlling
interest: The world of the multinational corporation [Videotape]. San
Francisco, CA: California Newsreel.

SAMPLE RESEARCH PAPER #1

Sexual Fulfillment in <u>The Awakening</u> and "The Storm" by Kate Chopin

by
Lavonne C. Cliff

Professor John Smith
Freshman Communicative Skills
ENC 1102-001
September 30, 1998

Lavonne Cliff
Dr. Smith
ENC 1102, Section 001
September 30, 1998

Sexual Fulfillment in <u>The</u> <u>Awakening</u> and "The Storm"
by Kate Chopin

Thesis Statement: Kate Chopin's protagonists, Edna Pontellier of <u>The</u> <u>Awakening</u> and Calixta of "The Storm" dared to express sexual ideas that were revolutionary to the early twentieth century.

I.   Many of Katherine Chopin's stories deal with women who feel trapped in their marriages and/or relationships.

    A.   Two women, Edna Pontellier of <u>The</u> <u>Awakening</u> and Calixta of "The Storm" feel trapped in their marriages.

    B.   Both characters are trying to find their identities.

II.   Edna Pontellier of <u>The</u> <u>Awakening</u> is considered to be one of Chopin's most revolutionary characters.

    A.   Edna tries to find her identity.

    B.   Edna discovers her feelings about marriage.

        1.   She believes that marriage should not be the end of sensuality.

        2.   She finds that her marriage is an entrapment.

        3.   She explores an extramarital affair.

            a.   Her affair leads her to depression.

            b.   She decides to end her life.

III.   Calixta of "The Storm" is considered to be another of Chopin's revolutionary characters.

Cliff 2

    A. Calixta has an extramarital affair.

    B. She is not ashamed of her love affair.

IV. Kate Chopin is not interested in the immoral, but in life.

    A. Her heroines are described with no remorse or shame.

    B. Katherine Chopin dreamed of a renewed birthright for women.

Cliff 3

Lavonne Cliff
Dr. Smith
ENC 1102, Section 001
September 30, 1998

Sexual Fulfillment in The Awakening
and "The Storm" by Kate Chopin

Many of Katherine Chopin's stories deal with women who in some sense feel

trapped in their marriages and/or relationships. Each comes to recognize that she

wants to explore other avenues of life. Among Chopin's stories, The Awakening

and "The Storm" are particularly descriptive of women who are beginning to

acknowledge their sexuality and independence outside of the "traditional institu-

tion" of marriage. The two women, Edna Pontellier of The Awakening and Calixta

of "The Storm" believe that there is something missing in their lives. In searching

for what is missing, the two women experience sexual fulfillment with a libera-

tion uncommon to their time. Kate Chopin's protagonists, Edna Pontellier in The

Awakening and Calixta in "the Storm" dared to express sexual ideas that were

revolutionary to the early twentieth century.

   Chopin's novel, The Awakening, is considered one of the most important

pieces of early twentieth century fiction about the sexuality of women, and the

first to fully face the fact that marriage did not end a woman's sensuality, but was

instead, an episode in her continuous growth. Ziff, a critic of The Awakening

said, "Though it was not meant to attack the institution of the family, it did reject

the family as an automatic equivalent of feminine self-fulfillment" (299-305). In

striving towards feminine self-fulfillment and identity, Edna found that a woman could be a good mother and wife without devoting all of herself to her family. Indeed, she realized that a wife should be able to find personal happiness and freedom, and not be content with what is traditionally expected of her. Edna Pontellier realized that her husband was dull, that marriage with him was boring and confining, and that being a mother was a form of bondage which she refused to accept. Bogard, another expert in the field observed, "Edna will awaken in the novel and discover that she is caged in a marriage that does not allow her to grow or to become a mature, self-assured woman with a mind of her own and a sexual body of her own" (15).

Edna's awakening takes the form of a growing awareness of the conflict between her life as "a conventional wife and mother and her emergent sense of self" (Bogard 16). At first, her decision to reject her traditional marriage seems to free her to love another and to be loved in return. She is beginning to feel the possibility that there might be something more to marriage than what she and Leonce, her husband, share something deeper in the relationship between a man and a woman than exists in her marriage. Leonce Pontellier regards Edna as a "valuable piece of personal property that has suffered some damage" (Bogard 20). Later in the novel, Edna discovers that she cannot be anyone's personal property, whether it was her husband or her children. Edna's emancipation starts with her physical attraction to Robert. After she and Robert kiss, she jokes that Leonce is generous; perhaps he might "give" her to Robert, an offer she finds absurd since no one can give her away (Seyersted 138-196). Edna is already free; she belongs to no one, except herself.

Although Edna "struggles with the sensual appeal of physical ripeness, and wanting her own independence to love, she finds out that the one she loves is unwilling to sacrifice himself to love her" (Eble 261). Edna then turns to the sea where "there are no goals, no roles, no boundaries . . . as a wife and mother she would stagnate losing all self-confidence and direction; thus she chooses to swim out to her death." She had to choose whether or not life was worth being lived, "on terms other than her own," and she decided that it was not. Swimming out to her death gives Edna a sense of dignity because the choice is hers (Bender 264). However, Ziff observed that The Awakening "raises the question of what a woman was to do with the freedom that she struggled towards" (300). The intensity and appreciation of personal freedom cannot be measured. That is why soldiers and others sometimes choose to die free instead of to live in bondage.

Calixta of "The Storm" is another of Chopin's liberated wives. Actually, "The Storm" is a sequel to Chopin's earlier short story, "At the Cadian Ball". In "At the Cadian Ball," Bibinot, a young Creole is in love with Calixta, who is described as a "little Spanish vixen," and Alcee Laballiere, a planter, is attracted to Clarisee. During the ball, Calixta and Alcee share an intimate moment that was interrupted by Clarisee who comes to take Alcee away from Calixta and later expresses her love for him. Later Bibinot shows up and Calixta agrees to marry him, since she could not have Alcee.

"The Storm" takes place four years later when both couples have already married. "It appears that Calixta's marriage to Bibinot is a kind of self-inflicted penance for . . . she must settle for a less prestigious man instead of a . . . socially prominent planter" (Arms 215).

The title "The Storm" has a double meaning. The first reference is to the summer thunderstorm which traps Bibinot and his son in town for the afternoon.

The second reference is to the relationship between Calixta and Alcee, who is seeking shelter from the storm, incidentally at Calixta's home. The two have not seen or spoken to each other since the events described in "At the Cadian Ball". They soon discover that the attraction they once shared has not diminished over the years. A fiery display of mutual passion that leads them to infidelity takes place on a couch in Calixta and Bibinot's living room. The affair seems inevitable, given Calixta and Alcee's feelings for each other before marriage and because of their own hum drum marriages.

"Mrs. Chopin displays the gradual arousal of a woman to the gratification and the peril of extramarital sexual satisfaction" (Arms 215). When Bibinot returns home expecting to be scolded for his dirty clothes, he finds Calixta in a happy mood. She treats him royally because the void of not knowing what it would have been like to be with Alcee has now been filled and has taken her to unexplored sexual heights. Calixta regains her old sexuality, something that was lost between her and Bibinot. Bibinot is pleased and delighted with his wife's actions for those pleasures have not been consistent in their marriage. Calixta feels no guilt, no sorrow, no regret for what she has done. If anything, it has enlightened her relationship with Bibinot.

Leary states that Katherine Chopin was not interested in the immoral, but in life as it comes, "in what she saw as natural or certainly inevitable . . . inside or outside of marriage" (176). She describes her heroines as remorseless and shameless after their extramarital affairs. Even though Edna commits suicide, Chopin describes her as casting off her garments before walking into the sea. Leary claims that this was symbolic of a rebirth and a search for spiritual freedom which was sought mostly by men (178).

Cliff 7

The <u>Awakening</u> and "The Storm" are remarkable for the freedom they assert in the face of the suffocating conventionality in the 1890's. Unconventionality in marriage whether it came in the form of infidelity or some other feelings meant liberation for the early twentieth century woman. The <u>Awakening</u> and "The Storm" demonstrate Kate Chopin's dream of woman's renewed birthright for passionate self-fulfillment. "Her work is thus no feminist plea in the usual sense, but an illustration of a woman's right to be herself, to be individual and independent . . . ." (Leary 188). A reader may miss Chopin's point if he or she confines his or her reading to only one of her stories, but the point that marriage should not entrap a woman cannot be missed when it is repeated in several of her stories. The <u>Awakening</u> and "The Storm" illustrate the insistence with which Chopin wanted to make her point.

Works Cited

Arms, George. "Kate Chopin's <u>The Awakening</u> in the Perspective of her Literary Career. <u>Essays on American Literature</u>. Ed. Clarence Gohdes. Chapel Hill: Duke University Press, 1967.

Bender, Bert. "Kate Chopin's Lyrical Short Stories." <u>Studies in Short Story Fiction</u>. Vol. XI, No. 3. Newberry: Newberry College, 1974.

Bogard, Carley. "The Awakening: A Refusal to Compromise." <u>University of Michigan Papers in Women's Studies</u>. Ann Arbor: The University of Michigan Press, 1977.

Eble, Kenneth. <u>Western Humanities Review</u>. Salt Lake City: University of Utah, 1956.

Leary, Lewis. <u>Southern Literary Journal</u>. Vol. I, No. 1. December 1968. 176-191.

Seyersted, Per. <u>Kate Chopin: A Critical Biography</u>. Baton Rouge: Louisiana State University, 1969.

Ziff, Larzer. <u>The American 1890's</u>. New York: West Publishing Company, 1971.

SAMPLE RESEARCH PAPER #2

Sarah Hyde

Dr. Fortune

ENC 1101, Section 4

28 November 1997

Real Medical Alternatives

Thesis: The face of alternative medicine is changing through a redefinition of the healing practices involved, through its wide variety of uses, and through validating research.

I. The definition of alternative medicine differs between fields

   A. Orthodox practitioners believe it to be a hoax.

   B. Advocates find it to be beneficial to medicine.

II. There are four main types of alternative therapy.

   A   The first is physical manipulation.

      1. Massage is used

      2. Reflexology is used.

      3. Yoga is used.

   B. The second is use of ingested substances.

      1. Home remedies are used.

      2. Herbs are used.

      3. Aromatherapy is used.

   C. The third is energy balancing.

      1. Reiki is used.

      2. Crystals are used.

   D. The fourth use is psychic and spiritual healing.

      1. Self-help groups are used.

    2. Hypnosis is used.

    3. Visualizations are used.

III. The perspectives on alternative medicine are changing.

    A. They are changing through developing research programs.

    B. They are also changing through government recognition.

Sarah Hyde
Dr. Fortune
ENC 1101, Section 4
28 November 1995

Alternative medicine has been called "New Age" medicine, quackery, and fraud. Medical professionals argue that alternative medicine is a money scam that takes advantage of desperate people. However, it has been in existence longer than any of the practices in use today. Many of the so-called "New Age" procedures that have been grouped together under that title are actually traditional medical practices found in cultures throughout history; African, Native American, and Oriental are just a few of alternative medicine's origins. These practices must have been abandoned by many in search for a more direct and prompt way to provide the health care solutions found in present-day America. Since the traditional practices have become more prevalent, the federal government and orthodox practitioners have scurried to determine the truth about what works and what does not. As tests are run and experiments are done, it is obvious that some aspects of medical acceptance will be changing, especially opinions on the place alternative medicine should hold in scientific circles. The face of alternative medicine is changing through a redefinition of the healing practices involved, through its wide variety of uses, and through validating research.

Alternative medicine has been called many names, including traditional medicine, unconventional medicine, and unorthodox medicine; all of which generally mean different from the accepted norm. While the rarely accepted idea of alternative medicine is used in most fields of medicine in the United States, it is being used widely among patients outside of medical supervision. Stehlin noted in 1990, one in three patients used some type of alternative therapy, and 80 percent of those were also using conventional medicine at the same time but did not inform their physicians about the use of the treatment (2).These statistics suggest that some aspects of alternative medicine are appealing to the patients, who may feel trapped in the midst of the highly structured and impersonal health care system.

Many conventional practitioners have been skeptical about this alternative practice of medicine. On the subject of an opening of the recently organized Office of Alternative Medicine on a Maryland college campus, medical opinions varied. Critics said that the opening of such an office would give the public the idea that alternative medicine practices are legitimate alternatives to conventional treatment before they have been scientifically proven to be effective. The American Medical Association, on the other hand, believed that although the majority of alternative therapies have not yet been proven effective, they should be given the opportunity to be evaluated (42). Isadora B. Stehlin stated, "Many physicians believe it is not unreasonable for someone in the last stages of an incurable cancer to try something unproven," yet these same physicians do not recommend " . . . abandoning a conventional therapy when there is a known response in the effectiveness of that therapy" (4).Biomedicine focuses on how to cure a patient through scientifically tested and proven effective strategies. However, alternative or holistic healers embrace a different perspective on healing.

As the number of alternative medicine advocates increases, the confidence in the power of alternative healing grows also. Believers and administers of alternative medicine (usually referred to as healers) have come forward to attest to the benefits of it. They believe, unlike the view held by the world of biomedicine, that the power to heal lies within the patient (Engebretson 51). Daniel Glick, from Newsweek, wrote "Most alternative practices focus on the whole individual rather than the ailment, and they stress a close link between body and mind to prevent disease" (52). Isadora Stehlin discovered the backbone of alternative medicine to be hidden in a simple act of faith. She wrote, "Many advocates of unproven treatments and cures contend that people have the right to try whatever may offer them hope, even if others believe the remedy is worthless" (2). In situations where people are faced with chronic or life-threatening diseases, it seems that alternative medicine is the only other option when all else has failed to be effective.

The many types and usages of alternative medicine have made it hard to define by advocates and opponents alike. "For many conditions," according to Stehlin, " . . . what's effective for one patient may not help another" (2). That is why there are a variety of types and usages tailored to fit the diversified needs of patients. According to Joan Engebretson, " . . . there can be no classification system that adequately describes the types of healers practicing in the United States . . . because healers were often practicing more than one type of healing and would frequently incorporate many different methods into their practice" (52). The types of alternative healing can, however, be classified into four general areas of practice.

The most accepted type of alternative therapy is physical manipulation. Some more popular forms of this type include massage, reflexology, and yoga. Massage therapy is physical manipulation of muscles throughout the body. This is accomplished by the kneading and rubbing of muscles by a licensed therapist. Massage

machines and accessories have been available for some time in many specialty and

department stores. Reflexology is the practice often referred to in the United States

as "zone therapy" (Engebretson 54). Engebretson states, "Reflexology practitioners

believe that each organ and gland in the body has a corresponding reflex point on

the bottom of the feet" (54). Yoga, on the other hand, can generally be done with-

out a therapist. "In the United States," says Engebretson, "{Yoga} classes usually

focus primarily on the movement and breathing techniques" (54). The benefits of

these manipulations, according to Engebretson, include relaxation, reduced stress

level, and enhanced energy levels (54).

Another kind of alternative healing that has become more accepted is the use

of healing substances. Home remedies are used to assist the body in healing

itself, herb therapy is used to relieve common ailments and in preventive medi-

cine, and aromatherapy is used for various physical and psychological properties

(Engebretson 54). Vitamins and dietary supplements, although not always viewed

by patients as drugs or therapies, are also used for their healing properties

(Nightingale 454). These types of therapies are not new to mankind, but can be

found throughout history long before all the synthetic materials in use today were

even thought of.

A more abstract form of alternative healing is energy balancing. This therapy

is evident in all types of healing in some form or another. The belief behind it is

that health is the product of a balanced energy system in the individual (Enge-

bretson 55). Everyone, according to Kathleen McLane, has his or her " . . . own

energy field via seven whirling centers on the body called chakras, the Sanskrit word for 'wheel' " (170). One way of directing or stimulating these energy fields is through a therapy called Reiki. It is used in conjunction with the chakras, says McLane, to balance the body, mind, and spirit (170). Crystals are also used to balance energy flow. They respond, says Engebretson, to a spectrum of emitted body energies (55). McLane says that the crystals imitate the movement of the chakras by spinning, and the energy "wheels" needing adjustment or direction can be distinguished through the strength, size, and shape of the different spins (170). This type of therapy, along with releasing energy in the form of stress, is used for self enlightenment and personal growth.

The last type of alternative healing is the use of psychic and spiritual healing. This therapy is not uncommon to believers in certain religions, but in the scientific world of biomedicine, the idea of God is not dealt with, and the term miracle is just nonsense to scientists. Self-help groups, hypnosis, and visualizations are a few examples of spiritual and psychic healing. Engebretson notes that benefits include personal growth and insight into the self through a higher being (55). Because these types of benefits are impossible to accurately measure, scientists have a difficult time believing that this type of alternative medicine could actually be used to some benefit in the medical field. Because many types of alternative healing cannot be scientifically tested or measured, many argue that the benefits are not even real; that they are imagined or even fraudulent. Tim Beardsley wrote that " . . . some scientists . . . wonder how a proposal to investigate a therapy with scant supportive evidence could go against a conventional research proposal in a fair competition" (44). A multitude of scientists share this belief that researching alternative medicine is a waste of money and time. They complain that money spent assisting research into alternative medicine will divert resources from their research projects (Beardsley 44). What they fail to recognize, however, is that at one time the road to medical discovery was unpaved for them also. At some point in history, the medical practices taken for granted today were just as scrutinized as alternative medicine is now.

Despite the majority of opponents to alternative practices, the idea is becoming more accepted. One program, funded by the W. K. Kellogg Foundation, has developed a community based parish nursing project (King 27)."Parish nursing," defined by Jean King, "plays an instrumental role in promoting health, healing, and wholeness among their congregation and the community (27). With organizations like these, although they adhere more to the rules set by the world of bio-medicine, it will not take long for more alternative medicine practices to be funded and expanded. The National Institutes of Health (NIH) found that life-style related diseases such as cancer, heart attacks, and high blood pressure could have been prevented through a healthy sense of spirituality and self-direction (King 30). This in itself is a statement giving unwarranted support for alternative medicine, whose central belief is the unity of body, mind, and spirit.

Even the government is recognizing the benefits of alternative medicine. A two million dollar congressional appropriation to the NIH has already begun to be used in research (Glick 58). Stehlin informs the public that alternative therapies that are currently under study are acupuncture, hypnosis, Ayurvedic herbals for Parkinson's disease, electrical currents, and imagery (53). Other agencies have also begun to participate in research. "The National Cancer Institute has evaluated more than 30,000 natural products in recent years for activity against

Hyde 9

cancer and the AIDs virus," says Beardsley (44). The Food and Drug Administra-

tion has also developed regulations for potential consumer hazards (Stehlin 4).

Soon, says Glick, insurance companies will find that paying for alternative medi-

cine will keep people healthier and medical bills lower (53). As the American

Medical Association said, the practice of alternative medicine deserves the

chance to be evaluated thoroughly and correctly (Beardsley 58).

After evaluations have been completed, the fakes will be weeded out from

the real alternatives. What worked in the past may not be accepted as yet by

society, but it should be an option for all. The benefits of alternative medicine are

plentiful; lowering medical bills, preventing disease, and promoting a healthier

life-style are just a few of those mentioned among the multitude of other alterna-

tive practices. With time, testing, and open-mindedness, the healing powers of

real alternative medicine will have the chance to show that they can be inte-

grated as a truly powerful force in the world of medicine.

Works Cited

Beardsley, Tim. "Fads and Feds. Holistic Therapy Collides with Reductionist Science." Scientific American Sept. 1993: 39, 42, 44.

Engebretson, Joan, and Dianne Wardell. "A Contemporary View of Alternative Healing Modalities. Nurse Practitioner Sept. 1993: 51-55.

Glick, Daniel. "New Age Meets Hippocrates. Medicine Gets Serious About Unconventional Therapy." Newsweek 13 July 1992: 58.

King, Jean M., Jean A. Larkin, and Jan Striepe. "Coalition Building between Public Health Nurses and Parish Nurses. Journal of Nursing Administration Feb. 1993: 27-31.

McLane, Kathleen. "Do You Give Good Vibes? Maybe You Need an Energy Tune-up. How to Adjust Your Aura." Mademoiselle Nov. 1995: 170, 183.

Nightingale, Stuart L. "Dietary Supplement Use: Significant Information in the Medical History." Editorial. Journal of the American Medical Association 28 July 1993: 454.

Stehlin, Isadora. "An FDA Guide to Choosing Medical Treatments." The Food and Drug Administration, 1995.

9

The Essay Examination

GENERAL ESSAY EXAMINATIONS

The time has come for you to take a state-mandated examination. You are nervous about it, especially the Essay Subtest, for it has been over a year since you have written a theme. To make matters worse, you do not have time to attend any help sessions, but you definitely need practice in writing. What are you going to do? Well, you can do nothing. Or you can take a few days to digest the helpful hints found within this unit and follow the simple steps outlined therein. Upon completion of this review guide, you will be ready to take and pass the state-mandated essay subtest.

Review Noteworthy Elements

Most of the essay topics for state-mandated tests require you to write about a person, thing, idea, or event that has gained prominence or fame in a particular societal area within a certain period of time. Granted, this is a world of material to cover, so just choose two or three from each broad category and jot down some main ideas about each. For instance, if a topic requires you to discuss a man or woman who is noted for a major breakthrough in the field of medicine, you would already have reviewed the accomplishments of such greats as Jonas Salk, Charles Drew, or Marie Curie. Therefore, you will not have to waste time trying to think of something or someone to write about. More than likely, you will already have some ideas in mind. You may take the time to look through some recent issues of magazines such as *Time*, *Newsweek*, or even *People*. Such publications often contain articles on very topical issues. Your journal (the one that you perhaps kept for Freshman Composition) could also be of help, depending upon what you were allowed to write about. However, if you are a well-read person who stays abreast of major issues, you probably do not need such a review as the one described here. Proceed to the next step.

Analyzing Simulated State-Mandated Exam Essay Topics

State-mandated exam essay topics can usually be found in your writing laboratory or English department. You (and your study mate(s)), if you have any, can even formulate your own, using some of the subject areas that you have thought of as you read various magazines, or you may use those topics at the end of this unit. Focus on the various restrictions and/or limitations that are built into them. Notice the examples below:

1. The main reason(s) for the rise in violent crime within the past ten years.

2. Why welfare should (not) be deleted from today's social system.

3. Why today's farmers should (not) use pesticides on their crops.

In topic one (1), the expressions "main reason(s)," "rise," and "violent crime" should get your immediate attention as you begin to formulate your thesis idea in your head. Such wording limits your writing realm. Also, you must remember your time constraint—"within the past ten years." This element also limits your reference span; but it, as well as the key expressions, helps you to focus and pull possible ideas together for development.

In topic two (2), the expressions "welfare," "deleted," and "social system" are the restricting elements; "today's" is the time constraint. In addition, topic two offers an alternative view—"should" or "should not." Once you choose your alternative and include it in your thesis idea, you are obligated to your reader to develop your essay along the lines of your choice of viewpoint. Furthermore, in developing topic two, because of its introductory word—*why*, you have the broad-based obligation to use reasons as the basic vehicle for development.

Topic three (3), like topics one (1) and two (2), has its limiting elements—"pesticides," "crops," and "farmers," and time constraint—"today"; and like topic two, it presents you the option to be for or against the stated idea. A second parallel that topic three has with topic two is the necessity to be developed by reasons.

Not all topics have to have several limiting elements, time constraints, or obligatory methods of development. You should read each topic closely to determine its individual specifications. After the appropriate determinations have been made about your chosen topic, you may formulate your thesis statement, often-times using much of the wording of the topic to construct this main idea. Topic three will be used to illustrate this point.

Thesis: Today's farmers should not use pesticides on their crops.

Notice that the thesis statement above uses the same wording that is found in its topic. Using such a tactic cuts down on the time that you would use trying to find the exact wording for your idea. It also assures adherence to the topic in the development of your paper. The main difference in the topic and the thesis is that in the thesis you show that you have taken a position—the farmer should not use pesticides. The reader can now expect the specific reasons for your stance to be given and developed.

Adding Prongs

Often the reasons (or any other means of development) are attached to the thesis statement itself. Such attachments are called prongs—two or more parallel ideas affixed to the thesis to show more specific avenues of development. Prongs should be well thought out and weighed to see if each can be adequately covered within a body paragraph of the essay. Notice the reasons—the prongs—that are considered for further development of the more general thesis idea above.

Because

(1) they often aggravate respiratory problems in humans.

(2) they tend to pollute the rivers and streams.

(3) they leave trace elements that cause reproductive problems in humans and animals.

(4) they kill vegetation not targeted for eradication.

After making a hurried jot list of possible prongs, you can then choose the two or three that you feel that you can develop most easily. Your previously open-ended thesis statement may now look like this:

> Today's farmers should not use pesticides on their crops because such chemical compounds often aggravate respiratory problems in humans, leave trace elements that can cause reproductive problems in both humans and other animals, and kill vegetation and animals that are not targeted for eradication.

In composing such a thesis statement, you have determined not only the focal point of your discussion, but the specific substance and order of your development as well. Thus, prongs can serve as significant allies in timed situations. In some instances, having prongs will preclude your having to construct a specific jot list for your essay—your basic ideas and order of development are already in place. However, if you feel the need to plan further before you begin to write, continue with the following step, which takes you through more detailed planning for getting started.

Going Through the Steps of the Writing Process

First, take one of the topics from the end of this unit and construct a thesis idea as we did above. Second, keeping both the subject and purpose of your thesis in mind, jot down some possible main thoughts that would help to give more specific detail to your thesis. Quickly check each potential main thought (which will serve as a topic sentence for a body paragraph) to see if you can generate (in your mind) significant discussion about it. If you are unable to develop an idea, this is the time to throw your chosen topic out and consider another one. *Do not try to make a formal outline.* Making such a construction would be far too time consuming, and graders do not consider planning efforts anyway. If you have two or three main thoughts that can each generate enough pertinent information for two or three well-developed body paragraphs, then place these ideas in an order that would reflect a particular process or mode of development, if necessary. Simply place a number beside each idea to establish your order of discussion. You may then add two or three secondary ideas (which will be used as basic development for the primary ideas) under each. None of the ideas on your jot list have to be written as a full sentence. Just write enough of the thought for you to remember. *Do not take the time to rewrite the jot list.* Do not forget that you have the option of making prongs from the main topics.

Write an *introduction* (of about 3-5 sentences), making sure that you get your reader's attention; that you give a bit of *general*, but *relevant*, background information; and that you include your thesis statement, preferably at the end. Your prongs or jot list already gives you the plan for your *body*, so just begin writing, using each main idea as a topic sentence. Your *conclusion* can be a paragraph of just two sentences—a paraphrasal of the thesis sentence and an additional sentence that lends a note of finality to the paper. Such a sentence can present a solution, resolution, or some other rather decisive idea, depending on the content of the theme. (See "The Writing Recipe" later in this section if you need to review a basic mode of theme and/or body paragraph development.)

Reviewing Your Major Error Tendencies

If you were chided quite frequently in Freshman Composition I and II for errors in such areas as subject-verb agreement, comma usage, or sentence structure, get out your handbook and review the area(s). Don't try, however, to correct all of your wrongs in a short period of time; just work on the most blatant ones. If time permits, attend a few lab sessions or have a conference with an English teacher for help with your problem(s). Check for these errors in the paper after you have written it.

Timing Yourself

Now that you have gone through the writing process in a step-by-step manner, you need to start considering the time factor. Write about five themes which are four or five paragraphs in length. Use the various topics at the end of this unit. (You may write four-paragraph themes for many state-mandated tests—an introduction, two body paragraphs, and a conclusion.) Allow yourself about fifteen minutes for planning (constructing a thesis sentence and making the jot list), thirty minutes for writing, and about five minutes for proofreading and making minor revisions. (Do not start to develop another topic after you have spent more than ten minutes on one; usually, time does not allow for such switching, and *do not* try to *write* and then *rewrite* your paper. Your first draft is very likely your last draft. Simply draw a thin line through an error or whatever you would like to change, and write the correction or new idea just above it. Do not make scratch marks! Write legibly and try to keep your paper neat.) If you spend more than the allotted fifty minutes on your first two themes, do not become too alarmed. But you should try to finish three consecutive themes within the time limit. However, the point should be made that graders focus more on *quality* than on *quantity*. Even if you have not *quite* finished, about five minutes before time is up, take the remaining time to read over what you have already written, making as many corrections as you can.

Making an Assessment of Your Essay

Since most state-mandated essays are graded holistically, it would be ideal to have an English teacher who is adept at grading holistically to evaluate each theme, indicating the score [ranging from one (1) to six (6)] that it merits. If such a situation is not possible, ask a writing lab instructor or specialist or someone who has already passed the Essay Subtest (with at least a total score of 8) to make the assessment for you. If this also fails, make the assessment yourself. The score descriptions below are illustrative of the kind of grading criteria often used to evaluate state-mandated tests.

(Scoring Criteria for the Essay Subtest)—a modification of the rubric sanctioned by the State of Florida.

- - - - - - - - - - - - - - - - - - -

Score of 1=F

Thesis—tends to present no thesis or a thesis that is an announcement or a thesis that presents two ideas to be developed.

Support—(when present) is usually irrelevant, vague, general and/or illogical.

Language—is often nonstandard and colloquial.

Errors—are numerous, consequently preventing effective communication.

- - - - - - - - - - - - - - - - - - -

Score of 2=D

Thesis—suggests a plan of development.

Support—presents a series of generalizations with unrelated ideas, therefore preventing effective communication.

Language—tends to be rudimentary.

Errors—are pervasive, hence interfering with communication.

- - - - - - - - - - - - - - - - - - -

Score of 3=C–

Thesis—has a thesis and often a plan of development that is superficial.

Support—is scant, with inconsistent development in paragraphs.

Language—is usually conventional.

Errors—appear sometimes in syntax, usage, punctuation, and mechanics, however, do not impede communication.

- - - - - - - - - - - - - - - - - - -

Score of 4=C+

Thesis—is explicit or implicit with reasonable support.

Support—tends to be detailed and consequently adequate.

Language—demonstrates competency in selecting appropriate diction but has occasional lapses in word choice and expression.

Errors—appear infrequently.

- - - - - - - - - - - - - - - - - - -

Score of 5=B

Thesis—is explicitly stated (or skillfully implied) and developed.

Support—presents thorough discussion of main points with sophistication.

Language—presents precise word choices and imaginative expression.

Errors—(if present) are minor, therefore not marring communication.

- - - - - - - - - - - - - - - - - - - -

Score of 6=A

Thesis—is well-focused and shows a very mature flair (expressed or implied).

Support—tends to have very substantive ideas which are extensively elaborated and show exceptional polish in development and in imagination.

Language—is polished.

Errors—are practically non-existent in the areas of grammar and punctuation. A few spelling errors may be present. The writer's ability to communicate his purpose must be very evident.

If your scores are not quite up to par, repeat the process. Otherwise, you have finished! You are fully prepared to pass any essay subtest. Get a good night's rest, have a good breakfast, and keep your nerve up. You will have no problems!

The Writing Recipe

The Writing Recipe below is not for everyone. If you have a good sense of organization and development, just omit this part. On the other hand, if you find yourself grasping for ideas and trying to find a place to put them, this illustration could help you a great deal. You should remember, however, that this recipe is basic; you might need to add or subtract a sentence or transitional marker at one place or another.

INTRODUCTION (3-5 SENTENCES)

Sentence 1: Attention getter
Sentence 2: (and perhaps 3 & 4);
  Bridge sentence(s)
Sentence 3: THESIS

I. (Transition) Topic Sentence	1st body paragraph
A. Primary sentence one:	Specific aspect of the topic sentence.
1. Secondary sentence:	Specific detail about primary sentence one.
2. Secondary sentence:	Specific detail about primary sentence one.
B. (Trans) Primary sentence two:	A specific aspect of the topic sentence.
1. Secondary sentence:	Specific detail about primary sentence two.

2. Secondary sentence: Specific detail about primary sentence two.

Paragraph Closure (This sentence is optional).

II. (Trans) Topic Sentence   2nd body paragraph

  A. Primary sentence one: Specific aspect of the topic sentence.

    1. Secondary sentence: Specific detail about primary sentence one.

    2. Secondary sentence: Specific detail about primary sentence one.

  B. Primary sentence two: Specific aspect of the topic sentence.

    1. Secondary sentence: Specific detail about primary sentence two.

    2. Secondary sentence: Specific detail about primary sentence two.

Paragraph Closure (This sentence is optional).

III. (Trans) topic sentence (You may omit this paragraph if your thesis does not dictate additional development and if your paragraphs one and two are extensively developed.

                                   3rd body paragraph

  A. Primary sentence one: Specific aspect of the topic sentence.

    1. Secondary sentence: Specific detail about primary sentence one.

    2. Secondary sentence: Specific detail about primary sentence one.

  B. (Trans) Primary sentence two: A specific aspect of the topic sentence.

    1. Secondary sentence: Specific detail about primary sentence two.

    2. Secondary sentence: Specific detail about primary sentence two.

Paragraph Closure (This sentence is optional).

CONCLUSION (2–3 SENTENCES)

Sentence one: A paraphrasal of the thesis

Sentence two: A solution, resolution, or any appropriate sentence that will give your essay a sense of finality.

Sample Essay

The theme below has been constructed to follow the recipe outlined above. See if you can identify specific sentences and transitions within it. Pay very close attention to the functions and relationships of each. The simulated state-mandated essay topic and its jot list have been included to illustrate the whole writing process.

> Essay topic: The one thing in life that means a great deal to most people, regardless of their age.
>
> Thesis: Love is the one thing that means a lot to almost all people—the old, the middle-aged, and the young.

Planning

Jot List:

Old people	Middle-aged people	Young people
pets	children	romantic partners
children and grands	spouses	parents, toys, and activities

DRAFT

A lot of women have cried for it. A lot of men have died for it. Most people spend a lifetime trying to find it. Even some animals and insects seem to value it a lot. What is this thing that means so much to so many? Why, it is love, of course. Love is the one thing that means a lot to most people—the old, the middle-aged, and the young.

First, love makes a great difference in the lives of many who are over sixty. For instance, the love of a pet usually makes them feel warm all over. There is nothing more important to them than coming home to the happy yelps and wagging tail of a dog. A cat purring and rubbing against a senior citizen's legs or curled up in his lap is a source of peace and joy. In addition, older folk also appreciate little acts of affection shown by younger relatives. A friendly call or a visit from a son or daughter makes the day brighter for them, especially for an elderly person who lives alone. A birthday card, a phone call, a brief note, or a photograph sent by a grandchild will be cherished by an older person for many years. Love indeed means quite a bit to elderly people.

Secondly, middle-aged people, those individuals who are between the ages of forty and sixty, also value love. Although they might not show it as readily as old people do, middle-agers also appreciate their sons, daughters, and grandchildren showing that they care. Many of them show their love for their family by working endlessly to prepare a Christmas or Thanksgiving dinner that everyone will enjoy. Also, there have been many people in their middle years who have emptied their savings accounts to help their children buy the house or car that they wanted. The parents do all of this in an effort to show love to and be loved by their children. Middle-age people appreciate the love shared with their children, but they also value the love shared with a spouse. A box of candy, a bouquet of roses, or a simple "I love you" means a lot when it comes from a husband or wife who has shared a person's life for many years. After about age forty-five, a lot of people start thinking about retirement. Having a loving partner to share the waning years with is a pleasing thought. Thus, it is evident that middle-aged people, like older people, place a high premium on love.

Finally, those in the under-forty group are renowned for their preoccupation with love. For instance, teenagers spend most of their waking hours thinking about their romantic partners. They write love notes, listen to love songs, read love magazines, and even buy T-shirts with love messages written on them, all with that special someone in mind. They often spend hours on end talking on the telephone to or about the present object of their affection. Even the older ones in this group are still caught up with the idea of having a romantic partner in their lives. They are especially marriage-minded at this time. The little ones, on the other hand, have parents and a few toys that are usually the center of their world. They hug and kiss mommies, daddies, and their favorite teddy bears. A pat on the head, a smile from a parent, or a red lollipop is all they need to feel special. Love means the world to those who are young.

In conclusion, people of all ages value love. The focus of their affection might be different, but the basic need for it is common to all.

This student's essay was given a total score of eight (8), four (4) points each by two holistic graders.

Simulated State-Mandated Essay Topics

1. A movie that most Americans have seen and enjoyed.
2. A non-religious book that many people read or make use of frequently.
3. A man or woman who has helped many Americans get and/or stay in shape physically.
4. A major disaster, occurring within the last ten years, that elicited the concern or sympathy of millions of people.
5. America's greatest source of embarrassment.
6. A television program that should be taken off the air.
7. The greatest military hero the world (America) has ever known.
8. A popular singing group that stands apart from all of the others.
9. Certain practices in American politics that should be changed or stopped.
10. A well-known non-American person who is (was) revered by many Americans.
11. A country that extensively affects the economy of the world.
12. A weekly or monthly news publication that most American adults deem reliable.

10

Observing Conventions

GLOSSARY OF USAGE

This glossary is intended to provide definitions and descriptions of selected word usages current in formal academic writing. In consulting this kind of glossary, writers should be prepared to make informed decisions about the meaning and the level of diction that is most appropriate to their writing project.

Many entries in this glossary consist of commonly confused homonyms—words that are pronounced almost alike but have different meanings and spellings.

a, an   Use *a* when the article precedes a noun beginning with a consonant. For example, *At last we found a hotel*. Use *an* when the article precedes a word beginning with a vowel or an unpronounced *h*. *It was an honor to receive an invitation*.

accept, except   Use *accept* when your meaning is "to receive." Use *except* when you mean an exception, as in *He invited everyone except Thuan*. You can also use *except* as a verb that means "to leave out," as in *The report excepted the two episodes of misconduct*.

adverse, averse   Use *averse* when you mean a person's feelings of opposition. Use *adverse* when you refer to a thing that stands in opposition or is opposed to someone or something, as in *I was not averse to taking the roofing job, but the adverse circumstances of a tight deadline and bad weather almost kept me from it*.

advice, advise   Use *advice* as a noun meaning "a recommendation," as in *Longfellow gave excellent military advice*. Use *advise* as a verb meaning "to recommend," as in *Many counselors advise students to declare a double major*.

affect, effect   If your sentence requires a verb meaning "to have an influence on," use *affect*. If your sentence requires a noun meaning "result," use *effect*. *Effect* can also be a verb, however. Use *effect* as a verb when you mean "to make happen," as in *He was able to effect a change in how the city council viewed the benefits of recycling*.

aggravate, irritate In formal writing, use *aggravate* when you mean "to make worse," as in *The smoke aggravated his cough.* Use *irritate* when you mean "to bother," as in *He became irritated when the drunken driver said the accident was not her fault.*

ain't Do not use *ain't* in formal writing. Use *is not, are not,* or *am not* instead.

all ready, already Use *all ready* when you mean "prepared" as in *He was all ready for an expedition to Antartica.* Use *already* when you mean "by this time," as in *The ushers at Symphony Hall will not seat you if the concert has already started.*

all right Do not use *alright*. It is simply a misspelling.

all together, altogether Use *all together* when you mean "as a group" or "in unison," as in *Once we got the family all together, we could discuss the estate.* Use *altogether* when you mean "entirely," as in *Some of the stories about Poe's addictions and personal habits are not altogether correct.*

allude, elude Use *allude* when you mean "to refer indirectly to." Use *elude* when you mean "to avoid or escape."

allusion, illusion Use *allusion* when you mean "an indirect reference," as in *The children did not understand the allusion to Roman mythology.* Use *illusion* when you mean "false or misleading belief of appearance," as in *Smith labored under the illusion that he was a great artist.*

a lot Do not use *a lot* in formal writing. Use a more specific modifier instead. When you use *a lot* in other contexts, remember that it is always two words.

among, between Use *between* when you are expressing a relationship involving two people or things, as in *There was general agreement between Robb and Jackson on that issue.* Use *among* when you are expressing a relationship involving three or more separable people or things, as in *He failed to detect a link among the blood cholesterol levels, the red blood cell counts, and the T-cell production rates.*

amongst Do not use *amongst* in formal writing. Instead, use *among*.

amount, number Use *amount* when you refer to a quantity of something that cannot be counted, as in *The amount of effort put into finding the cure for AIDS is beyond calculation.* Use *number* when you refer to something that can be counted, as in *The number of people who want to run the Boston Marathon increases yearly.*

an, and Use *an* when the article precedes a noun beginning with a vowel or an unpronounced *h*. Use *and* when your sentence means "in addition to."

and etc. Avoid using *etc.* in formal writing. When you must use *etc.* in nonformal writing, do not use *and. Et cetera* means "and so forth"; therefore, *and etc.* is redundant.

and/or Use *and* or *or,* or explain your ideas by writing them out fully. But avoid *and/or,* which is usually too ambiguous to meet the demands of formal writing.

anxious, eager Use *anxious* when you mean "worried" or "nervous." Use *eager* when you mean "excited or enthusiastic about the possibility of doing something."

anybody, any body; anyone, any one   Use *anybody* and *anyone* when the sense of your sentence requires an indefinite pronoun. Use *any body* and *any one* when the words *body* and *one* are modified by *any*, as in *The teacher was careful not to favor any one student* and *Any body of knowledge is subject to change.*

any more, anymore   Use *any more* to mean "no more," as in *I don't want any more of those plums.* Use *anymore* as an adverb meaning "now," as in *He doesn't work here anymore.*

anyplace   Do not use *anyplace* in formal writing. Use *anywhere* instead.

anyways, anywheres   Do not use *anyways* and *anywheres* in formal writing. Use *anyway* and *anywhere* instead.

apt, likely, liable   Use *apt* when you mean "having a tendency to," as in *Khrushchev was apt to lose his temper in public.* Use *likely* when you mean "probably going to," as in *We will likely hear from the Senator by Friday.* Use *liable* when you mean "in danger of," as in *People who jog long distances over concrete surfaces are liable to sustain knee injuries.* Also use *liable* when you are referring to legal responsibility, as in *the driver who was at fault was liable for the damages.*

as, like   Use *as* either as a preposition or as a conjunction, but use *like* as a preposition only. If your sentence requires a preposition, use *as* when you are making an exact equivalence, as in *Edison was known as the wizard of Menlo Park.* Use *like* when you are referring to likeness, resemblance, or similarity, as in *Like Roosevelt, Reagan was able to make his constituency feel optimism.*

as, than   When you are making a comparison, you can follow both *as* and *than* with a subjective- or objective-case pronoun, depending on meaning. For example, *We trusted O'Keeffe more than him [we trusted Smith]* and *We trusted O'Keeffe more than he [Jones trusted O'Keeffe]. O'Keeffe was as talented as he [was talented]* and *We found O'Keeffe as trustworthy as [we found] him.*

as to   Do not use *as to* in formal writing. Rewrite a sentence such as *The president was questioned as to his recent decisions in the Middle East* to read *The president was questioned about his recent decisions in the Middle East.*

assure, ensure, insure   Use *assure* when you mean "to promise" as in *He assured his mother that he would return early.* Use *ensure* when you mean "to make certain," as in *Taking a prep course does not ensure success in the SATs.* Use *insure* when you mean "to make certain" in a legal or financial sense, as in *He insured his boat against theft and vandalism.*

at   Do not use *at* in a question formed with *where*. For example, rewrite a sentence such as *Where is the class at?* to read *Where is the class?*

a while, awhile   Use *awhile* when your sentence requires an adverb, as in *He swam awhile.* If you are not modifying a verb, but rather want a noun with an article, use *a while,* as in *I have not seen you in a while.*

bad, badly   Use *bad* as an adjective, as in *Bad pitching changed the complexion of the game.* Use *badly* as an adverb, as in *The refugees badly needed food and shelter.* Use *bad* to follow linking verbs that involve appearance or feeling, as in *She felt bad about missing the party.*

being as, being that   Do not use either *being as* or *being that* to mean "because" in formal writing. Use *because* instead.

beside, besides   Use *beside* as a preposition meaning "next to." Use *besides* as an adverb meaning "also" or "in addition to" as in *Besides, I needed to lose the weight.* Use *besides* as an adjective meaning "except" or "in addition to," as in *Rosa Parks seemed to have nothing besides courage to support her.*

better, had better; best, had best   Do nut use *better, had better, best,* and *had best* for *should* in formal writing. Use *ought* or *should* instead.

between, among   See *among, between.*

breath, breathe   Use *breath* as a noun; use *breathe* as a verb.

bring, take   Use *bring* when you are referring to movement from a farther place to a nearer one, as in *The astronauts were asked to bring back rock samples.* Use *take* for all other types of movement.

broke   Use *broke* only as the past tense, as in *He broke the Ming vase.* Do not use *broke* as the past participle; for example, instead of writing *The priceless vase was broke as a result of careless handling,* write *The priceless vase was broken as a result of careless handling.*

bunch   Use *bunch* to refer to "a group or cluster of things growing together." Do not use *bunch* to refer to people or a group of items for formal writing.

burst, bust   Use *burst* when you mean "to fly apart suddenly," as in *The pomegranate burst open.* (Notice that the example sentence doesn't say *bursted;* there is no such form of the verb.)

but however, but yet   When you use *however* and *yet,* do not precede them with *but* in formal writing. The *but* is redundant.

but that, but what   When you use *that* and *what,* do not precede them with *but* in formal writing. The *but* is unnecessary.

calculate, figure, reckon   If your sentence requires a word that means "imagine," use *imagine.* Do not use *calculate, figure,* or *reckon,* which are colloquial substitutes for "imagine."

can, may   Use *can* when you are writing about the ability to do something, as in *He can jump six feet.* Use *may* when you are referring to permission, as in *He may rejoin the team when the period of probation is over.*

can't, couldn't   Do not use these contractions in formal writing. Use *cannot* and *could not* instead.

can't hardly, can't scarcely   See *not but, not hardly, not scarcely.*

can't help but   Use *can't help* by itself; the *but* is redundant.

censor, censure Use *censor* when you mean editing or removing from the public eye on the basis of morality. Use *censure* when you mean "to give a formal or official scolding or verbal punishment."

center around Do not use *center around* in formal writing. Instead, use *center on*.

chose, choose Use the verb *choose* in the present tense for the first and second person and for the future tense, as in *They choose [or will choose] their teams carefully*. Use *chose* for the past tense, as in *The presidential candidate chose a distinguished running mate*.

compare to, compare with Use *compare to* to note similarities between things, as in *He compared the Chinese wine vessel to the Etruscan wine cup*. Use *compare with* to note similarities and contrasts, as in *When comparing market-driven economies with socialist economies, social scientists find a wide range of difference in the standard of living of individuals*.

complement, compliment Use *complement* when you mean "something that completes," as in *The wine was the perfect complement for the elegant meal*. Use *compliment* when you mean "praise," as in *The administrator savored the compliment on her organizational skills*.

conscience, conscious Use *conscience* when your sentence requires a noun meaning "a sense of right or wrong." Use *conscious* as an adjective to mean "aware of" or "awake."

consensus of opinion. Do not use *consensus of opinion* in formal writing. Use *consensus* instead to avoid redundancy.

continual, continuous Use *continual* when you mean "constantly recurring," as in *Continual thunderstorms ruined their vacation days at the beach*. Use *continuous* when you mean "unceasing," as in *The continuous sound of a heartbeat, unceasing and increasing in volume, haunted the narrator*.

could of, would of, should of, might of, may of, must of In formal writing, avoid combining modal auxiliaries (*could, would, should, might, may,* and *must*) with *of*. Instead, write *could have, would have, should have, might have, may have,* and *must have*.

couple, couple of Do not use *couple* or *couple of* to mean "a few" in formal writing. Instead, write *a few*.

criteria Use *criteria* when you want a plural word referring to more than one standard of judgment. Use *criterion* when you are referring to only one standard of judgment.

data use *data* when you are referring to more than one fact, statistic, or other means of support for a conclusion. When you are referring to a single fact, use the word *datum* in formal writing, or use *fact, figure,* or another term that is specific to the single means of support.

different from, different than Use *different from* when an object or phrase follows, as in *Braque's style is different from Picasso's*. Use *different than* when a clause follows, as in *Smith's position on the deficit was <u>different</u> when he was seeking the presidency <u>than</u> it was when he was president.*

differ from, differ with Use *differ from* when you are referring to unlike things, as in *Subsequent results of experiments in cold fusion differed radically from results first obtained in Utah.* Use *differ with* to mean "disagree," as in *One expert might differ with another on a point of usage.*

discreet, discrete Use *discreet* to mean "respectfully reserved," as in *He was always discreet when he entered the synagogue.* Use *discrete* to mean "separate" or "distinct," as in *The essay was a discrete part of the examination and could be answered as a take-home assignment.*

disinterested, uninterested Use *disinterested* to mean "impartial," as in *An umpire should always be disinterested in which team wins.* Use *uninterested* to mean "bored" or "not interested."

doesn't, don't Do not use *doesn't* and *don't* in formal writing; instead, use *does not* and *do not.* In other contexts, use *don't* with the first and second person singular, as in *I don't smoke* and with the third person plural, as in *They don't smoke.* Use *doesn't* with the third person singular, as in *He doesn't ride the subway.*

done Use *done* when your sentence requires the past participle; do not use done as the simple past. For example, rewrite a sentence such as *Van Gogh done the painting at Arles* to read *Van Gogh did the painting at Arles.*

due to, due to the fact that Use *due to* to mean "because" only when it follows a form of the verb *be*, as in *The sensation of a leg falling asleep is due to pooling of the blood in the veins.* Do not use *due to* as a preposition, however. Also, do not use *due to the fact that* in formal writing because it is wordy.

eager, anxious See *anxious, eager.*

effect, affect See *affect, effect.*

elicit, illicit Use *elicit* to mean "to draw out," as in *the social worker finally elicited a response from the child.* Use *illicit* to mean "illegal," as in *Illicit transactions on the black market fuel an underground Soviet economy.*

emigrate, immigrate, migrate Use *emigrate* to mean "to move away from one's country." Use *immigrate* to mean "to move to another country." Use *migrate* to mean "to move to another place on a temporary basis."

ensure, assure, insure see *assure, ensure, insure.*

enthused, enthusiastic Use *enthusiastic* when you mean "excited about" or "showing enthusiasm." Do not use *enthused* in formal writing.

especially, specially Use *especially* when you mean "particularly," as in *Maria Mitchell was especially talented as a mathematician.* Use *specially* when you mean "for a specific reason," as in *The drug was intended specially for the treatment of rheumatism.*

et al., etc.   Do not use *et al.* and *etc.* interchangeably. *Et al.* is generally used in references and bibliographies and is Latin for "and others." *Et cetera* is Latin for "and so forth." Like all abbreviations, *et al.* and *etc.* are generally not used in formal writing, except that *et al.* is acceptable in the context of a citation to a source.

etc.   Do not use *etc.* in formal writing. Use *and so forth* instead. Or, preferably, be as specific as necessary to eliminate the phrase.

everybody, every body   Use *everybody* when you mean "everyone." Use *every body* when you are using *body* as a distinct word modified by *every*, as in *Is every body of water in Canada contaminated by acid rain?*

every day, everyday   Use *everyday* when your sentence requires an adjective meaning "common" or "daily," as in *Availability of water was an everyday problem in ancient Egypt.* Use *every day* when you are using the word *day* and modifying it with the adjective *every*, as in *Enrico went to the art gallery every day.*

everywheres   Do not use *everywheres* in formal writing. Use *everywhere* instead.

except, accept   See *accept, except.*

except for the fact that   In formal writing prefer the less wordy *except that.*

explicit, implicit   Use *explicit* when you mean "stated outright," as in *The Supreme Court rules on issues that are not explicit in the Constitution.* Use *implicit* when you mean "implied," as in *Her respect for the constitution was implicit in her remarks.*

farther, further   Use *farther* when you are referring to distance, as in *He was able to run farther after eating carbohydrates.* Use *further* when you are referring to something that cannot be measured, such as *Further negotiations are needed between the central government and the people of Azerbaijan.*

fewer, less   Use *fewer* when you are referring to items that can be counted, as in *There are fewer savings accounts at the branch office this year.* Use *less* when you are referring to things that cannot be counted, as in *The East German people have less confidence in the concept of unification than they had one year ago.*

figure   See *calculate, figure, reckon.*

fixing to   Do not use *fixing to* in formal writing. Use *intend to* instead.

former, latter   Use *former* and *latter* only when you are referring to two things. In that case, the former is the first thing, and the latter is the second. If you are referring to more than two things, use *first* for the first and *last* for last.

get   Do not overuse *get* in formal writing. Prefer more precise words. For example, instead of *get better*, write *improve*; instead of *get*, write *receive, catch,* or *become*; instead of *get done* write *finish* or *end.*

gone, went   Use *gone* when your sentence requires the past participle of *to go*, as in *They had gone there several times.* Use *went* when your sentence requires the past tense of *to go*, as in *They went to the theater Friday.*

good and   Do not use *good and* in formal writing. Use *very* or, preferably, a more precise modifier instead.

good, well   Use *good* as an adjective, as in *Astaire gave a good performance, but not one of his best*. Use *well* as an adverb, as in *He danced well*. You can also use *well* as an adjective when your refer to good health, as in *She felt well* or *She is well today*.

got, have; has/have got to   Do not use *got* in place of *have* in formal writing. For example, rewrite a sentence such as *I got to lose weight* to read *I have to [or I must] lose weight*.

had better, better; had best, best   See *better, had better*.

had ought   Do not use *had ought* in formal writing. Use *ought* by itself instead.

half   When you refer to half of something in formal writing, use *a half* or *one-half*, but do not use *a half a*. For example, rewrite a sentence such as *He had a half a sandwich for dinner* to read *He had a half sandwich for dinner*.

hanged, hung   Use *hanged* for the action of hanging a person, as in *The innocent man was hanged by an angry mob*. Use *hang* for all other meanings, such as *The clothes were hung on the line* and *The chandelier hung from a golden rope*.

he, she; he/she; his, her; his/her; him, her; him/her   When you are using a pronoun to refer back to a noun that could be either masculine or feminine, you might use *he or she* in order to avoid language that is now considered sexist. For example, instead of writing *A doctor must be constantly alert; he cannot make a single mistake* to refer generally to doctors, you could write *A doctor must be constantly alert; he or she cannot make a single mistake*. Or you could recast the sentence in the plural to avoid this problem: *Doctors must be constantly alert; they cannot make a single mistake*.

herself, himself, myself, yourself   Use pronouns ending in *-self* when the pronouns refer to a noun that they intensify, as in *The teacher himself could not pass the test*. Do not use pronouns ending in *-self* to take the place of subjective- or objective-case pronouns. Instead of writing, for example, *Joan and myself are good friends*, write *Joan and I are good friends*.

himself   See *herself, himself, myself, yourself*.

his/her   See *he/she*.

hisself   Do not use *hisself* in formal writing. In a context such as *He hisself organized the picnic*, recast the sentence to read *He himself organized the picnic*.

hopefully   Use *hopefully* when you mean "with hope," as in *Relatives watched hopefully as the first miners emerged after the fire*. Avoid using *hopefully* as a modifier for an entire clause or to convey any other meaning. For example, avoid *Hopefully, a cure for leukemia is not far away*.

hung, hanged   See *hanged, hung*.

if, whether   Use *if* to begin a subordinate clause when a stated or implied result follows, as in *If the court rules against the cigarette manufacturers, [then] thousands of lawsuits could follow*. Use *whether* when you are expressing an alternative, as in *Economist do not know whether the dollar will rebound or fall against the strength of the yen*.

illicit, elicit   See *elicit, illicit*.

illusion, allusion See *allusion, illusion*.

immigrate See *emigrate, immigrate, migrate*.

impact Use impact when you are referring to a forceful collision, as in *The impact of the cars was so great that one was flattened*. Do not use *impact* as a verb meaning "to have an effect on." Instead of writing *Each of us can positively impact waste reduction efforts*, write *Each of us can reduce waste*.

implicit, explicit See *explicit, implicit*.

imply, infer Use *imply* when you mean "to suggest without directly stating," as in *The doctor implied that being overweight was the main cause of my problem*. Use *infer* when you mean "to find the meaning of something," as in *I inferred from her lecture that drinking more than two cups of coffee a day was a health risk*.

in, into Use *in* when you are referring to location or condition. Use *into* to refer to a change in location, such as *The famous portrait shows a man going into a palace*. (See 23a.) In formal writing, do not use *into* for "interested in." For example, avoid a statement such as *I am into repairing engines*.

incredible, incredulous Use *incredible* to mean "unbelievable," as in *Some of Houdini's exploits seem incredible to those who did not witness them*. Use *incredulous* to mean "unbelieving," as in *Many inlanders were incredulous when they heard tales of white people capturing men, women, and children who lived on the coast*.

individual, person, party Use *individual* when you are referring to a single person and when your purpose is to stress that the person is unique, as in *Curie was a tireless and brilliant individual*. Use *party* when you mean a group, as in *The party of eight at the next table disturbed our conversation and ruined our evening*. The word *party* is also correctly used in legal documents referring to a single person. Use *person* for other meanings.

infer, imply See *imply, infer*.

in regards to Do not use *in regards to* in formal writing. Generally, you can substitute *about* for *in regards to*.

inside of, outside of Use *inside* and *outside*, without *of*, when you are referring to location, as in *The roller blades were stored inside the garage*. In formal writing, do not use *inside of* to replace *within* in an expression of time. For example, avoid a sentence such as *I'll have that report inside of an hour*.

insure, assure, ensure See *assure, ensure, insure*.

irregardless, regardless Do not use *irregardless*. Use *regardless* instead.

is when, is where Do not use *is when* and *is where* when you are defining something. Instead of writing *Dinner time is when my family relaxes*, write *At dinner time, my family relaxes*.

its, it's Use *its* when your sentence requires a possessive pronoun, as in *Its leaves are actually long, slender blades*. Use *it's* only when you mean "it is."

-ize   Do not use the suffix *-ize* to turn a noun into a verb in formal writing. For example, instead of writing *He is finalizing his draft*, write *He is finishing his draft* or *He is working on his final draft*.

kind, sort, type   Do not precede the singular words *kind*, *sort*, and *type* with the plural word *these*. Use *this* instead. Also, prefer more specific words than *kind*, *sort*, and *type*.

kind of, sort of   Do not use these phrases as adjectives in formal writing. Instead, use *rather* or *somewhat*.

later, latter   Use *later* when you refer to time, as in *I will go to the concert later*. Use *latter* when you refer to the second of two things, as in *The latter of the two dates is better for my schedule*. (See also *former, latter*.)

latter, former   See *former, latter*.

lay, lie   Use *lay* when you mean "to put" or "to place," as in *She lays the present on the table*. Use *lie* when you mean "recline," as in *She lies awake at night*, or when you mean "is situated," as in *The city lies between a desert and a mountain range*. Also, remember that *lay* is a transitive verb that takes a direct object.

learn, teach   Do not use *learn* to mean "teach." For example, rewrite a sentence such as *Ms. Chin learned us Algebra* to read *Ms. Chin taught us Algebra*.

leave, let   Use *leave* to mean "depart." Use *let* to mean "allow." You can use either *leave* or *let* when the word is followed by *alone*, as in *Leave her alone* or *Let him alone*.

less, fewer   See *fewer, less*.

liable   See *apt, liable, likely*.

lie, lay   See *lay, lie*.

like, as   See *as, like*.

like, such as   Use *like* to make a comparison, as in *Verbena is like ageratum in size and color*. Use *such as* when you are giving examples, as in *Many small flowers, such as verbena, ageratum, and alyssum, can be combined to create decorative borders and edgings*.

likely   See *apt, liable, likely*.

lose, loose   Use *lose* as a verb meaning "to misplace" or "to fail to win." Use *loose* as an adjective meaning "not tight" or "unfastened." You can also use *loose* as a verb meaning "to let loose," as in *They loosened the enraged bull when the matador entered the ring*.

lots, lots of   Do not use *lots* or *lots of* in formal writing. Use *many, very many, much*, or choose a more precise word instead.

man, mankind   Do not use *man* and *mankind* to refer to all people in general. Instead, consider using *people, men and women, humans*, or *humankind*.

may be, maybe   Use *maybe* to mean "perhaps." Use *may be* as a verb (or auxiliary verb), as in *William may be visiting tomorrow*.

may, can See *can, may.*

may of See *could of, would of, should of, might of, may of, must of.*

media Use a plural verb with *media*, as in *the media are often credited with helping the consumer win cases against large companies. Medium* is the singular form.

might of See *could of, would of, should of, might of, may of, must of.*

migrate See *emigrate, immigrate, migrate.*

moral, morale Use *moral* when you mean "an object lesson" or "knowing right from wrong." *What is the moral of the story?* Use *morale* when you mean "outlook" or "attitude." *The team's morale was high.*

Ms. Use *Ms.* to refer to a woman when a title is required and when you either know that she prefers this title or you do not know her marital status. An invented title, *Ms.* was intended to address the issue of discrimination or judgment based on marital status. In research writing, use last names alone, without any title, as in *Jenkins recommends. . . .* In this case, do not use a title for either a man or a woman.

must of See *could of, would of, should of, might of, may of, must of.*

myself See *herself, himself, myself, yourself.*

nor, or Use *nor* and *or* to suggest a choice. Use *nor* when the choice is negative; use *or* when the choice is positive.

not but, not hardly, not scarcely Do not use *not* to precede *hardly, scarcely,* and *but* in formal writing. Because *but, hardly,* and *scarcely* already carry the meaning of a negative, it is not necessary or correct to add another negative.

nothing like, nowhere near Do not use *nothing like* and *nowhere near* in formal writing. Instead, use *not nearly.*

nowheres Do not use *nowheres* in formal writing. Use *nowhere* instead.

number, amount See *amount, number.*

off of Do not use *off of* in formal writing. Use *off* or *from* alone instead, as in *She jumped off the bridge* or *He leaped from the rooftop.*

Ok, okay, O.K. Do not use *Ok, okay* or *O.K.* in formal writing as a substitute for *acceptable.*

on account of Do not use this as a substitute for *because.* Use *because* instead.

on, upon Use *on* instead of *upon* in formal writing.

or, nor See *nor, or.*

outside of, inside of See *inside of, outside of.*

party, individual, person See *individual, person, party.*

people, persons Use *people* to refer to a general group, as in *The people will make their voices heard.* Use *persons* to refer to a (usually small) collection of individuals, as in *The persons we interviewed were nearly unanimous in their opinion.*

per   Do not use *per* in formal writing. For example, instead of writing *The package was sent per your instructions*, it is better to write *The package was sent according to your instructions*. *Per* is acceptable in technical writing or when used with data and prices, as in *Charging $75 per hour, the consultant earned a handsome salary.*

percent (per cent), percentage   Use *percent* (or *per cent*) with a specific number. Use *percentage* with specific descriptive words and phrases, such as *A small percentage of the group did not eat meat.* Do not use *percentage* as a substitute for *part*; for example, rewrite a sentence such as *A percentage of my diet consists of complex carbohydrates* to read *Part of my diet consists of complex carbohydrates.*

person, party, individual   See *individual, person, party.*

plenty   Do not use *plenty* as a substitute for *quite* or *very.* For example, instead of writing *The Confederate troops were plenty hungry during the winter of 1864,* write *The Confederate troops were hungry [or starving] during the winter of 1864.*

plus   Avoid using *plus* as a conjunction joining independent clauses or as a conjunctive adverb. For example, rewrite *Picasso used color in a new way plus he experimented with shape; plus, he brought new meaning to ideas about abstract painting* to read *Picasso used color in a new way and he experimented with shape; moreover, he brought new meaning to ideas about abstract painting.* It is acceptable to use *plus* when you need an expression meaning "in addition to," as in *The costs of day care, plus the costs of feeding and clothing the child, weighed heavily on the single parent's budget.*

practicable, practical   Use *practicable* when you mean "capable of putting into practice," as in *Although it seemed logical, the plan for saving the zoo was very expensive and turned out not to be practicable.* Use *practical* when you mean "sensible," as in *Lincoln was a practical young man who studied hard, paid his debts, and dealt with people honestly.*

precede, proceed   Use *precede* when you mean "come before," as in *The opening remarks precede the speech.* Use *proceed* when you mean "go forward," as in *The motorists proceeded with caution.*

pretty   Do not use *pretty,* as in *pretty close,* to mean "somewhat" or "quite" in formal writing. Use *somewhat, rather,* or *quite* instead.

previous to, prior to   Avoid these wordy expressions. Use *before* instead.

principal, principle   Use *principal* when you refer to a school administrator or an amount of money. Use *principle* when you are referring to a law, conviction, or fundamental truth. You can also use *principal* as an adjective meaning "major" or "most important," as in *The principal players in the decision were Sue Marks and Tom Cohen.*

quotation, quote   Use *quotation* when your sentence requires a noun, as in *the quotation from Nobel laureate Joseph Goldstein was used to lend credence to the theory.* Use *quote* when your sentence requires a verb, as in *She asked Goldstein whether she could quote him.*

raise, rise   Use *raise* when you mean "to lift." Use *rise* when you mean "to get up." To help you understand the difference, remember that *raise* is transitive and takes a direct object; *rise* is intransitive.

rarely ever   Do not use *rarely ever* in formal writing. Use *rarely* or *hardly ever* instead.

real, really   Use *real* as an adjective and use *really* as an adverb.

reason is because   Do not use *reason is because* in formal writing. Rewrite your sentence to say, for example, *The real reason that the bomb was dropped was to end the war quickly* or *The bomb was dropped because Truman wanted to prevent Soviet influence in the Far East settlement.*

reckon   See *calculate, figure, reckon.*

regarding, in regard to, with respect to   In formal writing that is not legal in nature, use *about* or *concerning* instead of these terms.

regardless, irregardless   See *irregardless, regardless.*

respectfully, respectively   Use *respectfully* when you mean "with respect," as in *He respectfully submitted his grievances.* Use *respectively* when you mean "in the given order," as in *The chief of police, the director of the department of public works, and the director of parks and recreation, respectively, submitted their ideas for budget cuts.*

right   Do not use *right* as an intensifier in formal writing. For example, instead of writing that *The farmer was right tired after milking the cows,* write *The farmer was tired [or exhausted] after milking the cows.*

rise, raise   See *raise, rise.*

seen   Do not use *seen* without an auxiliary such as *have, has,* or *had.* For example, rewrite a sentence such as *I seen the film* to read *I have seen the film.*

set, sit   Use *set* when you mean "to place." *Set* is a transitive verb that requires an object, as in *I set the book on the table.* Do not use *set* to mean "to sit" in formal writing.

shall, will   Use *shall* instead of *will* for questions that contain the first person in extremely formal writing, as in *Shall we attend the meeting?* In all other cases, use *will.*

should of   See *could of, would of, should of, might of, may of, must of.*

should, would   Use *should* when you are referring to an obligation or a condition, as in *The governor's mansion should be restored.* Use *would* when you are referring to a wish, as in *I would like to see it repainted in its original colors.*

sit, set   See *set, sit.*

so   Do not use *so* in formal writing to mean "very" or "extremely," as in *He is so entertaining.* Use *very, extremely,* or, preferably, a more specific intensifier instead. Or follow *so* with an explanation preceded by *that,* as in *The reaction to the Freedom Riders was so violent that Robert F. Kennedy ordered a military escort.*

some   Do not use *some* to mean either "remarkable" or "somewhat" in formal writing. For example, rewrite a sentence such as *Babe Ruth was some hitter* to read *Babe Ruth was a remarkable hitter*, or use another more precise adjective to modify *hitter*. Also, rewrite a sentence such as *Wright's mother worried some about the kinds of building blocks her young child used* to read *Wright's mother worried a bit [or was somewhat worried about] the kinds of building blocks her young child used*.

somebody, some body; someone, some one   Use the indefinite pronouns *somebody* and *someone* when referring to a person, such as *There is someone I admire*. Use *some body* and *some one* when the adjective *some* modifies the noun *body* or *one*, as in *We will find the answer in some body of information*.

sometime, sometimes, some time   Use *sometime* when you mean "an indefinite, later time." Use *sometimes* when you mean "occasionally" or "from time to time." Use *some time* when *some* functions as an adjective modifying *time*, as in *His eyes required some time to adjust to the darkened room*.

sort   See *kind, sort, type*.

specially, especially   See *especially, specially*.

stationary, stationery   Use *stationary* to mean "standing still." Use *stationery* to mean "standing still." Use *stationery* to mean "writing paper."

such   Do not use *such* to mean "very" or "extremely" unless *such* is followed by *that*. For example, rewrite a sentence such as *It had such boring lyrics* to read *It had extremely boring lyrics* or *It had <u>such</u> boring lyrics* that *I almost fell asleep half way through the song*.

such as, like   See *like, such as*.

supposed to, used to   Do not use *suppose to* or *use to* in formal writing. Use *supposed to* or *used to* instead.

sure and, sure to; try and, try to   Do not use *sure and* and *try and* in formal writing. Instead, use *sure to* and *try to*. For example, rewrite the sentence *Be sure and bring your computer* to read *Be sure to bring your computer*.

sure, surely   Use *surely* instead of *sure* when your sentence requires an adverb. For example, rewrite a sentence such as *Robert Fulton was sure a genius* to read *Robert Fulton was surely [or certainly] a genius*.

take, bring   See *bring, take*.

than, as   See *as, than*.

than, then   Use *than* when you mean "as compared with," as in *The violin is smaller than the cello*. Use *then* when you are stating a sequence of events, as in *First, he learned how to play the violin. Then he learned to play the cello*. Also use *then* when you mean "at that time" or "therefore."

that there   See *this here, these here, that there, them there*.

that, which   Use *that* or *which* in an essential (or restrictive) clause, or a clause that is necessary to the meaning of the sentence, as in *This is the book that explains Locke's* *philosophy.* Use *which* in a nonessential (nonrestrictive) clause, or a clause that is necessary to the meaning of the sentence, as in *My library just acquired Smith's book on Locke, which is not always easy to find.*

their, there, they're   Use *their* as a possessive pronoun, as in *Their father prevented William and Henry James from being under the control of any one teacher for more than a year.* Use *there* to refer to a place, as the opposite of *here.* Use *they're* to mean "they are."

theirselves   Do not use *theirselves* in formal writing. Rewrite a sentence such as *They treated theirselves to ice cream* to read *They treated themselves to ice cream.*

them there   See *this here, these here, that there, them there.*

then, than   See *than, then.*

these here   See *this here, these here, that there, them there.*

these kind   See *kind, sort, type.*

this here, these here, that there, them there   Do not use *this here, these here, that there,* and *them there* in formal writing. Use *this, that, these,* and *those* instead.

thru   Do not use *thru* in formal writing. Use *through* instead.

thusly   Do not use *thusly* in formal writing. Use *thus* instead. (*Thus,* which is already an adverb, does not need an *-ly* ending.)

till, until, 'til   Do not use *'til* or *till* in formal writing. Prefer *until.*

to, too, two   Use *to* as a preposition meaning "toward"; use *too* to mean "also" or "excessively"; and use *two* as a number.

toward, towards   Use *toward* instead of *towards* in formal writing. *Towards* is the British form.

try and, try to   See *sure and, sure to; try and, try to.*

type of   Do not use *type* in formal writing when you mean "type of." For example, rewrite a sentence such as *He is an anxious type person* to read *He is an anxious type of person.* (See also *kind, sort, type.*)

uninterested, disinterested   See *disinterested, uninterested.*

unique   Do not modify *unique* in formal writing. Because *unique* is an absolute, you should not write, for example, *most unique* or *very unique.*

until   See *til, until, 'til; until* is the preferred form in formal writing.

use, utilize   When you need a word that means "use," prefer *use. Utilize* is a less direct choice with the same meaning.

used to   See *supposed to, used to.*

very   Avoid using *very* as an intensifier. Sometimes you will want to replace more than one word in order to eliminate *very.* For example, in the sentence *It was a very* *nice painting*, you could substitute more precise language, such as *It was a colorful [or provocative or highly abstract] painting*.

wait for, wait on   Unless you are referring to waiting on tables, use *wait for* instead of *wait on* in formal writing. For example, rewrite *We grew tired as we waited on Sarah* to read *We grew tired as we waited for Sarah*.

ways   Do not use *ways* in formal writing to mean "way." Use *way* instead.

well, good   See *good, well*.

where at   See *at*.

whether, if   See *if, whether*.

which, that   See *that, which*.

which, who   Use *which* when you are referring to things. Use *who* when you are referring to people.

who, whom   Use *who* when a sentence requires a subject pronoun, as in *Who can answer this question?* Use *whom* when a sentence requires an object pronoun, as in *Whom did you invite?*

who's, whose   Do not use *who's* in formal writing. Use *who is* instead. Use *whose* to show possession, as in *Whose computer did you use?*

will, shall   See *shall, will*.

-wise   Do not attach the suffix *-wise* to nouns or adjectives to turn them into adverbs in formal writing. For example, instead of writing *I am not doing well grade-wise*, you could recast the sentence to read *My grades are falling* or *My grades are low*.

would of   See *could of, would of, should of, might of, may of, must of*.

would, should   See *should, would*.

your, you're   Do not use *you're* in formal writing. Use *you are* instead. Use *your* to show possession, as in *Your CD player is broken*.

yourself   See *herself, himself, myself, yourself*.

AN A TO Z GUIDE TO REVISING AND EDITING*

We do not expect you to sit down and read this section straight through. Use this alphabetized index to get quick advice during your revising process. For the convenience of both you and your instructor, the entries are keyed to common correction symbols. Figure 10.1 presents a punctuation guide as a quick reference for determining correct punctuation. We have also included exercises in this guide so you can get some practice on especially knotty problems.

Our advice covers current standard English, the language used by educated people in our society. While standard English is not necessarily any better than the language you may hear at the grocery store or in your local bar (it may, in fact, be less

---

*   From *The Practical Writer's Guide*. Susan X. Day, Elizabeth McMahan, Robert Funk. Allyn and Bacon Publishers.

vigorous and colorful), standard English is the language usually required of college students and in the business world.

Abbreviation

    1. Abbreviate only the following terms in general or formal writing.

      A. *Personal Titles:* Mr., Ms., Mrs., Dr.

        Abbreviate doctor only before the person's name: Dr. Dustbin—but never "The dr. removed my appendix."

        By the same token: St. Joan—*but:* "My mother has the patience of a saint."

      B. *Academic degrees:* Ph.D., M.D., D.V.M., R.N., M.S., or all can be written without periods.

      C. *Dates or time:*   1000 B.C. or AD 150 (periods are optional here)

                    10:00 a.m., 3 p.m., or 10 A.M., 3:00 P.M.

                    (*but not:* "Sylvester succumbed to exhaustion in the early a.m.")

      D. *Places:* Washington, D.C. or DC, the U.S. economy (*but not:* "Ringo flew to the U.S. on a jumbo jet.")

      E. *Organizations:* IRS, FBI, ITT, UNICEF, YWCA.

Figure 10.1

Quick Punctuation Guide*

Between two whole sentences	Between a phrase or dependent clause and a whole sentence	In a whole sentence interrupted by a phrase or dependent clause	In a list or series
⊙ usually	⊙ if the phrase or dependent clause comes first and is long	◯–◯ no punctuation if the interrupter limits the meaning of the word before it	⊙ between each parallel item
⊙ if connected by *and, but, or, nor, yet, so, for*			⊙ between all items when one of the items already has a comma in it
⊙ if they are closely related in meaning	◯ no punctuation if the whole sentence comes first followed by a phrase or clause	⊙–⊙ if the interrupter simply adds information or detail	
⊙ if the second one restates the first		(⁓) to play down interrupter	
⊙ if followed by a conjunctive adverb (e.g., *however, thus, nevertheless*)		⊖–⊖ to stress interrupter	

* A glance at this table will solve most of (but not all) your punctuation quandaries. Decide which one of the four situations given in the column headings has you baffled and find the appropriate solution in the table.

Many organizations are commonly known by their abbreviations (usually written in capital letters without periods). If you are not certain whether your readers will recognize the abbreviation, write the name out the first time you use it, put the initials in parentheses following it, and use only the initials thereafter.

F. *Latin expressions:* e.g. (for example); i.e. (that is); etc. (and so forth)—but do not use etc. just to avoid thinking of other examples. In an essay, writing out the English phrase is preferred: it's OK to use abbreviations within parentheses.

2. **In Works Cited lists for papers that use sources, abbreviate the following (per MLA style).**

A. The month (except for May, June, and July)

B. The names of publishers (Yale UP for Yale University Press)

C. The names of states, if cited (Boston, MA)

D. The words *editor* (ed., eds.), *translator* (trans.), *compilers* (comps.), and *volume* (vol., vols.)

3. **Avoid using symbols (%, #, &).**

In scientific papers, however, you are expected to use both numerals and symbols.

See also *Numbers*.

Active Voice   See *Passive Voice*.

Adverb Adjective Confusion

1. **Adverbs usually end in -*ly*.**

Adjective	Adverb
beautiful	beautifully
rapid	rapidly
mangy	mangily

Naturally, there are exceptions—adjectives that end in -*ly* like *sickly, earthly, homely, ghostly, holy, lively, friendly, manly*—but these seldom cause difficulty. Also, there are adverbs that do not end in -*ly*—*now, then, later, there, near, far, very, perhaps*—but hardly anybody messes these up either.

2. **Adverbs modify, verbs, adjectives, and other adverbs.**

       subj.   *vb.*   *adv.*
A. *Standard:* The <u>car</u> <u>was</u> <u>vibrating</u> badly.

       subj.   *vb.*   *adj.*
Faulty: The <u>car</u> <u>was</u> <u>vibrating</u> bad.

subj.   vb.   adv.   adv.

B. *Standard:* The car was moving really rapidly.

subj.   vb.   adj.   adv.

Faulty: The car was moving real rapidly.

subj. vb. adv.   adj.

C. *Standard:* The car was badly damaged.

subj.vb.   adj.   adj.

Faulty: The car was damaged bad.

3. **Adjectives modify *nouns* or *pronouns*.**

   subj.vb.   adj.   n.

   A. Fido is a frisky pup.

   subj. vb.   adj.

   B. She looks frisky.

4. **Adjectives also follow linking verbs (*to be, to feel, to appear, to seem, to look, to become, to smell, to sound, to taste*) and refer back to the noun or pronoun subject.**

   subj. vb.   adj.

   A. Fido feels bad.

   subj.   vb.   adj.

   B. Fido smells bad.

   Notice that a verb expressing action requires an adverb in what appears to be the same construction, but the adverb here modifies the verb:

   subj. vb.   adv.

   C. Fido eats messily.

   subj.   vb.   adv.

   D. Fido scratches frequently.

5. **Some short adverbs do not need the *-ly* ending in informal writing.**

   Drive slowly!   Drive slow!

   Yell loudly.   Yell loud.

6. **The distinction between *good* and *well*.**

   Good is an adjective: it can be compared (*good, better, best*). *Well* can be an adverb (as in "Jamal writes well.") or an adjective (as in "Carla is well now.") What you want to avoid, then, is using *good* as an adverb.

A. *Wrong:* Jamal writes **good**.

  Right: Jamal writes **well**.

B. *Wrong:* Carla's job pays **good**.

  Right: Carla's job pays **well**.

Remember, though, that the linking verbs take predicate adjectives, so you are right to say:

```
        linking    pred.
subj.   vb.        adj.
```

C. Jamal <u>looks</u> <u>good</u>.

```
          linking pred.
subj.     vb.     adj.
```

D. Carla's attitude <u>is</u> <u>good</u>.

E. I <u>feel</u> <u>good</u>.

F. I <u>feel</u> <u>bad</u> about my grade.

"I feel badly" means "I have a poor sense of touch," though people mistakenly use it to mean "I feel bad" emotionally.

If in doubt, find a more precise expression.

Jamal looks healthy (or happy or handsome).

Carla's attitude is positive (or cooperative or hopeful).

I feel frisky (or energetic or great).

Agreement (Pronoun and Antecedent)

1. **Pronouns should agree in number with their antecedents (the words they stand in for).**

   A. Charlene shucked **her** sweater.

   B. Charlene and Bianca shucked **their** sweaters.

   C. Neither Charlene nor Bianca shucked **her** sweater.

   Some indefinite pronouns can be singular or plural, depending on the construction.

   D. *All* my <u>money</u> <u>is</u> gone.

   E. *All* my <u>pennies</u> <u>are</u> spent.

   F. *Some* of <u>this</u> <u>toast</u> <u>is</u> burned.

   G. *Some* of <u>these</u> <u>peas</u> <u>are</u> tasteless.

2. **Some *indefinite* pronouns *sound* plural but have been decreed grammatically singular.**

anybody	none	someone	neither
anyone	no one	everyone	either

Consider, for instance, the logic of these grammatically correct sentences:

Because everyone at the rally spoke Spanish, I addressed him in that language.

Everyone applauded, and I was glad he did.

After everybody folded his paper, the instructor passed among him and collected it.

Robert C. Pooley points out in *The Teaching of English Usage* that grammarians since the eighteenth century have been trying to coerce writers into observing this arbitrary, often illogical, distinction. Professor Pooley, in summarizing his findings on current usage, reports:

> It may be concluded, then, that the indefinite pronouns *everyone, everybody, either, neither,* and so forth, when singular in meaning are referred to by a singular pronoun and when plural in meaning are referred to by a plural pronoun. When the gender is mixed [includes both females and males] or indeterminate [possibly includes both sexes] the plural forms *they, them, their* are frequently used as common gender singulars.

Thus, we may now write in standard English,

A. *Everyone* should wear ***their*** crash helmets.

B. *Neither* of the puppies has ***their*** eyes open yet.

C. *None* of those arrested will admit ***they*** were involved.

That takes care of what used to be a really troublesome problem with pronoun agreement. But you should realize that there are still plenty of people around who will disapprove of this usage. Many people who learned standard English, say, twenty years ago will declare you wrong if you write *everyone* followed by *their*. If you prefer to avoid ruffling such readers, you can use both pronouns:

D. *Everyone* should wear ***his or her*** crash helmet.

E. *Neither* of the informers escaped with ***his or her*** life.

F. *None* of those arrested will admit ***he or she*** was involved.

There remains, too, the sticky problem of what pronoun to use if your indefinite pronoun is strictly singular in meaning. This dilemma occurs frequently because we are programmed to write in the singular. Some people would write

G. *Each* student must show ***his*** permit to register.

But the problem is easily solved by using the plural:

Students must show ***their*** permits to register.

or, try this:

Each student must show **a** permit to register.

The meaning remains the same, and you have included both sexes.

Occasionally, you may need to write a sentence in which you emphasize the singular.

H. **Each** individual must speak **his or her** own mind.

But the sentence will be just as emphatic if you write it in this way:

Each one of us must speak **our** own minds.

Try to break the singular habit and cultivate the plural. You can thus solve countless agreement problems automatically.

Agreement (Subject and Verb)

1. **Subjects and verbs should agree in** *number* (**singular or plural**).

   plural   plural
   subj.   vb.
   A. <u>Artichokes</u> <u>are</u> a struggle to eat.

   singular   singular
   subj.   vb.
   B. An <u>artichoke</u> <u>is</u> a struggle to eat.

   NOTE: *The* to be *verb* (am, was, were, being, been, etc..) *agrees with the subject (a noun before the verb), not the predicate nominative (a noun following the* to be *verb).*

   ---

                  subj.   pred. noun
   C. My favorite <u>fruit</u> <u>is</u> peaches.

      subj.   *pred. noun*
   D. <u>Peaches</u> <u>are</u> my favorite fruit.

2. **Most nouns add** -*s* **to form the plural.**

   snips and snails and puppy dogs' tails

   But with most verbs, the singular form ends in -*s* and you drop it to form the plural.

   one squirrel gnaws, several squirrels gnaw

3. **Do not let intervening modifiers confuse you.**

   Sometimes a modifier gets sandwiched in between subject and verb to trip the unwary, like this:

subj.   *vb.*

A. *Wrong:* The full <u>extent</u> of his crimes <u>have</u> now <u>been</u> discovered.

"Crimes have been discovered" sounds fine, but *crimes* is *not* the
subject of that sentence. The actual subject is the singular noun
extent, with *crimes* serving as object of the preposition *of*. The
sentence should read:

Right: The full <u>extent</u> of his crimes <u>has</u> now <u>been</u> <u>discovered</u>.

Here are more correct examples of sentences with intervening
modifiers.

subj.

B. The <u>bother</u> of packing clothes, finding motels, and searching

vb.

for restaurants <u>takes</u> the joy out of vacation.

subj.

C. <u>Pictures</u> showing nude women and men having sexual contact

vb.

<u>are</u> shocking.

subj.   *vb.*

D. <u>Books</u> full of adventure <u>are</u> what Lucy likes.

4. **Singular subjects connected by *and* require a plural verb.**

plural subj.   *plural vb.*

A. The <u>pitcher</u> and the <u>catcher</u> <u>are</u> both great players.

But sometimes we complicate matters by connecting singular subjects with *correlative conjunctions (not . . . but, not only . . . but
also, neither . . . nor, either . . . or)* instead of *and*. Then the verb
should be singular, although the idea may still come out plural.

B. Not only the pitcher but the catcher also is getting tired.

C. Neither the pitcher nor the catcher is still frisky.

D. Either the pitcher or catcher is slowing down.

5. **Compound *plural* subjects connected by *or* require a plural verb.**

<u>Fleas</u> or <u>ticks</u> <u>are</u> unwelcome.

6. **In the case of subjects joined by *or* or *nor*, if one subject is plural and
the other singular, the verb agrees with the subject closest to it.**

A. <u>Leather</u> or <u>hubcaps</u> <u>remind</u> me of you.

B. <u>Hubcaps</u> or <u>leather</u> <u>reminds</u> me of you.

WARNING: Some constructions appear compound but really are not. Singular subjects followed by words such as with, like, along with, as well as, no less than, including, besides *are still singular because these words are prepositions, not coordinating conjunctions. The idea in the sentence may be distinctly plural, but be advised that the subject and verb remain singular.*

C. My <u>cat</u>, as well as my parakeet, <u>is</u> lost.

D. <u>Seymour</u>, together with his St. Bernard, his pet alligator, and his piranha fish, <u>is</u> moving in with us.

E. <u>Claudia</u>, no less than Carlyle, <u>is</u> responsible for this outrage.

7. **Always find the grammatical subject, and make the verb agree.**

We do not always follow the usual subject-followed-by-verb sentence pattern.

      vb.   *subj.* *vb.*

A. Where <u>have</u> all the <u>flowers</u> <u>gone</u>?

If the sentence is longer, you may have trouble.

B. **Wrong:** Where has all the hope, gaiety, yearning, and excitement gone?

NOTE: The adverb where *can never be the subject of a sentence, so you must look further. The actual subject is compound: "hope, gaiety, yearning, and excitement," which means the verb should be plural.*

Right: Where <u>have</u> all the <u>hope</u>, <u>gaiety</u>, <u>yearning</u>, and <u>excitement</u> <u>gone</u>?

We often invert subject and verb for stylistic reasons.

                                      vb.   *subj.*

C. **Right:** In poverty, injustice, and discrimination <u>lies</u> the <u>cause</u> of Juan's bitterness.

             vb.   *subj.*   *subj.*

D. **Right:** Here <u>are</u> my friend <u>Seymour</u> and his cousin <u>Selma</u>.

Like the adverbs *here* and *where*, the word *there* often poses alluringly at the beginning of a sentence, looking for all the world like the subject. Do not be deceived. *There* can never be the subject; it is either an adverb or an *expletive* (a "filler" word that allows variety in sentence patterns). So before you automatically slide in a singular verb after *there*, find out what the subject really is.

>   *vb.*   *subj.*
> **E. *Right:***   There <u>is</u> great <u>hope</u> for peace today.
>
>   *vb.*   *subj.*
> **F. *Right:***   There <u>are</u> two great <u>hopes</u> for peace today.

The pronoun *it* can also be an expletive, but unlike *there*, it can be the subject of a sentence and always takes a singular verb, even when functioning as an expletive.

G. *Right:*   <u>It</u> <u>is</u> a mile to the nearest phone.

H. *Right:*   <u>It</u> <u>is</u> miles to the nearest phone.

8. **Collective nouns can be singular or plural.**

Some words in the language (*group, staff, family, committee, company, jury*) can be either singular or plural, depending on the context. To suggest that the members are functioning together as a single unit, you can write

A. The office <u>staff</u> <u>is</u> <u>working</u> on the problem.

B. The <u>jury</u> <u>has</u> <u>agreed</u> on a verdict.

Or to suggest that individual members are functioning separately within the group, you can write

C. The office <u>staff</u> <u>are</u> <u>debating</u> that proposal.

D. The <u>jury</u> <u>have</u> not yet <u>agreed</u> on a verdict.

Analogy

An analogy is a form of comparison, either brief or extended.

A brief analogy will be a metaphor or simile. (See *Figures of Speech.*) An extended analogy provides a more thorough comparison and can be a means of organizing a paragraph, perhaps even a whole essay. You use something familiar to explain something unfamiliar. Geologists, for instance, often describe the structure of the earth's crust by comparing the layers to the layered flesh of an onion. Sometimes writers use analogy in an attempt to persuade, as advocates of legalizing marijuana are likely to argue that the present laws are as ineffective and unnecessary as prohibition laws in the twenties. Although analogy is not purely logical, you can certainly use analogy persuasively—so long as your analogy is indeed persuasive.

Antecedent   See *Agreement (Pronouns and Antecedent).*

Apostrophe

1. **The apostrophe signals possession (except for the possessive pronouns, which do not need apostrophes: *ours, yours, its, theirs*).**

Clarence's car
the Joneses' junk
Yeat's yearnings or Yeats' yearnings

2. **An apostrophe signals that some letters (or numbers) have been left out.**

we've (for *we have*)
something's (for *something has* or *something is*)
mustn't (for *must not*)
class of '75 (for *class of 1975*)
o'clock (for *of the clock*)

3. **The *its/it's* confusion.**

Use the apostrophe only for the contraction. *It's* = *it is* or *it has.* If you use the apostrophe to form the possessive of *it* and write

That dumb dog chomped it's own tail.

you have really said

That dumb dog chomped it is own tail.

That dumb dog chomped it has own tail.

And your readers may wonder about you as well as the dog. Make a mental note to check every *its* and *it's* when you proofread if you tend to be careless about apostrophes. If you are writing on a computer, use the *search* command to find each *its* and *it's* and check them all.

REMEMBER: *its* = "of it"—*possessive   The dog chomped its tail.*
          it's = "it is"—*contraction   It's not an intelligent dog.*

---

4. **Apostrophes are optional in forming the plural of numbers, titles, letters, and words used as words.**

The 1970's [or 1970s] proved quieter than the 60's [or 60s].
We hired two new Ph.D.'s [or Ph.D.s]
Seymour makes straight A's.
Those two *and*'s [or and**s**] are ineffective.
You are learning the dos and don'ts of English usage.
Horace rolled three consecutive 7's [or 7s].

But no apostrophe in

Horace rolled three consecutive sevens.

Appositive

An appositive is a word or phrase that comes directly after a noun and identifies or supplements it. Appositives should have commas on both ends.

Stella, **the older sister,** was quite intelligent, while Blanche, **the younger sister,** was courageous.

Also see *Case of Pronouns*, number 3.

Article

Articles are words used to limit or identify nouns: *a, an, the.*

Bufflegab   See *Diction*, number 4.
          See *Diction*, number 4.

Balanced Sentence

1. **A sentence that has balanced (or *parallel*) structure includes a series or pair of elements that are grammatically similar.**

   A. Series of prepositional phrases

   The juggler tosses ninepins <u>over</u> his head, <u>behind</u> his back, and <u>under</u> his knee.

   B. Series of three adjectives

   <u>Ignorant</u>, <u>sullen</u>, and <u>mean-spirited</u>, the young man did not seem to be a promising father.

   C. Pair of clauses

   She hoped <u>that</u> <u>she</u> <u>argued</u> the case well and <u>that</u> <u>she</u> <u>achieved</u> justice quickly.

2. **Make items in series parallel.**

   Most of the time, similar grammatical constructions pair up naturally, but sometimes they get jumbled. You must then decide what grammatical construction you want and make the items in the series or pair fit that construction.

   A. *Jumbled:* She never got used to the drudgery, depression, and being so ill-paid for her work at the nursing home.

   That example has two nouns and a gerund phrase.

   Improved: She never got used to the drudgery, depression, and low pay of her work at the nursing home.

   Now all are nouns.

   B. *Jumbled:* This new kind of therapy promises to make you happy, to improve your love life, and that it will make your hair shiny.

   This one has two infinitive phrases and a clause.

Improved: This new kind of therapy promises to make you happy, to improve your love life, and even to make your hair shiny.

Now all three items are infinitive phrases.

C. *Jumbled:* The bell was about to ring, the students closed their books, and watched the clock anxiously.

The third item is not a clause.

Improved: The bell was about to ring, the students closed their books, and everyone watched the clock anxiously.

Now all the items are independent clauses.

3. **Balance sentences for effect and emphasis.**

Practice writing parallel constructions for their beauty and impact. These qualities shine in the conclusion of a review of Dee Brown's *Bury My Heart at Wounded Knee*, a book detailing the deplorable treatment of Native Americans by White Americans who desired their land. The paragraph is effective for several reasons, but mainly because of the balanced structure:

> The books I review, week upon week, report the destruction of the land or the air; they detail the perversion of justice; they reveal national stupidities. None of them—not one—has saddened me and shamed me as this book has. Because the experience of reading it has made me realize for once and all that we really don't know who we are, or where we came from, or what we have done, or why.
>
> —Geoffrey Wolff

Brackets

Use brackets as a signal for readers in the following cases.

1. **To change verb tenses in a quotation.**

Usually you can adjust your phrasing to suit a quotation, but if the quotation is past tense and you are writing in present tense (or vice versa), it is considerably easier to change the verb in the quotation than to rewrite your paper. If you want to make a past tense quotation about H. L. Mencken fit your present tense essay, do it like this:

Original in past tense

"He defended prostitution, vivisection, Sunday sports, alcohol, and war."

Changed to present tense

"He defend[s] prostitution, vivisection, Sunday sports, alcohol, and war."

2. To clarify any word in a quotation.

Jessica Mitford remembered, "In those days [the early 1940s] until the post-war repression set in, the [Communist] party was a strange mixture of openness and secrecy."

3. To enclose *sic*.

When you quote a passage that contains an error, you must copy the error. The word *sic* ("thus" in Latin) means, "Honest, it really was written that way."

One edition of Stephen Crane's "The Open Boat" reads this way:

> "The correspondent, as he rowed, looked down as [sic] the two men sleeping underfoot."

4. To enclose parenthetical material that is already within parentheses.

Use brackets this way only if you cannot avoid it, as in a scholarly aside, like this one:

> (For an informed appraisal of her relationship with the Rev. Mr. Wadsworth, see Richard B. Sewall, *The Life of Emily Dickinson* [New York: Farrar, 1974], 444–62.)

Capitalization

1. Begin each sentence with a capital letter, including sentences you quote.

Ambrose Bierce says that "Diplomacy is the patriotic art of lying for one's country."

2. Begin each line of poetry with a capital letter only if the poet has used capitals.

3. Always capitalize the pronoun *I*.

4. Use caution in capitalizing words to express emphasis or personification (Truth, Justice, Beauty) unless you are writing poetry.

5. Capitalize proper nouns—the names of specific persons, places, historical events and periods, organizations, races, languages, teams, and deities.

Lowercase	Capitalized
the town square	Washington Square
go to the city	go to Boston
our club secretary	the Secretary of State
traveling east	visiting the far East
a historical document	the Monroe Doctrine
reading medieval history	studying the Middle Ages
taking Latin, chemistry, and math	Latin 100, Chemistry 60, Math 240
an industrial town	the Industrial Revolution
a political organization	Common Cause
an ethnic group	a Native American
our favorite team	the Galveston Gophers
buttered toast	French toast
the gods	Buddha, Allah, Zeus

6. Most people capitalize pronouns referring to the Christian God or Jesus.

> Our Father, Who art in heaven, hallowed be Thy name . . .
> In His name, Amen.

7. When in doubt, consult your dictionary.

If the word is capitalized in the dictionary entry, you should always capitalize it. If you find a usage label, like "often cap." or "usually cap.," use your own judgment. Occasionally, a word will acquire a different meaning if capitalized.

Abraham Lincoln was a great democrat.

Lyndon Johnson was a lifelong Democrat.

The Pope is Catholic.

Carla's taste is catholic (all-encompassing).

8. Capitalize the *first* and *last* words of titles; omit capitals on articles, conjunctions, and prepositions of fewer than five letters.

> *Pride and Prejudice*
> *Gone with the Wind*
> *Shakespeare Without Tears*
> *Been Down So Long It Looks like Up to Me*
> *One Flew Over the Cuckoo's Nest*

9. Capitalize after colons.

Always capitalize the first word following the colon in a title.

> *Problems of Urban Renewal: A Reconsideration*

A capital letter on the first word after a colon in a sentence is optional—unless a question or quotation follows: then capitalize.

Case of Pronouns

1. Pronouns change form with function.

Although nouns do not change form to show case when they move from being subjects to objects, pronouns do. We can write

A. Kesha resembles my sister.

B. My sister resembles Kesha.

But with pronouns, alas, we must use a different form for subjects and objects.

C. *She* resembles my sister.

D. My sister resembles *her*.

The case forms are easy:

Subjective	Objective	Possessive
I	me	mine
he	him	his
she	her	hers
you	you	yours
it	it	its
we	us	ours
they	them	theirs
who	whom	whose
whoever	whomever	whosoever

Most of the time the possessives give no trouble at all, except for the confusion of the possessive *its* with the contraction *it's* (see *Apostrophe*, section 2). But problems like the following do come up.

2. When the subject or object is compound, drop the noun momentarily to decide which case to use.

A. *Faulty:*   Sylvester and *me* went to a lecture.

  Preferred: Sylvester and *I* went to a lecture.

B. *Faulty:*   Desiree sat with Sylvester and *I*.

  Preferred: Desiree sat with Sylvester and *me*.

If in doubt about which pronoun to choose, drop the noun momentarily and see how the pronoun sounds alone:

I went?	or	*me* went?
Desiree sat with *me*?	or	Desiree sat with *I*?

Your ear will tell you that "me went" and "sat with I" are not standard constructions.

Remember that although prepositions are usually short words (in, on, at, by, for), a few are deceptively long (through, beside, among, underneath, between). Long or short, prepositions always take the objective pronoun.

> between Homer and *me*
> among Homer, Martha, and *me*
> beside Martha and *me*

3. **When pronouns are used with appositives, drop the noun momentarily to decide.**
   A. *Faulty:*   *Us* cat lovers are slaves to our pets.
      Preferred: *We* cat lovers are slaves to our pets.
   B. *Faulty:*   Spring is a delight for *we* hedonists.
      Preferred: Spring is a delight for *us* hedonists.

Once more, if in doubt about which pronoun to choose, drop the noun and your ear will guide you: "*We* are slaves to our pets," not "*Us* are slaves to our pets"; "Spring is a delight for *us*," not "Spring is a delight for *we*."

4. **When pronouns are used in comparisons, finish the comparison in your mind.**
   Faulty: Demon rum is stronger than me.
   Preferred: Demon rum is stronger than I.

These comparisons are incomplete (or *elliptical*). If you finish the statement—at least in your mind—you will eliminate any problem. You would not be likely to write, "Demon rum is stronger than *me* am." Naturally, "stronger than *I* am" is standard English. How about "Henrietta's husband is ten years younger than her"? Younger than *her* is? No, younger than *she* is.

5. **When the choice is between *who* and *whom*, substitute *he* or *she* to decide the proper usage.**
   Colloquial usage now allows *who* in all constructions because when we begin a sentence in conversation, we scarcely know how it's going to come out.

   But in writing you can always see how your sentence comes out, so you need to know whether to use *who* or *whom*. When the choice occurs in midsentence, you can fall back on substitution. Replace the prospective *who* or *whom* with *she* or *her* in the following sentence, and your ear will tell you whether to choose the subjective or objective form.

   Kate Chopin was a superb writer (who, whom) literary critics have neglected until recently.

   Ask yourself

Critics have neglected **she?**

or

Critics have neglected **her?**

We would all choose *her*, naturally. Since *her* is objective, the sentence needs the objective *whom*:

Kate Chopin was a superb writer whom literary critics have neglected until recently.

There is also an easy way to avoid the choice. If you are writing an exam and have no time to think, try using *that*:

Kate Chopin was a superb writer **that** literary critics have neglected until recently.

Although some people still find this usage distasteful, it is now standard English. But do not ever substitute *which* for *who* or *whom*. Standard usage still does not allow *which* to refer to people.

Preferred: the woman **whom** I adore

Acceptable: the woman **that** I adore

Faulty: the woman **which** I adore

Preferred: the woman **who** adores me

Faulty: the woman **whom** adores me

Clauses and Phrases

A *clause* is a group of words that has both a subject and a verb: a *phrase* does not have both.

Clauses: after I <u>lost</u> my head
I <u>lost</u> my head
that I <u>lost</u> my head

Phrases: having lost my head
to lose my head
after losing my head

Infinitive and gerund phrases can have a subject but will not have a finite verb:

the <u>negatives</u> to be developed

the <u>film</u> being shown

The subject within each phrase is underlined.

Cliché See *Triteness.*

Coherence

Good writing must have *coherence*—a logical relationship among the parts. In short, it must *hang together*.

1. **Organize your ideas before, during, and after you write.**

   Each point should clearly follow the one before it. Make sure that all points pertain to the idea contained in your *thesis*, or main idea. (See also *Unity*.)

2. **Keep your audience in mind.**

   In order not to lose your readers when you move from one detail or example to the next (between sentences) or from one main idea to the next (between paragraphs), you must provide *transitions*—words like *for example, for instance, namely, next, besides, finally, otherwise, but, since, thus, therefore.*

3. **Use plenty of specific, concrete examples and discussion.**

   You cannot expect your readers to read your mind. Whenever you make a *generalization* (a general statement, a main point), be sure to follow it with specific examples of precise explanations to make sure that your readers can follow your thinking.

Collective Noun   See *Agreement (Subject and Verb)*, number 8.

Colloquial   See *Diction*.

Colon

1. **Use a colon to introduce lists of things: single words, phrases, or subordinate clauses.**

   A. A hawk sometimes catches small animals: chickens, rabbits, moles, and mice.

   B. "It is by the goodness of God that in our country we have those three unspeakably good things: freedom of speech, freedom of conscience, and the prudence never to practice either of them."

   —Mark Twain

2. **Use a colon to connect two independent clauses when the second enlarges on or explains the first.**

   A. The students had an inspired idea: they would publish a course guide.

   B. Only later did the truth come out: Bumper had gambled away his inheritance, embezzled the company funds, and skipped town with the manager's daughter.

If the second clause poses a question, begin with a capital letter.

The main question is this: What are we going to do about the nuclear arms race?

3. **In most cases, a colon should be used only after a complete sentence.**

    A. My favorite animals are the following: lions, tigers, aardvarks, and hippopotamuses.

    Many people, though, will stick in a colon without completing the first independent clause.

    B. *Faulty:*   My favorite animals are: lions, tigers, aardvarks, and hippopotamuses.

    Careful writers would eliminate the colon in that sentence.

    > *Right:*   My favorite animals are lions, tigers, aardvarks, and hippopotamuses.

4. **Use a colon (or a comma) to introduce a direct quotation when your leadin is a complete sentence.**

    Camus puts the matter strongly: "Without work all life goes rotten—but when work is soulless, life stifles and dies."

5. **Use a colon to separate numerical elements.**

Time:	9:35
Biblical chapter and verses:	Revelations 3:7–16 *or*
	Revelations III:7–16
Act and Scene:	II:2
Act, scene, and line:	IV:iii:23–27 *or*
	IV, iii, 23–27

6. **Use a colon after the salutation of business letters.**

    Dear Judge Ito:
    Dear Credit Manager:

7. **Use a colon between the title and subtitle of a book or article.**

    American Humor: A Study in the National Character

    "The Money Motif: Economic Implications in *Huckleberry Finn*"

Combine Sentences for Fluency

If your sentences tend to be fairly simple and monotonous in structure, combine one or two of them.

Say you are writing too many repetitious sentences like these:

Cucumber beetles begin their life cycle as white larvae. These larvae are hatched from yellowish eggs. The eggs are deposited in the soil around the cucumber plants.

What you need to do is combine the three ideas into a single sentence, like this:

Cucumber beetles, which begin their life cycle as white larvae, are hatched from yellowish eggs deposited in the soil around the plants.

Or, if you want to emphasize instead the larval stage, you could combine the material this way:

Cucumber beetles, which are hatched from yellowish eggs deposited in the soil around the plants, begin their life cycle as white larvae.

Comma   See also *Comma Splice*.

1. **Use commas to set off interrupters (nonrestrictive modifiers).**

   A word, phrase, or clause that interrupts the normal flow of the sentence *without changing the meaning* is nonessential or *nonrestrictive*. You need a comma both *before* and *after* the interrupter.

   A. Magnum Oil Company, our best client, canceled its account.

   B. Our instructor, who usually dresses conservatively, wore jeans and a headband today.

   C. "Being merciful, it seems to me, is the only good idea we have received so far."

   —Kurt Vonnegut

2. **Do not use commas around restrictive modifiers.**

   A. *Restrictive:*   Students who can't swim must wear life jackets on the canoe outing.

   B. *Nonrestrictive:* Melvin, who can't swim, must wear a life jacket on the canoe outing.

   Notice that "who can't swim" is essential to the meaning of the first example (it *restricts* the subject) but can easily be left out in the second without changing the basic meaning. Thus in sentence B the modifier "who can't swim" is nonrestrictive and is set off by commas. But commas around "who can't swim" in sentence A would mislead readers. The difference in meaning between restrictive and nonrestrictive modifiers should be clear in these two sentences:

   C. *Restrictive:*   Students who are lazy should be closely supervised.

   D. *Nonrestrictive:* Students, who are lazy, should be closely supervised.

3. Use a comma for clarity.

After any longish introductory element (like a dependent clause or a long phrase), a comma makes the sentence easier to read.

A. Since we've run out of lemons, we'll have to make do with limes.

B. After all the trouble of sneaking into the movie, Arnold didn't like the film.

Once in a while you may write a sentence that needs a comma simply to make it easier to read, like these:

A. The main thing to remember is, do not light a match.

B. Smoking permitted, the passengers all lit up.

Do not write unclear sentences, though, and depend on a comma to make them intelligible. If in doubt, rewrite the sentence.

4. A comma precedes a coordinating conjunction (*and, but, or, for, nor, yet, so*) that connects two complete sentences (*independent clauses*).

A. Myrtle splashed and swam in the pool, but Marvin only sunned himself and looked bored.

Notice, there are three coordinating conjunctions in that example, but a comma precedes only one of them. The *ands* connect compound verbs (splashed *and* swam, sunned *and* looked), not whole sentences the way the *but* does. Thus, a comma before a coordinating conjunction signals your readers that another complete sentence is coming up, not just a compound subject or object. Here are two more examples:

B. Curtis adores coconut cream pie, yet three times he has suffered ptomaine poisoning from eating it.

C. Harvey went to the library, so he may well be lost in the stacks.

5. Use a comma to separate independent clauses if they are *short* and *parallel in structure*.

A. "We shall fight on the beaches, we shall fight on the landing grounds, we shall fight in the fields and in the streets, we shall fight in the hills; we shall never surrender."

—Sir Winston Churchill

B. "It was the best of times, it was the worst of times. . . ."

—Charles Dickens

6. Use a comma before a phrase or clause tacked on at the end of a sentence.

A. "The universal brotherhood of man is out most precious possession, what there is of it."

—Mark Twain

B. I just failed another math exam, thanks to Rob's help at the local bar.

NOTE: You can use a dash instead of a comma for greater emphasis.

C. I just failed another math exam—thanks to Rob's help at the local bar.

7. **Use a comma to separate a direct quotation from your own words introducing it—if you quote a complete sentence.**

A. F. L. Lucas observes, "Most style is not honest enough."

Omit the comma if you introduce the quotation with *that* or if you quote only a part of a sentence.

B. F. L. Lucas observes that "Most style is not honest enough."

C. F. L. Lucas observes that in writing we are often "not honest enough."

If your introduction interrupts the quotation (as sometimes it should, for variety), you need to set off your own words with commas as you would any other interrupter.

D. "Most style," observes F. L. Lucas, "is not honest enough."

8. **Use commas to set off nouns of direct address and other purely introductory or transitional expressions.**

A. *Direct Address*

Mr. President, your proposal boggles the mind.
Your proposal, Mr. President, boggles the mind.
Your proposal boggles the mind, Mr. President.

B. *Introductory and transitional words*

Well, anywhere you go, there you are.
Yes, we are now hopelessly lost.
My, how the child has grown.
In the first place, we must clean up the environment.
We must, however, consider one thing first.
We must first consider one thing, however.

9. **Use commas to separate elements in series.**

A. Tabrina ordered tomato juice, bacon and eggs, pancakes, and coffee with cream.

B. Some of the old moral values need to be revived: love, pity, compassion, honesty.

NOTE: *For variety you can omit the and, as we did in sentence B. In sentence A the comma before and is now optional, but keep in mind it helps to avoid misreading.*

Another option: For emphasis, replace the commas with *ands.*

C. Some of the old moral values need to be revived: love and pity and compassion and honesty.

10. Use a comma to separate adjectives in series before a noun if you can insert *and* between them.

Suppose you want to write

Tigers have thick short orange and black striped fur.

Can you say *thick and short?* You can. Can you say *short and orange?* Yes. What about *orange and and?* No way. *And and black?* Surely not. *Black and striped?* Sure. *Striped and fur?* No. So you need only three commas:

Tigers have thick, short, orange and black, striped fur.

Some series of adjectives read smoothly with no commas between them:

Sheila has short black hair styled in forty funny little spikes.

11. Use commas to separate numerals and place names and to set off names of people from titles.

A. Eudora, who was born November 15, 1950, in Denver, Colorado, moved to Dallas, Texas, before she was old enough to ski.

B. You may write to Laverne at 375 Fairview Avenue, Arlington, TX 20036.

C. My friend Laverne lives in Arlington, Texas.

D. The committee chose Lola Lopez, attorney-at-law, to present their case.

See also *No Punctuation Necessary* for advice about where *not* to use a comma.

Comma Splice

A comma splice (or *comma fault* or *comma blunder*) occurs when a comma is used to join ("splice") two independent clauses together, instead of the necessary semicolon or colon.

1. **Use a semicolon or possibly a colon—*not a comma*—to separate closely related independent clauses.**

    These sentences are correctly punctuated:

    A. Morris has been listless all day; he appears to have a cold.

    B. It's tough to tell when Morris is sick: he just lies around all day anyway.

    C. Tonight he skipped dinner; Morris must be sick if he misses a meal.

    If you write comma splices, you are probably not paying attention to the structure of your sentences. You are writing complete sentences (independent clauses) without realizing it.

2. **Conjunctive adverbs cannot connect sentences.**

    There's another devilish complication that can produce comma splices. Conjunctive adverbs—transitional words such as *indeed, therefore, nevertheless, however*—sound for all the world like coordinating conjunctions, *but they are not*. They cannot connect two independent clauses with only a comma the way coordinating conjunctions can. The solution to this seemingly baffling difficulty is to memorize the coordinating conjunctions: *and, but, or, for, nor, yet, so*. Then all you have to do is remember that all those other words that *sound* like pure conjunctions really are not; hence you need a semicolon.

    A. It's tough to tell when Heathcliff is sick; indeed, he just lies around all day like a rug.

    One final word of warning: try not to confuse the conjunctive adverbs with subordinating conjunctions. A subordinating conjunction at the beginning of a clause produces a *dependent*, not an independent, clause. Thus, you do not need a semicolon in the following sentence because there is only one independent clause.

    B. It's tough to tell when Heathcliff is sick because he just lies around all day anyway.

3. **Independent clauses (except short, balanced ones) must be separated by something stronger than a comma.**

    You have all these options:

    A. *Use a semicolon.*

    Carlos feels better today; he's outside practicing chip shots.

B. *Use a period.*

Carlos feels better today. He's outside practicing chip shots.

C. *Use subordination to eliminate one independent clause.*

Carlos apparently feels better today since he's outside practicing chip shots.

D. *Use a comma plus a coordinating conjunction.*

Carlos feels better today, so he's outside practicing chip shots.

E. *Use a semicolon plus a conjunctive adverb.*

Carlos feels better today; indeed, he's outside practicing chip shots.

Common Noun   See *Proper Noun.*

Comparison. Degrees of   See *Adjectives* and *Adverbs.*

Comparisons. Incomplete or Illogical

1. **Comparisons must involve at least two things being compared.**

   A. *Incomplete:*   Calculus is the hardest course.

      Improved: Calculus is the hardest course I've ever taken.

   B. *Incomplete*   Eloise has fewer inhibitions.

      Improved: Eloise has fewer inhibitions now that she's Maybelle's roommate.

   While the comparison in "improved" sentence B is still only implied, the meaning is easy to understand. But if you want to avoid all possibility of confusion, state the comparison flat out, like this:

   Better: Eloise has fewer inhibitions than she did before becoming Maybelle's roommate.

2. **The second element of any comparison must not be ambiguous, vague, or illogical.**

   Illogical: A passionate kiss is Scarlett O'Hara and Rhett Butler in Gone with the Wind.

   Improved: A passionate kiss is one like Rhett Butler gives Scarlett O'Hara in Gone with the Wind.

3. **Do not compare words that denote absolutes, like *unique, omnipotent, infinite.***

   Illogical: Clovis came up with a very unique design.

   Improved: Clovis came up with a unique design.

Confused Sentence

Take care that every sentence you write makes sense.

Be careful not to begin a sentence one way, lose track in the middle, and finish another way.

> **A. *Confused:*** The first planned crime will tell how well a boy has learned whether or not he is caught to become a juvenile delinquent.
>
> ***Improved:*** Whether or not a boy is caught in his first planned crime may determine whether he will become a juvenile delinquent.
>
> **B. *Confused:*** When frequently opening and closing the oven door, it can cause a soufflé to fall.
>
> ***Improved:*** Frequently opening and closing the oven door can cause a soufflé to fall.

Usually, such sentences result for sheer carelessness. You should catch them when you revise. *Do not forget to proofread.*

Conjunctions, Coordinating   See *Comma Splice*, number 2.

Conjunctions, Correlative   See *Agreement (Subject and Verb)*, number 4.

Conjunctions, Subordinating

See *Comma Splice*, number 2.
See *Comma*, number 3.
For a list of subordinating conjunctions, see *Fragment* number 2.

Conjunctive Adverb

See *Comma Splice*, number 2.
For a list of conjunctive adverbs, see *Semicolon*, number 2.

Connotation and Denotation

Words are symbols that often carry two meanings:

> 1. **Denotative meaning—the actual definition; the person, thing, or abstract quality referred to;** the term *mother*, for instance, denotes a woman who gives birth to or adopts and cares for a child.
>
> 2. **Connotative meaning—those feeling usually associated with the word;** the term *mother* suggests to most of us warmth, love, security, comfort, apple pie.

Whether you choose to refer to the president as a *statesman* or as a *politician* may well reveal your political sympathies. Consider, for example, Frederick Lewis Allen's description of Woodrow Wilson as a "Puritan Schoolmaster . . . cool in a time of great emotions, calmly setting the lesson for the day; the moral idealist . . . , the dogmatic prophet of democracy. . . ." The word *Puritan* suggests a moralist with no human warmth. Allen could have said *high-minded* and lessened the chill factor. And what does the word *schoolmaster* suggest that the neutral word *teacher* does not? Again, a strict, no-nonsense, unsmiling disciplinarian. The word *cool* reinforces this same feeling, as does *calmly*. The term *moral idealist* sounds at first totally complimentary—but is it? We associate idealists with good intentions, but a tinge of daydreaming impracticality clings to the word. *Dogmatic* denotes closed-mindedness. And *prophet* suggests an aura of fanaticism, since the biblical prophets were always exhorting the fun-loving Old Testament sinners to repent of their evil ways or face the wrath of Jehovah. Allen has told us perhaps more through connotation in the sentence than he did through denotation. He uses connotative words to convey a picture of Wilson that he feels is accurate—the image of a cold, determined, perhaps misguided man with the best intentions.

Without the use of emotion-laden words, writing becomes lifeless. But you must be *aware* of connotations as you choose lively words, or you run the risk of producing unfortunate effects. Ignoring connotations can produce regrettable sentences, like this one:

Sandor moped around for a week before he killed himself.

The connotations of the phrase "moped around" are too frivolous for that statement (unless the writer has no sympathy whatsoever for Sandor). This sentence might be better:

Sandor was deeply depressed for a week before he killed himself.

Contraction	See *Apostrophe*, number 2.
Coordinating Conjunction	See *Comma Splice*, number 2.
Coordination	See *Subordination and Coordination*.
Corrective Conjunction	See *Agreement (Subject and Verb)*, number 4.

Dangling Modifier

A *modifier* is a word, a phrase, or a clause that describes, qualifies, or in some way limits another word in the sentence.

    1. Every modifier in a sentence needs a word to modify.

        A. *Dangling:*   Staring in disbelief, the car jumped the curb and crashed into a telephone booth.

Improved:	While I stared in disbelief, the car jumped the curb and crashed into a telephone booth.
B. *Dangling:*	When a girl of sixteen, we courted each other.
Improved:	When I was sixteen, we courted each other.
Improved:	When she was sixteen, we courted each other.
C. *Dangling:*	When only seven years old, her father ran off with another woman.
Improved:	When Marcella was only seven years old, her father ran off with another woman.

2. Be sure introductory elements have something to modify.

Unwise use of the passive voice often causes dangling modifiers. (In the last example here, *you* is understood as the subject of both *pin* and *cut*.)

Dangling:	After carefully pinning on the pattern, the material may then be cut.
Improved:	After carefully pinning on the pattern, you may then cut out the material.
Improved:	First pin on the pattern; then cut the material.

In order to avoid dangling modifiers, think carefully about what you are writing. You can eliminate many of your modifier problems by writing consistently in the active voice: "I made a mistake," rather than "A mistake was made."

Dash

The dash—which requires your readers to pause—is more forceful than a comma. You can use dashes to gain emphasis, so long as you use them sparingly.

1. Use a dash to add emphasis to an idea at the end of a sentence.

Emphatic:	LaBelle had only one chance—and a slim one at that.
Less emphatic:	LaBelle had only one chance, and a slim one at that.

2. Use dashes instead of commas around an interrupter to emphasize the interrupting material.

To take away emphasis from an interrupter, use parentheses.

Emphatic:	My cousin Caroline—the crazy one from Kankakee—is running for Congress.
Less emphatic:	My cousin Caroline, the crazy one from Kankakee, is running for Congress.

Not emphatic: My cousin Caroline (the crazy one from Kanka-kee) is running for Congress.

3. Use dashes around in interrupter if commas appear in the interrupting material.

All the dogs—Spot, Bowser, Fido, and even Old Blue—have gone camping with Cullen.

4. Use a dash following a series at the beginning of a sentence.

Patience, sympathy, endurance, selflessness—these are what good mothers are made of.

If you want to be more formal, use a colon instead of the dash.

NOTE: Do not confuse the dash with the hyphen. On your keyboard, strike two hyphens to make a dash. To use a hyphen when you need a dash is a serious mistake: hyphens connect, dashes separate.

Denotation   See *Connotation and Denotation.*

Diction

Diction (meaning which words we choose and how we put them together) is vitally important since it affects the clarity, accuracy, and forcefulness of everything we write and say. (See also *Connotation and Denotation, Triteness, Wordiness.*)

1. Select exactly the right word.

Inaccurate: I was **disgusted** because rain spoiled our picnic.

Accurate: I was **disappointed** because rain spoiled our picnic.

Accurate: I was **disgusted** by the mindless violence in the movie.

Use your dictionary to be sure the word you choose really means what you want it to mean. If you cannot think of the perfect word, consult your thesaurus for suggestions; then check the dictionary meaning of the term you select to be certain you have the right one. Even synonyms have different shades of meaning: you must keep thinking and looking until you find the precise word.

2. Do not confuse words because they sound alike or are similar in meaning.

Wrong word: Today's society has been **pilfered** with a barrage of legalized drugs.

Improved: A barrage of legalized drugs has ***proliferated*** in today's society.

3. **Use lively, concrete, specific terms.**

Limp: We got into the car.

Improved: All four of us piled into Herman's Honda.

Limp: This dog came up, all excited.

Precise: "[A dog] came bounding among us with a loud volley of barks and leapt round us wagging its whole body, wild with glee at finding so many human beings together."

—George Orwell, "A Hanging"

4. **Avoid bafflegab.**

Bafflegab (or gobbledygook) is inflated, pretentious language that sounds impressive but obscures meaning.

Bafflegab: The production of toxic and noxious residue by hydrochloric acid obviates its efficacious application since it may prove incompatible with metallic permanence.

Translation: Don't use hydrochloric acid: it eats hell out of the pipes.

5. **Avoid doublespeak.**

Doublespeak is language that deliberately obscures the meaning with intent to deceive:

"protection reaction strike" (meaning ***bombing***)
"to terminate with extreme prejudice" (to ***assassinate***)
"that statement is inoperative" (it is ***untrue***)

6. **Be selective with euphemisms.**

Euphemisms obscure meaning but in a benign way:

powder room (meaning ***women's toilet***)
unmentionables (***underwear***)
passed away (***died***)
sanitation engineer (***garbage collector***)

Consider your audience. If you think they would be shocked by blunt language, then use a harmless euphemism.

7. **Be careful with jargon and slang.**

Jargon can mean the same thing as gobbledygook. But *jargon* also means the technical language used in a trade, profession, or special interest group: *printer's jargon, medical jargon, sports jargon.* If you are certain your readers will understand such specialized language, go ahead and use it. Otherwise, stick to plain English, and define any technical terms that you cannot avoid.

Slang can contribute a lively tone to *informal* writing, but you need to be sure your readers will understand current slang. Remember also that today's slang is tomorrow's cliché. Do not write vague expressions, like these:

Maybelle is simply far out.
Clyde's a real cool cat.
That move just blew me away.

If you decide to use slang, do not apologize for it by putting it in quotation marks. Use it boldly.

8. Do not mix formal and colloquial language—unless you do so deliberately for effect.

You will give your readers a considerable jolt if you write a basically formal sentence and drop in a slang term.

One anticipates that the Boston Symphony will deliver its customary **dynamite** performance.

Digression   See Unity.

Doublespeak See Diction, number 5.

Ellipsis Dots

1. Use three space dots if your readers will be unable to tell that you have omitted words from a direct quotation.

  A. *Something left out at the beginning.*

   About advice, Lord Chesterfield wrote ". . . those who want it the most always like it the least."

   —Letter to his son, 1748

  B. *Something left out in the middle.*

   "The time has come . . . for us to examine ourselves," warns James Baldwin, "but we can only do this if we are willing to free ourselves from the myth of America and try to find out what is really happening here."

   —*Nobody Knows My Name*

  C. *Something left out at the end.*

   Thoreau declared that he received only one or two letters in his life "that were worth the postage" and observed summarily that "to a philosopher all *news*, as it is called, is gossip. . . ."

—*Walden*, Chapter 2

NOTE: *The extra dot is the period.*

---

2. **If you are quoting only a part of a sentence—and your readers can *tell*—do not use ellipsis dots.**

   Occasionally, like Eliot's Prufrock, we long to be "scuttling across the floors of silent seas."

   Judge William Sessions describes himself as a "West Texas tough guy" and subscribes to a law-and-order philosophy.

3. **Use either ellipsis dots or a dash to indicate an unfinished statement, especially in recording conversation.**

   "But, I don't know whether . . . ," Bernice began.

   "How could you . . . ?" Ferdinand faltered.

Elliptical Construction See *Case of Pronouns*, number 4.

Emphasis

Work especially hard on the beginnings and ends of things—of sentences, of paragraphs, of essays—because those are the positions that require the most emphasis.

   Any time you vary the normal pattern of your writing, you gain emphasis. Try the following variations:

1. **Periodic sentences.**

   Save the word or words conveying the main idea until the end (just before the period):

   One quality they definitely do not value in the military is individuality.

2. **Balanced sentences.**

   Make all grammatical elements balance precisely:

   > With this faith we will be able to work together, to pray together, to struggle together, to go to jail together, to stand up for freedom together, knowing that we will one day be free.

   —Martin Luther King Jr.

3. ***Ands* to separate a series.**

   Instead of commas, use *ands* to emphasize items in series:

> It is his privilege to help man endure by lifting his heart, by reminding him of the courage and honor and hope and pride and compassion and pity and sacrifice which have been the glory of his past.
>
> —William Faulkner

4. Dashes.

Set off with dashes elements you want to emphasize.

A. *At the beginning:*

Cardinals, blue jays, finches, doves—all come to frisk in the fountain.

B. *In the middle:*

> The trial allowed—indeed, required—a jury to pick between numerous flatly incompatible theories spun by credentialed experts.
>
> —George F. Will

C. *At the end:*

> Dandy ideas these—or so it seemed at the beginning.
>
> —John Hurt Fischer

5. Deliberate repetition.

Occasionally, repeat key words for emphasis:

> Her working-class, middle-aged life was buffeted by an abusive husband, an abusive son, and a series of abusive supervisors at a succession of low-level jobs.
>
> —Hugh Drummond, M.D.

6. Short sentences.

A short-short sentence following sentences of normal length will get attention:

> If there is to be a new etiquette, it ought to be based on honest mutual respect, and responsiveness to each other's needs. Regardless of sex.
>
> —Lois Gould

7. A one-sentence paragraph.

Punctuate a single sentence as a paragraph to make it extremely emphatic.

Euphemism   See *Diction*, number 6.

Exclamation Point

1. **Do not use exclamation points merely to give punch to ordinary sentences. Write a good, emphatic sentence instead.**

   Ineffective: LeRoy's room was a terrible mess!

   Improved: We declared LeRoy's room a disaster area.

2. **Use exclamation points following genuine exclamations:**

   > O kind missionary, O compassionate missionary, leave China! Come home and convert these Christians!
   >
   > —Mark Twain, "The United States of Lyncherdom"

   > I'm mad as hell, and I'm not going to take it anymore!
   >
   > —Paddy Chayefsky, *Network*

   NOTE: Avoid stacking up punctuation. Do not put a comma after an exclamation point or after a question mark.

   See also *Quotation Marks*, number 12.

Expletive

1. **An *expletive* can be an oath or exclamation, often profane.**

   You will have no trouble thinking of the four-letter ones, so we will mention some socially acceptable ones: Thunderation! Tarnation! Drat! Oh, fudge! Use only when reproducing conversation.

2. **The words *it* and *there,* also expletives, serve as "filler" words to allow for variety in sentence patterns.**

   It is raining.
   There are two ways to solve the problem.

   See also *Agreement (Subject and Verb)*, number 7.

Figures of Speech

Figures of speech involve the imaginative use of language and can give your writing greater vividness and clarity, if used effectively.

1. **Metaphors and similes.**

   These imaginative comparisons are characteristic of poetry but are used frequently in prose.

   A. *A metaphor is an* implied *comparison.*

   Clarence was a lion in the fight.

B. *A simile* is a stated *comparison (with* like *or* as*).

Clarence was like a lion in the fight.

The term *metaphor* now serves to describe both figures of speech. Here are some examples used in prose by professional writers:

New York is a sucked orange.

—R. W. Emerson

Like soft, watery lightning went the wandering snake at the crowd.

—D. H. Lawrence

His voice was as intimate as the rustle of sheets.

—Dorothy Parker

The medical case against smoking is as airtight as a steel casket.

—Barbara Ehrenreich

See also *Analogy.*

2. Extended metaphors.

Skillful writers sometimes write imaginative comparisons that go beyond a single comparison.

The intersection of IAA Drive and Vernon Avenue is like a heart attack waiting to happen. Clogged traffic arteries have prompted city officials to begin looking at ways to correct the monitoring aneurysm.

—Kurt Erickson

3. Mixed metaphors.

Be careful of metaphors that do not compare accurately, that start off one way and end another way.

A. Our quarterback plowed through their defense and skyrocketed across the goal lines.

B. The FTC does nothing but sit on its hands and fiddle while Rome burns.

C. The fan really hit the ceiling.

REMEMBER: Figures of speech should clarify the meaning through comparisons that increase understanding. Ambiguity fascinates the mind in poetry but tries the patience in expository prose. So, be creative: but when you revise, be sure that your metaphors clarify rather than confuse.

---

4. Personification.

Personification means giving human characteristics to nonhuman things (objects or animals). Use with restraint.

The missiles lurk in their silos, grimly waiting for the inevitable day when at last they will perform their duty.

5. Avoid *trite* figures of speech. See *Triteness.*

Formal Usage   See the discussion of usage in the Glossary.

Fragment

1. A sentence fragment is only part of a sentence punctuated as a whole.

Many professional writers use fragments for emphasis, or simply for convenience, as in the portions we have italicized in the following examples.

> Man is the only animal that blushes. *Or needs to.*
>
> —Mark Twain

> I did not whisper excitedly about my Boyfriends. *For the best of reasons.* I did not have any.
>
> —Gwendolyn Brooks

> No member [of Congress] had ever been challenged or even questioned about taking the exemption. *Until my nomination.*
>
> —Geraldine Ferraro

> *Easy to say, but hard to practice.*
>
> —F. L. Lucas

> So Shelly asked her what was "real" and the student responded instantly. "Television." *Because you could see it.*
>
> —Harlan Ellison

2. Avoid fragments in formal writing (term papers, business reports, scholarly essays).

Fragment: Pollution poses a serious problem. Which we had better solve.

Complete: Pollution poses a serious problem—which we had better solve.

Complete: Pollution poses a serious problem which we had better solve.

NOTE: If you write fragments accidentally, remember that a simple sentence beginning with one of the following subordinating words will come out a fragment:

after	if	though	where
although	only	till	whereas
as, as if	since	unless	which
as far as	so as	until	while
because	so that	when	
before	still	whenever	

Fragment: Although I warned him time after time.

Complete: I warned him time after time.

Complete: Although I warned him time after time, Clyde continued to curse and swear.

NOTE: Words ending in -ing and -ed can cause fragments also. Although such words sound like verbs, sometimes they're verbals— actually nouns or adjectives. Every complete sentence requires an honest-to-goodness verb.

Fragment: Singing and skipping along the beach.

Complete: Juan went singing and skipping along the beach.

Fragment: Abandoned by friends and family alike.

Complete: Alice was abandoned by friends and family alike.

Complete: Abandoned by friends and family alike, Alice at last recognized the evils of alcohol.

3. **Use fragments in asking and answering questions, even in formal writing:**

When should the reform begin? At once.

How? By throwing self-serving politicians out of office.

4. **Use fragments for recording conversation, since people do not always speak in complete sentences:**

"I suppose that during all [my sickly childhood] you were uneasy about me?"

"Yes, the whole time."

"Afraid I wouldn't live?"

After a reflective pause, ostensibly to think out the facts, "No—afraid you would."

—Mark Twain, *Autobiography*

5. **Be sure that two constructions connected with a semicolon are complete sentences.**

Questionable: He looked a lot like Quasimodo; although I couldn't see him too well.

Improved: He looked a lot like Quasimodo, although I couldn't see him too well.

Improved: He looked a lot like Quasimodo; I couldn't see him too well, though.

Fused Sentence   See *Run-on Sentence.*

Generalizations   See *Coherence,* number 3.

Hyphen

Unlike exclamation points, hyphens are in fashion today as a stylistic device.

1. **Hyphenate descriptive phrases used as a whole to modify a noun.**

   George needs to get rid of his holier-than-thou attitude.

2. **Hyphenate compound adjectives when they come before the noun.**

ivy-covered walls	up-to-date entries
high-speed railroads	lighter-than-air balloon

3. **Omit the hyphen if the descriptive phrase comes after the noun.**

walls covered with ivy	Entries that were up to date
railroads running at high speed	a balloon lighter than air

4. **Hyphenate most compound words beginning with *self-* and *ex-*.**

self-employed	ex-wife
self-deluded	ex-slave
self-abuse	ex-President

5. **Never use a hyphen in the following words.**

yourself	himself	itself
themselves	herself	selfless
ourselves	myself	selfish
oneself (or one's self)		

6. **Consult your dictionary about other compound words.**

   Some words change function depending on whether written as one word or two:

   Verb: Where did I slip up?

Noun: I made a slipup somewhere.

7. Use a hyphen to divide words at the end of a line.

Divide only between syllables. Consult your dictionary if in doubt. Never put a hyphen at the beginning of a line.

8. Use no hyphen between an adverb ending in *-ly* and an adjective.

Beauregard is a hopelessly dull person.

Idioms

Idioms are expressions peculiar to the language for which there are no grammatical explanations. For instance, we say, "I disagree **with** that statement," but "I disapprove **of** that statement." Most of the time native speakers have no trouble with idiomatic prepositions, the ones which cause considerable grief for adults trying to learn the English language from scratch. But sometimes even native speakers choose the wrong proposition and write bothersome sentences like this one:

Unidiomatic: The young couple soon became bored **of** each other.

That should read,

Correct: The young couple soon became bored **with** each other.

If you sometimes write unidiomatic expressions, you should, during the editing process, find someone to read your paper who can tell you if your prepositions are correct.

Idioms Often Misused*

Wrong	*Right*
comply to	comply with
to my opinion	in my opinion
regardless to	regardless of
insight to	insight into
to dispense of	to dispense with
first step of success	first step toward success
opportunity of work	opportunity to work
to identify to	to identify with
job on the field	job in the field
aptitude toward	aptitude for
education depends of	education depends on
satisfied of	satisfied with
on the future	in the future
insight on	insight into

*Adapted from Mina Shaughnessy, *Errors and Expectations* (New York: Oxford UP) 192–93.

Interjection	See *Exclamation Point*.
Italics	See *Underlining*.
Jargon	See *Diction*, number 7.

Linking Verb

Linking verbs connect the subject of the sentence with the complement.

The most common linking (or copulative, as they used to be bluntly called) verbs are these: *to be, to feel, to appear, to seem, to look, to become, to smell, to sound, to taste.* See also *Adverb/Adjective Confusion*, number 4.

Logic

In order to write convincingly, your thoughts must be logical. You should be aware of the most common pitfalls of slippery logic so that you can avoid them in your own thinking and writing, as well as detect them in the arguments of others.

1. **Avoid oversimplifying.**

   Most of us have a tendency to like things reduced to orderly, easily grasped *either-or* answers. The only problem is that things are seldom that simple. Be wary of arguments that offer no middle way—the "either we outlaw pornography or the nation is doomed" sort of reasoning.

2. **Avoid stereotyping.**

   Stereotypes involve set notions about the way different types of people behave. Homosexuals, according to the stereotype are all neurotic, promiscuous, immoral people bent only on sex and seduction. Such stereotypes seldom give a truthful picture of anyone in the group and could never accurately describe all the members.

3. **Avoid faulty (sweeping or hasty) generalizations.**

   You will do well to question easy solutions to complex problems. A faulty generalization (broad statement) can result from stating opinion as fact.

   Acid rock music causes grave social problems by creating an attitude of irresponsibility in the listener.

   The statement needs evidence to prove its claim, and such proof would be nearly impossible to find. Since you cannot avoid making general statements, be careful to avoid making them without sufficient evidence. At least, *qualify* your statements.

Sweeping: All Siamese cats are nervous.

Better: Many Siamese cats are nervous.

Statements involving *all, none, everything, nobody,* and *always* are tough to prove. Instead, try, *some, many, sometimes,* and *often.*

4. Watch for hidden premises.

Another sort of generalization that is likely to deceive involves, a *hidden premise* (a basic idea underlying the main statement). This observation, upon first reading, may sound entirely plausible:

> If those striking workers had left when the police told them to, there would have been no trouble, and no one would have been injured.

The hidden premise here assumes that all laws are just and fairly administered: that all actions of the government are honorable and in the best interest of all citizens. The statement presumes, in short, that the strikers had no right or reason to be there and hence were wrong not to leave when told to do so. Such a presumption overlooks the possibility that in a free country the strikers might legitimately protest the right of the police to make them move.

5. Do not dodge the issue.

People use a number of handy fallacies in order to sidestep a problem while appearing to pursue the point. One of the most effective—and most underhanded—involves playing on the emotional reactions, prejudices, fears, and ignorance of your readers instead of directly addressing the issue.

> If we allow sex education in the public schools, the moral fiber of the nation will be endangered, and human beings will become like animals.

That sentence, which contains no evidence whatever to prove that sex education is either good or bad, merely attempts to make it sound scary.

In a variation of this technique (called "*ad hominem*"), people sometimes attack the person they are arguing with, rather than the issue being argued. They call their opponents "effete, effeminate snobs" and hope nobody notices that they have not actually said anything to the point.

Another favorite dodge is called "begging the question" or "circular argument." You offer as evidence arguments which assume as true the very thing you are trying to prove. You say that pornography is evil because pornography is evil, but you have to say it fancy, like this:

> If we want a society of people who devote their time to base and sensuous things, then pornography may be harmless. But

if we want a society in which the noble side is encouraged and mankind itself is elevated, then I submit that pornography is surely harmful.

—John Mitchell

6. Keep an open mind.

Thinking is your best defense against logical fallacies. Think while you are reading or listening and think some more before you write. Be prepared to change your mind. Instead of hunting for the facts to shore up your present opinions, let the facts you gather lead you to a conclusion. And do not insist on a nice, tidy, clear-cut conclusion. Sometimes there isn't one. Your conclusion may well be that both sides for various reasons have a point. Simply work to discover what you honestly believe to be the truth of the matter, and set that down, as clearly and convincingly as you can.

See also *Analogy, Coherence, Connotation and Denotation,* and *Unity.*

Misplaced Modifier

Keep modifiers close to what they modify (describe, limit, or qualify).

Faulty:	I had been driving for forty years when I fell asleep at the wheel and had an accident.
Improved:	Although I have driven safely for forty years, last night I fell asleep at the wheel and had an accident.
Faulty:	DARE is sponsoring a series of presentations on drugs for local college students.
Improved:	DARE is sponsoring for local college students a series of presentations on drugs.

Mixed Construction

See *Confused Sentence.*

Modifiers

See *Dangling Modifier.*
See *Misplaced Modifier.*

Nonrestrictive Clause

See *Comma,* number 2.

No Punctuation Necessary

Commas do not belong wherever you would pause in speaking. That rule doesn't always work; we pause far too often in speech, and different speakers pause in different places. Here are some situations where people are tempted to add unnecessary commas.

1. When main sentence parts are long.

Some writers mistakenly separate the subject from the verb or the verb from the complement, like this:

A. *Wrong:* Tall people with large feet, are particularly good auto-harp players.

B. *Wrong:* By the end of the year we all understood, that using too many commas would make us grow hair on our palms.

Neither of those sentences should have a comma in it. In sentence B, the clause serves as the direct object of the verb *understood* and thus should not be set off with a comma.

2. When a restrictive clause occurs in the sentence.

Putting a comma on one end of an adjective clause and no punctuation at all on the other end is never correct. Nonrestrictive clauses always need punctuation on both ends (see *Comma*, number 1), and restrictive ones need no punctuation. Avoid errors like this one:

Wrong: Aretha's poem that compared a school to a prison, was the most moving one she read.

No comma is necessary in that sentence.

3. When the word *and* appears in the sentence.

Some people always put a comma before the word *and*, and they are probably right more than half the time. It's correct to put a comma before *and* when it joins a series or when it joins independent clauses. But when *and* does not do either of those things, a comma before it is usually inappropriate. This sentence should have no comma:

Wrong: Mark called the telephone company to complain about his bill, and got put on "hold" for an hour.

Numbers

1. **Spell out numbers one hundred and under.**

2. **In general, write numbers over one hundred in figures.**

3. **Spell out round numbers requiring only a couple of words (two hundred tons, five thousand dollars).**

   If a series of numbers occurs in a passage, and some of them are over one hundred, use figures for all of them.

4. **Always use figures for addresses (27 White's Place), for times (1:05 P.M.), for dates (October 12, 1950), and for decimals, code**

and serial numbers, percentages, measurements, and source references.

EXCEPTION: *Never begin a sentence with a numeral: spell it out or rewrite the sentence.*

Overburdened Sentence

Do not try to cram more into one sentence than it can conveniently hold.

> The plot concerns a small boy, somewhat neglected by his mother, a recently divorced working woman, who is evidently having a difficult time keeping her family, her emotions, and her household together, who discovers by mysterious means and befriends a small, adorable extraterrestrial creature.

That's just too much. It should be divided into two more graceful sentences.

> Two of the story's characters are a small boy and his somewhat negligent mother, a recently divorced working woman who is evidently having a difficult time keeping her family, her emotions, and her household together. By mysterious means, the boy discovers and befriends a small, adorable extraterrestrial creature.

Paragraph

The proofreader's mark ¶ means that your instructor thinks you should indent to begin a new paragraph at that point. When all your sentences are closely related, sometimes you forget to give your readers a break by dividing paragraphs.

Remember to indent when you shift topics or shift aspects of a topic. For instance, look at the break between the preceding paragraph and this one. Both of these paragraphs are on the same subject (paragraphing), but the topic shifts from *why* to begin a new paragraph to *when* to begin a new paragraph. Because of this shift, we indented.

When you notice that you have written a paragraph over eight sentences long, it may be time to look for places to break it into two separate paragraphs.

Parallel Structure   See *Balanced Sentences.*

Parentheses

1. **Use parentheses around parts of a sentence or paragraph that you would speak aloud as an aside.**

   A slight digression or some incidental information that you do not particularly want to emphasize belongs in parentheses.

   A. John Stuart Mill (1806–1873) promoted the idea of women's equality.

   B. Although Clyde has lapses of memory (often he forgets what he went to the store to buy), he is the best auditor in the company.

2. Use parentheses around numerals when you number a list.

Her professor did three things that bothered her: (1) he called her "honey," even though he didn't know her; (2) he graded the class on a curve, even though there were only ten students; (3) he complained that male students no longer wore suit coats and ties to class.

3. Punctuation goes inside the parentheses if it punctuates just the words inside.

Consumers can use their power by boycotting a product. (The word *boycott* is from Captain Charles C. Boycott, whose neighbors in Ireland ostracized him in 1880 for refusing to reduce the high rents he charged.)

4. Punctuation goes outside the parentheses if it punctuates more than just the enclosed material.

The comma does this in example 1B above. A numbered list, like that in number 2, is the *only* case in which you may put a comma, semicolon, colon, or dash before an opening parenthesis.

Participle Endings

Do not omit the *-ed* from the ends of participles.
An adjective formed from a verb is called a participle. Examples are

a tired writer (from **tire**)
an embarrassing moment (from **embarrass**)
a delayed reaction (from **delay**)

Many of the participles ending in *-ed* are said aloud without the *-ed* sound; thus, sometimes you forget to put the ending on in writing. Some typical examples of this error are

old fashion ice cream
air condition theater
vine ripen tomatoes
prejudice attitudes

Those phrases should read:

old-fashioned ice cream
air-conditioned theater
vine-ripened tomatoes
prejudiced attitudes

Passive Voice

Passive voice contrasts with active voice as you can see in the following examples:

A. *Active:* My daughter solved the problem.

B. *Passive:* The problem was solved by my daughter.

C. *Passive:* The problem was solved.

In active voice, the agent of the action (the person who does the solving, in this case) is also the subject of the sentence. In passive voice, the agent of the action is not the subject of the sentence. In both example B and example C, even though the daughter did the solving, *problem* is the subject of the sentence, and in example C, the daughter is left out altogether and gets no credit for her ingenuity.

Period

Use a period at the end of a complete declarative sentence and after most abbreviations (see *Abbreviation*).

If a sentence ends with an abbreviation, let its period serve as the final period of the sentence: Do not double up.

Personification   See *Figures of Speech.*

Phrase

A phrase is a string of words that does not include a subject and verb combination.

Point of View   See *Shifts in Tense and Person.*

Possessives   See *Apostrophe.*
See *Case of Pronouns,* item D.

Possessives with Gerunds

1. **A gerund is a verbal ending in *-ing* that serves as a noun in a sentence.**

   A. Squishing mud between your toes is a sensual pleasure.

   Squishing is the subject of the sentence, and thus acts as a noun.

   B. He got back at the telephone company by folding his computer billing card each month.

   Folding is the object of a preposition, and thus acts as a noun.

2. **Use possessive nouns and pronouns before gerunds because gerunds act as nouns.**

   You probably would not forget to use a possessive before a regular noun in a sentence like this:

   A. I was embarrassed by John's coarse manners.

   But you may forget to use the possessive before a gerund. The preferred usage is as follows:

   B. I was embarrassed by John's snapping his fingers to attract the waitress's attention.

Not "*John* snapping his fingers."

C. I disapproved of his acting so rudely.

Not "*him* acting so rudely."

If you have other problems with possessives, see *Apostrophe.*

Predicate

The predicate of a sentence is the verb plus the complement (if there is one).

Predication, Faulty

1. **This error comes from not rereading your sentences closely enough.**

   A sentence with faulty predication is one whose predicate adjective or predicate noun does not match the subject in meaning.

   A. *Faulty:* Your first big city is an event that changes your whole outlook if you grew up in a small town.

   B. *Faulty:* The importance of graceful movement is essential when doing ballet.

   C. *Faulty:* Smoothness and precision are among the basic problems encountered by beginning dancers.

   In sentence A, a city is not really an event; in B, the writer probably did not want to say something as banal as "importance is essential"; and in C, smoothness and precision are not problems.

   To correct such errors, you can revise the subject, the predicate, or both to make them match up better. Here are possible revisions of our problem sentences:

   A. *Improved:* Your first visit to a big city is an experience that changes your whole outlook if you grew up in a small town.

   B. *Improved:* Graceful movement is essential when doing ballet.

   C. *Improved:* Roughness and imprecision are among the weaknesses of beginning dancers.

2. **Your prediction can be merely weak instead of utterly illogical.**
   Important words should appear as the subject and predicate.

   Weak: One important point of his speech was the part in which he stressed self-reliance.

   The key subject and predicate words are *point . . . was . . . part,* which do not carry much meaning in the sentence. Here's an improvement:

Improved: At one important point, his speech emphasized self-reliance.

Now the key subject and predicate words are *speech . . . emphasized . . . self-reliance,* which are more meaningful.

Pronoun   See *Agreement (Pronoun and Antecedent).*
See *Case of Pronouns.*
See *Reference of Pronouns.*

Proper Noun

A common noun names a class (*dog, city*); a proper noun names a specific person, place, or thing (*Rover, Chicago*).

Qualification

Avoid making absolute statements in writing:

Avoid: My gym instructor is never wrong.

Avoid: Cats are finicky.

Instead, qualify your remarks.

Better: My gym instructor is seldom wrong.

Better: Cats are often finicky.

Better: My cats are finicky.

Quotation Marks

1. **Put quotation marks around words that you copy just as they were written or spoken, whether they are complete or partial sentences.**

   A. "Gloria, please don't practice your quacky duck imitation while I'm trying to do my income tax," she said.

   B. She said that Gloria's barnyard imitations made her "feel like moving to New York for some peace and quiet."

2. **A quotation within a quotation should have single quotation marks around it.**

   I remarked, "I've disliked him ever since he said I was 'a typical product of the midwest,' whatever that means."

NOTE: *Do not panic if you read a book or article that reverses double and single quotation marks (that is, uses single around quotations and double around quotations within quotations). The British do it the opposite the American way, so that book or article is probably British.*

---

3. **If you paraphrase (i.e., change words from the way they were written or spoken), you are using indirect quotation and you need not use quotation marks.**

   A. She said that Gloria's pig grunt was particularly disgusting.

   Her actual words were, "Gloria's pig grunt is the worst of all."

   B. He told me that he loathed levity.

   He actually said, "I despise levity."

4. **When you write dialogue (conversation between two or more people), give each new speaker a new paragraph. But still put related nondialogue sentences in the same paragraph.**

   After our visitor finally left, I was able to ask my question. "What did he mean by 'a typical product of the midwest'?" I said.

   "Maybe he meant you were sweet and innocent," Mark suggested.

   "Fat chance," I replied. "He probably meant I was corny." I doubt that he was that clever, though.

5. **Put quotation marks around tiles of words that you think of as *part* of a book or magazine rather than a whole by itself: articles, stories, chapters, essays, poems, T.V. episodes.**

   Do not put quotation marks around titles of your own essays.

   Examples:

   "Petrified Man," a short story by Eudora Welty

   "We Real Cool," a poem by Gwendolyn Brooks

   "My View of History," an essay by Arnold Toynbee

6. **Underline the titles of works you think of as a *whole*: books, magazines, journals, newspapers, plays, T.V. series, and movies (*Walden,* The *New York Times, Star Trek, Casablanca*). Also underline the names of works of visual art (Dali's painting, *Civil War*).**

   NOTE: Italics in print mean the same thing as underlining by hand or on a keyboard.

7. **Do not use underlining or quotation marks around Preface, Appendix, Index.**

8. **Underline or put quotation marks around words used as words.**

   A. You used <u>but</u> and <u>and</u> too often in that sentence.

   B. He thought "sophisticated" referred only to stylishness.

9. **In general, do not put quotation marks around words that you suspect are too slangy.**

   A. *Weak:*   Phys ed was really a "drag."

   B. *Weak:*   On the first day of class, my philosophy instructor showed that he was really "hot" on the subject.

   Do not use quotation marks as a written sneer, either. Learn to express your feelings in a more exact way.

10. **Periods and commas always go inside quotation marks.**

    A. "Never eat at a restaurant named *Mom's*," my brother always said.

    B. In James Joyce's story "Eveline," the main character is at once frightened and attracted by freedom.

    C. "I must admit," Cosmo said, "that Gloria sounds more like a rooster than anyone else I know."

11. **Colons and semicolons always go outside the quotation marks.**

    If at first you don't succeed, try, try again"; "It takes all kinds"; "You can't get something for nothing": these shallow mottos were his entire philosophy of life.

12. **Exclamation points and question marks go inside the quotation marks if they are part of the quotation and outside if they are not.**

    A. "That man called me 'Babycakes'!" Sandra screeched.

    B. He said, "Hey there, Babycakes, whatcha doin' tonight?"

    C. Isn't that what my father calls "an ungentlemanly advance"?

Redundance

Do not accidentally pile up two or more words that say the same thing.

emotional feelings
round in shape
earthtone shades of color
fatally murdered

To avoid this redundance, just *emotions, round, earthtones,* and *murdered* would be fine.

Redundant prepositions

Avoid using a preposition at the end of any sentence involving *where*.

Colloquial:	Can you tell me where the action's at?
Standard:	Can you tell me where the action is?
Colloquial:	Where is our money going to?

Standard: Where is our money going?

Reference of Pronouns

1. **Make sure pronouns have clear antecedents.**

   Pronouns are useful words that stand in for nouns so that we do not have to be forever repeating the same word. Occasionally pronouns cause trouble, though, when readers cannot tell for sure *what* noun the pronoun stands for (or refers to). Say you write.

   A. Seymour gave Selina her pet parrot.

   There's no problem: *her* clearly means Selina. But suppose you write instead

   B. Seymour gave Clyde his pet parrot.

   Instant ambiguity: *his* could mean either Seymour's or Clyde's. In order to avoid baffling your readers in this fashion, you must rephrase such constructions in a way that makes the pronoun reference clear.

   C. Seymour gave his pet parrot to Clyde.

   or

   D. Clyde got his pet parrot from Seymour.

   If you have difficulty with vague pronoun reference, start checking pronouns when you proofread. Be sure each pronoun refers clearly to only *one* noun. And be sure that noun is fairly close, preferably in the same sentence.

2. **Use *this* and *which* with care.**

   Whenever you use the word *this*, try to follow it with a noun telling what *this* refers to. Too often *this* refers to an abstract idea or to a whole cluster of ideas in a paragraph, and your readers would require divine guidance to figure out exactly what you had in mind. So, if you write

   A. The importance of this becomes clear when we understand the alternatives.

   at least give your reader a clue: "this *principle*," "this *qualification*," "this *stalemate*" or "this *problem*."

   Which causes similar problems. Often this handy pronoun refers to the entire clause preceding it. Sometimes the meaning is clear, sometimes not. Suppose you write

   B. Jocasta has received only one job offer, which depresses her.

   That sentence can be interpreted in two different ways.

C. Jocasta is depressed about receiving only one job offer, even though it *is* a fairly good job.

or

D. Jocasta has received only one job offer—a depressing one, at that.

Look up *Agreement (Pronoun and Antecedent)* for a discussion of more pronoun problems.

Repetition

Carefully designed repetition of terms can add emphasis and coherence to a passage, as it does in this one by Dr. Hugh Drummond:

> I watched a woman slip into madness recently. Her working-class, middle-aged life was buffeted by an abusive husband, an abusive son, and a series of abusive supervisors at a succession of low-level jobs. She would come home day after day, year after year from her file-clerk tedium, exhausted by the subway commute and the stained city's air, only to begin caring for her indulged, soured men; with their impatient appetites and their bottom-rung entitlements, they waited for her like beasts in a lair.

The repetition reflects the tedious repetitiousness of the woman's life.

Careless repetition, though, lends emphasis to a word or phrase awkwardly and unnecessarily:

A. After the performance, we went to Karl's house to discuss whether or not it was an effective performance.

B. The length of his hair adds to the wild appearance of his hair.

Those sentences need revision because the repeated words have no reason to be emphasized.

A. After the performance, we went to Karl's house to discuss whether or not our production was effective.

B. The length of his hair adds to its wild appearance.

Restrictive Clause   See *Comma*, number 2.

Run-on, Fused, or Run-together Sentence

Do not run two sentences together without a period between them.

Fused: Horace has a mangy dog without a brain in his head his name is Bowser.

When you proofread, make sure that each sentence really *is* an acceptable sentence.

Revised: Horace has a mangy dog without a brain in his head. His name is Bowser.

Those sentences are standard English, but a good writer would revise further to avoid wordiness.

> *Revised:* Horace has a mangy, brainless dog named Bowser.

Semicolon

> **The semicolon, which is similar to a period, means stop briefly; then go ahead.**
>
> Complete sentences connected by semicolons should be closely related.

> When angry, count four; when very angry, swear.
>
> —Mark Twain

2. **Use a semicolon (instead of only a comma) when sentences are joined with a conjunctive adverb rather than with a coordinating conjunction (*and, but, or, for, nor, yet, so*).***

   Here is a list of the most commonly used conjunctive adverbs.

accordingly	indeed	nonetheless
besides	instead	otherwise
consequently	likewise	then
furthermore	meanwhile	therefore
hence	moreover	thus
however	nevertheless	too

---

* This rule may seem senseless, but there *is* a reason for the distinction. A conjunctive adverb is not a pure connective in the way a coordinating conjunction is. *However*, it can be picked up and moved to several other spots in the sentence. You could write:

The prisoners have a valid point; I can't, however, condone their violence.

or

I can't condone their violence, however.

or even

I, however, can't condone their violence.

You cannot take such liberties with the coordinating conjunctions without producing nonsentences like these:

I can't, but, condone their violence.

I can't condone their violence, but.

I, but, can't condone their violence.

---

3. **The following sentences appear to require identical punctuation, but in standard usage the first requires a semicolon, the second only a comma, because *however* is a conjunctive adverb and *but* is a coordinating conjunction.**

   The prisoners have a valid point; however, I can't condone their violence.

   The prisoners have a valid point, but I can't condone their violence.

It's easy to tell the difference between the pure conjunctions and the conjunctive adverbs if you'll just memorize the seven coordinating conjunctions: *and, but, or, for, nor, yet, so.* Then all the other words that seem like coordinating conjunctions are actually conjunctive adverbs.

4. **Do not use a semicolon to connect an independent clause with a dependent clause (a fragment).**

   Faulty: He looked a lot like Robert Redford; although I couldn't see him too well.

   Improved: He looked a lot like Robert Redford, although I couldn't see him too well.

5. **The semicolon substitutes for the comma in separating items in series when any of the items listed *already contain commas.***

   Ann went to college and dropped out; lived with per parents for a year; worked as a veterinarian's assistant, a teacher's aide, and a clerk; and finally found her niche as an organic farmer.

   Sometimes the series may follow a colon.

   Cosmo made several New Year's resolutions: to study harder, sleep longer, and swear less; to eat sensible, well-balanced meals; and to drink no more rum, tequila, or gin.

Sentences   See *Chapter One.*

Shifts in Tense and Person

Sometimes your prose gets rolling along, and you shift into the wrong gear while you are moving, which results in an unpleasant grinding noise in your readers' heads. These shifts occur in tense and point of view.

1. **Choose either present or past tense and stay with it unless you have a reason to change.**

   Here's an example of faulty tense switch.

   Faulty: Maris was quietly cleaning the dining room when in comes Sue with a bunch of her loud friends and puts on her Nine Inch Nails CD at full volume. Maris had to go upstairs and sulk.

   There's no call for the change from past to present tense. If Maris *was cleaning*, then Sue *came* in and *put* on the CD. You can, of course, switch tenses to indicate a change occurring in time:

   Revised: Maris was cleaning the dining room, but now she is sulking.

   Just be sure that you do not mix tenses without meaning to.

2. **When you are writing about literature, be especially careful about mixing past and present tense in your discussion of what happens in the book.**

It's traditional to describe literary happenings in the present tense (called the "historical present"):

Kingsley Amis's hero, Lucky Jim, *has* an imaginative humor that constantly *gets* him in trouble.

3. **Shifting *point of view* in a passage is a similar error.**

Faulty: As students we learn the ghastly effects of procrastination. You find out that you just cannot assimilate ten chapters of geography the night before a test. Most students know the grim thud in the gut that they feel when they stare at an exam and do not even understand the questions.

In that example the writer refers to the students in three different ways: *we* (first-person plural), *you* (second person), and *they* (third-person plural). To revise the passage, stick to one pronoun.

Revised: As students, we learn that ghastly effects of procrastination. We find out that we just cannot assimilate ten chapters of geography the night before a test. We become familiar with the grim thud in the gut that we feel when we stare at an exam and do not even understand the questions.

Simile   See *Diction.*

Slang   See *Diction.*

Spelling

Use your spell-checker or your dictionary.

If you get certain pairs of words confused, like *accept* and *except,* or *affect* and *effect*, the Glossary of Usage, beginning on page 281, will help you.

Subject   See *Agreement (Subject and Verb).*

Subordination and Coordination

1. **You can enrich a sentence or series of sentences by subordinating some of the clauses—that is, by changing independent clauses to dependent ones or phrases.**

Plain simple and compound sentences may be the easiest ones to write, but they do not always get across the relationships between your ideas in the clearest way possible. And if you use simple sentences too often, you will have a third-grade writing style. Here are a couple of plain simple sentences.

Lucy forgot how to spell *exaggerated.* She used the word *magnified* instead.

The idea in one of those sentences could be subordinated in these ways:

A. *By using subordinating conjunctions and adverbs (after, when, because, if, while, until, unless, etc.)*

<u>Since</u> <u>Lucy</u> <u>forgot</u> <u>how</u> <u>to</u> <u>spell</u> <u>exaggerated</u>, she used the word *magnified* instead.

B. *By using a participial phrase or an adjective*

Lucy, <u>who</u> <u>forgot</u> <u>how</u> <u>to</u> <u>spell</u> <u>exaggerated</u>, used the word *magnified* instead.

C. *By using a participial phrase or an adjective*

<u>Having</u> <u>forgotten</u> <u>how</u> <u>to</u> <u>spell</u> <u>exaggerated</u>, Lucy used the word *magnified* instead.

2. **Avoid stringing together simple sentences with coordinating conjunctions.**

Subordinate some of the ideas, using parallel structure (see also *Balanced Sentence*).

Ineffective: Phoebe got a hot tip on the phone, and she grabbed her tape recorder and hurried to the corner and an angry mob was gathered there, and she ran to a phone booth and called the paper's photographer and said, "Dave, get down here quick!"

Improved: After getting a hot tip on the phone, Phoebe grabbed her tape recorder and hurried to the corner where an angry mob was gathered. She ran to a phone booth, dialed the paper's photographer, and said, "Dave, get down here quick!"

Thesis Statement

A successful essay needs a *thesis,* or controlling idea, either expressed in a single sentence in the introduction or implied, as in narrative or descriptive writing.

1. **Narrow the topic.**

If you're assigned a 500-word paper on "Solving the Energy Shortage," you need to find a suitable thesis idea that you can handle within the word limit. You might, for instance, focus on the need to develop alternative energy sources. But that still is too broad a topic to cover in 500 words. You could then narrow your idea to one neglected source, like solar energy. But you will need an approach—a *focus*—for your paper.

2. **Give the direction of your thinking.**

   Your thesis should state more than just your general topic. Do not settle for just "solar energy" or even "the need for solar energy." Write a complete sentence—with a *verb* as well as a subject—to indicate what you plan to say about the subject. You might propose the need for solar energy like this: "Our economy needs to convert to solar power because it remains our only nonpolluting source of energy."

3. **Make all ideas relate to your thesis.**

   Once you've decided on a clear, concise thesis statement, make sure that every major and minor point in the paper relates directly to that controlling idea so that your essay will be unified.

4. **Be flexible.**

   As you write your paper, be prepared to broaden, narrow, or change your thesis if you discover a better direction of focus.

This and Which   See *Reference of Pronouns*, number 2.

Title Tactics

Your title should tell the readers, so far as possible, what the paper is about.

1. **Do not use a complete sentence but give more than a hint about your topic.**

   Vague: The Teacher and Research

   Better: The Teacher and Research in Education

   Good: Practical Research Ideas for High School Teachers

2. **Experiment with a colon.**

   > Grass Roots Organization: A Key to Political Success

   > Legal Liability: What Everyone Needs to Know about Mercy Killing

3. **Do not put quotation marks around your own essay title.**

   See also *Quotation Marks*, numbers 5, 6, and 7, for advice on punctuating other people's titles.

Topic Sentence

The topic sentence expresses the central idea of a paragraph. Most of your paragraphs should have one.

Transitions

1. **Transitional words are verbal signals that help your readers follow your thought.**

   Some of the most useful ones function this way:

   A. *To move to the next point:* also, besides, too, furthermore, moreover, next, in the first place, second, third, again, in addition, further, likewise, finally, accordingly, at the same time, first, to begin with.

   B. *To add an example:* for instance, for example, in the same manner, such as, that is, in the following manner, namely, in this case, as an illustration.

   C. *To emphasize a point:* in fact, without question, especially, without doubt, primarily, chiefly, actually, otherwise, after all, as a matter of fact.

   D. *To contrast a point:* yet, although, after all, but, still, on the other hand, on the contrary, nevertheless, contrary to, however, nonetheless, conversely, granted that, in contrast, in another way.

   E. *To conclude a point:* thus, therefore, in short, consequently, so, accordingly, then, as a result, hence, in sum, in conclusion, in other words.

2. **Use special transitional techniques when moving from one point to the next.**

   A. Occasionally, you can pose a question for yourself and answer it, like this:

   > How does vitamin E work to repair body tissues? Nobody knows for sure, but . . .

   B. A more useful method is the **echo transition** in which you touch on the idea from the previous paragraph as you introduce the idea for your next one, like this:

   > He also **gave us coffee, cigarettes, and alcohol.**
   > Despite **this new health program,** Sylvester continued to be depressed until . . .

Triteness

A *cliché* is a worn-out series or words which usually expresses a simple-minded or trite idea: "It takes all kinds to make a world." But you can express superficial ideas without using clichés too. Here is an example of a sentence your reader might think trite.

> Motherhood is a joyful experience that no woman should miss.

The writer has not thought very deeply about the idea. Is motherhood joyful for a poor woman with nine children? Are women's personalities so alike that such a generalization could be true?

We all find ourselves mindlessly writing down unexamined ideas once in a while. A thoughtful rereading of whatever you write can help you avoid making this weakness public.

Underdeveloped Paragraphs

A friend of ours says that throughout college she got her papers back marked with "Underdeveloped ¶" in the margins. To correct this problem, she would carefully restate the topic four or five different ways in each paragraph, and she would still get "Underdeveloped ¶" marked in her margins.

Our friend finally realized, too late, what *underdevelopment* meant. She resents the fact that her teachers never wrote in her margins, "Add an example or illustration here," or, "Give some specific details," or "Describe your reasoning step by step." She would have understood *that*.

When you find one of your skimpy paragraphs marked *undernourished* or *lacks development,* you will know what it means: add examples, provide specific details, describe your reasoning, or do all three.

Underlining

Underlining by hand or on a keyboard is the same as italics in print. It is used three ways:

1. **To indicate titles of long works.**

   See *Quotation Marks* for a list of what titles to underline and what titles to enclose in quotation marks.

2. **To point out words used as words.**

   A. Manipulative behavior is my therapist's favorite phrase.

   B. You have used twelve in other words's in this paragraph.

3. **To indicate foreign words.**

   In informal writing, you do not have to underline foreign words that are widely used, like et cetera or tortilla or tango.

But underline foreign words when they are less familiar or when you are writing formally.

After graduation, Jocasta seemed to lose her joi de vivre.

Unity

Unity is something we never require of casual conversation: it's find if you wander a little off the track and tell about the Bluebird Saloon in Denver in the middle of a discussion about Humphrey Bogart films.

But in an expository essay, unity is important: you must not go on about the Bluebird in the middle of an essay about Bogart films, even though you had a beer there after seeing *The Maltese Falcon* at a nearby theater. Such a departure from the main subject is called a "digression." A paragraph or essay has unity if it sticks to the main point. It lacks unity if it wanders across the street for a drink.

See also *Coherence.*

Usage   See *Glossary of Usage,* pages 281–296.
                 See *Diction.*

Verb   See *Agreement (Subject and Verb).*
                 See *Linking Verb.*

Word Division See *Hyphen.*

Wordiness

A *wordy* sentence has words and phrases that add nothing to its meaning; in fact, extra verbiage can actually blur the meaning and spoil the style of a sentence. See the example below.

> Mary had to stand at the bus stop fifteen minutes to wait for the bus to come to take her to her mother's house to visit her mother.

PRACTICE EXERCISES IN ENGLISH LANGUAGE SKILLS

Following is a group of exercises on some of the most common skills errors that appear in student essays.

Fragments

Exercise #1

Some of the constructions in the paragraph below are fragments. Correct each fragment by connecting it to the sentence before *or* after it, by adding a subject and/or a predicate, or by deleting a subordinating word-whichever procedure is more appropriate for the desired sense of the passage. Take care to punctuate correctly. Place each correction beside its corresponding number at the bottom of this sheet.

1) I am a person who loves to give to those who are less fortunate than I am. 2) For example, giving clothing to small children. 3) Whose parents are out of work. 4) In addition, I like to place money into the outstretched hands of the homeless. 5) Because they need money for food and shelter. 6) And even for clothing and medication. 7) Also, whenever organizations like the Red Cross, the American Cancer Association, or even the Benevolent Police Society are soliciting funds, I want to write them a generous check. 8) Knowing that the money that I give will help someone who is suffering. 9) Or will put a smile on someone's face. 10) Giving to others makes me very happy. 11) Also, a feeling that I am doing something to help my fellow man.

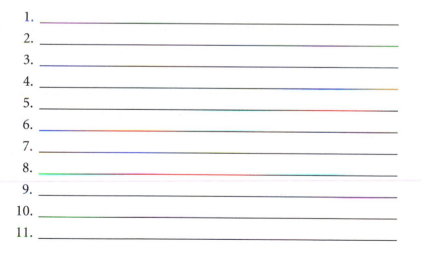

1. _____
2. _____
3. _____
4. _____
5. _____
6. _____
7. _____
8. _____
9. _____
10. _____
11. _____

Exercise #2

Directions: This is a partnership assignment: two of you will complete it together. First, decide which type of fragment is in each word group and place the number beside the fragment description in the space beside the sentence. Second, focusing on the means of correction described in the text, correct the fragment, underlining the part that you correct. Third, explain your means of correction. If there is no fragment in a sentence group, place 5 beside it. Make no effort to change the sentence.

FRAGMENT DESCRIPTION

1. Dependent-word fragment
2. *-ing* and *to* fragment
3. Added—detail fragment
4. Missing—subject fragment
5. No fragment error

EXAMPLE:

___4___ Chenise lost her keys on Tuesday. And found them on Wednesday.

Correction: Chenise lost her keys on Tuesday *and* found them on Wednesday.

Explanation: Deleted the period and made a lower case *a* for *and*.

_____ 1. Morris was patient. Waiting in line at the bank.

Correction:

Explanation:

_____ 2. The president waved as he left the building. Then got into the car and drove away.

Correction:

Explanation:

_____ 3. My roommate Tonya is an excellent skater. She has won many trophies for skating.

Correction:

Explanation:

_____ 4. Juan was bored. Listening to his sister complain so much.

Correction:

Explanation:

_____ 5. Although competition increased. The sales staff was still getting customers.

Correction:

Explanation:

_____ 6. Many people attended my party. Among them, Dr. Hill and his wife, my mother-in-law, and my pastor.

Correction:

Explanation:

_____ 7. To reach my life's goal. I must study really hard and discipline myself.

Correction:

Explanation:

_____ 8. I am majoring in English because I want to become a journalist.

Correction:

Explanation:

Run-ons And Comma Splices

Exercise #1
Determine which word groups below contain a comma splice (CS) or a run-on (RO) sentence. If a group does contain a comma splice or a run-on sentence, place CS or RO in the provided space, and make the necessary change(s) in punctuation and/or capitalization to make the group correct. If a group contains no comma splice or run-on sentence, place *C* (for correct) in the provided space. Attempt to make NO changes for the correct groups.

_____ 1. I was lost, therefore, I had to stop and ask a policeman for directions.

_____ 2. The man died instantly, he never knew that the truck was coming.

_____ 3. Certain animals can be more than just pets, for instance, dogs can be used to guide the blind or help the police track criminals.

_____ 4. I want to join the military; however, I would like to attend college first.

_____ 5. Luke went to church this morning, after the services, he went to see his ailing mother, who is in a nursing home.

_____ 6. Clarence paid three thousand dollars for the land—a small price to pay for beach-front property.

_____ 7. They sell fruit in the fall they also sell fruit in the winter.

_____ 8. Rabbits multiply quickly they, therefore, are seldom in short supply.

_____ 9. Chipper wanted to buy a car, but he did not have enough money to buy even a bicycle.

_____10. You must study very hard, also, you must turn your assignments in on time.

Exercise #2
Some of the sentences in the paragraph below are either run-on sentences or contain comma splices. Correct each error by supplying the

appropriate punctuation and/or capitalization. Make no changes to sentences that are already correct.

1) I spend Sunday afternoons preparing various dishes for my family to eat during the week.   2) For my husband, I usually prepare rice and sausage, he loves this odd combination.   3) In addition, I bake my husband several pastries, such as apple turnovers or lemon tarts.   4) My daughter is a very picky eater she, I must say, likes very few things.   5) However, she loves red beans and rice and roasted chicken wings she also loves brownies and plum wedges, therefore, I make sure that I prepare these dishes for her.   6) My two sons, although they are identical twins, do not have the same tastes in food.   7) One son has a sweet tooth, he likes as many desserts as he can get.   8) I fix him strawberry shortcake and blue-berry muffins.   9) The other son likes bread, thus, he must have his share of rolls, muffins, and bread sticks.   10) Cooking for my family makes my Sunday afternoons very busy, but I enjoy doing it.

Adjectives/adverbs: Comparative and Superlative

Exercise #1
Some of the sentences below contain faults in the use of the comparative or the superlative form. If a sentence contains an error in the superlative form, write an "S" in the blank that precedes the sentence. If a sentence contains an error in the comparative form, write a "C" in the blank that precedes that sentence. If a sentence contains no error in the superlative or comparative forms, leave the space preceding the sentence blank.

_____ 1. Mr. John picked ten bushels of apples; they were the most juiciest apples I had ever tasted.

_____ 2. Which was the warmest month, July or August?

_____ 3. December with its Christmas holidays was more busier than the Thanksgiving holidays in November.

_____ 4. 1997 was the worse year of my life because I had to learn to adjust to college away from home.

_____ 5. Between my sister and me, I do the best job.

_____ 6. Of the two pieces of gossip I had heard, the one about my seeking positions I cannot manage was the most insensitive.

_____ 7. That type of computer was invented in 1996, but it sells better now than when it was first invented.

_____ 8. How particles of dirt raised themselves off the earth and created a new dance was the oddest idea I had ever heard of in a poem.

_____ 9. Of gladioli, daffodils, and roses, roses are more difficult to grow.

_____10. Your line was straighter than Joe's, yet the judge ruled that he had won the prize for the better science project among all the schools.

Exercise #2

Some of the following sentences contain faults in the use of the comparative or superlative form. In the space provided before the sentence, place the letter "S" if there is a fault in the use of the superlative, or the letter "C" if there is a fault in the use of the comparative. If there is no fault in the use of the comparative or the superlative form, leave the space blank.

_____ 1. People who live in cold climates are most likely to be prepared for storms than people who live in warm climates.

_____ 2. The eighth basket contained more apples than all the other baskets.

_____ 3. For us to improve our record in 1998 over the ones for 1997 and 1996, we must control the use of alcohol best than in previous years.

_____ 4. One argument was bad, maybe even worst than the other.

_____ 5. The store was managed more inefficiently by all of the past owners than by the present owner.

_____ 6. We were received most warmly by our host family than by the airline and immigration representatives.

_____ 7. Sam's disagreement with Jane today was worse than those of the past.

_____ 8. After inspecting all of the paintings, we had to conclude that Jane's was the more excellent of all.

_____ 9. Mary modeled several exquisite dresses, but her more alluring one stayed in the closet.

_____10. We tend to become more greedier for new technology as the years go by.

Pronoun Case

Exercise #1

Some of the sentences below contain an error in pronoun case. If a sentence does contain such an error, draw a line under the error and write its correction in the provided space. If a sentence contains no such error, place *C* (for correct) in the provided space.

_____ 1. Pam and I will give Lois and she a second chance to pass the test.

_____ 2. Nobody knows the misdeeds that they and their children have suffered.

_____ 3. It was Leila and I who had to rescue the people who the storm had left homeless.

_____ 4. Ask whoever comes in first to help you move the desk.

_____ 5. After Tim and she had left for their honeymoon, us girls tidied up the church.

_____ 6. Before you and me can leave, we must first inform our mothers.

_____ 7. Him and his brother have been tutoring us students for years.

_____ 8. The Cowboys played better football than them.

_____ 9. Two of us–Christy and me–met George at the bus station.

_____ 10. The award was given to the three best players-Rachel, Sylvia, and I.

_____ 11. I don't know who John is taking to the prom.

_____ 12. They asked we students to help them prepare the final examination.

_____ 13. The committee members and we voted for whomever the president recommended.

_____ 14. The chairperson and I would like to have a conference with both you and she.

_____ 15. Both you and her have been invited to the party hosted by the department.

_____ 16. She asked me to please see who was at the door.

_____ 17. Dave asked the committee–Katie, LaRoche, and I–to call a meeting immediately.

_____ 18. Missy is only two months older than me.

_____ 19. I detest him singing in the shower.

_____ 20. The girls who will go to Hawaii are Pamela and Me.

Exercise #2

Some of the sentences in the paragraph below contain an error in pronoun case. *Underline* the error, and write its correction above it. Be able to justify your change. If a sentence contains no error in pronoun case, do nothing to the sentence.

1) Cheryl and me are on the prom committee.   2) Betty, the chairperson, has given Cheryl and me the responsibility of preparing the decorations.   3) It is Cheryl and me who must buy the flowers and the various colored ribbons.   4) Us girls must also find a person who we can trust to take us down town to shop for the items that are needed.   5) We must give whomever will help us with stringing the lights proper instructions.   6) My brother might just help "we damsels in distress."

7) Cheryl and me will give him and anyone who helps him all the praise. 8) On prom night, Dave and Tom will surely help us determine if everything is in order. 9) Them two guys are very dependable. 10) Considering all of the energy that Cheryl and I must put into decorating for the prom, we are sure that the prom hall will be its prettiest ever.

Pronoun Reference

Exercise #1

The sentences below contain various errors in pronoun reference. Identify the error and revise the sentence to eliminate the error.

1. Some people get married and then realize that it wasn't really love.
2. When Gina finished Lara's manicure, she sprinkled them with moisturizers.
3. Registration is often a frustrating experience because they don't have sufficient personnel to accommodate the process.
4. In a relationship, individuality is important if it is going to last.
5. Rude behavior seems to be increasing, which we all seem resigned to accept.
6. In Faulkner's "A Rose for Emily," he focuses on a woman who becomes isolated from her community and eventually goes insane.
7. On the evening news, it stated that the new 401k options will increase retirement benefits for some people.
8. Warren gave Clyde his cellular phone yesterday, but he lost it.
9. Ultimately, adventure brings fun to a friendship, which makes it a requirement for a long-lasting relationship.
10. The family which moved away last week is returning to Houston.

Exercise #2

Revise the following paragraph to correct all errors in pronoun reference.

When communication begins to fade in a relationship, it leaves one person open to make assumptions. When assumptions have to be made, chances are that they will assume the worst possible option must be true. One person may begin to believe that his partner no longer wants to continue the relationship because he has no clear idea what his mate might be thinking. Clear and constant communication closes the door to assumption. It strengthens the relationship by helping each person to know his or her position in the relationship. That promotes better decision-making by each person involved in it. Because of this, it is imperative that people involved in relationships, platonic or romantic, continue to talk to each other-especially if it is worth saving.

Subject-Verb Agreement

Exercise #1

Read each sentence below carefully. Some of the sentences contain errors in subject-verb agreement, and some are correct. If a sentence contains an agreement error, write the correct verb in the blank provided to the left of the sentence. If a sentence has correct agreement, write *C* in the blank provided.

_____ 1. The setting of the movies, the characters, and the story lines of these movies is very important.

_____ 2. The setting of the movies are important.

_____ 3. If a member of the family need money, my family always finds a way to help that relative out.

_____ 4. People have forgotten what it means to be faithful to one another in the 90's.

_____ 5. In this area, you may see your neighbor occasionally, and the only word that you might exchange is hello.

_____ 6. Normally, there is three guests on the show.

_____ 7. Today, traffic lights throughout the world use the same devices and colors that Garrett A. Morgan used in his invention of the traffic light in 1923.

_____ 8. There's clothes piled up on the floor.

_____ 9. Clothes, books, shoes, and everything one can think of is scattered on my roommate's side of the room.

_____10. At the movie, one may sit between two people that talks a lot.

Exercise #2

Each sentence below is numbered. Read each sentence carefully, paying special attention to subject-verb agreement. If a sentence contains an error in agreement, write the correct verb in the blank provided. If a sentence has correct agreement, write *C* in the blank.

1)Saturdays are my favorite day of the week.   2) For one thing, on Saturdays, I am able to sleep as late as I want to, unless Claire, one of my best friends, call me.   3)But on some mornings, I rise early, about 7:30, to begin my flea market shopping with my shopaholic friends, Patrice and Jan, who knows all of the good bargain spots in town.   4)One of our favorite places are Daisy's Curb.   5) At Daisy's there is unique items, such as tapestries, homemade quilts, and glass figurines.   6) Then, on those days when I don't go shopping, I prepare a barbeque dinner and invites a few friends over to eat with me.   7) We sit on the deck and feast, laughing and talking, licking our fingers and dancing in our seats to pop, hard rock, R&B, and jazz tunes that blare from my CD player. 8) And we crown this weekend revelry by eating homemade ice cream and chocolate cake, which are my favorite dessert.   9) Everyone know what I am doing on Saturdays.   10) Let others spend the day cleaning, planting flowers, or running into the office to do "catch up" work; I enjoy myself!

1. _____

2. _____

3. _____

4. _____

5. _____

6. _____

7. _____

8. _____

9. _____

10. _____

Pronoun Agreement

Exercise #1

Read each sentence below carefully. Some of the sentences contain errors in pronoun agreement. If a sentence contains an agreement problem, write the correct answer in the blank provided to the left of the sentence. If a sentence has correct agreement, write *C* in the blank.

_____ 1. When one is alone, they have a lot of time to reminisce about the past and dream about the future.

_____ 2. I am sure that everyone's family is important to them.

_____ 3. Inner beauty comes from one who is giving and who cares about others besides himself or herself.

_____ 4. A person is beautiful if they are intelligent, caring, and well-groomed.

_____ 5. When someone uses the terms "woman" and "girl" interchangeably, they are mistaken.

_____ 6. The last thing that distinguishes a lady from a woman is that she will wait for a man to approach her for a date.

_____ 7. During the weekends, college students have more time to do things which are important to us to do besides studying.

_____ 8. To be happy, a person needs some type of love in their life or that individual will live a life filled with sorrow.

_____ 9. Clothing can make a person or break them.

_____ 10. When I am at home, there are many distractions that prevent you from studying.

_____11. People are never aware that someone you trust could betray them.

_____12. If everybody had the opportunity to change something personal, they would.

_____13. The local news is a regular television program that is primarily informative because they cover the news, weather, and sports-three subjects most people want to know about.

_____14. Racism may be defined as disliking another person because of the color of their skin.

_____15. Everyone thinks their family is great.

_____16. Corporal punishment is needed in today's public schools to help a child behave and respect their teachers.

_____17. In a friendship you trust someone to let them hold your most prized possession.

_____18. Before a person is hired to work for the school system in our town, a criminal check must be run on him or her.

_____19. If Jake or Elton arrives before I return, tell them to begin reading the galleys.

_____20. Either Ms. Fisher or the Shaw sisters will model their designs in the fashion show.

Exercise #2
Rewrite the paragraph below to correct the errors in pronoun agreement.

With the frequent reports of drive-by shootings, home invasions, and public denigrating attacks on political and religious leaders, one often concludes that the world is a cold place where no one cares about anybody except themselves. But occasionally, if one is lucky, he will witness human beings being kind to each other for the sake of spreading warmth, love, and joy alone. I was fortunate to witness this behavior just recently as I worked as a volunteer with a Habitat for Humanity building project. There I stood at 8:00 a.m. on a Saturday morning, watching people from different backgrounds coming together to build homes for two separate families. There were people of different races–African Americans, Caucasians, Asians, and Latinos. There were different socioeconomic groups represented, including housewives, clerical workers, teachers, contractors, businessmen, students, and a college president. There were adolescents, young adults, the middle aged, and senior citizens. And various religious denominations were represented, including but not limited to Episcopalians, Presbyterians, Baptists, Methodists, and nondenominational–all different yet intrinsically the same, a person with a desire to share their skills, talents, and time to help others. I rejoiced as I thought, "Disaster and tragedy are not the only ties that bind people together, nor is benevolence a contagion of the harvest and yuletide seasons. All is not lost; everyone can work together peacefully with their brothers and sisters, even on ordinary Saturday mornings."

Verb Form

Exercise #1
Determine which sentences below contain faults in verb form. If a sentence contains a fault in verb form, place *VF* in the provided space, and write in the correct form of the verb. If the sentence is correct, place *C* in the provided space.

_____ 1. They should have came straight to our house when they arrived in Chicago.

_____ 2. While we were at the club last night, someone had entered our apartment and had went through all of our belongings.

_____ 3. The students had ate all of the hors d'oeuvres before the party had ever started.

_____ 4. I taken two Tylenols and went to bed early last night.

_____ 5. Although I always wanted to attend college, I never stop to determine if I had the skills to function in college.

_____ 6. The balloon bursted as soon as the temperature rose.

_____ 7. Unfortunately, we drank more beer than we should have at the party last night.

_____ 8. Marion should have forgave Troy when he asked for forgiveness.

_____ 9. When I returned from the Army, I found out that my mother had gave away all of my old clothes.

_____ 10. They should have chose the red car, not the blue one.

_____ 11. The milk was to be drunk by the baby, not by his father.

_____ 12. When we returned to the old house in which we had grown up, we found weeds and vines covering the entire place.

_____ 13. You were not suppose to tell our secret.

_____ 14. The posse hung the murder suspect before he ever went to trial.

_____ 15. The hot cheese clang to the roof of my mouth when I ate the pizza.

_____ 16. We should have took the Amtrak to New Orleans.

_____ 17. As soon as Mickey had throwed the rock at the window, he wished that he hadn't.

_____ 18. I laid down early last night, but I didn't fall asleep until the wee hours of the morning.

_____19. That flower pot has set by the front door for well over two years now.

_____20. After Bob had placed his jacket on the bed, it lay there until the next morning.

Exercise #2

Some of the sentences in the paragraph below contain errors in verb tense. There are those that contain more than one such error. Find each error, draw a line through it , and write its correction above it.

1) Tony should have never went into the Army.   2) First of all, he has never been good at following orders.   3) Even when he was a little boy, he never wanted to do the chores that were assigned to him by his parents,   4) and he never set down in school when he was told to do so by his teachers.   5) Secondly, he was always a stay-at-home person; 6) therefore, everyone was surprised when he choose a profession that was bound to take him thousands of miles from his parents' house.   7) But when the train for Fort Rucker, Alabama, blowed its whistle one Saturday morning, Tony jumped on it and wave goodbye to his family and friends.   8) Finally, Tony never liked to work hard.   9) Once he digged a hole in which to bury his pet dog.   10) The hole was only six inches long and five inches wide.   11) The dog had growed to be two feet tall and eleven inches long before he was ran over by the truck that kill him. 12) Somehow, Tony cram the big dog into the small hole and covered him up.   13) A mild-wind come along and blowed away the little dirt that Tony had place over the puppy.   14) Both the dog's feet and head begun to stick out of the shallow grave.   15) When Tony seen that this had happen, he drug a tree limb over and put it on top of the puppy. 16) Tony always swore that hard work would never kill him.   17) Because of Tony's shortcomings, he should have became a teacher, lawyer, or even a doctor, but never a soldier.

Tense Shifts

Exercise #1

Some of the sentences below contain tense shifts. If a sentence contains an incorrect tense shift, place "TS" in the space provided and write in the correct verb form. If the sentence is correct, write "C" in the space.

_____ 1. After John wrecked the car, he sat down at the curb and starts to cry.

_____ 2. The two suspects could not deny that they had stolen the tape deck from John's wrecked car.

_____ 3. Yesterday's weather was excellent, but today as I walk home, the weather was terrible.

_____ 4. I used to love to listen to and view Andy Williams' live concerts, but now I have to be satisfied with playing his tapes and CDs because I no longer heard any announcements of his live concerts.

_____ 5. The birds seemed lively and happy as they chirp this morning at my window, but, for some reason, this evening they are silent.

_____ 6. Today many of us may be happy; however, since most of us cannot predict the future accurately, we will not know what tomorrow would have bring us.

_____ 7. I held my nose, jumped into the pool, and find a hundred dollars.

_____ 8. A new type of camera that took eight years to develop is introduced earlier this year.

_____ 9. Two seconds before the buzzer sounded, John scored a basket from mid-court, and the crowd goes wild.

_____10. We improved the quality of our teaching, graded harder, disciplined more, and see positive results.

Exercise #2
Some of the sentences in the paragraph below contain tense shifts. Correct each error by supplying the appropriate tense. Make no changes to sentences that are already correct.

1) Participating in sports and games, going camping, throwing bait for fish, watching movies, and lounging on beaches all bring big smiles to my face.   2) My friend, Mike, knows that I am a man for rugged living, so he calls me up any day and asked, "Hey, John, wanna go fishing tomorrow at Alligator Point?"   3) My response without a doubt was "Sure, what time?"   4) All my friends knew how highly energetic and active I am, so yes, it was a stupid question.   5) This is not obvious to my mom.   6) She often thought I should stay home and read a book instead.   7) My reply to her, while running out the door is usually, "Sure thing, mom, next time!"   8) Reading was like torture to me most of the time.   9) Since I read *Tom Sawyer*, however, I now had a different perspective.   10) This book is my favorite.

Comma Faults

Exercise #1
Read each sentence below to determine if commas have been used incorrectly or if needed commas have been omitted. If there is a comma fault, rewrite the sentence, correctly punctuating it or removing any unnecessary commas. If a sentence is correctly punctuated, write "C" in the blank provided instead of rewriting the sentence.

_____ 1. Some people believe, that they are better than everyone else.

_____ 2. Some people will not even socialize with others, unless those people are in their, so called "class."

_____ 3. To disassociate yourself from people because you feel they are inferior, is the best example of being "stuck up."

_____ 4. When you label a guy as a romantic you are basically saying that he is a true lady's man.

_____ 5. My very neat dresser sits on the left side of my bed.

_____ 6. Respect, is something that should not be taken for granted.

_____ 7. Driving in afternoon traffic can be frustrating not to mention dangerous.

_____ 8. The slang term "word" is not useful in a formal, or business-like atmosphere.

_____ 9. There is no correct definition of something, the meaning of a word is relative.

_____10. If we do not show our children love, they may do harsh things to other people.

_____11. According to most parents education is the most important concern in the world.

_____12. If a woman takes care of what she has for instance her hair, then she will be beautiful.

_____13. A true lady would know what to say at the boss's party, and which fork to use at a fancy restaurant.

_____14. My first grade teacher, made an impact on my life, that I will never forget.

_____15. They always want to improve, or be improved.

_____16. In the March on Washington in 1963, the leader as you already know, was the late Dr. Martin Luther King, Jr.

_____17. When I am in the dorm, I usually eat food like, sausage, hash browns, and a bowl of cereal for breakfast.

_____18. The things we need to live today are not the same things people needed to live yesterday.

_____19. Where there is no love, there is no trust, where there is no trust, there is no togetherness.

_____20. Yes, I admit that I am afraid of the dark sometimes, aren't you?

Exercise #2
Rewrite the paragraph below to correct errors in comma usage.

If I could become any other creature, I would become a bird. Why a bird? Well let me see, there are numerous reasons why I would choose to be this creature. The ability to soar, must be a wonderful feeling.

Imagine the freedom birds must feel, imagine floating in the air. Consider the sacredness of being closer to the Creator, and the heavens. Consider the sights, the beautiful sights-a closer view of the warm, peaceful, blue sky; a closer view of the bright sun and its merry rays; and a closer view of luminous drops of rain falling softly upon my face and refreshing my tongue before the thunderous waterfall swooshes down upon other earthlings. What a sense of power I would feel to be able to look down on tips of mighty trees, towering buildings, and man who thinks the earth was made for him and his kindred. But most joyful, most beneficial to me, would be the opportunity to escape the pettiness and mean-spiritedness of human beings occasionally. To be able to run, to be able to escape to a place where I could not be disturbed or spiritually wounded, nor see others thusly assaulted, would be the ultimate reward of being a bird. What a flight! What a fantasy!

Apostrophes/Plurals

Exercise #1

Read each sentence below carefully. Some of the sentences contain errors in use of the apostrophe. If a sentence contains an error, write the correct word (s) in the blank provided at the left of the sentence. If a sentence has correct apostrophe use, write "C" in the appropriate blank.

_____ 1. Dear, do not forget to buy two dollars worth of peaches for the cobbler.

_____ 2. I have wanted to meet your famous cousin's for an eternity!

_____ 3. It's my fault that I failed to follow instructions on the algebra examination.

_____ 4. All college students must realize that if they are to be successful, the responsibility is solely theirs'.

_____ 5. As a result of our intensive recruitment activities, we've fifty-five members in our recently organized "Return Ethics to the Campus Society."

_____ 6. I have been unable to shake this feeling that something's wrong, ever since I glanced out of my dorm window and saw my girl strolling through "Lovers' Lane" with my best friend.

_____ 7. If you want to make all A's in your major courses, you mustn't make a habit of cultivating close friendships with chronically negative peers.

_____ 8. As a member of the current freshman class of '97, I am working and planning for the day that I will be awarded my college diploma-in front of my professors- with all their Ph.D.'s.

_____ 9. Do you mean its already time for me to be in class?

_____10. Some people still feel that humility is it's own reward.

Exercise #2
Read the paragraph below that contains errors in use of the apostrophe. Then, rewrite the paragraph, correcting apostrophe errors.

Kenyatta Spencer and Chris Johnson were asked to present their research papers in class today. Kenyattas paper, "School Prayer: "To Be Or Not To Be," addressed the various issues concerning the need for prayer in public schools and the impact prayer would have on students' and school personnel. He presented many arguments by both proponents and opponents of this highly debated issue. Many students in the class laughed and cheered when Kenyatta, the class-clown, raised his' hand, as if mimicking the Statue of Liberty, and said, "I, Kenyatta Spencer, do hereby agree with the constitution when it separates the state from the church. Further, I proclaim on this glorious day that no one should be forced to accept any ones religious preference, nor will any one have to accept mine's." Chris paper, "Does a Child's Home Environment Affect His' Potential to Do Well in School?" wasnt as entertaining as Kenyatta. In his presentation, Chris discussed the effect home life has on one's school performance. He reported that its important that a child lives in a clean and healthy home environment. Chrises presentation was very informative, but it was too long and boring. The teacher stated that he was very pleased with Kenyatta and Chris's presentations; however, he was very upset with a few students who were unprepared to present their's. Also, the teacher told the class that there were only three As (90, 93, and 95) and four Bs (83,84, and two 88s) on the presentations.

Usage

Exercise #1
Read each sentence below carefully. Some of the sentences contain errors in usage. If a sentence contains an error in usage, write the correct word (s) in the blank provided at the left of the sentence. If a sentence has correct usage, write "C" in the appropriate blank.

_____ 1. Don't except expensive gifts from people, unless you know them well.

_____ 2. "Girl, sit down and let a man of the world advice you on this essential matter," the pompous upperclassman said to the freshman.

_____ 3. "Whether or not the teacher comes to class does not effect me," the apathetic student remarked.

_____ 4. If the professor gets irritated by student's incomplete assignments, students would do well not to further aggravate the situation by being arrogant.

_____ 5. Although my cousin and I were both starving, we agreed to share a orange, an action that meant a lot to both of us.

_____ 6. The amount of people who write well these days is dwindling.

_____ 7. Being that you are my dearest relative, I am going to share this secret with you.

_____ 8. Hanson said he can't hardly wait for the holiday weekend to begin.

_____ 9. When you've reached a milestone in your life you can't help but doing what achievers do.

_____ 10. The university choir sang good at the Annual Spring Gospel Extravaganza last night.

Exercise #2

Each sentence below is numbered. Read each sentence carefully, paying special attention to usage. If a sentence contains an error in usage, write the correct word (s) in the blank provided. If a sentence has correct usage, write "C" in the appropriate blank.

1) This written comment is sent in regards to your inquiry of April 4, 1998.   2) Irregardless of your personal feelings, I think you should do the right thing.   3) Unfairness is when people who are fully qualified for a position are passed over because someone does not like them.   4) My parents say when such unfairness exists, it's time for someone in strategic places to "lay down the law."   5) On account of this widespread practice, legislators can no longer ignore the need for positive change. 6) As a matter of fact, they should of listened to the grassroots people long ago.   7) Farther, if our elected law makers would do their jobs, problems like these would not occur.   8) However, as registered voters, we can easily learn our legislators a lesson.   9) We can let them know that just as we helped them win a previous election, we can help them loose the next one.   10) I bet such a notice would get lots of attention and the appropriate legislation.

1. _____

2. _____

3. _____

4. _____

5. _____

6. _____

7. _____

8. _____

9. _____

10. _____

Sentence Structure: Modification

Exercise #1

Revise the sentences below to repair faulty modification (dangling and misplaced modifiers).

1. After completing a computer course, more opportunities will be available.
2. A price-chart greeted me upon entering the room.
3. Soaring majestically above the statehouse grounds, the soldier saluted the U. S. Flag.
4. There are many examples of alumni who have become famous in the book.
5. Jensen is a woman with tremendous talent that is beautiful as well.
6. Consisting of explicit sexual references and violent images, teenagers currently spend thousands of dollars on popular music.
7. The statement is true that opposites attract.
8. Gillian is taking a course on witchcraft at the University of Atlanta.
9. After losing his money while running for the bus, his stomach growled noisily during his classmates's presentation.
10. Seeing her give so much time and patience to her patients, that nurse must love her job.

Exercise #2

The paragraph below contains errors in modification. Revise the paragraph to eliminate dangling and misplaced modifiers.

When he was twelve years old, Joe's father decided to enroll him in a junior basketball camp. After saving the money, it was time to select a camp for Joe to attend. Having superior knowledge about such camps, the decision about an appropriate camp was made by Joe's father and Joe obediently attended. Joe's father believed that Joe might play professionally as he grew into a young man and a better basketball player. However, Joe's father neglected to ask Joe what he wanted to do professionally. In his father's eyes, Joe began to realize that his wishes did not matter. Although Joe loved basketball, his greater love was animals. He had hoped to become a veterinarian. When it was time for Joe to enroll in college, his father insisted that he choose a non-demanding major so that he could focus on his athletic career. But Joe followed his own mind, uncharacteristically. He played basketball for two years and then quit the team so that he could focus on his major in veterinary science. Today, Joe is a respected and well-loved animal doctor in his hometown. And Joe's father is proud of him.

Sentence Logic: Mixed Constructions and Faulty Predication

Exercise #1
Revise the sentences below to eliminate faulty predication, mixed construction, and awkward coordination.

1. No two people are exactly alike and in attempts to be someone else usually doesn't work out.
2. Being an individual constitutes as a learning experience and can be quite helpful to both parties.
3. In America, there is more room for advancement than any other place.
4. Everyone loves when that special person shows he is loved.
5. The treatment of children is horrible and to some should not be done.
6. The author explained cloning in his book and the morality issue.
7. People should not be able to take responsibility away, but may accept what they have gotten themselves into.
8. By my mom trying to control my behavior, it just made or relationship more strained.
9. Tolerance is when you are patient with someone else.
10. Forgiveness is a requirement that will require a lot of compassion if a marriage is to survive.

Exercise #2
Revise the paragraph below to eliminate errors in sentence logic.

Boredom is when people find themselves frustrated by the lack of interesting entertainment or intellectual involvement/stimulation. While the world is filled with astonishing technology which enables us to choose from a myriad of entertainment options, to be bored is a puzzling phenomenon. Traditional forms of entertainment—television, music, movies, sports—have been enhanced in so many ways that even the less imaginative among us can find something to command our interest for at least a short period of time. By our failing to do so suggests that perhaps we are bored with our entertainment technology. When playing the same video games again and again can make our movements in from of that screen become robot-like because there is no mental challenge. Seeing so many plotless special-effects movies is how we realize that we can guess their endings. Although deep down we must somehow know that it is our mindless entertainment that bores us, but we continue to engage in it. Maybe the reason is because we simply refuse to look for challenges to stimulate us.

ENGLISH LANGUAGE SKILLS TEST

Pre-Test

This test is designed to test your knowledge of English language skills. Out of the thirty-five (35) items in the test, you must get at least twenty-eight (28) correct to demonstrate competency. You should be able to complete this test in thirty (30) minutes.

I. Some of the following sentences use incorrect grammar. Select the letter that appears in parentheses before the incorrect usage.

1. The nurse left the patient (A) laying (B) on the floor when she heard the patient from the (C) other bed scream.

2. Although the store will be closed for (A) repairs, (B) but you may shop as (C) usual.

3. (A) Because we cannot walk any (B) further, we must (C) take the boat.

4. At the graduation party, we (A) drunk more than we would have (B) normally (C) done.

5. My brother and (A) me (B) toured the islands (C) during our spring break.

6. (A) Whose coming (B) with (C) us to the football game?

7. (A) If we had not lived in a dormitory (B) before, we would not have been (C) use to such small quarters.

8. The person who (A) rammed that car must (B) have bought (C) their license.

9. A poor (A) grade is (B) not (C) nothing I would want to deal with at the end of the semester.

10. Coming out of (A) it's shell did not seem (B) to be a simple (C) matter.

II. Errors in punctuation appear in the following sentences. Identify the errors by selecting the parenthetical letter that precedes the error. Only one error exists in each sentence.

11. (A) "Will you go to the prom with me (B)?" he asked (C)?

12. The entire audience realized (A), that the play, (B) based on Jonathan's script, (C) was absurdist.

13. I did not (A) have my usual cheesy, (B) burger at lunch (C), only some fries.

14. The registrar said (A), (B) "I think you will find everything in order, (C)" Mr. Lott.

15. We laughed and cried (A), we knew that our friendship would never die (B), not (C) under any circumstances.

III. From the choices provided, select the correct word to complete the sentences below.

16. We had a large _____ of students applying for scholarships.
    A. amount
    B. number
    C. bevy

17. I am definitely _____ when I see children rummaging for food in the garbage dumps.
    A. effected
    B. affected
    C. nonchalant

18. A steady buzzing noise in my head always _____ me.
    A. irates
    B. irritates
    C. aggravates

19. It was not easy for me to _____ the award on behalf of Jim, who had attended school with me every day of his life, except for the last day.
    A. except
    B. excess
    C. accept

20. The _____ was not pleased when she saw the snake that Johnny had brought to school.
    A. principle
    B. principal
    C. baby sitter

21. The head of my department gave me sound _____ when I registered as a freshman.
    A. device
    B. advise
    C. advice

22. The house _____ belonged to an old couple who moved to Tampa.
    A. formally
    B. formerly
    C. firstly

23. The child sat _____ her mother in the doctor's office.
    A. besides

B. beside

C. outside

24. The rowdy fraternity brothers'_____behavior was reason for the neighbors to call the police.

    A. coarse

    B. course

    C. amicable

25. I do not want to have cause to look back at my _____ with disgust.

    A. pass

    B. past

    C. passed

IV. Some of the following sentences contain errors and some are correct. No sentence has more than one error. When you find an error, circle the letter that comes before it. If there is no error, circle NE at the end.

26. Our wonderful group of students (A) have decided to (B) undertake a difficult but (C) meaningful project. (NE)

27. This test is (A) different (B) to the (C) others. (NE)

28. After dropping (A) a rose at my feet (B), he ran (C) of before I could thank him. (NE)

29. Everyone said it (A) was (B) her who (C) stole the money. (NE)

30. Anyone knowing (A) him, (B) should not place (C) their trust in him. (NE)

Select the word nearest in meaning to the underlined word in each sentence.

31. The interns are less <u>zealous</u> than those of former years.

    A. patient

    B. willing

    C. enthusiastic

32. A survey of the needs of the area was conducted and a plan for solutions was <u>formulated</u>.

    A. executed

    B. planned

    C. devised

33. He spoke with extreme caution and avoided giving a <u>biased</u> opinion on the matter at hand.

    A. ambiguous

    B. prejudicial

    C. doubtful

34. The home team, cheered on by the spectators, adopted an approach to the game that may be described as <u>belligerent</u>.

    A. defensive

    B. aggressive

    C. tactical

35. The chairperson of the committee gave <u>confirmation</u> to the views expressed by members.

    A. recognition

    B. approval

    C. loyalty

EDITING

Assignment I

The following is an observation essay written by a student. Edit the essay.

Sample Essay 1

YESTERDAY'S LOVE

It was an average day after school. Classes were boring during school, so I needed something, anything to excite me. A certain aroma tackled the spicy chicken smell coming from the kitchen. It was the aroma of newly blossomed flowers. The trees were spreading there joy all over the many yards. The birds were singing. The dogs were barking. the neighborhood kids were all participating in a game of frisbee. An old lady sat on her porch an drank tea, while she watched her husband and grandson play checkers. Then it appeared as if the wind begin to blow. Time seem to be of no essence. As the evening sun rays bounced off of the pavement, she appeared. One could not hardly see her. As she got closer, my heart begin to pound, beating faster and faster with anticipation. Shocking as it may seem, she entered my yard.

She was covered in gold. The gold was glowing as the sun's rays reflected off of her. All eyes were on her. She didn't have to do nothing. Her looks said it all. I wanted her. In time I would have her. I touched her gentlely. Then I began to run my hands all over her. Her surface was as smooth as silk. She was kind of warm. I couldn't resist the temptation. I jumped right in, head first, not caring who were watching. I was all smiles. She smelled so good. I asked my mom for her name. She said Betsy. I looked at my mom curiously and replied, "Wasn't that the name of our old car."

We jumped in as if there were no tomorrow. I guess I knew how to push the right buttons, because she began to sing to me, clearly with a wonderful pitch. She did whatever I wanted her to do. The car drove so quietly. As far as I was concerned, people were all lined up along the road as if we were in a parade. Betsy was more than a car, she was a work of art, crafted with precision the cars first owner must have treated her like a queen She was clean and sweet. She now belong to me and I guess the rest of my family.

It wouldn't be too long before our relationship would stand the test of time. I received my first true freedom with her as a teenager. It was she that performed so well as I got my license. She was the orchestra and I was the leader. At times, Betsy was stubborn. She just wouldn't perform up to par.

Now look at her, father time has taken its toll on her. The car is a dinosaur compared to the younger, swifter cars. The car's graceful motion has been replaced by a limp. Her smooth, silky, golden surface has had its share of knocks and bruises. A band-aid couldn't cure but only treat the various ailments. The quiet sound she made as she passed by others of her kind is now a roar of anger. It sounds like she has a cold, along with sinus congestion. Betsy no longer smells like fragrance of poupouri but instead smell like the grease from body shops. There use to be a time when it didn't cost very much to satisfy her thirst but now she behaves like an alcoholic. She insist of having the finest and most expensive beverage offered. If not, she doesn't feel so good.

As I look at her, I have mixed feelings. On one hand, she was my ticket to all of the nearby activities. On the other hand, I had my first encounter with the law.

At least I don't have to share her with anyone else. She's all mine. Who was it that said "never judge a book by its cover" or "it's not what's on the outside but what's on the inside?" Whoever said these things doesn't have to see a dinosaur parked next to a new specie. There was once a time when people thought New Yorker was inscribed on the car because it was from New York. May be it's time to retire her. If I traded her in, I may get seven hundred dollars. I don't think I will. Nowadays, they give Betsy and others a face lift that would remind you of yesterday. May be that's what I'll do.

EDITING

Assignment II

Edit the following letter to correct errors in grammar, punctuation, and mechanics.

November 15, _____
Blank Circle Circle Sorority, Inc.
Your University or School
Your Town

Dear Committee,

I am please to write this letter in support of Ms. Daisy Doe nomination for a scholarship by your're find organization. I have known Ms. Doe for several years now and can attest to her acceptional scholastic ability an unimpeachable character.

During her tenure as an English major. She has maintained an overall GPA of 3.23, and will do her student intenship next semester. Because of her pass performance in her studies'. I have no doubt that she will excel in the classroom as teacher and graduate as expected during the Spring (Year) Commencement.

Besides being a model student, Ms. Doe is a roll model for other students here at _____. Not only is she responsible in completeing her studies she is a friendly, respectable and mature young woman whom is all ready making a worthy contribution to her school and community. She is a active member of the Baldwin Literary Guild, jane eyre society, and Brighte Honor Society. Indeed Ms. Doe has a promising future as a professor of english and valuable member of society. Any assistance your organization can provide her now and in the future will be a worhtwhile investment.

Sincerely,

Your name

Title

EDITING

Assignment III

The essay below is a contrast of love and hate. Correct the errors in this paper. One type of error is made repeatedly. What is it? Also pay special attention to development. Has the writer proved his thesis? Revise this essay.

A THIN LINE BETWEEN LOVE AND LUST

Being in love is one of the most beautiful part of life. Being that love is difficult to define, most people simply assume that they know they're in love. These are the people that have successfully been able to differentiate between love and lust. Attitude toward a relationship, desire to please, and feelings toward a person are three items by which to make such a differentiation.

When being in love, one's attitude toward their relationship is full of optimism and hope. When being infatuated, one's attitude is more careless and that of little concern. When in love, a person makes an effort to try to make the relationship work well. When infaturated, a person isn't too concerned whether the relationship will work just as long as they are enjoying it now.

One's desire to please is another way by which to differentiate between love and infatuation. When a person is in love, they have an utmost desire to please their significant other. When a person is infatuated, their main concern is to please themselves. In love, a person is always willing to be there when there are sacrafices made by a person to be there for the other.

Finally, one can differentiate between love and infatuation by one's feelings toward a person. When someone is in love, their feelings for a person are quite deep and emotional. When infatuated, a person's feeling are that of lust. They are superficial and represent one's physical desires of the other. A person in love will get out of their bed at 4:00 in the morning if their partner needs someone to talk to. Someone who is infatuated will only get out their at that time for reasons other than talking.

The difference between love and infatuation are quite evident though they are often confused. If someone is unsure about whether they are in love, they should ask themselves if they comply with the previous items.

EDITING

Assignment IV

Revise the paper below. Be certain to check the MLA documentation section in text to make corrections in the Works Cited section.

SUMMARY OF THE BLUEST EYE

The first novel published by Miss Toni Morrison, "The Bluest Eye", has a simple yet complex storyline. The story is simply about a young black girl on the edge of puberty who wishes to have blue eyes. The complexity comes when one discovers her reasons for desiring the blue eyes. Pecola Breedlove feels that she is ugly. This theory is reinforced by her parents distance from her as well as the disdain and abuse she suffers at the hands of her classmates. Twice in the novel she appeals to possible allies/saviors (Maureen and Geraldine), and both times she is rebuffed and confronted with her "blackness" and "ugliness". She experiences no true companship, even from Claudia and Frieda, only pity. Finally, in the climax of the novel, her drunken father, Cholly Breedlove, rapes her. Pecola is shocked out her reason by this event. She then consults a spellman, Soaphead Church to give her blue eyes. Pecola's insanity is hinted at by her belief that she actually does possess blue eyes. It is confirmed after the death of her baby, folowing which she loses all appearances of sanity. It is a story of a child asking the biggest question of all, "why?".

Pecola's life is affected by the indifference of her mother, who desires to make her job her life, and her father, who is bitter at the world for his circumstances and seeks solace in a bottle. Frieda and Claudia represent to her a home life entirely different from her own. Maureen is viewed as an idol, a potential savior until she reveals that she too thinks Pecola ugly. The three whores China, Poland, and Miss Marie are the most accepting of Pecola throughout the entire novel. Finally, Soaphead Church is seen as her savior as he is the one who is able to gift her with blue eyes.

One theme of the story could be that beauty is in the eye of the beholder. Another could be that the answer to one's dreams may not be the answers to one's problems. The setting is the town of Lorain in Ohio. It takes place in the Autumn of 1941. The tone of the story is rather objective as the author does not try to arouse pity for her characters, she merely tells a tale. The majority of the imagery in the story is used to display the difference in classes (various skin colors).

Toni Morison was born Chloe Anthony Wofford on February 13, 1931, in Lorain, Ohio. After an extensive education, marriage, and divorce, she penned her first novel, "The Blues Eye" in 1970. During the course of her upbringing she was exposed to people and situations which directly parallel her writings. Like many of her characters, Miss Morrison has cleaned for whites and experienced racial incidents. Miss Morrison uses her writings as a means to expose and express her view of African American circumstances during that particular era.

Works Cited

1.   Bloom, Harold, ed. *20th Century American Literature.* 9 vols. USA: Chelsea Publishing House, 1987. 5:2762-71.

2.   Draper, James P., ed. *Black Literature Criticism.* 3 Vols. Detroit, Michigan: Gale Research Inc., 1992. 3:1422-45.

3.   Mainiero, Lina, ed. *American Women Writers.* 5 vols. USA: Fredreick Unger Publishing Co. Inc., 1981. 3:113-14.

4.   Popkin, Micheal. *A Library of Literary Criticism, Modern Black Writers.* USA: Frederick Unger Publishing Co. Inc., 310-13.

5.   Shockley, Ann Allen and Sue P. Chandler. *Living Black American Authors.* USA: R. R. Bowker Co., 1973. 112-113.

EDITING

Assignment V

Below you will find a statement of purpose written by a student seeking financial assistance. Read the statement carefully. How can you improve this statement? Rewrite the statement so that the problem or need is clearly identified, conventional English skills are employed, and so that the tone will be more serious, more appropriate for the request made.

The Mark of Excellence Scholarship Program

Statement of Purpose

Name _____ Date_____

Use the space below to write a 250-300 word statement regarding your need for the two-year academic scholarship to enhance your education.

I am currently a sophomore business major with a minor in Biology. I am a very good student, as my GPA of 3.7 verifies. Being that I am a sophomore, I have only two more years of college before I can graduate. I want desperately to graduate with my classmates, but I fear I will not if I can not come up with some more money to pay for my expenses.

Right now I am working a twenty-five hour part-time job and you know how I must feel trying to study and go to work. I tried to make it without working at first but you cannot imagine how hard that was! My bad. I got a job and have been working ever since. Therefore, this scholarship will allow me to study full-time without having to worry. And my parent neither. I need sixty more hours to graduate, so I plan to follow this schedule for the next two years, provided that i get the scholarship; take 21 hours in the fall and 21 in the spring; then 12 in the fall of my senior year and 6 hours during the spring, my last semester at Gadsden State. I am thinking about pledgeing during the fall of my last year here at GSU and I cannot imagine studying hard, pledgeing, and working too. Most people want to take it kind of easy during their last semester of college, you know. Word. So I'm planning to study and enjoy myself before I enter the real world.

I do hope that you will strongly consider giving me this scholarship because I have certainly proven myself scholastically. Maintaining one of the highest GPA's in my Department. Last but not least, if I can finish my B.A. in the next two years, I will be able to start to work on my masters during the summer. At least that is my plan now.

ENGLISH LANGUAGE SKILLS EXAM

Post-Test

Directions: The passage below contains several errors. Read the passage. Then answer each item by choosing the test option that corrects an error in the italicized portion. Refer to the passage as necessary. No more than one underlined error will appear in each item. If no error exists, choose "No change is necessary."

Comedians of the 90s cater to the baser instincts of their audiences. Unlike comedians of the 60s, such as Bill Cosby, whose routines were insightful vignettes on family life, or comedians of the 70s, like Richard Pryor, whose routines were seriocomic social commentaries today's comedians often use sex and mean-spirited ridicule as the basis of their humor. HBO, programming torch-bearer of the future, airs "Def Comedy Jam" and "Loco Slam," two ethnic oriented half-hour showcases in which up and coming comedians do five minute sets rife with profanity and sexual gesturing. The comics, both males and females, use their five minutes to graphically relate "stories" about sexual experiences, to explicitly proclaim their sexual prowess, to insensitively insult audience members, and exploit the cruel misfortunes of the famous. And the audiences love it. They cheer; they whoop; they bark there approval. These cable comedians have only marginal competition from those comedians relegated to network television. These mainstream comedians forced to use cleaner language compensate by increasing the sexual innuendo and the mean-spirited reference to those larger-than-life "celebrities" among us. Reviewing the "news of the day," they do not hardly ever miss an opportunity to exploit a misfortune or connect the dots of sexual implication in any of those news tidbits. Of course, comedians have always used sex, and the famous as a part of their routines, just not as explicitly or as cruelly as they do today. And, it seems, once upon a time, there was a point to using it. Yet, in all fairness, maybe today's comics also have an agenda—a hidden one. Or perhaps these bright and industrious comedians simply have not got anything else to say.

1. Comedians of the 90s *cater to* the baser instincts of their audiences.

   A. adhere to
   B. succumb to
   C. live up to
   D. No change is necessary.

2. Unlike comedians of the 60s, such as Bill Cosby, whose routines were insightful vignettes on family life, or comedians of the 70s like Richard Pryor, whose routines were seriocomic social *commentaries today's* comedians often use sex and mean-spirited ridicule as the basis of their humor.

   A. commentaries; today's
   B. commentaries. Today's
   C. commentaries, today's
   D. No change is necessary.

3. HBO, programming torch-bearer of the future, airs "Def Comedy Jam" and "Loco Slam," two ethnic oriented half-hour showcases in which *up and coming comedians* do five minute sets rife with profanity and sexual gesturing.

A. up, and coming comedians
B. up, and coming, comedians
C. up-and-coming comedians
D. No change is necessary.

4. These comics, both males and females, use their five minutes to relate "stories" about sexual experiences quite graphically, (A) *to proclaim their sexual prowess very explicitly,* (B) *to insult audience members in a very insensitive manner,* and (C) *exploit the cruel misfortunes of the famous.*

A. to proclaim their sexual prowess very implicitly.
B. insulting audience members in a very insensitive manner.
C. to exploit the misfortunes of the famous cruelly.
D. No change is necessary.

5. And the audiences love it. They cheer; they whoop; they bark *there* approval.

A. their
B. they're
C. they
D. No change is necessary.

6. These cable comedians have *only* marginal competition from those comedians relegated to network television.

A. from only
B. only from
C. only have
D. No change in necessary.

7. These mainstream comedians (A) *forced to use cleaner language* (B) *compensate* by increasing the sexual innuendo and the mean-spirited reference to those (C) *larger-than-life* "celebrities" among us.

A. ,forced to use cleaner language,
B. compinsate
C. Larger-then-life
D. No change is necessary.

8. (A) *Reviewing* the (B) *"news of the day,"* (C) *they do not hardly ever miss* an opportunity to exploit a misfortune or connect the dots of sexual implication in any of those news tidbits.

A. Reveiwing
B. "news of the day",
C. they hardly ever miss
D. No change is necessary.

9. Of course, comedians (A) *have* always used (B) *sex, and* the famous as (C) *a part* of their routines, just not as explicitly or as cruelly as they do today.

    A. had
    B. sex and
    C. apart
    D. No change is necessary.

10. And, it seems, once upon a time, there was a point to using *(it)*.

    A. that
    B. them
    C. this
    D. No change is necessary.

11. Yet, in all fairness, (A) *maybe* today's comics also have (B) *an* (C) *agenda*—a hidden one.

    A. may be
    B. and
    C. addendum
    D. No change is necessary.

12. Or perhaps these bright and industrious comedians simply *(have not got anything else to say)*.

    A   don't have nothing else to say.
    B. have nothing else to say.
    C. do not have nothing else to say.
    D. No change is necessary.

PASSAGE TWO

The night air carried the strong scent of sweet roses from the rose garden next door, but Jefferson Sloan could care less about roses or their scent as he hid behind an oak tree. The scent of the roses were only another reminder of his being such a fool. He had sent roses to his wife whenever he thought she was feeling down or for no other reason than to let her know that he loved her. Without a doubt, all of his romantic notions and thoughts of love was destroyed by his unfaithful wife. In addition Jefferson had learned that his best friend, Franklin Price, who was like a brother to him, was the other man. However, all the lies, all the deceit, and all the pain would end tonight. Silently, he eased around to the back of Franklin's house, found the back door key underneath the doormat, placed the key gently into the lock, turning the knob carefully so as not to alert anyone inside. While inside the house and walking toward the staircase, waves of laughter echoed from upstairs. As Jefferson followed the laughter, he stumped his toe on the corner of the first step, and pain electrified his foot and raced through his body. Determined, he slowly continued up the winding stairs. Which were covered with a slick, stained carpet. Finding his way to Franklin's bedroom, Jefferson took a deep breath and threw hisself against the door. The door collapsed under his weight and a women's scream sent shock waves throughout the house.

13. The night air carried the strong scent of sweet roses from the rose garden next (A) *door, but* Jefferson Sloan (B) *could care less* about roses or their (C) *scent as* he hid behind an oak tree.

    A. door but
    B. could not care less
    C. scent, as
    D. No change is necessary.

14. The scent of the roses (A) *were* only (B) *another* reminder of (C) his being such a fool.

    A. was
    B. the other
    C. him
    D. No change is necessary.

15. He had sent roses to his wife (A) *whenever* he thought she was (B) *feeling down* (C) *or* for no other reason than to let her know that he loved her.

    A. whenever
    B. feeling depressed
    C. are
    D. No change is necessary.

16. Without a doubt, all of his (A) *romantic* notions and thoughts of love (B) *was* (C) *destroyed* by his unfaithful wife.

    A. Romantic
    B. were
    C. distroyed
    D. No change is necessary.

17 (A) *In addition* Jefferson had learned that his best (B) *friend,* Franklin (C) *Price, who was like a brother to him,* was the other man.

    A. In addition,
    B. friend
    C. Price who was like a brother to him
    D. No change is necessary.

18. However, all the lies, all the (A) *deceit, and* all the (B) *pain* (C) *would end* tonight.

    A. deceit and
    B. pain, would
    C. would be ended
    D. No change is necessary.

19. Silently, he eased around to the back of (A) *Franklin's* house, found the back door key underneath the doormat, placed the key (B) *gently* into the lock, (C) *turning* the knob carefully so as not to alert anyone inside.

    A. Franklins'
    B. gentally
    C. and turned
    D. No change is necessary.

20. While inside the house and walking toward the staircase, (*waves of laughter echoed* from upstairs.)

    A. the waves of laughter echoed
    B. waves of laughter could be heard echoing
    C. he heard waves of laughter echo
    D. No change is necessary.

21. As Jefferson followed the (A) *laughter; he* stumped his toe on the corner of the first (B) *step, and* pain electrified his (C) *foot and* raced through his body.

    A. laughter,
    B. step and
    C. foot, and
    D. No change is necessary.

22. Determined, he slowly (A) *continued* up the winding (B) *stairs which were covered* with a (C) *slick, stained* carpet.

    A. continues
    B. stairs, which were covered
    C. slick stained
    D. No change is necessary.

23. Finding his way to Franklin's bedroom, Jefferson took a deep (A) *breath* and (B) *throws* (C) *hisself* against the door.

    A. breathe
    B. threw
    C. himself
    D. No change is necessary.

24. The door collapsed under (A) *his* weight and a (B) *women's* scream sent shock waves (C) *throughout* the house.

    A. its
    B. woman's
    C. through out
    D. No change is necessary.

Directions: Choose the sentence that contains no errors in usage and which most correctly expresses the idea.

25. A. Being that we are composition teachers, our writing should be flawless.
     B. Because we are composition teachers, our writing should be flawless.
     C. Being composition teachers, our writing should be flawless.

26. A. John Hurley, a physicist at my university, stated that the tail of Hale-Bopp is as bright as, if not brighter than, other comets.
     B. John Hurley, a physicist at my university, stated that "the tail of Hale-Bopp is as bright as, if not brighter than, the tails of other comets."
     C. John Hurley, a physicist at my university, stated that the tail of Hale-Bopp is as bright as, if not brighter than, the tails of other comets.

27. A. Hazel's reason for getting a divorce was because her ex-mate was insanely jealous.
     B. Hazel's reason for getting a divorce was that her ex-mate was insanely jealous.
     C. Hazel's reason for getting a divorce being that her ex-mate was insanely jealous.

Directions: Choose the underlined word or phrase that is unnecessary to express the meaning of the sentence or to convey sentence sense.

28. Terry's (A) *most* (B) *biggest* dream was to find a (C) *very* (D) *beautiful* house and settle down.
     A. most
     B. biggest
     C. very
     D. beautiful

29. We, (A) *those of us who are members of Delta Zeta Phi Sorority,* have gone out into the community to plan (B) *healthy,* low-fat diets for (C) *very fat* obese people.
     A. those of us who are members of Delta Zeta Phi Sorority
     B. healthy
     C. very fat

30. Dr. Roman's (A) *English* class is offered too late (B) *in the evening,* and it is (C) *boring* and uninteresting.
     A. English
     B. in the evening
     C. boring

Directions: Choose the most effective words to complete the sentences below.

31. The lawyer _____ various high-profile cases in an effort to convince the jury.
    A. cited
    B. sighted
    C. sited

32. For twenty _____ service, my father was given a silver watch and a firm handshake.
    A. year's
    B. years'
    C. years

33. James' lawyer did not believe that a man's uncle could be a _____ witness.
    A. creditable
    B. credible
    C. credulous

34. When Mr. Jonas was shaving, he was careful not to cut _____.
    A. hisself
    B. his self
    C. himself

Directions: In each sentence below, find what is incorrect, if anything. Possible errors are underlined and lettered. Assume that all other elements of the sentence are correct and cannot be changed. If there is an error, circle the appropriate letter of the underlined part.

35. (A) <u>Most</u> all students spend (B) <u>their</u> time doing everything (C) <u>except</u> studying their lesson. (D) No error.

36. (A) <u>Less</u> than ten people (B) <u>were</u> present at (C) <u>John's</u> recital last night. (D) No error.

37. (A) <u>Waiting to Exhale</u>, a novel by Terri McMillan, was exciting. (B) Its characters were very colorful and (C) <u>its</u> storyline very contemporary. (D) No error.

Directions: Choose the sentence that logically and correctly expresses the comparison.

38. A. Jean's hair is as long as Sherry.
    B. Jean's hair is as long as, if not longer than, Sherry.
    C. Jean's hair is as long as Sherry's.

39. A. The colt's mane looked shinier after he had been brushed vigorously.

    B. The colt's mane looked more shinier after he had been brushed vigorously.

    C. The colt's mane looked its shiniest after he had been brushed vigorously.

40. A. Many experts agree that giving birth to a child does not help one to become a good parent any more than adoption or foster care.

    B. Many experts agree that children do not help one become a good parent any more than adoption or foster care.

    C. Many experts agree that birthing a child does not help one become a good parent any more than adopting a child or acting as a foster parent does.

Index